THEOLOGICAL FOUNDATIONS

VOLUME TWO

THEOLOGY
AND
CULTURE

ROBERT M. DORAN

MARQUETTE
UNIVERSITY
PRESS

Library of Congress Cataloging-In-Publication Data

Doran, Robert M., 1939–
    Theological foundations / Robert M. Doran.
      p. cm. — (Marquette studies in theology ; no. 8–9)
    Includes bibliographical references.
    ISBN 0-87462-632-3 (pbk. : v. 1). — ISBN 0-87462-633-1
    (pbk. : v. 2)
    1. Theology, Doctrinal. 2. Christianity—Psychology. 3. Man
    (Christian theology) 4. Sociology, Christian (Catholic) 5.
    Catholic Church—Doctrines. I. Title. II. Series: Marquette
    studies in theology ; #8-9.
    BT78.D56 1995
    230'.01—dc20   95-41772

MARQUETTE STUDIES IN THEOLOGY No. 9

Cover design by Clare Tallon.
Photo by Andrew J. Tallon

Printed in the United States of America

MARQUETTE UNIVERSITY PRESS
MILWAUKEE

The Association of Jesuit University Presses

Contents

I

Preface to Volume 2

The first volume in this collection, *Intentionality and Psyche*, consisted mainly of essays from the 1970s that, by and large, relate the development of the notion of psychic conversion. The essays in this second volume are from the 1980s, and shift to social, political, and cultural concerns. Insofar as I can trace my own development, I would say that the intimate link of the two concerns, which all along I knew existed, started to find expression while I was working on the book *Psychic Conversion and Theological Foundations* (Scholars Press, 1981), and is there spelled out in some detail in the context of an attempt to link a methodical theology to a radical reorientation of the human sciences. The present volume reflects as well an explicit encounter with the concerns of hermeneutics and an inching toward praxis as a thematic issue, though only in *Theology and the Dialectics of History* (University of Toronto Press, 1990) does the latter topic come to center stage.

Two of these essays (chapters 3 and 11) are previously unpublished. 'Psychic Conversion and Spiritual Development' is the text of a lecture that I was asked to give at a symposium on Lonergan and spirituality at Mount Angel Abbey near Portland, Oregon, in 1984. It shows the transition from the psychological to the social and cultural interests. 'Cosmopolis and the Situation' reflects the concern with the postmodern issues that I came to see as establishing the context that a contemporary systematics

must address. It is left as it was written, as a contribution
distributed at one of the Boston College Lonergan Workshops in the mid-1980s. The major statement to date on
postmodernism from a Lonergan perspective is Fred
Lawrence's 1993 paper in *Theological Studies*, 'The Fragility
of Consciousness and the Postmodern Concern for the
Other.' My contribution to the issue, both here and in
Theology and the Dialectics of History, is far more elementary. I intend only to affirm that postmodernism is the
context to be addressed in a contemporary systematic theology, and that the movement that springs from Lonergan
represents a genuine postmodern option.

The essays appear here, not in the order in which
they were either written or published (as was the case with
the essays in volume 1), but, in keeping with the fine suggestion of two preliminary readers, arranged into different
parts depending on different emphases. Several were written for Boston College Lonergan Workshops, but one of
the more important papers that I gave at the Workshop is
not reprinted here: '*Insight* and the Ontology of Meaning'
became chapter 19 of *Theology and the Dialectics of History*.

Systematics remains my objective, and all of the essays in both volumes of this set are preparatory, clearing a
ground. It is a ground on which I hope others will join me,
for a contemporary systematics is best done in collaborative fashion. But that is not up to me, and I wish only to
thank those who have asked that these essays be collected
and published together.

Robert M. Doran
13 December 1993

Acknowledgments

The following articles are reprinted here with permission:

'Report on a Work in Progress,' *Searching for Cultural Foundations*, ed. Philip McShane (Lanham, MD: University Press of America, 1984) 44-64.

'From Psychic Conversion to the Dialectic of Community,' *Lonergan Workshop* 6, ed. Fred Lawrence (Atlanta: Scholars Press, 1986) 84-107.

'Duality and Dialectic,' *Lonergan Workshop* 7, ed. Fred Lawrence (Atlanta: Scholars Press, 1988) 59-84.

'Jung and Catholic Theology,' *Catholicism and Jungian Psychology*, ed. J. Marvin Spiegelman (Phoenix: Falcon Press, 1988) 41-73.

'Theological Grounds for a World-cultural Humanity,' *Creativity and Method: Essays in Honor of Bernard Lonergan, S.J.*, ed. Matthew L. Lamb (Milwaukee: Marquette University Press, 1981) 105-22.

'Suffering Servanthood and the Scale of Values,' *Lonergan Workshop* 4, ed. Fred Lawrence (Scholars Press, 1983) 41-67.

'Theology's Situation: Questions to Eric Voegelin,' *The Beginning and the Beyond: Supplementary Issue of Lonergan Workshop*, vol. 4 (Scholars Press, 1984) 69-91.

'Bernard Lonergan: An Appreciation,' *The Desires of the Human Heart*, ed. Vernon Gregson (Mahwah, NJ: Paulist Press, 1988) 1-15.

'Common Ground,' *Communication and Lonergan: Common Ground for Forging the New Age*, ed. Thomas J. Farrell and Paul A. Soukup (Kansas City, MO: Sheed & Ward, 1993) ix-xvi.

'Education for Cosmopolis,' *Method: Journal of Lonergan Studies* 1 (1983) 134-57.

'Self-knowledge and the Interpretation of Imaginal Expression,' *Method: Journal of Lonergan Studies* 4 (1986) 55-84.

'Psychic Conversion and Lonergan's Hermeneutics,' *Lonergan's Hermeneutics: Its Development and Application*, ed. Sean E. McEvenue and Ben F. Meyer (Washington, DC: The Catholic University of America Press, 1989) 161-216.

'The Analogy of Dialectic and the Systematics of History,' *Religion in Context: Recent Studies in Lonergan*, ed. Timothy P. Fallon, S.J. and Philip Boo Riley (Lanham, MD: University Press of America, 1988) 35-57.

Part One

Transitional Essays

1   Report on a Work in Progress

1   Introduction

After nearly a year of wrestling with the question of how to integrate a process of psychic self-appropriation, involving a good deal of dream analysis, with the dimensions of interiorly differentiated consciousness promoted by the work of Bernard Lonergan, in February of 1973 a basic insight occurred to me that I have been laboring to articulate, develop, test, and amplify ever since. The insight was to the effect that there is a fourth aspect of foundational subjectivity, and so of conversion, beyond the three instances — intellectual, moral, and religious — whose objectification constitutes in Lonergan's work the theological functional specialty 'foundations.'[1] I have called this fourth aspect of conversion 'psychic conversion.' Quite recently I have been moved to clarify for myself where my work is going from here, and so to locate the work of the past nine years within a new and more inclusive context.[2] In the present paper I will describe this newly explicit context and will then offer an interpretation of the two stages through which my work of the preceding nine years has passed.

This new context is one neither of method nor of psychology, as the previous two phases, respectively, have been, but explicitly one of theology, and more precisely of systematics. I am beginning work on a systematics that I will entitle *A Theology for a World-cultural Humanity.* The

3

first volume of this work will be devoted to two themes: the cultural matrix of a contemporary systematics and the meaning of integrity or authenticity within that matrix.[3] It will present a vision of a religiously and theologically transformed cosmopolis. The section dealing with integral interiority will include a statement, more thorough and refined than any that appears in my previous work, regarding the structure of a psychology of orientations.[4] But — and this is the most important point — the context even of this psychological theory is explicitly theological.

The cultural matrix with which a contemporary Christian systematics must mediate the significance and role of the Christian religion is global. I understand the global cultural matrix of our age as constituted by several competing and escalating sets of totalitarian ambitions, which for purposes of hypothetical generalization or at least of 'ideal-type' articulation, can be reduced to variations on one or other of the two major myths of post-Machiavellian modernity: the progressionist myth of automatic expansion, unlimited progress, and exponential growth, whose paradigmatic resultant in our day is found in transnational corporational capitalism, and the myth of class conflict as the indispensable and infallible means to social harmony and justice, the myth that finds similar paradigmatic expression in the Marxist states.[5] A common structural error regarding the order of values infects both of these sets of ideological assumptions and their corresponding and competing social-systemic objectifications: namely, a subordination of the cultural values in terms of which groups live in a world mediated and constituted by meaning to the social values that constitute a particular social order. I understand the significance and role of Christianity, then, within such a global cultural matrix to consist in the promotion of a mentality that would become incarnate in alternative communities and that would proceed in the order of praxis on the grounds of a rectified conception and articulation of the genuine order of values. In such a conception religious values condition the possibility of personal integrity, personal integrity conditions the possibility of genuine cultural values, such cultural values condition the possibility of a just social order, and a just social order conditions the possibility of an equitable distribution of particular goods. The network of alternative communities arising from the praxis of such a mentality must extend across both cultural and religious boundaries. I adopt Lewis Mumford's expression 'world-cultural humanity' as an appropriate denomination.[6]

The ground of the values that motivate a world-cultural humanity I locate in the four aspects or modalities of conversion — religious, moral, intellectual, and psychic — whose objectification constitutes 'theological foundations.'[7] The conversions will ground the praxis of world-cultural humanity. This praxis will be both superstructural and infrastructural. The superstructural praxis will consist in the interdisciplinary collaboration required to reorient the human sciences. My work up to this point indicates what the reorientation of one of these sciences, depth psychology, entails, and argues that this particular reorientation is itself a dimension of theological foundations. The infrastructural praxis of world-cultural subjects is intent on the transformation of the myriad varieties of common sense by integrating the cosmological, anthropological, and soteriological modes of spontaneous self-understanding that constitute the authentic heritage of the various cultural traditions, and by reversing the mechano-morphic self-understanding that informs the common sense of totalitarian societies.[8] The bulk, if not the totality, of my intellectual energies will be devoted, for the foreseeable future, to working out a theology that can mediate Christian faith with the global cultural matrix in such a way as to promote the emergence of a world-cultural community.

My work of the previous nine years I now understand as a methodological, and consequent psychological, preface to a theology for a world-cultural humanity. Methodologically, this work complements Lonergan's objectification of the interiority of the integral human subject, and so further specifies what constitutes authenticity. Thus it is heading toward a specification of the grounds of orthopraxis. Psychologically, this work articulates the aesthetic sensitivity of the converted subject. I have moved to this articulation by way of a dialectical confrontation with Jungian depth psychology. Thus both of the aspects or phases of my work are a fitting preparation for my present concerns: the methodological aspect because of the transcultural structure of consciousness disengaged in Lonergan's writings, and the psychological because of the potential of Jung's insights for promoting crosscultural understanding. The scope of my attempt to reorient Jung's work is limited to articulating the nature of converted psychic sensitivity. This articulation is obviously dependent upon Lonergan's understanding of self-transcendence. Thus the methodological phase of my work precedes the psychological, and grounds the latter in an extension of Lonergan's notion of generalized empirical method. Let me add that I believe that a reorientation of much of twentieth-century depth psychology could follow from my attempt to outline the structure of a psychology of orientations. But I have decided to turn my own energies to the theological task consequent upon the first two phases of my work.

I have not yet proceeded very far in pursuing this goal. My book *Psychic Conversion and Theological Foundations*[9] specifies the superstructural dimensions of the endeavor to form a global alternative to the totalitarianisms.

It speaks of the reorientation of the human sciences on the foundation of the objectification of authenticity. But I have yet to relate my understanding of the global cultural matrix to various prevalent interpretations of culture and politics or to begin constructing a systematic theology to mediate Christian faith with this matrix. I have written very little about the infrastructural transformations that would be promoted by a world-cultural humanity, though I have received much encouragement concerning my ideas in this regard from my students in a course on 'Religion and Culture' at Regis College in Toronto.[10] I was fortunate enough to have a class in which twelve distinct cultural backgrounds were represented, so I consider the encouragement something of a confirmation that I should continue along the path of my explorations.

2   Background

Prior to the completion of any of my work to date, my concerns went through two stages, which are reflected in the two phases of the written work itself. The first concern emerged between May of 1972 and October of 1973, when, with the assistance of Dr. Charles Goldsmith in Milwaukee, I began a process of dream analysis that promoted a process that I call psychic self-appropriation. During these months I resolved to begin in my doctoral dissertation the work of complementing Lonergan's intentionality analysis with the psychic self-appropriation that I was about. This stage of concern is reflected in the first, or methodological, phase of my written work to date, which includes the book *Subject and Psyche*[11] and the articles 'Psychic Conversion'[12] and 'Subject, Psyche, and Theology's Foundations.'[13] The principal function of this phase is to generate categories for expressing an understanding of the psyche that would be continuous with Lonergan's articulation of intentionality. I also argue in these works that these new categories are foundational.[14] They are expressive of a dimension of converted subjectivity, and so they articulate an aspect of foundational reality. I became convinced at this time that these categories afford a necessary complement to Lonergan's account of this reality, and so that his notion of foundational reality was to this extent incomplete. This claim, which I still maintain, has proved to be the most controversial aspect of my work among Lonergan's students. Put briefly, my conviction is that the self-knowledge that is gained through psychic analysis is just as transformative as is that acquired through intentionality analysis, and that *the latter can neither supply nor substitute for the former.* Four new foundational categories are generated during this phase of my work: second immediacy, the imaginal, psychic conversion, and the anagogic.

My second conviction, which is as controversial among Jungians as the first is among students of Lonergan, is that Lonergan's intentionality analysis is needed if one is critically to ground a psychic analysis that avoids the perils of self-deception concerning our authentic possibilities. This conviction reached articulable form which I was in Zürich from October to December of 1974. There I came to see that, while psychic analysis is a necessary *complement* to Lonergan's intentionality analysis, the latter stood in a relationship of *dialectic* with Jung's science of the psyche. Jungian depth psychology, as it stands, is not complementary to Lonergan's intentionality analysis, and the problem lies in mistaken assumptions on Jung's part concerning the three aspects of foundational reality that Lonergan had articulated: knowledge, morality, and religion. Jungian psychology needed to be reoriented on the basis of Lonergan's intentionality analysis. While this conviction is clearly present even in the writings of the first phase of my work, the actual task of attempting the reorientation could not be undertaken until I had arrived at the notion of the anagogic, and had distinguished the anagogic from the archetypal. These developments emerge in the last work of the first phase, the paper 'Subject, Psyche, and Theology's Foundations.' The second phase begins to display positively what a reoriented depth psychology would be, and thus I refer to this phase as psychological. The concerns of the third phase, which I described in the introductory section above, begin to become apparent in some of the later works of this period.

3   The Methodological Phase

The generation of additional foundational categories is the preoccupation of *Subject and Psyche*. These categories would serve to integrate psychic self-appropriation with Lonergan's account of method, and so would fill a need that was left unaddressed by Lonergan and that had to be met before the structure of foundations was complete. Since my first thorough absorption in Lonergan's work in 1967, I had been engaged in the slow and laborious process of explanatory self-knowledge. In May of 1972 I began with Dr. Goldsmith a similarly intense journey through another dimension of inner life. It did not take long before I realized that the process of recovering, telling, and making the story of my life in which I was engaged bore striking resemblances to some of the work that I had been engaged in under Lonergan's tutelage for some five years, and was definitely aided by what I had learned about myself from Lonergan, but also that the dimension of interiority that I was now coming to understand and take responsibility for was different from the one to which Lonergan had introduced me. Thus I began to formulate the question of how I could integrate these two processes of self-exploration, not simply in the unthematic manner of living from the basis of both, but in the thematic manner of articulating their integration in a theoretic or explanatory fashion. *Subject and Psyche*, completed in 1975, was the first articulation of my convictions that Lonergan's account of foundational subjectivity had to be complemented by a depth psychology, and that psychic interiority was indeed important and significant enough to deserve to be considered a dimension of 'foundational reality.' The opening of my own intentional consciousness to a willingness to negotiate psychic sensitivity in an intelligent, reasonable, and responsible fashion was such a change in myself, and instituted such a new horizon, that I felt justified in referring to it as a fourth mode of conversion, which I called psychic conversion.

I have already referred to a second concern that appeared but was left undeveloped in *Subject and Psyche*. In Zürich I became quickly disillusioned with Jungian psychology, which previously I had thought could be integrated in a fairly straightforward way with Lonergan's thought. I had supposed that the integration would require little more than a purging from Jungian thought of its at least implicit Kantianism in the realms of epistemology and metaphysics. But in Zürich I saw that much more was demanded, that the existential problems in Jungianism were far more profound than the cognitional difficulties, and that in fact a quite radical religious and moral crisis lies behind the epistemological and metaphysical counterpositions in Jungian literature. In effect, a *new* psychology had to be proposed, if Lonergan was to be appropriately complemented by psychological self-knowledge. My own readiness to carry out this task was quite incomplete at the time of writing *Subject and Psyche*, and so I deliberately contented myself with indicating the scope of the problem, and then devoted my attention to the first concern of suggesting the manner in which Lonergan's thought left itself open to, and demanded, a psychological complement which it had already begun to anticipate.

The anticipation to which I refer is found in *Method in Theology*, where Lonergan speaks of the relations, first, between feelings and values,[15] and then, in a distinct context, between feelings and symbols.[16] I concluded to a relation between values and symbols, because of their common relatedness to feelings, and I claimed that the spontaneous symbols that emerge from the psychic depths of the subject, particularly in dreams, but also in such deliberately undertaken exercises as those proposed by Ira Progoff,[17] provide significant help in the appropriation of that level of intentional consciousness whose distinctness from the cognitional emerges in Lonergan's later work: the fourth or existential level. The relationship consists in the fact that psychic analysis is one necessary key to the appropriation of the fourth level of intentional consciousness. Psychic analysis helps one to know what one actually wants, what one truly values, the real state and orientation of one's desires. The spontaneous symbols of the sensitive psyche constitute the principal data for the differentiation of one's existential orientation to the objectives that constitute the human good, objectives whose pursuit or neglect constitutes world-constitutive and concomitant self-constitutive praxis.

This insight serves to integrate psychic conversion with the other dimensions of foundational reality. When Lonergan speaks of intellectual, moral, and religious conversion, of their order of emergence and of their reverse order of sublation,[18] he creates a problem that he leaves unanswered, in my view. For intellectual conversion, at least as this expression is usually used in his work, is in fact intellectual self-appropriation.[19] It is a precise, theoretic, explanatory self-understanding that guides a responsible self-determination in matters cognitional. But religious and moral conversion precede intellectual conversion thus conceived, and so they are not a matter of explanatory — or, for that matter, even descriptive — self-thematization. But if they are to sublate intellectual conversion, they must be raised out of their compactness and be subjected to the process of self-appropriation, the process that leads to interiorly differentiated consciousness. Only then will cognitional theory find that higher integration in existential world-constitutive agency that is implied when one speaks of sublating intellectual by moral conversion. Now it is psychic conversion that makes moral self-appropriation possible, and so that enables the sublation of intellectual by moral conversion. The dominant theme of *Subject and Psyche* is the following: by exploiting the clue mentioned earlier — the relation of feelings both to values and to symbols — one can develop a depth psychology, integrate this psychology with Lonergan's intentionality analysis, and raise moral and religious conversion into the stage of meaning governed by interiorly differentiated consciousness.

The integration of psychic analysis with intentionality analysis, as I have stated, gave rise to three new foundational categories in *Subject and Psyche* — second immediacy, the imaginal, and psychic conversion — and to a fourth that emerged a bit later, the anagogic.

Second immediacy can be explained by contrasting it with the spontaneously operative infrastructure of the subject-as-subject that I call primordial immediacy. Primordial immediacy is the immediacy of the operating and feeling consciousness to the symbols, concepts, and judgments through which the world is mediated and constituted by meaning, and to the evaluations through which the world is motivated by values. The operational aspect of primordial immediacy is mediated in Lonergan's work. My proposals speak of a complementary mediation of the affective dimensions of immediacy. Both mediations result in objective self-knowledge, the subject-as-object. But the subject-as-object is not yet what is meant by second immediacy. The latter emerges as objectivity in one's own regard *changes one's spontaneity* as a subject as a result of one's *decisions* to operate in a manner consistent with what one has come to affirm regarding one's most authentic possibilities. New habits of perception, insight, judgment, feeling, and deliberation begin to be formed, the habits that constitute interiorly differentiated consciousness. When this most subtle of all differentiations becomes habitual, it establishes one in a condition that I call second immediacy and that I describe as the probably always asymptotic recovery of primordial immediacy through method. Lest such a claim appear either outlandish or gnostic, let me emphasize that what one becomes asymptotic *to* is wrapped in the non-luminosity that is the very reason that primordial immediacy is, as I put it in my later writings, a search for direction in the movement of life. We are not speaking here of anything continuous with the *lumen gloriae*, the luminosity in which we shall know even as we are known, but of a differentiated appropriation of our own nescience, and so of the process of inquiry through which, step by step, we discover the direction that is to be found in the movement of life. In the humility that reflectively owns its own nescience in a differentiated fashion is to be found the integral foundation of theology, of human science, and of world-cultural humanity.

A discussion of Paul Ricoeur's understanding of the symbol precedes my treatment of *the imaginal*. I find Ricoeur's efforts to mediate the conflict between restorative and reductive hermeneutics essential for my own insistence on psychic analysis as an intrinsic ingredient of existential self-appropriation. I also find his discussion of the structure of the symbol quite illuminating. But I take issue with him on three counts. First, I do not accept his insistence that self-appropriation is to be mediated radically by an encounter with the externalized objectifications of religious and cultural history; I propose rather that, however contributory such an encounter is to our self-understanding, our very interpretation of these expressions is grounded in our understanding of ourselves, and so that the grounds of the hermeneutic of symbolic expressions lie in our understanding of our own spontaneous symbolic experience. Second, I find that Ricoeur mistakenly undervalues the symbolic power and worth of dreams. Finally, I propose that the teleological counterpole to the Freudian archeology of the subject must be found in the same dimensions of the psyche itself, and not in the fictive Hegelian *Geist* to which Ricoeur appeals, nor even in the very real dimensions of intentionality, however much the teleology of the psyche may be explained in terms of its orientation to a participation in the objectives of our intentional operations. Jung has correctly insisted on a teleological orientation within the psyche itself, and so on the inclusion of teleological considerations in any science of the psyche, even if he misplaces and in fact dislocates the direction of psychic intending. The dialectic of archeology and teleology is experienced in sensitivity itself. This is due to the psyche's intermediate status or position between and participation in the schemes of recurrence of the bodily organism, on the one hand, and the unrestricted reach of intentionality, on the other hand. The symbols released in our dreams are exploratory of the dialectic of the subject within the dialectic of history. But they can be produced as they are only because of the dialectic within the psyche itself. That dialectic, I later came to see, can be understood in Lonergan's terms of limitation and transcendence.[20]

The imaginal is that sphere of being that is known in true interpretations of elemental symbolic productions. I extend the processes of sublation to the imaginal, in an effort to account for how such interpretations are possible. Thus the dream is sublated into waking experience by memory, into intelligent consciousness by interpretation, into rational consciousness by reflection, and into existential consciousness by decision. The decision has to do with how I am to deal with the self-knowledge gained in the interpretation of the dream. In this way, and through the negotiation of the interpreted materials, the sensitive psyche is gradually conscripted into the self-transcendent dynamism of intentionality. The teleology of the psyche is to be understood in terms of its potential orientation to and participation in the objectives of intentional consciousness. This potential is actualized only as the detachment and disinterestedness of ordered intentionality permeates one's affectivity.

This specification of psychic teleology differs from the Jungian position. The elemental symbols of our dispositionally conscious energies reflect the emergence or non-emergence of the subject as an originating value. Their ground theme consists in the conflict between the intention of the transcendentals and the flight from genuine humanity. This drama is a priori, in Lonergan's operative-heuristic sense of 'notions' rather than in the content-objective sense of Kant's categories. In the first volume of *A Theology for a World-cultural Humanity*, I will elaborate its theological, and so most radical, meaning.[21]

Psychic conversion, the third foundational category presented in *Subject and Psyche*, is the process that enables a person consciously to sublate imaginal data by intentional process. The psychically converted subject has learned to sublate the elemental symbols that reflect his or her affective orientations in a world mediated and constituted by meaning and motivated by value. In the article 'Psychic Conversion,' I spoke of this process as one in which the undertow of sensitive consciousness is subjected to the same kind of self-appropriation as in Lonergan's work was brought to bear on cognitional activity. This means that psychic self-appropriation as I am conceiving it is a matter of interiorly differentiated consciousness. It corresponds to the philosophic variety of intellectual conversion that results from answering correctly the three questions, What am I doing when I am knowing? Why is doing that knowing? What do I know when I do that? It would be artificial and arbitrary to try to elaborate parallel questions to promote the process of psychic conversion. It is more accurate to say instead that the detachment and disinterestedness of the notions of being and value which the process of philosophic conversion reveals as constitutive of authenticity move one to the further question of how one can negotiate one's affective spontaneities so that they further the emergence of genuineness in one's own conscious behavior rather than obstructing that emergence. Where self-knowledge becomes explanatory, as it does in philosophic conversion, one wants the same rigor of interiorly differentiated consciousness to extend to one's familiarity with one's psychic spontaneities. 'Psychic conversion,' then, as I am using this term, refers to more than the spontaneous affective self-transcendence of the well-ordered psyche, or even the spontaneous sublation and correction of affective energies by the morally good person, just as 'intellectual conversion' in Lonergan's work usually refers to more than the cognitive genuineness of a person who happens to be using his or her mind intelligently and rationally as it is meant to be used. 'Psychic conversion' means rigorous, explanatory appropriation of one's sensitive psychic experience and of its existential meaning just as 'intellectual conversion' means rigorous, explanatory appropriation of one's intellectual and rational activity.

The fourth foundational category presented in my early work is that of *the anagogic*. It is introduced, not in *Subject and Psyche*, but in the article 'Subject, Psyche, and Theology's Foundations.' It is further elaborated in many of the articles of the second or psychological phase of my work, where my concern shifts from that of complementing Lonergan to that of reorienting Jung. Jung spoke of two kinds of elemental symbolism: the personal symbols of the personal unconscious and the archetypal symbols of the collective unconscious. I want to speak of a third variety, which Jung includes under the rubric of archetypal symbols, but which I consider quite distinct. Archetypal symbols are taken from nature and imitate nature in a generic and highly associative way. They correspond to the symbolization that Eric Voegelin calls cosmological. Anagogic symbols, on the other hand, while they may be borrowed from nature or from history, express the relation of the person, the world, or history to the reality disclosed by the anthropological and/or soteriological 'leaps in being' by which consciousness is explicitly related, through philosophy or faith, to a world-transcendent measure of integrity. This distinction enabled me to address myself to the reorientation of Jungian psychology, and more specifically to come to grips with the moral and religious crises that lie behind the epistemological and metaphysical counterpositions in Jung's thought. The crucial issue in Jung's work is the problem of evil. The symbolism of the negotiation of evil is anagogic, not archetypal, and the resolution of the problem of evil calls, not for an integration of evil with good in such a way that both good and evil can be cultivated, as would be the case if they were archetypal contraries, but for the decision between contradictories, a decision made in the freedom that we are given by our relation with the world-transcendent and redeeming measure of our integrity.

With the emergence of this fourth category, the first phase of my work, that of complementing Lonergan's intentionality analysis with an account of the structure of psychic analysis, comes to a close, and the second phase, that of suggesting a reorientation of Jungian psychology, begins.

4   The Psychological Subject

My efforts at reorienting Jungian psychology began in an article that I wrote for a *Festschrift* honoring Frederick E. Crowe on the occasion of his sixtieth birthday.[22] Jung had written a number of works in which he treated the symbolic significance of the person of Christ. His late work *Aion*[23] contains perhaps the most thorough presentation of his thought in this regard. Here he tries to understand Christ's psychological importance and meaning by considering Christ as an archetype of the self. Now, for Jung, wholeness, conceived as the integration of opposites, is the paradigm for understanding the self. Good and evil are for him among the opposites that must be integrated. Christ functions as a symbol of the self-as-good, and Satan as a symbol of the self-as-evil. Wholeness demands that Christ's psychic significance be complemented by and integrated with Satan's, through the cultivation of dimensions of the self that Christianity had rejected as evil during the astrological Age of Pisces, in which the warring fishes symbolized the conflict of opposites. The emerging Age of Aquarius will witness the cessation of the conflicts, the reconciliation of the warring elements, the *rapprochement* of Christ and Satan. I contend that Jung limited himself to archetypal or cosmological symbolizations as expressions of the reality of God. God for him is to be understood as emergent within the world, in a manner not unlike Hegel's Absolute Spirit; in fact God is to be redeemed from unconsciousness by individuating persons. God's unconsciousness is to be attributed to the exclusion from God's conscious being of the fourth personal element of divinity, of God's shadow, that is, of Satan. As human subjects integrate good and evil in themselves, Satan will be reintegrated into the conscious being of God, and God will be at rest with God's own self.

The leap in being to a world-transcendent God who redeems human subjects and communities from evil seems never to have been taken by Jung. There is for him no further dimension of symbolism beyond the archetypal, for there is nothing beyond the cosmological to be symbolized. His autobiographical *Memories, Dreams, Reflections* records a dream in which Jung is invited to acknowledge the transcendent God into whose mystery we are introduced by, among other things, the experience of innocent suffering.[24] But in the dream Jung refused the invitation. The dream itself is anagogic in its symbolism; but, paradoxically, it reflects the choice in which Jung ruled out an acknowledgment of the relations to which anagogic symbols refer. The irony is that Jung has provided a superb avenue to an appropriation of the dimensions of our inner being that stand in need of God's redemptive love, and yet he missed or rejected the connection between his own discoveries and the Christian life of grace. The problem of evil is resolved, not by an apocatastatic reconciliation of evil with good, but only by the transformation of evil into a greater good by participation in the 'just and mysterious law of the cross.'[25] Jung has penetrated so deeply into the recesses of the psyche that he has uncovered the need for a theological grounding of depth psychology. But he did not acknowledge the necessary grounding, and so he ends up offering a system of thought that must, in the last analysis, be regarded not as a complement but as an alternative to Christian theology and to Christian religious praxis.

Another article written at the same time, 'The Theologian's Psyche: Notes toward a Reconstruction of Depth Psychology,'[26] pursues the question of the transformation that Jungian psychology will undergo when it is encountered dialectically by an analysis of intentional self-transcendence. In this article the Jungian notion of the self is examined. This notion, as we saw, was central to Jung's critique of the Christian ethos in *Aion*. I redefine the self as the subject, and I understand the subject as inextricably involved in the dialectic of authenticity and inauthenticity. I speak of good and evil, respectively, as the intelligent, reasonable, and responsible negotiation of the tension of limitation and transcendence, matter and spirit, on the one hand, and the failure or refusal so to negotiate this tension, and thus its displacement to one or other pole, on the other hand. Thus I argue that good and evil cannot be listed among the *contrary* opposites to be negotiated by a process that establishes their complementarity, that is, the opposites that can be discussed under the general rubric of limitation and transcendence. Rather, good and evil are qualifications of that very process of negotiation itself, depending on whether it has or has not been characterized by the genuineness that is constituted by the taut balance of limitation and transcendence. There is no 'both/and' here, but only an 'either/or.'

Further nuances are introduced in the two papers 'Aesthetics and the Opposites' and 'Aesthetic Subjectivity and Generalized Empirical Method.'[27] The first of these papers speaks of the context of psychic self-appropriation as being quite beyond the narrow psychotherapeutic framework that my earlier works are still presupposing. Furthermore, it correlates the psychic or aesthetic dimension of subjectivity with the dramatic character of world constitution and self-constitution. The appropriation of this dimension will thus take the form of a narrative which may or may not require a psychotherapeutic setting to get one started, but whose purpose is 'beyond therapy.' The second paper proposes that the differentiation of the psyche is more accurately conceived as a process of developing one's aesthetic sensitivities than as a matter of psychotherapy as we usually think of the latter, and of developing these sensitivities primarily in the area of artistry in which all of us are inevitably involved, the dramatic artistry of making a work of art out of our own lives.

This theme is resumed in 'Dramatic Artistry in the Third Stage of Meaning,'[28] where psychic conversion is argued to be the key to a self-appropriating genuineness, that is, to a genuineness that reflectively mediates the duality of limitation and transcendence. Sensitive participation in both the organism's schemes of recurrence and the spirit's intention of objectives that are not restricted by space and time makes of the psyche the locus in which the tension of limitation and transcendence is experienced. This paper also proposes that in psychic conversion the healing and creative vectors of conscious development are conjoined. The retrieved genuineness that results from the mediation, through interiorly differentiated consciousness, of limitation and transcendence involves sensitivity itself in the divinely originated solution to the problem of evil. This sensitive participation is manifest especially in the spontaneous release of the anagogic symbols that reflect the penetration of *gratia sanans* to the physiological level of the person.

The world-constitutive praxis of the converted subject has been emerging as a more central theme in these last few papers. In 'Metaphysics, Psychology, and Praxis,'[29] it comes to center-stage. The debate with Jung continues in this paper as well, for the question with which the paper deals has to do with the contribution of a transcultural psychology of orientations to the emergence of a world-cultural humanity. In my response to this question I insist on the penetration of sensitive consciousness by the detachment that makes one able to think and choose on the level of history. Such detachment is quite other than what develops if one submits to Jung's prospective swallowing up of intentionality and its objectives within the horizons of a merely archetypally symbolizing psyche. Jung's discovery of archetypal symbols is an important contribution to crosscultural communication. But equally important is the insight, the act of understanding, that in all cultures authenticity consists in the participation of the sensitive psyche in the pursuit of the transcendental objectives of intentionality.

Most of the remaining articles in the second phase resume the central task of reorienting Jungian psychology. 'Primary Process and the Spiritual Unconscious'[30] recasts the Freudian notion of primary process so that it includes the operations of intentional consciousness as well as all of the motivations and orientations of the sensitive psyche. Thus it becomes, not libido, but the search for direction in the movement of life. It is constituted by the tension of limitation and transcendence. 'Secondary process,' then, becomes a term referring to all attempts to objectify primary process. Among these attempts are those which issue from philosophic and psychic conversion, and so which admit into consciousness in an explanatory fashion the ineluctable tension, *felt* in the sensitive psyche, between the schemes of recurrence of a body-bound sensitivity whose imaginal horizons are constituted by time and space, on the one hand, and the intention of the true and the good, the notions of being and value, on the other hand, which are unrestricted by time and space. The philosophies that we adopt in secondary process have a constitutive influence on the psyche and its symbolic deliverances. This explains why persons undergoing different kinds of psychotherapy will experience different kinds of dreams — 'Freudian,' 'Jungian,' etc. And this means that a therapy of *pneumopathology*[31] is more radical than a therapy of psychopathology, and that an accurate science of the psyche is dependent on a critical retrieval of spiritual intentionality. One's imaginal experience depends on one's fidelity or infidelity to the transcendental precepts, which, along with grace, are the ultimate operators of one's psychic development: Be attentive, Be intelligent, Be reasonable, Be responsible. One implication of this is that the Jungian symbols of wholeness, such as the mandala, symbolize only temporary plateaus of integration. They will be continually and relentlessly dissolved by the self as operator, in favor of more comprehensive integrations that are reached only through the difficult process of advancing differentiation. Jung's compacting of all transpersonal symbolism into the archetypal images of wholeness reflects too one-sided an emphasis on the self-as-integrator and a relative neglect of the unceasing process of differentiation as this process moves to an ever more comprehensive synthesis of the tripartite self — bodily organism, sensitive psyche, and spiritual intentionality. When wholeness is overemphasized, the danger is incurred that the person will be derailed from the search for direction in the movement of life. What should be regarded as the goal of psychic development is, not wholeness, but the affective self-transcendence which enables the psyche to participate ever more spontaneously in the person's fidelity to the transcendental precepts, to the normative order of inquiry through which direction is found. Wholeness is a relative and temporary integration of various stages of development along the way.

'Jungian Psychology and Lonergan's Foundations: A Methodological Proposal'[32] lists the changes that would take place in Jungian psychology if it were to be reoriented on the basis which I am suggesting. The operative heuristic notion guiding the process of individuation would become, not wholeness, but self-transcendence. Jung's romantic mysticism, where affectivity bogs down in intracosmic archetypal symbolization, would be replaced by an intentionality mysticism that would be reflected in the anagogic images released by a psyche that participates in the spirit's openness to a world-transcendent and redeeming God. These images would themselves be negotiated 'anagogically.' That is, they would not be clung to, but would lead one beyond themselves to participation in the very life of God. Moreover, the symbols of our dreams, whether personal, archetypal, or anagogic, would be regarded as a narrative whose theme is the emergence of the authentic world-constitutive agent. In the theoretic realm, the psyche would be more sharply differentiated from the spirit. The spirit is not an unknowable *Ding an sich*, but is rather what one knows when one affirms oneself as the subject of intelligent, rational, and responsible operations. The issue of good and evil would be understood in terms of one's emergence as a self-transcendent agent. The integration proposed by Jung would become patently absurd, for one cannot be simultaneously and willingly both an intelligent, rational, and responsible person and a stupid, silly, sociopathic drifter. The symbolic significance of Christ and Satan reflects the ultimate context of grace and sin, where the problem of evil is decided, not by the cultivation of darkness in the illusory hope of integrating it with the light, but by the ever further transformation of the realm of our darkness by the therapeutic vector of redemptive love.

I published in *Review for Religious* three less technical articles on Jungian psychology and Christian spirituality.[33] They conclude with the affirmation that the divinely originated solution to the problem of evil invites us to the existential decision to 'let ourselves fall into the incomprehensibility of God as into our own true fulfillment and happiness' (Karl Rahner).[34] This is precisely what Jung's dream, referred to above, shows that he would not let himself do. This existential refusal is the root of the most serious intellectual problems in his psychology. No clearer instance can be provided of the spiritual causation of the psyche's symbolic manifestations. By the time of the article 'Psyche, Evil, and Grace,'[35] then, I am calling for the construction of a new psychology that would articulate the psychic dimension that permeates all intentional orientation. I have been presenting the outline of this psychology in my course at Regis College on 'Psychic Conversion and Contemporary Spirituality,' and I will include it in the book that I am now writing, in the context of a discussion of authenticity within the global cultural matrix that invites the formation of a world-cultural communitarian alternative to the competing and escalating totalitarian systems.[36]

5   Psychic Conversion and Theological Foundations

The anticipation of a world-cultural community begins to take more definitive shape in my second book, *Psychic Conversion and Theological Foundations*. The book is essentially a sustained argument to the effect that the processes of intellectual, psychic, moral, and religious self-appropriation must ground not only a contemporary doctrinal, systematic, and practical theology, but also an interdisciplinary collaboration geared to the reorientation of the human sciences on the basis of the positions in which authentic subjectivity is objectified. This collaboration will constitute the superstructural dimension of the cosmopoli-

tan alternative to totalitarianism. The first of the human
sciences to be reoriented is depth psychology, because its
data are among the data of interiority whose explanatory
objectification constitutes the foundations of further endeavor in the human sciences. In this sense the book re-
turns to the concerns of the first phase of my work, that of
complementing Lonergan's methodological positions. I
begin to draw out the implications of Lonergan's suggestions regarding a scale of values, and I root totalitarianism
in the instrumentalization of rationality and the concomitant neglect of psychic sensitivity that coincide with the
collapse of the scale of values into the two levels of the
good of order and the acquisition and distribution of particular goods. As I argued in the first section of this paper,
this collapse is predicated on a neglect of the manner in
which religious values condition personal integrity, personal integrity conditions cultural values, and cultural values condition a just social order. A global alternative to
competing totalitarianisms will take its stand on the integrity of the full scale of values. It is in terms of this full scale
of values that I wish in the near future to discuss as well
the infrastructural dynamics of a world-cultural community. But I intend as well to ground these dynamics in an
advancing position on interiority, in which there would
occur an integration of the truth of the cosmological, anthropological, and soteriological symbolizations through
which various cultures have expressed their experience of
the search for direction in the movement of life.[37] This
integration depends above all on a reversal of the
mechanomorphic symbolizations of the totalitarian systems, that is, of symbolizations that result from the utili-
tarian collapse of the scale of values and that threaten a
deaxialization of history, a regression to a compactness that
would forget even the limited but essential ecological truth
of the cosmological or archetypal symbolizations.

Two further attempts to complement Lonergan's work appear in *Psychic Conversion and Theological Foundations*. The first draws out the implications of the distinction made in *Method in Theology* between the notion of being and the notion of value. This distinction is not as clear in *Insight*, for Lonergan had not yet arrived at the differentiation of the fourth level of consciousness, the intention of value, from the three levels that constitute the cognitive intention of truth. When existential consciousness emerges as a distinct level that is both the ground and the objective of cognitional praxis, the notion of value is no longer interchangeable with the notion of being. The real human world as it is and the good human world as it ought to be are not coincident. With this distinction, and perhaps only with it, transcendental method moves definitively beyond a classicist orientation, and so beyond the danger of its becoming an agent, however unwilling, of right-wing ideologies. Moreover, with this distinction, psychic self-appropriation, as the key to the objectification of the fourth level, becomes the narrative through which we express what we do when we strive to transform the human world as it is into the human world as we judge it ought to be. With this qualification, psychological self-knowledge transcends the narcissistic concerns that, as Peter Homans has argued, undermine the Jungian enterprise from beginning to end.[38]

Secondly, I attempted to draw an explicit link between the sensitive psyche and the transcendental notion of the beautiful. The beautiful is the objective of affective intentionality. In beauty there is articulated in sensible form the splendor of truth and goodness. Thus one more argument is forged for the assertion that the sensitive psyche cannot be brought to the realization of its own proper objective except to the extent that the person remains faithful to the spiritual exigences that prompt us to be intelli-

gent, reasonable, responsible, and in love. The paradigmatic enjoyment of and creative participation in beauty
lies in the affective integrity of the subject who has been
healed by redemptive love and thus freed to implement
the creative vector of consciousness through whose operations one's constitution of the world and of oneself becomes a work of art.   .

Notes

1 See Bernard Lonergan, *Method in Theology* (latest reprint,
Toronto: University of Toronto Press, 1994) 237-44.

2 1993 note: The 'nine years' referred to here are those from 1973
to 1982, when this paper was written. Most of the papers referred to
here have been reissued in volume 1 of this collection, *Intentionality and
Psyche*.

3 1993 note: This first volume appeared as *Theology and the Dialectics of History* (Toronto: University of Toronto Press, 1990). I consider
it still a work in foundations, preparatory to the systematic volumes
that I am now beginning to assemble.

4 1993 note: See ibid., chapters 6-10.

5 1993 note: Obviously this situation has changed dramatically
and unexpectedly since many of these papers were written. Nonetheless the vision of a world-cultural humanity remains an alternative to
the dominant paradigms of globalization that hold sway in our time,
and that was the point of the proposal from the beginning.

6 Lewis Mumford, *The Transformations of Man* (New York: Harper
Torchbooks, 1956) 137-68.

7 1993 note: I would now add a social dimension to conversion,
based on the relations among the levels of value. Its significance will
become apparent in later essays in this volume.

8 On cosmological, anthropological, and soteriological self-understanding, see Eric Voegelin, *Israel and Revelation*, vol. 1 of *Order and History* (Baton Rouge: Louisiana State University Press) 56. The term 'mechanomorphic' is Matthew Lamb's. I first heard Lamb use this term in class lectures that he delivered at Marquette University.

9 Robert M. Doran, *Psychic Conversion and Theological Foundations: Toward a Reorientation of the Human Sciences* (Chico, CA: Scholars Press, 1981).

10 See Robert M. Doran, 'Theological Grounds for a World-cultural Humanity,' in *Creativity and Method: Essays in Honor of Bernard Lonergan*, ed. Matthew L. Lamb (Milwaukee: Marquette University Press, 1981) 105-22 (chapter 6 below).

11 Robert M. Doran, *Subject and Psyche: Ricoeur, Jung, and the Search for Foundations* (Washington, D.C.: University Press of America, 1977); a second, revised edition, without the subtitle, was published by Marquette University Press, Milwaukee, in 1994.

12 Robert M. Doran, 'Psychic Conversion,' *The Thomist* (1977) 200-236; reprinted as chapter 2 in *Intentionality and Psyche*.

13 Robert M. Doran, 'Subject, Psyche, and Theology's Foundations,' *Journal of Religion* (1977) 267-87; reprinted as chapter 3 in *Intentionality and Psyche*.

14 1993 note: The notion of 'foundational categories' may seem somewhat anomalous, in that it is one of the functions of foundations to derive categories. What I mean by 'foundational categories' is what Lonergan means by 'basic terms and relations.' See Lonergan, *Method in Theology* 286.

15 Lonergan, *Method in Theology* 30-34.

16 Ibid. 64-69.

17 Ira Progoff, *The Symbolic and the Real* (New York: McGraw-Hill, 1973); *The Practice of Process Meditation* (New York: Dialogue House Library, 1980).

18 Lonergan, *Method in Theology* 241-43.

19 Ibid. 238-40.

20 Bernard Lonergan, *Insight: A Study of Human Understanding* (San Francisco: Harper & Row, 1978; Collected Works edition, vol. 3 of Collected Works of Bernard Lonergan, ed. Frederick E. Crowe and Robert M. Doran, Toronto: University of Toronto Press, 1992) 472-79/ 497-504. I will follow the same convention here as in *Intentionality and Psyche*, of referring first to the page numbers in the Harper & Row edition of *Insight*, and then to those in the Collected Works edition. But all quotations from *Insight* will be from the latter, critical edition.

21 1993 note: Some of this, in fact, was done in part 2 of *Theology and the Dialectics of History*. But more remains to be done in a distinctly systematic anthropology.

22 Robert M. Doran, 'Christ and the Psyche,' in *Trinification of the World*, eds. Jean-Marc Laporte and Thomas A. Dunne (Toronto: Regis College Press, 1978) 112-32; reprinted as chapter 5 in *Intentionality and Psyche*.

23 C.G. Jung, *Aion: Researches into the Phenomenology of the Self*, trans. R.F.C. Hull, vol. 9ii in Collected Works of C.G. Jung (Princeton: Princeton University Press, 1968).

24 C.G. Jung, *Memories, Dreams, Reflections*, trans. Richard and Clara Winston (New York: Vintage Press, 1961) 217-20.

25 See Bernard Lonergan, *De Verbo incarnato* (Rome: Gregorian University Press, 1964) 552-93.

26 Robert M. Doran, 'The Theologian's Psyche: Notes toward a Reconstruction of Depth Psychology,' in *Lonergan Workshop* 1, ed. Fred Lawrence (Missoula, MT: Scholars Press, 1978) 93-141; reprinted as chapter 6 in *Intentionality and Psyche*.

27 Robert M. Doran, 'Aesthetics and the Opposites,' *Thought* (1977) 117-33; reprinted as chapter 4 in *Intentionality and Psyche*; and idem, 'Aesthetic Subjectivity and Generalized Empirical Method,' *The Thomist* (1979) 257-78; reprinted as chapter 9 in *Intentionality and Psyche*.

28 Robert M. Doran, 'Dramatic Artistry in the Third Stage of Meaning,' in *Lonergan Workshop* 2, ed. Fred Lawrence (Chico, CA: Scholars Press, 1981) 147-99; reprinted as chapter 7 in *Intentionality and Psyche*.

29 Robert M. Doran, 'Metaphysics, Psychology, and Praxis,' paper distributed at the 1978 Lonergan Workshop at Boston College. 1993 note: Most of this paper is almost identical with material included in 'Insight and Archetype: The Complementarity of Lonergan and Jung,' which appeared for the first time as chapter 8 in *Intentionality and Psyche*, and so I have not included the paper in these volumes. But the very last subsection adds the world-constitutive theme mentioned here, and so I quote this part of the paper. The subheading is 'Existential Responsibility in the Third Stage of Meaning.'

'Attentiveness in any stage of meaning is for the sake of intelligent inquiry, reasonable reflection, and responsible decision in the interests of the promotion of the human good. But attentiveness in the third stage of meaning, the attentiveness of the psychically converted subject, is for the sake of the specific exigences of intelligence, rationality, and choice that impose themselves on an epochal juncture in the history of consciousness. Those exigences demand that one conceive, affirm, and implement the integral heuristic structure of proportionate being, that one move to the explicit semantics of all that can be said or done that is critical metaphysics. The implementation of the heuristic structure of proportionate being constitutes the existential and indeed the political responsibility of consciousness in the third stage of meaning. This responsibility is existential in that, by exercising it, one constitutes oneself as a self-appropriating subject. But it is also political, in that what it calls for is the reorientation of science and common sense, so that the explanation of all data and the management of all human affairs proceed in accord with the basic positions on knowing, on valuing, on transcendence, on being, on objectivity. The reorientation of common sense occurs through psychic conversion, through dramatic artistry in the third stage of meaning, through the release of the capacity to negotiate with full intentionality the dialectic of the dramatic subject and the more dominant dialectic of community that 'gives rise to the situations that stimulate neural demands and ... molds the orientation of intelligence that preconsciously exercises the censorship' (*Insight* 218/243) that selects materials for intelligent, reflective, and deliberative activity. The reorientation of science is instanced in my own attempts in this paper and elsewhere to integrate depth psychology with transcendental method. Both reorientations are politically significant, in that the theoretical and practical exercise of intelligence, rationality, and freedom alone promote the individual and social process that is the human good.

'Beyond the foundational questions of *Insight*, then — the questions, What am I doing when I am knowing? Why is doing that knowing? What do I know when I do that? — there emerges a fourth question for a consciousness that follows Lonergan in the way of self-appropriation to the point of explanatory mediation, not of knowledge, but of moral responsibility. The fourth question is, What do I do when I know all that, that is, when I have answered with Lonergan the three foundational questions of *Insight* and their existential and religious analogues. The existentially and politically responsible answer calls for the commitment of all one's energies to the implementation of the integral heuristic structure of proportionate being. If explanatory self-appropriation is indeed an epochal control of meaning, the future not only of civilized humanity but of proportionate being itself hangs in the balance of the tension that this fourth form of the foundational question introduces into one's conscious development as a human subject.'

30 Robert M. Doran, 'Primary Process and the Spiritual Unconscious,' *Lonergan Workshop* 5, ed. Fred Lawrence (Chico, CA: Scholars Press, 1985) 23-47; reprinted as chapter 15 in *Intentionality and Psyche*.

31 See Eric Voegelin, *The New Science of Politics* (Chicago: University of Chicago Press, 1952) 186.

32 Robert M. Doran, 'Jungian Psychology and Lonergan's Foundations: A Methodological Proposal,' *Supplement to the Journal of the American Academy of Religion* (1979) 23-35; reprinted as chapter 11 in *Intentionality and Psyche*.

33 Robert M. Doran, 'Jungian Psychology and Christian Spirituality,' *Review for Religious*, July, 1979, 497-510; September, 1979, 742-52; November, 1979, 857-66; reprinted as chapters 12-14 in *Intentionality and Psyche*.

34 Karl Rahner, 'Thomas Aquinas on the Incomprehensibility of God,' in *Celebrating the Medieval Heritage: A Colloquy on the Thought of Aquinas and Bonaventure*, ed. David Tracy, *Journal of Religion Supplement* (1978) S107-S125.

[35] Robert M. Doran, 'Psyche, Evil, and Grace,' *Communio* (1979) 192-211; reprinted as chapter 10 in *Intentionality and Psyche.*

[36] 1993 note: See chapters 6-10 in *Theology and the Dialectics of History.*

[37] 1993 note: See chapters 15-17 in *Theology and the Dialectics of History.*

[38] See Peter Homans, *Jung in Context: Modernity and the Making of a Psychology* (Chicago: University of Chicago Press).

2   From Psychic Conversion to the Dialectic of Community

1   Introductory Narrative

This paper is based on the first of four lectures that I delivered at Boston College in March of 1985 during the spring 'minisession' of the Lonergan Workshop. In this lecture I set forth in autobiographical fashion some of the factors that led me to move from earlier reflections on the psyche and on Lonergan's significance for the reorientation of the science of depth psychology to more recent work on society and culture. It seems that some have asked whether there is not some discontinuity in my work, and I would like to take this opportunity to show that there is not, that the development is consistent, and that the movement was demanded by the very logic of the ulterior purpose that I had in mind all along, namely, to begin work on the development of a contemporary Christian systematic theology. From the dialogue that transpired during the March workshop itself, which I found very helpful, I have learned to regard the work that I am about in the book on which I was lecturing, not yet as systematics itself, but still as foundations, and more precisely as that dimension of foundations devoted to the derivation of some of the principal categories that will be employed when I do get around to doing systematics. One must 'grow into' systematics. One must not try to hasten the process. One must be patient. As a result of the insights gained during the workshop, I have decided as to adopt a more modest title for the book on which I was speaking. I had intended to entitle it *A Theology for a World-Cultural Humanity*, Volume One: *The Situation*. I now will call it *The Analogy of Dialectic: Categories for a Systematic Theology*.[1]

The systematic theology that I am anticipating is to be a theology of history, through and through. This means that the realities named by the special categories will have to be understood in relation to history, or, better, as they affect history. And so a preliminary task consists in working out a theory of history. The book offers the principal categories of that theory. It will demonstrate, I hope, that I have not left behind the earlier work on the psyche, but have rather tried to integrate it, under the rubric of the dialectic of the subject, into a more complete synthesis.

The question of culture and society is not a new interest of mine; in fact it precedes in many ways my interest in psychology, at least in the technical sense in which I have tried to do psychology over the past twelve years or so in explicit dependence on Lonergan's thought. Strictly speaking my interest in psychology goes back to a time prior to my encounter with Lonergan, back to my days as a Jesuit novice in the mid-1950s. It was then that I was introduced to the spiritual life. Our novitiate was a relatively rare phenomenon in those days, in the sense that it was comparatively sane. In particular, there was some encouragement to face both existentially and somewhat theoretically such questions as those about the right way to live, the flourishing of persons in community, the development of an affective relationship to the living person of Jesus, and the primacy of an unfeigned charity in the Christian life. We had a Director of Novices, Fr. Joseph Sheehan, who, though not a professional theologian and certainly not a budding methodologist, would have had no difficulty with the proposition that Romans 5.5 more or less does name the ultimate foundation of all else, and who, on the basis of that conviction, was able quite deftly to give us some working knowledge of how to sort out intentional affective responses to genuine values from either intentional affective responses to mere satisfactions or such aberrations of feeling as *ressentiment* and lesser perversions which can do and have done so much to give religion a bad name. From my late teens and early twenties, then, I had developed a very serious interest, both practical and theoretical, in the relationship of psychology to the Christian life, to grace and the indwelling of the Holy Spirit; and I did make, I believe, an early commitment, however generic, to devoting a good deal of time and energy to working this out with some precision.

Nevertheless, in terms of the framework provided by Lonergan, and of the horizon shift that his work effects, it was chapter 7, not chapter 6, of *Insight* that got me started, and it will be in terms of what he says there that my own proposals about culture and society will have to be judged. I had finally got this far in *Insight* in the summer of 1967. And I believed then, as I still do today, that chapter 7 was the most important piece of literature that I had ever read; that it was the product not only of philosophic genius, which I already knew from earlier chapters, indeed from the first page of the preface, but also of prophetic vision, and so of grace, of a certain holiness, and no doubt a good deal of suffering. The call to conversion that is at the heart of all of Lonergan's writings began to make its singular impact on me in the reading of this chapter. I can recall reading and rereading and being stirred as I never had been before to a profound sense of what it would be worth while to devote my life to. For the first time, I think, I had found concretely something of which I could say, 'This is worth a lifetime.'

The time was ripe, of course, for a person of my age
to be affected in this way by what Lonergan was saying in
this chapter, and if I had read it a few years earlier it might
not have meant as much. Who knows? At any rate, 1967
was a time of profound social change, unrest, upheaval,
confusion, and also grace-inspired stirrings for far-reaching structural transformations in society, semantic transformations in culture, personal transformations in subjects,
and religious transformations in the life and ministry of
the church. Lonergan, for me, spoke to those coincidental
manifolds in history calling for higher integration in a way
and to a depth that nobody else did. And he also impressed
upon me the fact that meeting the problems of our latter
day at their roots in general bias would be a slow and laborious process demanding nothing short of what he calls,
elsewhere in the book, the reorientation and integration of
the sciences and the reorientation and integration of the
myriad instances of common sense. In a globally generic
way I was ready to throw myself into this task, but the
concrete specifics of how and in what order were not yet
clear.

I was ordained a priest in 1969, and a year later was
asked whether I would interrupt my doctoral studies for a
couple of years to assume the responsibility of organizing
and launching a new program of campus ministry at
Marquette University. Shortly after I had agreed to do so
and had assembled a staff of people to help me, but before
we had officially begun to operate, the Vietnam War spread
to Cambodia, and several students were killed in protests
at Kent State University. Campuses around the country
were in turmoil, and Marquette was no exception. Although
we had as yet no official position in the University, we found
ourselves challenged by both external events and inner
promptings to assume some role not only among the
students but also with the faculty and administration in

responding to the crisis. For the first time in my life I found myself not an observer but a participant in a situation where contrary ideologies and their accompanying emotions were the major components of the spiritual air that we breathed.

I was to find myself in such straits a few times too often in the course of my two years in campus ministry, over issues not only political but also pastoral, ecclesial, and Jesuit. And I realize, as I look back on this time now, that perhaps I was too young and inexperienced to be put in the middle of such an unsettled environment and asked to assume some institutional responsibility for a genuinely pastoral and fundamentally intelligent, non-opiate, religious response. I was only incipiently equipped with the power of that psychically transformative 'mystery that is at once symbol of the uncomprehended and sign of what is grasped and psychic force that sweeps living human bodies, linked in charity, to the joyful, courageous, whole-hearted, yet intelligently controlled performance of the tasks set by a world order in which the problem of evil is not suppressed but transcended.'[2] At any rate we did what we could, and no major disasters occurred. But at the end of this time I knew that there were dimensions of myself that I needed to come to know better and to negotiate more calmly if I was to be able to live an adult life in the latter third of the twentieth century, responding with at least some integrity as a person, a theologian, a priest, a Christian to the situation in which we all participate for better or for worse.

Before moving to a more or less full-time dedication to attempting to understand that situation itself, I had other business to attend to, and began to spend a period of some eighteen months, about two or three times a month, being introduced to my own sensitive psyche, my feelings and my dreams, with the help of Dr. Charles Goldsmith, a Christian psychologist of basically — though, thank God,

not dogmatically — Jungian persuasion: a man who gave
similar assistance, by the way, to a number of persons interested in Lonergan's work at that time in Milwaukee,
and who also got a basic introduction to Lonergan as a
result! It was an exciting time at Marquette, as a number
of us in close contact with each other shared in a community of discourse on the common grounds of Lonergan,
our introduction to depth psychology, and our cultural,
political, and social questions: no doubt the most closely
knit and intellectually fertile community I have ever experienced, and the one that has contributed most to my own
development.

2   Psychic Conversion

It was out of this environment and the living questions that sustained it that I arrived at the notion of psychic conversion. I had returned to doctoral studies, and I
was working on a paper on Heidegger's influence on
Bultmann. I was reading and rereading *Kant and the Problem of Metaphysics*, taking extensive notes, and was keenly
aware that some insight was emerging, when suddenly it
began to come together: there is another dimension of interiority besides the intentional operations that Lonergan
discloses in *Insight* and *Method in Theology*; it may at times
and in some people require a change that bears the features of what Lonergan calls a conversion, if they are to be
able to bring their intentional operations to bear upon it,
understanding it correctly and negotiating it responsibly.
A conversion is 'an about-face; it comes out of the old by
repudiating characteristic features; it begins a new sequence
that can keep revealing ever greater depth and breadth and
wealth.'[3] It is 'a transformation of the subject and his world,'
a 'change of course and direction. It is as if one's eyes were
opened and one's former world faded and fell away. There

emerges something new that fructifies in interlocking, cumulative sequences of developments on all levels and in all departments of human living.'[4] These descriptions seemed to fit what I was undergoing, and so it seemed that I could call it a conversion. Yet it was not exactly religious or moral or intellectual, even if closely related to all of these. Eventually I called it psychic, and I spent the greater part of the next decade in attempts, some successful and some not, to conceptualize and articulate it.

The first relatively successful attempt came in Zürich in the late fall of 1974 while I was working on my dissertation. I had distributed a paper the previous summer at the Lonergan Workshop which had not hit things off correctly, and I had to write to Fred Lawrence from Zürich and ask that, if publication plans on that Workshop were going ahead, this paper be withheld from publication. For until later in 1974 I had not yet accurately grasped and articulated the relation of the psyche to the intentionality that Lonergan discloses; and on that insight and articulation everything else depends. I had had previous indications that my observations were still coincidental. For instance, when I shared my work with Lonergan in late 1973, he asked (rhetorically, I now think) whether it manifested the same position on feelings and symbols that he had expressed in *Method*. I answered 'Yes,' of course, but I had not yet worked out how this was the case; I knew only that it did not conflict with his position. Then the following summer at the Workshop, Fred Lawrence said something to the effect that the difficulty he had with my paper was with the place of the *question* in the whole picture: I had seemed, in my haste and enthusiasm to sponsor and promote the psyche and its symbols, to shortchange the crucial and transformative role of intelligent inquiry, critical reflection, and moral deliberation. I can recall now how I went through at least four or five more months of such conceptual muddle and maybe even existential capitulation to the rhythms and processes of the psyche until I finally began to get it straight. I have told the story before of the dream that I had in Zürich of meeting Lonergan on the stairs. I was going down, and he was coming up. We met between the first and second floors, and so at that point where empirical consciousness gives way to intelligent consciousness. I was intending to go down to the basement — that is, to muddle some more among the images and archetypes — and Lonergan, knowing my intentions, said to me, 'If you really want see some images, come with me!' He took me to the top floor of the house, where we entered a large room, sat down, and began to watch a movie. Fourth-level consciousness, and the aesthetic detachment that it entails from the psychic basement, was the place from which to negotiate the kaleidoscope of symbols emerging from the neural depths. From there I was able to go on to articulate the basic position of *Subject and Psyche*, linking what Lonergan says about feelings and values in chapter 2 of *Method in Theology* with what he says about feelings and symbols in chapter 3, and so articulating at least a first approximation to an adequate theory of the psyche within the overall framework provided by intentionality analysis.

I was occupied for the next few years in trying to articulate this basic point more clearly, and to bring my position more fully to bear on Jungian psychology, where, I had become convinced in Zürich, the position on intentionality was lacking, and where the lack was responsible not only for a kind of epistemological idealism, half Kantian and half Hegelian, but also, and more seriously, for a somewhat Nietzschean and thoroughly disastrous moral relativism. These efforts led to what I felt were clearer expositions, both of what I meant by psychic conversion, through a clarification by contrast or what Philip McShane calls random dialectic, and also of its relation to religious, moral, and intellectual conversion; and they led as well to a more explicit effort at linking my work not only with *Method in Theology* as I had done earlier, but also with *Insight*.

Through this latter work I came to what is perhaps the clearest definition of psychic conversion that I have been able to arrive at: psychic conversion is the transformation of what Lonergan (following Freud but with a somewhat different meaning) calls the censor, from a repressive to a constructive intrasubjective agency in personal development. In this sense, it is a key to the integrity of what in *Insight* Lonergan calls the dialectic of the dramatic subject, where the linked but opposed principles of change are neural demand functions and the *orientation* of intelligence as the latter, in collaboration with imagination, preconsciously exercises a censorship over the former. Dramatically patterned intelligence and imagination exclude certain elements of the neural undertow from emerging in consciousness in the form of images and concomitant affects coherent with the images. Images, of course, are for the sake of insight. A constructive censor will exclude psychic materials that are irrelevant to the insight that one wants. It is an instrument of character, in Philip Rieff's sense of the restrictive shaping of possibilities. Such censorship

> ... selects and arranges materials that emerge in consciousness in a perspective that gives rise to an insight; this positive activity has by implication a negative aspect, for other materials are left behind, and other perspectives are not brought to light; still, this negative aspect of positive activity does not introduce any arrangement or perspective into the unconscious demand functions of neural patterns and processes.[5]

Unfortunately, however, 'just as insight can be desired, so too it can be unwanted. Besides the love of light, there can be a love of darkness,'[6] and besides the constructive activity of the censor, there can be a repressive activity.

> ... its positive activity is to prevent the emergence into consciousness of perspectives that would give rise to unwanted insights; it introduces, so to speak, the exclusion of arrangements into the field of the unconscious; it dictates the manner in which neural demand functions are not to be met; and the negative aspect of its positive activity is the admission to consciousness of any materials in any other arrangement or perspective.[7]

Psychic conversion, again, is a conversion of the censor from a repressive to a constructive agency in one's personal development. As such it is obviously dependent on other dimensions of a full conversion process: proximately, perhaps, on a prethematic intellectual conversion to the desire for insight and truth; and, with successive degrees of remoteness, on a moral conversion that shifts the criterion of what one wants from satisfactions to values, among which is truth, including the truth about oneself; and on a religious conversion that is the ultimate ground of sustained moral living. And its articulation is dependent on a quite thematic intellectual conversion as the latter promotes the self-appropriation of intentional operations.

But, however much it is a function of these other and in a sense more radical transformations, it also is something distinct from them. It is a conversion that affects the first level of consciousness, the dramatically patterned experiential flow itself, whereas intellectual conversion affects the second and third levels of consciousness, the levels of intelligent inquiry and critical reflection; moral conversion affects the fourth level of consciousness; and religious conversion affects or perhaps even creates (in the sense of created grace) a fifth level of consciousness.[8] This is not to say, however, that psychic conversion cannot also have its effects on these other dimensions of conversion, strengthening and confirming one in the general orientation of converted living, and functioning, as it were, as a defensive circle around the other conversions. The gift of grace that is responsible for the whole thing is rooted, as Thomas Aquinas knew, in the spiritual dimension of the person, and only from there does it extend its influence to the sensitive desires. But that extension consolidates a habituation in the orientation of converted living, until in the saint there is realized the more or less complete coincidence of satisfaction with an ordered and at times differentiated hierarchy of values, and one can truly love God and do what one wills, and even, for the most part, what one desires. This is the height of the affective conversion of which Lonergan spoke in some of his late papers.[9] Psychic conversion is related to affective conversion in that it renders available for conscious negotiation some of the materials with which one must work as one moves toward the threefold permanent commitment to love in the family, love in the community, and the love of God above all else that constitutes affective conversion.

3   The Dialectic of the Subject and the Dialectic of Community

I began to work out some of these refinements in *Psychic Conversion and Theological Foundations*, employing the basic framework of Lonergan's 'Healing and Creating in History.' And as I did so, the earlier themes of history

itself, of society, culture, and politics, which had been
placed on the back burner, began to return, and I began to
deal with the question of the relation between what I had
been doing on the subject and the whole realm of cultural
and social values. Obviously, the scale of values presented
on pages 31-32 of *Method in Theology* was pertinent here,
and I began to unpack the scale of values in the same book,
viewing the penultimate and ultimate phases of the longer
cycle — liberalism and totalitarianism — as a function of
the collapse of the whole scale of values to the two most
basic levels, and insisting that the root of this general
cultural derailment was to be located not only in general
bias but also in a concomitant neglect of the sensitive
psyche characteristic of modernity. This position implied,
and in fact was rooted in, a more basic position on the role
of the sensitive psyche vis-à-vis intentionality. In
expounding this more basic position I drew on Eric
Voegelin's articulation in 'The Gospel and Culture' of the
experience of life as a movement with a direction to be
found or missed. I related this articulation of what might
be called the 'original experience' to Lonergan's attempt
in *Insight* to bring his readers to locate insight and judgment in 'the pulsing flow of life' itself. For me, Lonergan
had disengaged the normative order of the search for direction in the movement of life, and what in a sense remained to be done, and could be done by what I was calling psychic conversion, was the disengagement of the
movement of life itself in which the direction is to be found.

The movement of life changes with, and is dependent on, the performance of the operations constitutive of
the normative order of inquiry. Sensitive consciousness is
transformed as one moves through the tension of inquiry
to insight, and it changes again as reflection arises only to
give way to reasonable judgment. Most obvious are the
changes that occur in sensitive consciousness in the course

of existential deliberation and decision. It is precisely about these changes that Ignatius wrote in his rules for discernment and his counsels about the three times for election. In a couple of courses at Regis College on psychology and spirituality I engaged in an interpretation of the rules for discernment in terms of these changes in the sensitive psyche. I employed as a basic grid Lonergan's articulation in chapter 15 of *Insight* of the conscious tension of limitation and transcendence. I identified the tension of limitation and transcendence in the sensitive psyche's experience of the movement of life with the condition of equanimity in which, Ignatius says, decisions can be made by a rational weighing of the pros and cons of the various alternatives. Because we are not always in this condition of creative tension when we have to make decisions, other rules are provided to help us determine the movements of consolation and desolation, where consolation is a movement that would lead us to a creative tension of limitation and transcendence, desolation a movement that would skew the balance in the direction of limitation, and false consolation a movement that would distort the same balance in the direction of transcendence.

The tension of limitation and transcendence is rooted ontologically in the disproportion of the schemes of recurrence of the bodily organism, on the one hand, and of intentionality with its unrestricted objective, on the other hand. The psyche participates in both schemes of recurrence, and experiences their tension. Psychic vitality is a matter of remaining in the tension of limitation and transcendence, in such a manner that the orientation is always toward the transformation of the self as integrator by the self as operator, through the emergence of further questions. It is a delicate negotiation. The displacement of the psychic tension in the direction of limitation heads in the limit to depression; the displacement in the direction of transcendence to schizophrenia. Most human beings settle for a slight displacement in the direction of depression: Kierkegaard's 'too little possibility.'[10] But it is easy to slip over as well to a displacement toward 'too much possibility,' to lose the ground under one's feet, to dispense with the roots in bodily existence, and to soar into schizophrenic fantasy. The creative tension of limitation and transcendence is experienced by the sensitive psyche, as are its displacements in one direction or the other. The tension itself is the key to discernment: when one is abiding in the tension itself, the way to proceed in making decisions is by the rational weighing of the pros and cons of the various alternatives; when one is not so abiding, but is being moved by the various pulls and counterpulls in different directions, one is to choose the way that leads to the establishment of the tension itself of limitation and transcendence.

The changes in the sensitive psyche as the normative order of inquiry either is or is not followed faithfully can be found as well even in our dreams. Lonergan speaks in *Method* of 'a transvaluation and transformation of symbols' and relates these to 'affective development, or aberration.' 'What before was moving no longer moves; what before did not move now is moving. So the symbols themselves change to express the new affective capacities and dispositions ... Inversely, symbols that do not submit to transvaluation and transformation seem to point to a block in development.'[11] My point goes a bit further than what is explicitly stated by Lonergan, though it is implicit in the connection of what I have just quoted with his mention of what is 'most significant from a basic viewpoint' about the dream, namely 'the existential approach that thinks of the dream, not as the twilight of life, but as its dawn, the beginning of the transition from impersonal existence to presence in the world, to constitution of one's self in one's world.'[12] It is that the dream life can be a source of data on the transvaluation and transformation, or lack of these, in the symbols that awaken determinate affects and the feelings that evoke symbolic images. Certain significant dream symbols will undergo transformation as a result of the subject's conscious performance in waking life of the operations constitutive of the normative order of the search for the direction to be found in the movement of life. These successive transformations are data on, and offered by, the very movement of life itself, indicating what is happening to it under the influence of the operations of the creative vector of intentional consciousness.

The same existential approach establishes the link between these reflections on the subject and the questions of society and culture that I try to treat in my work on the situation of a contemporary Christian systematic theology. In the remainder of the present paper, I will relate the several steps that led me into direct confrontation with some of the problems of social, political, and cultural theory.

The first step, and the one to which I will devote the greatest attention here, was to think through the statement in *Insight* about the relation between the dialectic of the dramatic subject and the dialectic of community. Let me quote in full what Lonergan says there about this issue:

> In two manners [the] dialectic of community differs from the dialectic of the dramatic subject. First, there is a difference in extent, for the dialectic of community regards the history of human relationships, while the inner dialectic of the subject regards the biography of an individual. Secondly, there is a difference in the level of activity, for the dialectic of community is concerned with the interplay of more or less conscious intelligence and more or less

conscious spontaneity in an aggregate of individuals, while the dialectic of the subject is concerned with the entry of neural demands into consciousness. Accordingly, one might say that a single dialectic of community is related to a manifold of individual sets of neural demand functions through a manifold of individual dialectics. In this relationship the dialectic of community holds the dominant position, for it gives rise to the situations that stimulate neural demands, and it molds the orientation of intelligence that preconsciously exercises the censorship. Still, as is clear, one must not suppose this dominance to be absolute, for both covertly and overtly neural demands conspire with an obnubilation of intelligence, and what happens in isolated individuals tends to bring them together and so to provide a focal point from which aberrant social attitudes originate.

This raises the basic question of a bias in common sense.[13]

This passage was to be the basis from which I was able to move from prolonged reflection on the dialectic of the subject to an attempt to understand the other dialectical processes constitutive of the historical process. The dialectic of the subject, I found, may be rearticulated as the dialectic of the movement of life with the normative order of the search for direction in that movement. Human interiority is twofold. There are the operations of conscious intentionality, and there are the affective compositions and distributions of sensitively conscious energy that constitute what we usually call the psyche. There is the search for direction in the movement of life, and there is the movement itself in which direction is found or missed or lost. Changes in the movement provide the required indications as to whether we are succeeding or not in finding the direction. Intentionality analysis would articulate the search, psychic analysis the movement. Together they would constitute interiorly differentiated consciousness.

Ira Progoff and Ernest Becker have documented a progressive realization in the great architects of depth psychology, from Freud through Adler and Jung to Rank, of the relations that obtain between these two dimensions of interiority, a progressive movement toward what Eric Voegelin, writing in a quite different context, calls a psychology of orientations as contrasted with a psychology of passional motivations.[14] The latter, Voegelin says, is descriptive only of a certain *pneumo*pathological type of person. It is as a function of the operations of the spirit that the sensitive psychic experience of the movement of life changes. The psyche permeates, participates in, and is affected by, these operations, but the capacity to question is not a function of the sensitive psyche, but of conscious intentionality.

Depth psychology did not begin with such a distinction, and so has been lacking a precise objectification of what precisely it is that makes people well. Its insights into psychic well-being are often genuine, but remain for the most part coincidental and, as I found with Jung, subject to derailment when the issues to be confronted are distinctly spiritual, such as the question of good and evil. An intentionality analysis is required for a psychology of orientations.

The passage I have quoted from Lonergan, however, provides a framework for understanding better why the human spirit itself sometimes goes astray, why we miss the mark. Ontologically, as both Lonergan and Ricoeur argue, the condition of the possibility of sin lies in the very constitution of the triple compound of bodily organism,

sensitive psyche, and spiritual intentionality that is the
human person, and more specifically in the disproportion
of intentionality and the complex of body and psyche. But
if this is the formal cause of fallibility, there is also a historical course of events in which sin occurs, the social situation becomes absurd, and the distorted dialectic of community exercises a certain dominance over the dialectic of
the subject. That dominance, again, gives rise to the situations that stimulate neural demands and molds the orientation of intelligence that preconsciously exercises the
censorship. The relation of the subject to society can begin
to be understood precisely in terms of these relations
between the distorted dialectic of community and the distortions that occur in the unfolding dialectic of the subject. Let us try to understand *some* of these relations.

First, then, there *is* a derailment that is specifically
psychic. The sensitive psyche must be free to cooperate in
the search for direction in the movement of life; it must be
endowed with an affective self-transcendence that matches
the self-transcendence of the operations of the creative
vector. As Lonergan remarks in the lectures on the philosophy of education, as one moves into a practical pattern of experience, one can preserve the detachment and
disinterestedness of the pure desire only by reason of the
gift of charity, of what in *Insight* he calls universal willingness.[15] One source of derailment lies in the affective blockages that will not submit to transformation, that resist insight, judgment, decision. These affective obstructions are
among the compositions of sensitively psychic energy that
Jung called complexes. Complexes support the creative
vector when they provide us with the images needed for
insight, or when they offer us memories that help us discover ways of responding to new situations, or when they
spontaneously acquiesce to the process of reflection that
anticipates judgment, or when, through their agency, we

apprehend genuine values in an affectively charged manner that leads to action consonant with the values so apprehended. But our psychic energy can be blocked, fixed in inflexible patterns, driven by compulsions, plagued by obsessions, weighted down by general anxiety or specific fears, resistant to insight, true judgment, responsible action. Then we are derailed from the integral performance of the operations that constitute the normative order of the search for direction in the movement of life.

Second, then, genuine psychotherapy is a dissolving of the energic complexes that often are responsible for the derailment. And third, the first step in the dissolution is the recognition that autonomous negative complexes are always victimized compositions of energy formed as the consequence of our inevitable participation in the distortions at work in one's community and one's culture. The violence done to one's psyche may be the issue of one's own self-destructiveness, of course. But it may issue as well from one's social environment or from the cultural values of one's milieu. It is in fact more often than not the complex function of social, cultural, and personal factors. But the point is that psychic spontaneity as such is never morally responsible for its own disorder. The psyche's order and disorder are rooted in action affecting it from beyond itself. Disordered complexes are always the victims of human history: of significant others, of social situations emergent from the distortions in one's community, of derailed cultural values, of one's own freedom, or of some combination of these various sources. The complex itself is the victim. It is not responsible for the genesis of its own disorder. The various compositions and distributions of our energic affectivity begin to be set for us, without our personal choice, from very early on in life. We may even speak of a certain generational bondage, through which a family can be affected over generations by the same psy-

chic pattern. One's psychic complexes are always in part
set by the agenda operative in the community and the culture, and that agenda will always be more or less distorted.
Psychic disorder usually reaches back into areas of our
experience that we cannot even remember (though the
question, What is your earliest memory? may well be very
illuminating), or that we have blocked from recall. And it
is usually reinforced by our acquiescence to patterns established without our self-constitutive contribution. ·

The fourth step in understanding the relations of the
dialectic of the subject to the wider community is to find
some way of determining the extent to which a subject's
total derailment from the direction to be found in the
movement of life is a function of these social factors beyond his or her control and the extent to which it is a function of freedom as freedom contributes to psychic disorder. Psychic disorder in itself, remember, is always a function of victimization. But the source of the victimization
may be more or less resident in the dominant dialectic of
community or more or less a default for which one's conscious intentionality and its orientations are responsible.
Lonergan's discussion of the various biases is helpful in
providing some better understanding of the various sources
of psychic disorder.

Lonergan distinguishes four varieties of bias: a general bias of ordinary common sense against theoretical
questions, the individual bias of the egoist, the group bias
of the clique or class or nation, and the dramatic bias of
the neurotic. First, we can see rather easily, I think, that
there is an increasing dominance of psychic as opposed to
spiritual features involved in the genesis and functioning
of the bias as one moves from general bias through individual and then group bias to dramatic bias. Dramatic bias
is the effect of autonomous complexes beyond the reach
of immediate self-determination. The functioning of the

psychic factor of spontaneous intersubjectivity is quite predominant in group bias. But psychic factors become less important and spiritual factors more important in the individual bias of the egoist (quite distinct from the dramatic bias of the narcissist, by the way), and they are least significant in the general bias of common sense, which clearly is a function more of intellectual than of psychological truncation.

The genesis of the biases follows this same sequential analysis. Dramatic bias is most affected by autonomous psychic complexes victimized originally by factors beyond one's control, and frequently associated with obstacles to sexual development through a disorientation of one's relationship to one's body. Group bias is more a blend of psychic disorder with character disorder; character disorder is the dominant feature in individual bias; and general bias requires conversion that is specifically intellectual or theoretic if it is to be transcended. As we move from dramatic through group and then individual to general bias, we are moving from psychopathology to what Voegelin called pneumopathology, from a sickness of the psyche to a sickness of the spirit. The element of personal default increases. It is least operative in dramatic bias, whose genesis often lies in part in events that precede even our earliest memories. It is more operative in group bias, where there is a capitulation of personal responsibility to the interests of a narrowly defined group bent on its own advantage. It is more dominant still in the egoist's choice of his or her own advantage over the common good and even over one's spontaneous involvement in normal intersubjective communicative action. It is most dominant when general bias instrumentalizes intelligence and reason so as to pervert the disinterested inquiry of the search for direction through the arbitrary brushing aside of relevant but difficult, ultimate, long-range, theoretical, disturbing questions.

In general, the more dominant the psychic factor in the bias, the more is its ultimate source to be located in the community and the culture rather than in the pneumopathological exercise of one's own freedom. This at least is a general rule of thumb. Dramatic bias is more a function of energic disturbances due to the victimization of the psyche by others or by distorted social and cultural situations beyond the control of the individual. Group bias entails a capitulation of the ego to, or an overwhelming of the ego by, spontaneous and psychically rooted inter-subjective connections. It results in a subordination of personal responsibility to the interests of a narrowly conceived group bent on its own advantage. Its genesis and functioning are more a blend of psychopathology and pneumopathology. Individual bias is a function of an erroneous negotiation of the emergence of the individual ego from the systemic relations that inform the group. Its genesis may involve a desperate reaction formation vis-à-vis intersubjective connections that seem to threaten the individual. One is confused in one's negotiation of these connections because of the powerful psychic factors involved in spontaneous intersubjectivity. Yet to name a bias egoistic is also to impute responsibility and guilt, and so to assign to the formation and functioning of the bias a certain degree of self-victimization. But the pneumopathological element is most pronounced in general bias, which is a function of a personal default of intelligence and freedom for which one is to be held accountable in a more pronounced way, an instrumentalization of reason that, by the arbitrary brushing aside of relevant and ultimate but difficult questions, perverts the disinterested inquiry through which direction can be found.

In fact, to discuss the various forms of bias separately is by and large to engage in abstractions. Thus the discussion must move on to the recognition that victimization by others and self-victimization usually conspire with one another in the cumulative production of personal and, through personal, historical disorder. To give one example, a person may be dramatically predisposed to egoism by a narcissistic disorder whose origin and genesis lay beyond that person's control. But the person may still be capable of assuming responsibility for the redirection of the energies locked up in narcissistic complexes. If not, it is a mistake to regard the person as an egoist, a term which implies personal responsibility and freedom.

Now, to the extent that one can assume such responsibility, pneumotherapy, a healing and conversion of the spirit, will be the more radical requirement before psychotherapy can have any effect in the healing of the disorder. Egoism is an unwillingness; narcissism is an inability. To the extent that they are distinct factors conspiring to distort personal integrity, the establishment of integrity will involve the conversion of unwillingness into willingness as a constitutive element in and precondition of the treatment of narcissistic energic complexes. On the other hand, to the extent that the person's derailment from the direction that can be found in the movement of life cannot be understood either in its genesis or in its reinforcement as the product of self-victimization for which the person is to be held accountable, psychotherapy will be the condition of the possibility of pneumotherapy. The underlying psychic inability will have to be radically affected before the appropriate willingness to cooperate with the process of further healing can emerge. Again, in either instance, *psychic* disorder as such is not responsible for its own genesis. *I* may be responsible for a good deal of my own affective disorder, but only insofar as I am capable of intelligent, reasonable, and responsible operations in its regard and fail or refuse to exercise such care. The constitution and genesis of affective disorder will vary from one person to another. No general, exhaustive, or exclusive mode of origination may be assigned. All that can be said is that there is always victimization.

Fifth, some insight is thus gained regarding the relation of the psyche to moral impotence. Lonergan's treatment of moral impotence is from the viewpoint of the incompleteness of intellectual and volitional development. As the reflections summarized above would suggest, his understanding can be complemented by a consideration of the incompleteness of psychic development. The victimized psyche lives in what John Dunne has called the hell of the night of private suffering. This is distinct from the night of the suffering of compassion and forgiveness. Between the two one has experienced the bliss of a day that overcomes the hell of the night of private suffering and that cannot be overcome by the night of the suffering of compassion and forgiveness.[16] But how does one emerge into that day that divides the two nights? The question can be put in another way. There are three ways to negotiate psychic darkness. In the hell of the night of private suffering, though, only two of them are available to us: repression and moral renunciation. Neither of these works, nor does either of them represent an intelligent way of proceeding. The third manner of negotiating psychic disturbance, compassionate negotiation of what has been victimized, is intelligent, reasonable, responsible; but this is precisely what we cannot be because of the psychic darkness. How do we gain that capacity for compassionate negotiation of our own darkness? We must be met by love, if we are to move from the hell of the night of private suffering to the capacity for the suffering of compassion and forgiveness. And, I submit, the compassion begins with regard to our own victimized darkness, and the forgiveness with regard to the factors that have brought it on. The love that must meet us can be mediated by others, but only if they are beyond getting caught in the darkness, only if they are capable of suffering from the darkness without being trapped by it into the hell of the night of their own private suffering, only if they are themselves capable of the suffering of compassion and forgiveness. And one will know oneself to be healed, to be beyond the hell of the first night and capable of the suffering of the second night, only when one can suffer precisely the same injury that brought about the first night without being driven again into the hell of private suffering. Then one can oneself be a medium of healing for others, for one has moved beyond the first night and into the second, and is on the way to the agapic charity of the affectively converted 'suffering servant,' whose catalytic agency is the goal and summit of the development of the person.

Perhaps I have said enough to indicate the manner in which reflection on psychic conversion leads through the process of further questions to a concern both for the structures of culture and society that are involved in some psychic victimization, and also for those structures that promote psychic well-being. Since I am concerned only to indicate how my own interests moved from the psychic to the social, I will not pursue the present line of investigation further here. I want rather to indicate a few other connections between my earlier work on the psychological dimensions of theological foundations and the present work moving toward a systematic theology of history, culture, and society.

4 Culture and Praxis

The first factor has to do with a satisfactory strategy for reversing the social and cultural decline responsible for, among other things, psychic disorder on such a massive scale. I stated a position in *Psychic Conversion and Theo-*

logical Foundations that finds further support in the book I am working on now, to the effect that an adequate doctrine of praxis includes, in a quite central fashion, an emphasis on superstructural interdisciplinary collaboration intent on the reorientation of the human sciences. This position, of course, is dependent on Lonergan's prophetic insistence — I think it is no overstatement to call it that — on the influence of the cultural superstructure on the social infrastructure; or, negatively put, on the deleterious effect vis-à-vis the social good of order of a major surrender of intelligence at the superstructural level. In this sense I came to understand Lonergan's own life's work, as well as the psychological work I had been engaged in on the basis of Lonergan's achievement, as themselves social praxis in the strictest possible sense of that term. Moreover, the human sciences are to be reoriented precisely on the basis of the interiorly differentiated consciousness that Lonergan's work makes possible, and on no other basis. And if that is the case, the science of depth psychology should be the first to undergo the purification and transformation that Lonergan's work makes possible, since it is itself concerned with the self-appropriation of one dimension of interiority. A reoriented depth psychology would thus be a dimension of the foundations of the reorientation of the other human sciences. But from there one must move to the cultural and political and social sciences, and begin to exercise an analogous critical, dialectical, and normative intelligence in their regard. There is, then, a quite spontaneous and natural movement from the suggestion of a reorientation of depth psychology to the task of providing some of the fairly basic categories for understanding culture, the political specialization of common sense, and the elements and structures of society.

Second, besides the reorientation and integration of the sciences, there is the reorientation and integration of the myriad instances of common sense. This, too, is social praxis. And a reoriented depth psychology is not without its implications for what I like to call a post-interiority mentality at the level of common sense, analogous to the post-systematic, post-scientific, and post-scholarly mentalities that Lonergan speaks of in *Method in Theology* as transformations of common sense consequent upon superstructural transformations in the differentiation of consciousness. From the time that I prepared to teach an undergraduate course at Marquette University on religion and culture, I have been convinced of the transcultural implications both of Lonergan's own work, and also of a reoriented Jungian approach to the psyche. No small part of the motivation behind my attempts both to understand and, where necessary, correct Jung, and to integrate a reoriented Jungianism with Lonergan's intentionality analysis, has been in the interests of specifying the major constituents of a world-cultural mentality at the level of common sense, a mentality that flows from successful communication to the wider culture on the part of the specialists in interiorly differentiated consciousness. What is required in our situation is a global alternative to present distortions in the dialectic of community. Such an alternative is dependent on transformations at the level of culture, in the generation of cultural values that are capable of informing the way of life of a global network of alternative communities intent on a different way to live. Those cultural values are themselves a function of the self-appropriation of the transcultural constituents of personal integrity. And to that self-appropriation both intentionality analysis and reoriented psychic analysis have constitutive contributions to make. The contributions of intentionality analysis are clear to any who have followed Lonergan in his relentless search for a transcultural base for the general and special categories. The contributions of psychic analysis are clear to any who have discovered that Jung, however deficient may have been his articulation, was not entirely wrong in insisting that the psyche's symbols include a crosscultural archetypal dimension that simply cannot be accounted for within the narrow confines of Freudian dogmatics. The link to culture and society became more clear to me as I reflected on Eric Voegelin's discussion of anthropological and cosmological symbolizations of the direction to be found in the movement of life. From this reflection, I went on to posit a dialectic of culture at the level of cultural values, analogous to the dialectic of the subject at the level of personal value and to the dialectic of community at the level of social value: hence, 'the analogy of dialectic.'

Two final sources of influence should be mentioned. One of them lies in the discussions at several Lonergan Workshops between Fred Lawrence and Matthew Lamb regarding political philosophy. I tried to find in the scale of values a way to contribute to that discussion, and perhaps to mediate a resolution of it that might be acceptable to both by honoring the emphases of each. A second lies in reflection on the option of the Society of Jesus at its thirty-second General Congregation to define its mission today in terms of the service of faith and the promotion of justice. Again, the scale of values was to prove helpful. Faith is a religious value, justice as understood in this option a social value; and intermediate between religious and social values are personal and cultural values. The connections, I am convinced, have to be made explicit and operative if the Society's option is to bear fruit that will last. At the moment the option is leading, I am afraid, to a gradual abandonment of the Society's intellectual and educational apostolates, and to a process of training for younger Jesuits that is not governed by a consistent set of objectives that can inspire a clear-headed commitment to long-range goals and consequent strategies. There is at present a sequence of ever less comprehensive syntheses; and this is the characteristic, not of progress but of major decline. Reversal of decline is the function of culture, and the integrity of culture is a function of a creative minority of authentic persons. Such practical problems, very close to home, have certainly been a further source of the movement of my own reflection beyond the realm of psychological considerations to the arena of the cultural and the social.

Notes

[1] In fact, the book came to be called *Theology and the Dialectics of History* (see above, chapter 1, note 3).

[2] Bernard Lonergan, *Insight* (see above, chapter 1, note 20) 723-24/745.

[3] Bernard Lonergan, *Method in Theology* (see above, chapter 1, note 1) 237-38.

[4] Ibid. 130.

[5] Lonergan, *Insight* 192/216.

[6] Ibid. 191/214.

[7] Ibid. 192-93/216.

[8] 1993 note: For a development of this latter point, see Robert M. Doran, 'Consciousness and Grace,' *Method: Journal of Lonergan Studies* 11:1 (1993) 51-75.

[9] See Bernard Lonergan, 'Natural Right and Historical Mindedness,' in *A Third Collection*, ed. Frederick E. Crowe (Mahwah, NJ: Paulist Press, 1985) 169-83, esp. 179.

10 See Ernest Becker, *The Denial of Death* (New York: The Free Press, 1973) chapter 5.

11 Lonergan, *Method in Theology* 66.

12 Ibid. 69.

13 Lonergan, *Insight* 218/243.

14 See Ira Progoff, *The Death and Rebirth of Psychology* (New York: McGraw-Hill, 1973); Becker, *The Denial of Death*; Eric Voegelin, *The New Science of Politics* (see above, chapter 1, note 31) 186.

15 See Bernard Lonergan, *Topics in Education*, ed. Robert M. Doran and Frederick E. Crowe, vol. 10 in Collected Works of Bernard Lonergan (Toronto: University of Toronto Press, 1993) 91.

16 See John S. Dunne, *The Way of All the Earth* (New York: Macmillan, 1972) 49-62.

3   Psychic Conversion and Spiritual Development

I will begin by locating personal development as a whole, which is a development of both intentionality and psyche, in the scale of values, and especially in the context of that scale of values as the latter is pertinent to the challenges that confront the human family under God in our time in history. Then I will attempt to locate precisely in what spiritual and psychological development consist, given this context. Finally, I will point to the place of depth psychology and psychic conversion in the emergence of the Christian subject precisely within this historical context. Given the limitations of time imposed by a short lecture, I can do no more than this, even though my treatment may leave you with more questions than answers. But perhaps that is enough, given the fact that conversation is possible, and that we have the time for further discussion in a more informal atmosphere.

I take this approach to the question because much talk of spirituality in our day, and especially of spirituality and psychology, is too thin, without substance, vacuous, and above all self-centered and narcissistic. The issue of personal development has to be placed in a context that is social and cultural, and, yes, even political, if it is to be more than a matter of effectively denying self-transcendence as the criterion of authenticity, and so of subtly seeking self rather than the personal authenticity through which one becomes a principle of benevolence and beneficence,

an agent of genuine collaboration and true love in the real
world as that world is mediated by the meanings and motivated by the values operative in one's community. Our
consideration here, then, turns first to the question of personal value in its relation to the other levels of value; then
to the goal of the process of personal development and so
of the entire conversion process of which psychic conversion is only one part; and finally to a general discussion of
the relation of spiritual development and psychological
development in the full conversion process.

1   **Personal Value**

Let me begin by quoting what Lonergan says about
the integral and normative scale of values.

> Not only do feelings respond to values. They
> do so in accord with some scale of preference.
> So we may distinguish vital, social, cultural,
> personal, and religious values in an ascending
> order. Vital values, such as health and strength,
> grace and vigor, normally are preferred to
> avoiding the work, privations, pains involved
> in acquiring, maintaining, restoring them. So-
> cial values, such as the good of order which
> conditions the vital values of the whole com-
> munity, have to be preferred to the vital values
> of individual members of the community. Cul-
> tural values do not exist without the underpin-
> ning of vital and social values, but none the
> less they rank higher. Not on bread alone doth
> man live. Over and above mere living and op-
> erating, men have to find a meaning and value
> in their living and operating. It is the function
> of culture to discover, express, validate, criti-

cize, correct, develop, improve such meaning and value. Personal value is the person in his self-transcendence, as loving and being loved, as originator of values in himself and in his milieu, as an inspiration and invitation to others to do likewise. Religious values, finally are at the heart of the meaning and value of man's living and man's world.[1]

Now, when we speak of personal development or spiritual development or psychological development, of the development of operations or the development of feelings, we are speaking directly of personal value, of the development of the person in his or her self-transcendence, as loving and being loved, as originator of values in self and milieu, as a principle of benevolence and beneficence, as an inspiration and invitation to others to do likewise. And yet to place this development in a scale of values is to raise the question of the relation of the development of the subject to the other realms or levels of value. By answering that question, we can locate spirituality and psychology in a wider context and address them from a higher viewpoint than is too often the case in the contemporary church. And by answering that question as concretely as possible, we can locate spiritual and psychological development in a *contemporary* context. And from that context we can gain some appreciation of the criteria of authentic personal development in our situation, our *kairos*, our time in history under God. Let us try, then, to think through the relations that obtain among the various levels of value.

We can think of the relations among the levels both from below and from above. From below, problems at more basic levels can at times be met only by changes at higher levels. From above, these changes at higher levels are the conditioning source of effective activity at the more basic

levels. Our first step toward concreteness, consequently, is
one of getting these relations straight as best we can.

Vital values are, basically, the goods required to live,
and to live well, where 'well' refers not to affluence or abun-
dance, but to dramatically artistic living. Our first work of
art is our own living. Life is experienced as a movement
with a direction that can be found or missed. To the extent
that a person finds the direction in the movement of life,
he or she is creating a work of art out of one's life, that is,
is so shaping the materials of one's life as to make of one's
life and of one's contribution to the constitution of the
human world a dramatically artistic enterprise. Living well,
then, requires freedom not only from hunger and misery,
but, as Habermas has said, also from servitude and personal degradation.[2] For the latter as well as the former are
enemies of life, and in fact can kill just as effectively, if
more subtly and more slowly, as can poverty, famine, and
war.

At any rate, the equitable distribution of vital values
to an entire community is a function of the second level of
values, of the social order, with its network of 'if-then' relationships. The social order, the level of social values, can
be broken down further to include the institutions of technology with their principal function of capital formation,
the economic order, and the political dimension of social
living. I could devote an entire lecture and more to trying
to disengage the relations that obtain among the elements
constitutive of this level, and to contrasting my position
with the major alternative position in our time, the Marxist theory of society.[3] But that would take us too far afield,
given our present purposes. My point is that there are times
when problems at the level of vital values can be met only
by changes at the level of social values: by a new alignment
of technological forces, under a new economic order,
governed by new legal and political agreements. A problem

at the more basic level of vital values, namely, their maldistribution within the community, thus creates the conditions which invite a series of changes at the higher level of social values.

These changes may be effected, of course, in several manners, revolutionary or orderly. In any case they will involve a change in the meanings and values informing a given way of life. And to the extent that this change is acknowledged as constitutive of the new order, human energies can be applied to bringing it about rather than to effecting a violent revolution with all of its attendant miseries and subsequent dangers of injustices of a new and perhaps contrary kind. In any event, social change of a major kind does not occur without cultural change, without a transformation of the meanings that people find in or give to their living and operating. Culture so understood informs the social order with the meanings and values that 'explain' to people why they do what they do, why they live as they live. If major transformations of the technological, economic, and political institutions of a community are to occur, there must be effected a change in the meanings and values that would inform a given way of life. Concretely, in our situation, we might think of the profit *motive*, precisely as a motive. Perhaps it is the case that the economic order will not be changed in such a way as to effect a change in the distribution of vital goods unless the profit motive is effectively removed from the way in which we think about and evaluate the economic order. But this means a transformation at the level of cultural values, precisely for the sake of the needed social order that would see to the equitable distribution of vital goods.

This example also highlights a major problem connected with cultural transformation, the problem of education. Culture functions at two levels. There is a spontaneous, everyday level of meanings and values informing

our ordinary human living. And there is a reflexive, superstructural level at which scientific and theoretical work is
conducted regarding the everyday level. Thus, we have not
only social relationships at the everyday level, but also the
science of sociology at the reflexive level; not only economic transactions at the everyday level, but also the science of economics at the reflexive level; not only political
persuasion at the everyday level but also political science
and political philosophy at the reflexive level, etc., etc. And
within the very realm of cultural values, then, there is required at times a major overhaul of the reflexive level of
culture, for the sake of the everyday level of culture. Economic transactions pursued under the motivation of maxi-
mizing profit are the manifestation, not of a supposed law
of economics, but also of a particular economic *theory*
whose practical implications have been successfully communicated to the everyday level. A change at the everyday
level will sometimes depend upon a change at the reflexive level, and upon the successful communication of that
change, through education, to the everyday level.

Personal value comes into play precisely at this point.
A change in the meanings and values which inform the life
of the community depends on a change in persons, on the
conversion of persons to authentic living in their constitution of the human world, and concomitantly of themselves.
Cultural values are changed, Lonergan has said, by the
work of a creative minority of persons who have effected
the changes in themselves which are required if they are to
assume responsibility for a new order of things in the mentality of the community; and then by the conversion of the
members of the wider community to a new orientation in
personal and communal living. And the more thorough
this personal conversion is, the more it is able to affect the
culture in all of its dimensions. When the problem is theoretical, as ultimately it is in the economic example we have

cited, the conversion required of some is not only religious and moral, but also intellectual. A cosmopolitan intellectual collaboration is required at the superstructural level of culture, a reorientation and integration of human science. And this collaboration is grounded in a conversion of intelligence and rationality to habits of authentic cognitional praxis, precisely for the sake of the mentality of the community, its operative meanings and values, its culture. Personal value, then, the person in his or her self-transcendence at every dimension of one's being, conditions the possibility of authentic cultural values. The latter, again, are required for the functioning of a social order that would see to the equitable distribution of vital values to the whole community.

Religious values, as Lonergan says, are at the heart of human living and the human world, precisely because the personal self-transcendence that is required if the scale of values is to function in an integral fashion is itself a function of divine grace: of the habitual grace through which the form of human living is the form of supernatural charity, hope, and faith; and of the actual grace, the *auxilium divinum*, the inner promptings and sustainment, that give rise to the particular acts by which the human person cooperates with God in the concrete working out of the divinely originated solution to the mystery of evil.

So far we have been engaged in a fairly abstract spelling out of the relations that obtain among the levels of value. This can now be concretized further. Not only do the conditions at the more basic levels of value call for changes at higher levels if they are to be met. Not only are these changes the condition of possibility for the effective functioning of the more basic levels. In addition, the proportions of the problematic conditions at the lower levels establish the dimensions that must be satisfied by the higher integration if the more basic problems are successfully to be resolved. With this insight, we are able to move to a contemporary context for personal, and so for both spiritual and psychological, development, and within this context to specify the relations of psyche and spirit in a very concrete fashion.

Now the problem of the maldistribution of vital goods is today not only factually but also recognizably global in its proportions. The factors responsible not only for the facts but also for our ability to recognize the facts as globally pervasive are multiform, and time does not permit us to go into them in any great detail. Let us simply accept as a given the *recognizably* global proportions of human misery, degradation, and injustice in our time.

Global injustice can be met only by a globally effective social order, and more concretely by a global network of communities intent on a way of living alternative to the competing and escalating imperialistic systems that are responsible for the current maldistribution of vital goods: intent, then, on alternative technologies, an alternative economic order, and an alternative mode of political praxis that would preserve the technological and economic institutions of society in a taut balance or poised equilibrium with the intersubjective spontaneity that is the ineradicable base of all human community. The theoretical developments that are required to institute such alternative technologies, economies, polities are a function of culture, and so there is demanded a superstructural transformation at the level of cultural values if the social infrastructure is to be constituted by the integral balance of practicality and intersubjective community that would institute an effective alternative to prevailing monstrosities. But, in addition, for there to be a global network of such alternative communities, there is required the crosscultural generation of a new set of cultural values to inform not simply the way of life of individual communities but also the communication among these communities by which they are enabled to collaborate in the institution of global 'if-then' relationships in the social order. There is required what Lonergan calls the transformation and integration of the myriad instances of common sense, so that a new set of meanings and values, generated by intercultural communication and collaboration, can inform the very infrastructure of social order itself. There is required a crosscultural generation of the cultural values that would inform the living of a world-cultural network of communities.

What does this mean for the *personal values* that are the condition of the possibility of authentic cultural values? What must occur at the level of the person in his or her self-transcendence if a crosscultural set of cultural values is to be generated? Basically, the answer is simple, but implementing it, realizing it, is a work of great difficulty. There is required the self-appropriation of the crosscultural constitution of personal authenticity or integrity. There is required on the part of a creative minority of subjects the achievement of interiorly differentiated consciousness. And then there is required a post-interiority mentality at the level of common sense, an attention to and recognition of the factors that make for authentic living and genuine progress, including cultural advance, on a crosscultural or transcultural basis. As far as religious values are concerned, we may offer, first, the hypothesis that what divine grace is doing in the world in our time includes this movement to interiorly differentiated consciousness as the condition of the possibility of a world-cultural network of alternative communities intent on a better way to live; and second, the persuasion that the dialogue among the major religions of the world will be one major arena both of the achievement of interiorly differentiated consciousness and of the crosscultural generation of world-cultural values.

2   **Interiorly Differentiated Consciousness and the Law of the Cross**

The process of self-appropriation has two dimensions: intentional and psychic. Its goal is the achievement of interiorly differentiated consciousness. I have located that goal in the context of a far wider consideration of the goals of humanity in our time, and so in the context of the responsibility for a global communitarian alternative to the monstrosities spawned by the competing and escalating imperialistic systems, whose conflicts have currently assumed effective control of the social order of the vast majority of the human race. If the goal of self-appropriation, then, is interiorly differentiated consciousness, there is also an ulterior finality to the whole process of interiorly differentiated consciousness itself. That ulterior finality is the precise kind of self-transcendence that can assume responsibility for the global cultural and social changes that are required if the human race can be and is to be saved from collective suicide.

Self-appropriation, then, does not supplant self-transcendence as the goal of the process of human development. It is rather a means to that goal, a means that will be increasingly required if the ecumenic community of humankind is to be raised to the next level of social evolution, to the planetization of the noosphere concerning which we receive such illuminating and inspiring images in the profoundly creative vision of Pierre Teilhard de Chardin. Personal value is the person in his or her self-transcendence. But the proportions to be met by that self-transcendence are set by the concrete problems of human cultural and social development that must be met if the human world is to be worthy of human habitation. And today those proportions demand that self-transcendence be a matter of self-appropriation, precisely for the sake of generating the transcultural meanings and values that can inform the life of a global network of alternative communities intent on a better way to live than that emergent from the exploits of competing and escalating systems of imperialistic domination.

In what, then, does the required self-transcendence itself consist? What is its immanent intelligibility, the form of its inner order? What precisely is the self-transcendence for the sake of which the arduous process of self-appropriation at the levels of both intentionality and psyche is to be undertaken, and in fact is becoming something of a moral imperative for an increasingly broad segment of human persons? That is the question that we must address in a concrete and contemporary discussion of the relation of psychic conversion to spiritual development.

The answer, I believe, is to be found most concretely in the primary sources themselves of Hebrew and Christian revelation. More specifically, of course, one might say that the required self-transcendence is precisely an integral fidelity to the normative scale of values, and such an answer is correct. But that fidelity is itself coincident with and to be understood in terms of a fidelity to the just and mysterious law of the cross that has provided the central religious category of the entire Christian spiritual tradition and that is present and available as well in what I will regard, with Eric Voegelin, as the summit of the revelation to Israel, the deutero-Isaian symbolic vision of the suffering servant of God.[4] Conversely, fidelity to the law of the cross, a living out of the vision of the suffering servant of God in our time, is to be identified with integral fidelity to the normative scale of values. Suffering servanthood under the just and mysterious law of the cross, then, is to be identified as the summit of self-transcendence, the goal of personal development, the intrinsic measure of both spiritual and psychological development, and in our time the genuine reason for undertaking the arduous process of intentional and psychic self-appropriation.

This is a hard doctrine, and is no doubt the point at which some will abandon the effort to follow my thought, if they have not already done so for other reasons. But it is also the point toward which everything that I have said thus far has been oriented, and it is the point from which all else will flow. The problem of evil is to be understood, to the extent to which we can approach any understanding of what in the last analysis is a surd, in terms of a breakdown of the integral scale of values and of the normative relations among the levels of values that I tried to portray in very compendious fashion in the previous section of the present lecture. The solution to the problem of evil is not available on the basis of human resources alone. If there is any solution at all, it must be a divinely originated solution, and a matter of collaboration with the divine partner in the search for direction in the movement of life. And the inner form of that collaboration has been demonstrated for all to see in the pattern adopted by the divine measure of all human integrity become flesh in human history. That inner form is available in the deutero-Isaian symbolic or mythic vision of redemptive suffering. But myth becomes history in the incarnation of the Word, of the measure, and the incarnation of the measure is the obedience unto death, even death on a cross, that this measure assumed as the goal of his life when he did not think equality with God something to be clung to. Conformity to the cross of the divine measure become human flesh is the summit of the process of achieving self-transcendence under the conditions of a human history shot through with the surd of evil and sin.

Limitations of time confine me here to stating this position, at once doctrinal and systematic, in a somewhat kerygmatic or proclamatory fashion. A sustained theological argument can be offered both for the extent and range of human moral impotence and so of the inability of human beings in community to find and live a solution to the problem of evil on the basis of human resources alone, and for the character of the divinely originated solution itself and for its genuine catalytic capacities vis-à-vis the human situation. It is not possible in the scope of the present lecture to present this argument in any detail (though we will touch on moral impotence and the character of the solution in the next section), and so I must be content with stating my belief in this regard, and moving on to the kind of discussion of spiritual and psychic development that is consonant with such a belief. The belief, again, is that there is a problem of evil, that it consists in the breakdown of the integral and normative scale of values, that its solution must be a matter of grace effecting the requisite self-transcendence, that the proportions of that self-transcendence will be determined by the proportions of the problem of evil to be met, that today these proportions demand the formation of a global network of alternative communities intent on a different way to live, that such a network will demand the generation of transcultural meanings and values, that the generation of such cultural values demands the arduous process of self-appropriation, and that under these conditions, as under any and all other conditions of human living in history, the self-transcendence required of human subjects if they are to collaborate with God in effecting the redemption of the situation from the surd of evil lies in their conformity to the just and mysterious law of the cross, to the suffering servanthood revealed by the divine measure itself become incarnate in the person of Jesus of Nazareth.

Before I move on to the implications of this statement of my position for the issue of personal spiritual and psychological development and for the relations of psy-

chic conversion to spiritual development, it is all-impor-
tant to stress that the point I am making is not a masoch-
istic glorification of human suffering. John Dunne has distinguished two types of human suffering. There is the hell
of private suffering, the hell of the suffering of isolation
and victimization; and there is the suffering of compassion and forgiveness. Both of these he calls a night of suffering. But between them, and making the difference between them, is the experience of the bliss of a day that
supplants the night of the hell of private suffering and that
cannot be supplanted by the night of the suffering of compassion and forgiveness. The participation in the law of
the cross, in the pattern of the deutero-Isaian suffering
servant of God, a participation that consists precisely in
integral fidelity to the normative scale of values in the living of one's life in history, is an experience of the night of
the suffering of compassion and forgiveness. It is not an
experience of the night of the hell of private suffering and
destructive victimization. The night of the hell of private
suffering is not redemptive. The night of the suffering of
compassion and forgiveness is redemptive. And between
them is the bliss of the day that supplants the first night
and that is not supplanted by the second. To this day between the two nights Lonergan refers when he writes such
things as the following:

> There is the context of growth, in which one's
> knowledge of human living and operating is
> increasing in extent, precision, refinement, and
> in which one's responses are advancing from
> the agreeable to vital values, from vital to so-
> cial, from social to cultural, from cultural to
> personal, from personal to religious. Then there
> prevails an openness to ever further achieve-
> ment. Past gains are organized and consolidated

but they are not rounded off into a closed system but remain incomplete and so open to still further discoveries and developments. The free thrust of the subject into new areas is recurrent and, as yet, there is no supreme value that entails all others. But at the summit of the ascent from the initial infantile bundle of needs and clamors and gratifications, there are to be found the deep-set joy and solid peace, the power and the vigor, of being in love with God. In the measure that that summit is reached, then the supreme value is God, and other values are God's expression of his love in this world, in its aspirations, and in its goal. In the measure that one's love of God is complete, then values are whatever one loves, and evils are whatever one hates so that, in Augustine's phrase, if one loves God, one may do as one pleases, *Ama Deum et fac quod vis*. Then affectivity is of a single piece. Further developments only fill out previous achievement. Lapses from grace are rarer and more quickly amended.[5]

Again:

There is the love of God with one's whole heart and whole soul, with all one's mind and all one's strength (Mark 12.30). It is God's love flooding our hearts through the Holy Spirit given to us (Romans 5.5). It grounds the conviction of St. Paul that 'there is nothing in death or life, in the realm of spirits or superhuman powers, in the world as it is or the world as it shall be, in the forces of the universe, in heights or depths — nothing in all creation that can

separate us from the love of God in Christ Jesus
our Lord' (Romans 8.38-39.).

As the question of God is implicit in all
our questioning, so being in love with God is
the basic fulfillment of our conscious intentionality. That fulfillment brings a deep-set joy that
can remain despite humiliation, failure, priva-
tion, pain, betrayal, desertion. That fulfillment
brings a radical peace, the peace that the world
cannot give. That fulfillment bears fruit in a
love of one's neighbor that strives mightily to
bring about the kingdom of God on this earth.
On the other hand, the absence of that fulfillment opens the way to the trivialization of human life in the pursuit of fun, to the harshness
of human life arising from the ruthless exercise of power, to despair about human welfare
springing from the conviction that the universe
is absurd.[6]

If we are to understand psychic conversion in its role
as contributing to the emergence of the person whose life
is in conformity with the pattern of suffering servanthood
assumed and revealed by the divine measure of integrity
become human flesh, we must first understand its role,
then, in the emergence of the dynamic state of being in
love with God. And if the dynamic state of being in love
with God is what characterizes the day that supplants the
night of the hell of private suffering and that is not supplanted by the night of the suffering of compassion and
forgiveness, we must relate our considerations to the crucial issue of the healing of the night of private suffering. To
that central element, then, in the emergence of the subject
in Christ Jesus we now turn.

3   Creating and Healing

In a very significant development in his thinking, one yet to be appreciated sufficiently, Lonergan, in a paper delivered in Montreal at the Thomas More Institute in 1975, distinguishes between two vectors in intentional consciousness.[7] There is a creative vector that moves from below upwards, and there is a healing vector that moves from above downwards.

The articulation of the creative vector occupied most of Lonergan's attention. It is what enabled him to distinguish the levels of consciousness that emerge as the process of inquiry moves from experience through insight and judgment to decision. It is characterized by the two dimensions of intentionality and psyche. Spirit or intentionality is the capacity to raise and answer questions: the capacity to discover meaning, to affirm truly, to decide responsibly, and to rest in the mystery of love that alone satisfies this capacity. The psyche is the stream of sensitive consciousness that constitutes the empirical level permeating the spiritual operations and changing as these operations move from one level to the next.

This upwardly moving vector is creative: one is effecting a series of cumulative and progressive changes in the world in which one lives and concomitantly in oneself to the extent that one's consciousness proceeds smoothly and uninterruptedly from experience to insight, from insight to judgment, from judgment to decision, from decision to new experiences, insights, judgments, decisions, etc., etc., with the whole process sustained and guided and in fact rendered possible in the first place because of the gift of love from and for the source, goal, and partner of our search for direction in the movement of life. One is constituting the world and oneself, in an integral creative process. But if one or more of these essential steps is missing or incomplete or goes astray, if, for example, a person or group does not correctly understand a situation, or leaps to judgment without passing through understanding, the creative process is derailed, and the actions of that person or group will miss the mark, will err, will depart from the direction to be found in the movement of life. The creative process and its imperatives mark out a path, and that path is nothing other than the normative order of the direction that is to be found, but that also can be missed, in the movement of life.

What, then, is the source of derailment? Why do we go astray? Why do we miss the mark? What can be done about it?

These questions are complex, and no simple answer is possible. With each of the levels of questioning promoting one's consciousness to a higher stage, there is a further degree of self-transcendence. Not only do we feel differently as we move from one level to the next, but also the psyche must participate in the self-transcendence of the spirit if we are to be capable of consistent performance of the requisite operations. The psyche, then, must be free to cooperate in the search for direction in the movement of life, in the questions for insight, for truth, and for the good through which that search is incrementally satisfied. Without psychic self-transcendence the very operations of the creative vector are inhibited. Affective self-transcendence, known in various spiritual traditions as detachment, is required for the integral functioning of creativity. One source of the derailment of the creative process, then, surely lies in the affective blockages that constitute a dimension of resistance to insight, judgment, decision, and self-sacrificing or agapic love. These blockages constitute the night of the hell of private suffering. Ultimately they are in the way not only of the normal creative operations of intentional consciousness, but also of the capacity for the suffering of compassion and forgiveness. There must emerge first the bliss of the day which supplants the night of the hell of private suffering and which cannot be supplanted by the night of the suffering of compassion and forgiveness.

In *Insight* Lonergan writes about moral impotence. His emphasis is on other dimensions of resistance than those that I am highlighting here, on the nearly inevitable occurrence of human sin because of the very structure of our *intellectual* and *volitional* development. It is important to keep this in mind as we proceed in the present discussion. Affective aberration and underdevelopment is not the only source of derailment in the search for direction in the movement of life. Or, in the terms that Lonergan uses in *Insight*, dramatic bias is not the only bias. There are biases of intelligence and existential orientation themselves, the biases that Lonergan calls group, individual, and general bias, and these too are factors to be accounted for in any theoretical treatment of error and sin. The self-appropriation of the creative vector of intentionality itself will bring to light these devices of the flight from *understanding*. But complementing the self-appropriation of the creative vector of intentionality there is a depth-psychological discovery and healing of the affective obstructions to creativity constituted by certain compositions of psychic energy that form sources of resistance to the pursuit of direction in the movement of life.

Feelings are sensitively conscious energy. Psychic energy is distributed into units, into various associated or fragmented compositions, each with a central core or nucleus affected by a person's previous development. Jung calls these units complexes. They affect our consciousness through the feelings that permeate the movement of consciousness from one level of the creative vector to another. The whole of the sensitive psyche is constituted by these compositions of psychic energy. Some of them aid one's performance as a creative human being, and others interfere with, subvert, block, derail the search for direction in the movement of life. Complexes support the creative vector when they provide us with the images needed for insight, or when they offer us memories that help us to discover ways of responding to new situations, or when they spontaneously acquiesce to the process of reflection that anticipates judgment, or when, through their agency, we apprehend genuine values in an affectively charged manner that leads to action consonant with the apprehended value. But our psychic energy can be blocked, fixed in inflexible patterns, driven by compulsions, plagued by obsessions, weighted down by general anxiety or specific fears, resistant to insight, true judgment, responsible action. And then it will divert or derail us from the self-transcendent participation in the humble but exhilarating search for direction in the movement of life. It can render us unable, or unwilling, or both, to function at one or other level of the creative vector in certain areas of our lives. Then one must take a detour through the disturbing set of complexes and release the inhibiting energy. The alternative is a blind alley, a dead end, a cul-de-sac, a breakdown in one's constitution of the world and oneself, even a cessation of desire, a decadent routine whose underlying rhythm is the slow beat of existential despair. In John Dunne's words, one is dragged through life rather than walking through life upright.

    The creative vector, then, requires an affective flexibility and detachment that match the self-transcendent capacities of conscious intentionality. Our feelings have to be as free from disorder as is required by our native orientation to intelligibility, truth, and the good. This freedom from disorder is not lifeless indifference but questioning commitment to insight, rational judgment, and responsible decision in every area of our lives, and to the self-sacrificing love of the servant of God in the face of the mystery of evil. It is a freedom from other inclinations so that we are able effectively to desire insight, truth, and the good. This detachment is identical with what in the Ignatian tradition of discernment is called freedom from inordinate affections. But now we are able to understand inordinate affections as complexes that derail one from the integral performance of the operations that constitute the normative order of the search for direction in the movement of life.

Affective development is a matter of psychic participation in a commitment of the whole person to the objectives of intentional consciousness. It is a matter of matching desire with the objectives of the creative vector. Freedom from affective disorder is freedom for the adventure of creativity in world constitution and self-constitution. Affective development is measured by the degree to which we are able to rejoice in the beautiful, the intelligible, the true, the good, the divine self-communication, with a joy that is both spontaneous and self-possessed as one engages in the process through which a flourishing person and a human world that genuinely is worth while are constituted. Its summit is the condition of complete simplicity of which Eliot writes at the end of the *Four Quartets*, a condition that costs not less than everything.

Genuine psychotherapy, then, is a healing of the complexes that derail one from the spontaneous performance of the operations that constitute the normative order of the search for direction in the movement of life. It is the dissolving of the energic blockages whose rigidity and autonomy prevent the self-transcendent exercise of the operations constituting the creative vector.

Our next step in understanding psychic resistance to self-transcendent inquiry is to acknowledge that the autonomous psychic complexes that prevent one from participating in the creative adventure of pursuing and finding direction are *victimized* compositions formed as the consequence of one's community and one's culture. The violence done to one's psyche, of course, may be the issue of one's own self-destructiveness. But it may issue as well from one's social environment or from the cultural values of one's milieu. In fact, it usually is a complex function of social, cultural, and individual factors. But the point I want to make is that psychic spontaneity as such is not morally responsible for its own disorder. The psyche's order and disorder are caused by action affecting it from beyond itself, whether that action be that of others or of oneself. Disordered complexes are the victims of human history: of significant others, of social situations emergent from the distortions in one's community, of derailed cultural values, of one's own freedom or of some combination of these various sources. The complex itself is the victim. It is not responsible for the genesis of its own disorder. The various compositions and distributions of energic affectivity begin to be set for us, without our personal choice, from very early on in our lives. We may even speak of a generational bondage, through which a family can be affected over generations by the same psychic patterns. One's complexes are set by the agenda operative in the community and the culture, and that agenda will always be more or less distorted. Psychic disorder usually reaches back into areas of our experience that we cannot even remember, or that we have blocked from recall, and it is usually reinforced by our acquiescence to patterns established without our self-constitutive contribution.

Lonergan's discussion of bias, which I just mentioned, provides a great deal of help toward distinguishing the various sources of psychic disorder. I do not have the time to go into his discussion here, beyond the point of saying, for those of you already familiar with his discussion, that there is an increasing dominance of psychic as opposed to spiritual features involved in the genesis and functioning of the bias as one moves from general bias through individual and then group bias to dramatic bias. There is a bias, which Lonergan calls dramatic, that is the effect of autonomous psychic complexes beyond the reach of immediate self-determination. It is the obstacle most affected by or due to autonomous complexes victimized originally by factors beyond one's control. The other biases — group, individual, and general — display successively greater degrees of *character* disorder and not simply the psychic derailment of the neurotic. In general, we may say that the more dominant the psychic factor in the bias, the more is its source to be located in the community and the culture rather than in the pneumopathological exercise of one's own freedom. Victimization by others and self-victimization, of course, usually conspire with one another in the cumulative production of personal and, through personal, of historical disorder. And to the extent that a person *can* assume responsibility for one's own psychic disorder, a healing and conversion of the spirit will be the more radical requirement before a therapy of the psyche can have any effect in the healing of the disorder. But whatever the causation and whatever the requirements for healing, the point to be made here is simply that *psychic* disorder precisely as such is always a victim of human freedom, never the source of its own disorder.

Now, our usual manner of negotiating psychic darkness is inadequate. We tend to adopt one of two postures toward affective disorder: either repression of it or moral renunciation of responsibility for its transformation. In either case we are simply further victimizing the distorted set of complexes. Repression constricts the psychic energy composing the complex, until eventually it explodes, either in relatively small but frequent outbursts of unpredictable or at least uncontrollable expression, or in the volcanic eruption of an act of violence either to self in a breakdown or to others in sociopathic behavior. Moral renunciation, on the other hand, which often follows upon futile attempts at repression, is a capitulation to the power of the energies constituting the disordered psyche. One begins simply to act out the disorder, abandoning as hopeless the task of transforming and then integrating the disordered energies. Such renunciation, moreover, sometimes is justified by the rationalization that the acting out of the disordered complex will result in its being dissolved or, even worse, will bring about some higher integration beyond good and evil. This, of course, is a demonically destructive illusion, but it is operative more or less overtly in a number of contemporary approaches to psychotherapy. Such a stance simply increases the power of the disordered complexes, further establishing them in the distorted rigidity and autonomy that give them their power. It simply makes it more difficult for one to move to a new position beyond the disorder, simply fixes one's energies more rigidly in the disturbing pattern.

From a theological point of view, victimized psychic complexes are the fruit of the sin of the world, a dimension of what the Scholastics called *peccatum originale originatum*. To the extent that we have freely conspired in their formation, they are the fruit as well of our own sin as a dimension of the sin of the world. Again from a theological point of view, the redemption of the energies bound up in these complexes over which we have so little power must be effected by a healing love that meets one at the depth where the disorder resides. The victimized dimension of our psyches must be met ultimately not by judgment and condemnation, but by mercy and gentleness. Judgment may be directed against our freedom, but not against what our freedom has freely victimized, even in ourselves. Redemptive love must reach to the wound itself, and even deeper, and touch it in a manner contrary to the action responsible for the victimization. And one is healed, and can know it, when one endures the same type of psychic violence but without being destroyed.

This means that there is a third way of negotiating psychic disorder besides repression and moral renunciation. It entails several steps, through which we cooperate with the compassion of redemptive love in our own regard. First is the recognition that the disturbed complex or set of complexes is a victim, whether of oneself or of others, so that one can cease hating oneself for what one *feels*. Second is the adoption of an attitude of compassion in its regard. Third is the emergence of a willingness to cooperate with whatever redemptive forces are available for the healing of the disorder and its transformation, and even for the consolidation of its energies into the self-transcendence of the search for direction in the movement of life. Victimized complexes can respond to such attention, and normally will, to the extent that the redemptive love, with which we can cooperate, truly reaches to the disorder and begins to work its transformation.

But the solution is not at all as simple as it sounds. For in suggesting this alternative manner of negotiating psychic darkness, we come head-on against the problem of moral impotence in the form in which the latter has a predominantly psychic causation. To adopt the posture of therapeutic compassion toward the negative emotional forces that derail us from the direction that can be found in the movement of life is to be intelligent, reasonable, and morally responsible in their regard. But the force and power of these complexes is precisely such that they inhibit the possibility of intelligent, reasonable, and responsible action. The antecedent willingness required to take compassion on our own affective disorder is a function in part of a certain degree of affective self-transcendence. But the disorder is a disorder precisely insofar as it inhibits such self-transcendence. The willingness to negotiate emotional darkness in an intelligent, reasonable, and responsible fashion depends on a freedom from that very emotional darkness; and that is precisely the self-transcendence that is not at one's disposal. The dilemma of moral impotence at this point is that, although the solution is clear, one is unable to avail oneself of it, because the requisite ability to do so is lacking. The steps of the analysis of this particular instance of moral impotence are the following: first, the integrity that is human flourishing depends on the self-transcendence of the operations through which we seek and find meaning, truth, and the good, and finally through which we acquiesce to the basic law of integrity in a sinful history, which is the law of the cross; second, the self-transcendence of these operations depends on the self-transcendence of our affectivity; third, reaching the self-transcendence of our affectivity depends on being able to do whatever is necessary to cooperate in the healing of its disorder and darkness; and fourth, that very ability is itself a function of a degree of affective self-transcendence with which we are not endowed because of our psychic disorder. We seem doomed to adopt a self-destructive posture. We cannot emerge from the vicious circle of disordered affective development.

We cannot — unless the very capacity to treat compassionately yet responsibly our own darkness is itself given to us. We cannot find this capacity in the creative vector of our own consciousness, which is impaired precisely because of the psychic darkness. That freedom must come from beyond the creative vector, from an agency that is independent of the immanent sources of our own self-constitution. Moral impotence is the statistically almost inevitable result of the meeting between the structure of human development and the fruit of the sin of the world. Perhaps only in the sinlessness of Jesus and the condition defined by the doctrine of the immaculate conception of his mother have these statistics been fully defied. And if this is the case, then the statistics are at least altered only by another movement than the creative movement from below upwards in human consciousness. At any rate, moral impotence means the impossibility of sustained development on the basis of our own resources. And that impossibility implies the near inevitability of further sin, further waywardness, and so of further victimization in history. The social surd into which new generations are born is simply further accentuated.

Is there, then, another movement besides the creative vector from below upwards in consciousness? Is there another agency that meets us as we are, but that has the power to dissolve the obstacles to integral creativity by moving from above downwards in consciousness? Is there an agency that lets our victimized darkness itself rest in being loved? Only if there is, can we adopt a new posture in our own regard, for only then is a new movement initiated in consciousness, only then can our vain striving to constitute ourselves with resources inadequate to the task cease, only then is the good that I have striven for given to me, and the longing of my consciousness fulfilled. Only then am I free to love in return, even in the face of the awful and demonic power of *ressentiment.* There is a whole new field of exploration opened up for appropriation by the affirmation that there is a healing vector in consciousness as well as a creative vector, that this healing vector moves not from below upwards but from above downwards, that it is a gift, that it meets me first at the highest level of consciousness, where values are apprehended in feelings before they are pursued by deliberation, chosen in decision, and implemented in actions in conformity with good decision. The gift of healing love affects first of all and most radically the very affective *capacity* to apprehend the good. Affective space is opened by this gift, and one becomes at last free to assume responsibility for what previously one could not negotiate. Another lecture would be required for an initial exploration of the dynamics of the healing vector in human consciousness. I must stop here, in terms of a formal lecture, simply inviting you to ask whether there is not this other movement in consciousness, whether its movement is not primarily affective, whether it is not the source of the needed affective detachment, whether it and it alone is not the reason that we can experience the bliss of a day that supplants the night of the hell of private suffering and that cannot itself be supplanted by the suffering of compassion and forgiveness. All of the rules for discernment provided by St. Ignatius in the *Spiritual Exercises* can be reinterpreted as guides toward the self-appropriation of the movement from above in consciousness, a movement that, while it prompts us to and sustains operations of the creative vector, is primarily the movement of the healing vector. And only the framework opened up by such an affirmation is adequate to the task of locating the significance and import of the science of depth psychology. These affirmations need a far more extensive treatment if they are to be explicated in a manner that does justice to the complexities of their content. But perhaps I have been able at least to open a horizon from which the place of depth psychology in the development of the subject in Christ Jesus can be appreciated, and if I have done this much then perhaps we have sufficient material for further discussion as our weekend together proceeds.

Notes

[1] Bernard Lonergan, *Method in Theology* (see above, chapter 1, note 1) 31-32.

[2] See Jürgen Habermas, 'Labor and Interaction: Remarks on Hegel's Jena *Philosophy of Mind*,' in Habermas, *Theory and Practice*, trans. John Viertel (Boston: Beacon Press, 1973) 169.

[3] 1993 note: Several times in the course of this volume, references will appear to the Marxist theory of society as the principal alternative to the theory advocated here. If these essays were being written today, while I would continue to contrast my position with Marxism, for the sake of clarification, I would not accord the Marxist position the political importance that it enjoyed when the essays were written. But I have decided not to change the essays so drastically as to eliminate these references to the very context in which they were written.

[4] See Eric Voegelin, *Israel and Revelation* (see above, chapter 1, note 8).

[5] Lonergan, *Method in Theology* 39.

[6] Ibid. 105.

[7] See Bernard Lonergan, 'Healing and Creating in History,' in *A Third Collection* (see above, chapter 2, note 9) 100-109.

4 Duality and Dialectic

I Introduction

Bernard Lonergan concludes his treatment of common sense in *Insight* with an observation on method. He says, first, that, since his purpose has been to direct attention to an event that occurs within consciousness, his method has not been that of empirical science, whose data lie in sensible presentations. Rather, his method is 'a generalized empirical method that stands to the data of consciousness as empirical method stands to the data of sense.'[1] The treatment of common sense has brought to light the nature of this generalized method. When applied solely to the data of consciousness, it bears an analogy to classical empirical method, for then 'it consists in determining patterns of intelligible relations that unite the data explanatorily. Such are the biological, artistic, dramatic, and intellectual forms of experience.'[2] But when extended beyond the data within a single consciousness to study 'the relations between different conscious subjects, between conscious subjects and their milieu or environment, and between consciousness and its neural basis,'[3] it demands the introduction of a new factor. This new factor consists of the procedures of dialectic.

Even with the introduction of these procedures, however, there remains an analogy to empirical science. For 'dialectic stands to generalized method as the differential equation to classical physics, or the operator equation to the more recent physics.'[4] Dialectic is thus a component 'from above' in the heuristic structure of human science, to be employed when this science studies data beyond those that are to be found within a single consciousness, whether these have to do with the relations of consciousness with the unconscious, with the relations among different conscious subjects, or with the relations between conscious subjects and their historical milieu.

If this is so, then if one would 'take a professional interest in the human sciences and make a positive contribution to their methodology,'[5] as Lonergan says contemporary theology must do, and if theology is to draw on the human sciences for some of its general categories, it is extremely important to get straight just what Lonergan means here by dialectic and to understand how it is to perform its heuristic office. Just as one who studies physics without knowing the relevant mathematics is not really studying physics,[6] so one who engages in human science without knowing how to use the procedures of dialectic will arrive at results that are less than scientific. I hope this paper might offer some minimal contribution to the interpretation of some of Lonergan's texts in *Insight* on dialectic, and display some of the applications that these texts have for reorienting human science, as well as for deriving some of the general categories of a contemporary systematic theology and for providing a context for the methodical employment of the special categories in a theology that would mediate between faith and culture.

2   Thesis

Dialectic is a major organizing principle of *Insight*. The problem of empirical human science in its relation to theology 'in a large measure has dictated the structure' of *Insight*.[7] Clarity on the meaning of dialectic, then, is a necessary condition for understanding *Insight*, and, because *Insight* is an essay in aid of self-appropriation, for understanding oneself in the dimensions of the self to which dialectic is applicable — the relations of consciousness to the unconscious, to other conscious subjects, and to the social environment.

The notion of dialectic in *Insight* is a complex notion. My thesis is that the complexity can be controlled if we understand dialectic on the foundation of the distinction between consciousness and knowledge. I do not think there are several notions of dialectic in *Insight*.[8] There is, rather, one complex notion that can be reduced to some manageable clarity by speaking of its integral and distorted realizations. The understanding of these realizations constitutes differentiations of the one complex notion of dialectic, not two distinct notions. But the differentiation has a grounding in the quite sharp distinction drawn between consciousness and knowledge.

3 The Principal Text

The most complete statement of the complexity of the notion of dialectic appears in the observation on method at the end of chapter 7 of *Insight* to which I have already referred.

> ... dialectic is a pure form with general implications; it is applicable to any concrete unfolding of linked but opposed principles that are modified cumulatively by the unfolding; it can envisage at once the conscious and the nonconscious either in a single subject or in an aggregate and succession of subjects; it is adjustable to any course of events, from an ideal line of pure progress resulting from the har-

monious working of the opposed principles, to
any degree of conflict, aberration, breakdown,
and disintegration; it constitutes a principle of
integration for specialized studies that concentrate on this or that aspect of human living,
and it can integrate not only theoretical work
but also factual reports; finally, by its distinction between insight and bias, progress and
decline, it contains in a general form the combination of the empirical and the critical attitudes essential to human science.[9]

Dialectic is a pure form, and nothing but that: it provides 'no more than the general form of a critical attitude.'[10]
Nonetheless, it will be extremely helpful to the various
departments of human science as they work out their specific criteria, for it will enable each department to distinguish 'between the purely intellectual element in its field
and, on the other hand, the inertial effects and the interference of human sensibility and human nerves.'[11] The
hope is expressed that a fuller study of the human mind
'will provide us with further general elements relevant to
determining a far more nuanced yet general critical viewpoint.'[12] The major burden of that fuller study, of course,
is borne by the succeeding chapters of *Insight* and the consequent developments in Lonergan's work. But for the
moment we will concentrate on the passage just quoted
and on related texts, and will try to unpack some of their
principal elements.

4   Interpretation

Dialectic constitutes an a priori element in the heuristic structure of the study of processes characterized by
the concrete unfolding of linked but opposed principles of

change, where the principles are modified cumulatively by the unfolding.[13] In the chapters on common sense, some implications of this general form of a critical attitude are drawn for the dramatic subject and the social community. We will focus on the dramatic subject, and later will suggest an analogy of dialectic that will enable us to understand both the community and, perhaps, culture, along the same lines.

I have argued elsewhere that with the emergence of Lonergan's differentiation of the fourth level of consciousness, the notion of the dramatic pattern of experience, of dramatic artistry in world constitution and self-constitution, must be given a more important position than is accorded it prior to this development in Lonergan's thought.[14] For the dramatic pattern is the pattern of experience operative in fourth-level operations, in existential, interpersonal, and historical agency, in praxis. In more recent work I have amplified this contention into an artistic paradigm of praxis. But if the dramatic pattern becomes the principal pattern, where before it played a subordinate role as constitutive of the world of undifferentiated Heideggerian *Sorge*, its own immanent constitution remains what it was in the sixth chapter of *Insight*. That is, the dramatic subject is immanently constituted by the dialectical unfolding of the linked but opposed principles of neural demands for conscious integration and psychic representation, on the one hand, and, on the other hand, the concern of dramatically patterned intentionality and imagination for dramatic artistry in world constitution and self-constitution.

Dramatically patterned orientation exercises either a constructive or a repressive censorship over neural demands. If the censorship is constructive, *Sorge* becomes character, the restrictive shaping of possibilities in the creative finalistic tension of limitation and transcendence; it is the responsible exercise of conscious finality. One develops, and one does so along a line of progress, to the extent that the opposed principles of neural demands and dramatically patterned existential intentionality are working harmoniously with one another. The development cumulatively modifies the opposed principles themselves, so that the underlying neural manifold becomes a more pliable support and instrument of artistic world constitution and self-constitution, and the censorship becomes character, habit, virtue.

But if, for whatever reasons or conditioning occasions, the censorship is repressive — and the most serious reasons are precisely those identified by Lonergan with the flight from understanding and responsibility — one's development becomes aberrant and heads in the limit to the breakdown, disintegration, and collapse of the *artiste manqué*. One is dragged through life by the forces, now of Kierkegaardian 'shut-up-ness,' now of the vengeful return of the repressed. The two opposed principles are not working harmoniously, and while the symptoms of the aberration are most manifest in 'the inertial effects and the interference of human sensibility and human nerves,'[15] the radical historical source is a disorientation of intentionality, a pneumopathology, conspiring with an oppressed imagination, a psychopathology, in the exercise of an intrasubjective domination over materials that, were they to become conscious, would be data for insight into the discrepancy between the self that one is and the self that one could, might, or should be. The disintegration is a cumulative modification of precisely the same two principles that develop along the lines of progress under the exercise of character. Cumulative fragmentation of the neural manifold occurs as affects are unhinged from their appropriate imaginal counterparts and cathected with incongruous cognitive elements; and the orientation of the dramatic pattern itself becomes ever more fixed in the schemes and determinisms of waywardness. In the limit one destroys oneself, and the roots of the self-destruction lie in the lack of antecedent willingness for insight, in the love of darkness, in the renunciation of the artistic constitution of the first and only edition of oneself.

Let us take this instance of dialectic as paradigmatic, not only because it is the first instance discussed by Lonergan, but also because it is foundational of other instances. True, the dialectic of community exercises a certain dominance over the dialectic of the subject, but that dominance is relative.[16] Distortions in the dialectic of community are reversed best by the transformation of subjects and the contributions of converted subjects to the reorientation of culture.

In the light of the general methodological observation at the end of chapter 7 of *Insight*, the dialectic of the dramatic subject provides a heuristic element for understanding the relations between consciousness and its neural basis. We may consider it an application of the pure form of dialectic to the conscious and nonconscious in a single subject. The dialectic is 'adjustable to any course of events, from an ideal line of pure progress resulting from the harmonious working of the opposed principles, to any degree of conflict, aberration, breakdown, and disintegration.'[17] The linked but opposed principles that, normatively, are to work harmoniously with one another are neural demand functions and the exercise of the censorship. These principles are the sources of events of a determinate kind, namely, the contents and affects emerging into consciousness. The link between the two principles is that one (the neural) is what is patterned, and the other (the censorship) is what is responsible for the patterning. The changes that occur are cumulative, in that the exercise of the censorship and the neural demands to be met at any time depend on previous interactions of the two principles and provide the basis of their future workings.[18] Since the censorship can be repressive, and repression results in neglected neural demands forcing their way into consciousness in ways that disrupt the dramatic project of artistic self-constitution, the opposition can result in a distortion of the dialectic, and 'the essential logic of the distorted dialectic is a reversal. For dialectic rests on the concrete unity of opposed principles; the dominance of either principle results in a distortion, and the distortion both weakens the dominance and strengthens the opposed principle to restore an equilibrium.'[19]

My interpretation of Lonergan's position on dialectic in the sixth and seventh chapters of *Insight* rests to a large extent on my understanding of the passage just quoted and of the methodological observations at the end of chapter 7. These two passages lead me to affirm that Lonergan holds out both the possibility of a dialectic that would not be distorted and that of a dialectic that is distorted. Clearly he speaks of the latter, for he writes that 'the essential logic of the distorted dialectic is a reversal.'[20] Does he also at least suggest the former? Well, he speaks of 'dialectic rest[ing] on the concrete unity of opposed principles.' It is not the opposition as such, but 'the dominance of either principle,' that 'results in a distortion.' The distortion undermines the dominance and 'strengthens the opposed principle to restore an equilibrium.'[21] Is it possible, then, to speak of the equilibrium, or the concrete unity of opposed principles, as an undistorted or integral instance of dialectic, and of the breakdown of that unity as a distorted dialectic? This will be my position. It receives further confirmation from the methodological observation at the end of chapter 7 of *Insight*. The pure form of dialectic is applicable to, can envisage, and is adjustable to, *both* 'an ideal line of pure progress resulting from the harmonious working of the opposed principles' and 'any degree of conflict, aberration, breakdown, and disintegration.'[22] The first of these possibilities is what I have chosen to call an integral dialectic, the second what Lonergan calls a distorted dialectic.

5   Foundations

I said at the beginning of this paper that my interpretation can be connected with the distinction that Lonergan draws between consciousness and knowledge. The distinction in itself is too familiar to require extended comment here. What perhaps does require some elaboration is the contention that there is a duality not only of knowledge but also of consciousness, and that the duality is to be negotiated in a different manner in each case. The duality of knowledge is a principal fact to be affirmed as a result of the reading of *Insight*.

> ... in each of us there exist two different kinds of knowledge. They are juxtaposed in Cartesian dualism with its rational *Cogito, ergo sum* and with its unquestioning extroversion to substantial extension. They are separated and alienated in the subsequent rationalist and empiricist philosophies. They are brought together again to cancel each other in Kantian criticism. If these statements approximate the facts, then the question of human knowledge is not whether it exists but what precisely are its two diverse forms and what are the relations between them. If that is the relevant question, then any departure from it is, in the same measure, the misfortune of missing the point. But whether or not that is the relevant question can

be settled only by undertaking an arduous exploratory journey through the many fields in
which men succeed in knowing or attempt the
task but fail.[23]

Again,

... the hard fact is that ... there exist in
man two diverse kinds of knowing, that they
exist without differentiation and in an ambivalent confusion until they are distinguished explicitly and the implications of the distinction
are drawn explicitly.[24]

Now it is explicitly established in Lonergan's work
that consciousness and knowledge are distinct; but it can
also be documented from *Insight* that there is a duality to
each of them. It follows that one way of departing from
the 'relevant question,' and so one instance of 'the
misfortune of missing the point,' would be to consider the
duality of consciousness in the same way as one treats the
duality of knowing. What is needed is a different posture
suitable to the distinction of consciousness from knowledge.
Perhaps the suitable posture in regard to the duality of
consciousness is a necessary condition for the appropriate
negotiation of the duality of knowledge.

The appropriate negotiation of the duality of knowledge is spoken of by Lonergan in terms of 'breaking' it.
'Breaking' here means 'explicitly distinguishing kinds, and
drawing the implications of the distinction.'

... unless one breaks the duality in one's knowing, one doubts that understanding correctly
is knowing. Under the pressure of that doubt,
either one will sink into the bog of a knowing
that is without understanding, or else one will
cling to understanding but sacrifice knowing

on the altar of an immanentism, an idealism, a relativism. From the horns of that dilemma one escapes only through the discovery — and one has not made it yet if one has no clear memory of its startling strangeness — that there are two quite different realisms, that there is an incoherent realism, half animal and half human, that poses as a halfway house between materialism and idealism, and on the other hand that there is an intelligent and reasonable realism between which and materialism the halfway house is idealism.[25]

But on my reading of *Insight*, an essential element in breaking the duality in one's knowing, and so in affirming that understanding correctly is fully human knowing, and in drawing the implications of that affirmation, lies not in breaking but in affirming, maintaining, and strengthening *consciousness as duality of sensitive psyche and pure desire to know*. Both the 'bog of a knowing that is without understanding' and clinging to 'understanding that sacrifices knowing on the altar of an immanentism, an idealism, a relativism' are consequences of breaking the duality of consciousness by opting for one or other of the opposed principles rather than for the concrete unity of the two.

Lonergan speaks explicitly of the *unity* of consciousness and maintains not only that this unity is given, but also that if it were not given it would have to be postulated.[26] But this unity is a 'concrete unity of opposed principles,'[27] both of which are 'I' rather than one being 'I' and the other 'It.'[28] The duality of human consciousness is not the duality of two things, nor does it call for the choice of one principle and the exclusion of the other. It *does* demand discrimination of the two constituent elements, but for the sake of their harmonious cooperation, not for the sake of the elimination of one and the dominance of the other.

The duality that is also a concrete unity of opposed principles is the duality of the sensitive psyche and spiritual intentionality, or the pure desire. The position on knowing, where 'the self as affirmed is characterized by such occurrences as sensing, perceiving, imagining, inquiring, understanding, formulating, reflecting, grasping the unconditioned, and affirming,'[29] implicitly acknowledges the duality of consciousness as constitutive of full human knowing. The two general forms of the counterpositions on knowing break this duality of consciousness; in empiricism this results in 'the bog of a knowing that is without understanding,' and in idealism in the clinging to 'understanding that sacrifices knowing.'

Breaking the duality of consciousness results in conflict, aberration, breakdown, and disintegration in the unfolding of the linked but opposed cognitive principles of psyche and spirit. But preserving the duality of consciousness results in the cognitive progress consequent upon the harmonious working of these principles. It strengthens the unity of consciousness. More existential implications appear in the following passage, which I will interrupt with a couple of parenthetical remarks that will indicate my meaning.

> Nor are the pure desire and the sensitive psyche two things, one of them 'I' and the other 'It.' [To regard them as two 'things' is what I mean by breaking the integral duality, or concrete unity of opposed principles.] They are the unfolding on different levels of a single, individual unity, identity, whole. Both are 'I,' and neither is merely 'It.' [To regard both as 'I' is what I mean by affirming the duality of consciousness

as a concrete unity of opposed principles.] If my intelligence is mine, so is my sexuality. If my reasonableness is mine, so are my dreams. If my intelligence and my reasonableness are to be thought more representative of me than my organic and psychic spontaneity, that is only in virtue of the higher integration that in fact my intelligence and reasonableness succeed in imposing on their underlying manifold, or proleptically, in virtue of the development in which the higher integration is to achieve a fuller measure of success. [Existentially, to co-operate with the finality that heads toward this higher integration is to affirm and strengthen the duality of consciousness.] But no matter how full the success, the basic situation within the self is unchanged, for the perfection of the higher integration does not eliminate the integrated or modify the essential opposition between self-centeredness and detachment. The same 'I' on different and related levels of operation retains the opposed characters.[30]

As *Insight* proceeds beyond the discussions of dialectic in chapters 6 and 7, the notion of dialectic comes to be used more exclusively in the sense of the philosophical method that advances positions and reverses counterpositions. All positions are rooted in the basic position on knowing, and all counterpositions in some form of the basic counterposition on knowing. The philosophical use of the notion of dialectic as *Insight* proceeds regards 'conflict, aberration, breakdown, and disintegration'[31] of the duality-as-integral-dialectic of consciousness. A distorted dialectic of consciousness yields a counterposition on knowing; dialectical method reverses the counterposition on knowing precisely by reversing the distorted dialectic of consciousness and appealing to the integral dialectic of consciousness as constitutive of full human knowing. The integral dialectic of consciousness, and so the concrete unity of linked but opposed principles which is not to be broken but only brought into consciousness and abided in, involves the sublation and so enrichment of the sensitive psyche, but not its elimination as a constitutive element of one's being, one's knowing, and one's self-understanding.

6   Applications

1   The preservation of the unity-in-duality of consciousness is a realization of the law of limitation and transcendence which Lonergan discusses in his treatment of the heuristic structure for studying human development.[32] This law, he says, is one of tension, and so the equilibrium of linked but opposed principles is to be conceived, not as a mere homeostatic balance, but as conscious finality, in which 'the operator is relentless in transforming the integrator.'[33] Psychic spontaneity heads toward the transforming enrichments effected by successive sublations caused by spiritual intentionality raising questions, first for intelligence, then for reflection, and finally for deliberation.

These questions are principles of movement, and the insights, judgments of fact, and judgments of value respectively emergent from them are principles of rest.[34] The movement and rest are experienced at the level of the sublated sensitivity, and this experience changes with the emergence of insight, then of the grasp of the virtually unconditioned, and finally of the grasp of the fulfillment of conditions for a judgment of value. The psyche's rest in intelligibility, truth, and the good is a manifestation and sign, indeed a criterion, of the integrity of the process of inquiry. This has long been realized in the tradition of discernment in Christian spirituality, where what is at stake is integrity in that form of inquiry that culminates in judgments of value and decision. But further study would show something analogous regarding the scientific and philosophical inquiry that specialize, respectively, in explanatory understanding and truth. Rest in the process of inquiry is in each instance a new level on which the creative tension of limitation and transcendence is *felt*, and on which one abides in that tension. The feeling of the creative tension is the affective indication of integrity in the process of inquiry whereby one arrives at the intelligible, the true, and the good.

The cumulative process of movement and rest is, among other things, a continuous and relentless transformation of the sensitive psyche, until one's living in the dramatic pattern is dominated by the detachment and disinterestedness of the pure desire. Thus Lonergan speaks of the importance of 'disinterested feelings' that 'recognize excellence.'[35] But the displacement of the tension between limitation and transcendence that constitutes a failure in genuineness[36] can occur *in either direction*. Lonergan emphasizes, perhaps, the displacement toward limitation, for it is this particular breaking of the unity-in-duality of consciousness that is responsible for the counterposition that conceives knowing and objectivity as analogous to ocular vision. But he does not overlook the danger that the perfection of the higher integration might try to eliminate the integrated;[37] he speaks of the mistake of supposing that there are no limits to the versatility and flexibility of neural demands;[38] and he refers to the neglect of the sensitive component of our orientation into the known unknown as hybris.[39]

To speak, then, of the integral as opposed to the distorted dialectic of diverse sets of linked but opposed principles of change, and to emphasize that distortion can occur by a dominance of either principle, is not to promote a counterposition, as long as one keeps in mind that the integral dialectic is based on a certain duality, not of knowledge, but of consciousness. The distortion of the integral dialectic of consciousness in either direction is the root of the basic counterpositions, which arise from the 'ambivalent confusion' about what it is to know. The use of the complex notion of dialectic as a philosophical tool for the advancement of positions and the reversal of counterpositions that becomes predominant as *Insight* proceeds is an application of this complex notion to these basic counterpositions in epistemology, metaphysics, ethics, and theology. But the root of the power of the one complex notion of dialectic to reverse counterpositions and advance positions is the unity-in-duality of consciousness. It is to be affirmed, promoted, and strengthened as a unity by maintaining the integrity of its duality. Then it is the source of progress, not only in philosophy and human science, but also and first in the life of the dramatic subject and the transactions of the intersubjective community.

2   From this basis we can proceed to an understanding of what I have called psychic conversion and of its function, not only in dramatic living but also in the establishment of the basic positions of philosophy. I understand psychic conversion as a release of the capacity for the internal communication that occurs in intelligent, reasonable, and responsible negotiation of the sensitive psychic component of consciousness. It is a transformation that primarily occurs in and with regard to the dramatic pattern of experience. For in its immanent intelligibility it is a transformation of the censorship over neural demands from a repressive to a constructive function in one's development.

The affects emergent from neural demands for conscious representation and psychic integration are sublated by all the levels of conscious intentionality, and change with the performance of the operations at each level. These changes, precisely as affective, are indications of the relative integrity or inauthenticity of the subject in his or her performance of the operations of intentional consciousness. We have an experience of the very movement of life given in the sensitive psychic concomitant of the operations of question and answer through which we pursue direction in that movement. If this experience is one of creative finalistic tension between the dialectic opposites of limitation and transcendence, it indicates authenticity in the search. But when it is displaced in the direction of either too little or too much possibility, it indicates a failure in character; and it restricts the shaping of possibilities that ought to mark the self-constitution of one who knows his or her place in the universe of being and faithfully and resolutely implements that knowledge.

Psychic conversion is conversion to attentiveness to that stream of sensitive consciousness, to internal communication with it, to responsible activity in its regard, and to an openness to negotiate it persuasively and patiently. The close connection between images and affects renders the dream a royal road to psychic conversion. For the dream provides images that represent the affects that are to be negotiated, transformed, refined, purified, and conscripted into the artistic forging of a work of art out of one's world, one's relations with others, and one's very self. That negotiation, transformation, refinement, purification, and conscription help the subject to move toward what Lonergan calls 'affective conversion,' conversion to being in love in the family, in the community, and with God.[40]

While the occurrence of psychic conversion is most likely to occur in, and affect directly, the dramatic pattern, its role as an aid to arriving at and abiding in the basic position on knowing should not be overlooked. If the concrete unity-in-duality of the psyche and the spirit have been strengthened through the internal communication of intentionality with the psyche, the integral dialectic of consciousness is consolidated by habits emergent from repeated sublation, and fortified against the breaking or displacement of the tension of psyche and spirit in either direction that is operative in the development of the counterpositions. The tendency to displacement in either direction assigns a precise meaning to Karl Rahner's special theological category of 'concupiscence'; and Rahner's 'gnoseological concupiscence'[41] can be pinned down with greater precision through Lonergan's delineation of the basic counterpositions. Establishing a relative integrity of limitation and transcendence in the dialectic of consciousness would contribute to the foundations in the subject for advancing positions and reversing counterpositions.

     3   The apprehension of values in feelings can also be illuminated by what we have been saying. What precisely is the structure of the evaluative process of Lonergan's fourth level of consciousness? Where in that process does the apprehension of value in feelings occur? What is the function of that apprehension in the process of arriving at judgments of value and decisions?

     Although these questions demand more work than I am able to give them at this time, I would suggest that the place of feelings in the evaluative process depends on the character of the feelings. The apprehension of value in the feelings of one who is affectively converted to love in the family, love in the community, and the love of God is related to judgments of value as reflective understanding is related to judgments of fact. That is, it is analogous to the grasp of the virtually unconditioned.

     But more often the apprehension of value in feelings is to judgments of value what insight is to judgments of fact. Then it is only the apprehension of *possible* value. It must be followed by such questions as, Is it really or only apparently good? Is it genuinely better than another object or course of action? These questions are to judgments of value what questions for reflection are to judgments of fact. The movement to a true *and effective* judgment of value will be mediated by feeling in the same way as the movement to a true judgment of fact is mediated by reflective understanding. But the feeling being described here is the feeling of one living in the finalistic tension of limitation and transcendence, that is, the feeling of one who is genuine. To arrive at genuineness one has to work on one's feelings, and this work may and often will reveal that what one first apprehended as a value was not a value at all.

4   These two instances of the apprehension of value in feelings can be related, it seems to me, to the 'times' which Ignatius Loyola proposes for election in the *Spiritual Exercises*. He proposes three such times. Only the first, as instanced by the conversion of Paul and the calling of Matthew, involves an immediate apprehension of value in feelings in which there are no further questions and one knows there are no further questions. Such times, he says, are rare. By extension, we can say without distorting Ignatius's meaning that Augustine's 'Love God and do what you will' is speaking of a condition in which one's affectivity is so refined that values are whatever one loves and evils whatever one hates. But this condition is almost as rare as are the extraordinary moments to which Ignatius refers. Usually we are involved in one of the other two 'times.'

The second time is one in which we are affectively drawn in various directions, or drawn in a particular direction without yet being in the solid condition of creative finalistic equilibrium. Our inclinations are moved, now to this object or course of action, and now to that, or to one object rather than another but in a manner not marked by the unity-in-duality of the psyche and authentic intentional orientation. We are not in the condition that Ignatius refers to as equilibrium, but are moved by the pulls and counterpulls of conflicting inclinations.

In the third time, on the other hand, we are in a state of equilibrium, but without a strong inclination in one direction rather than in another; nor are we affected by conflicting inclinations. We are open to the persuasion of intelligent and rational consciousness, and are to make our decision on that basis.

The correct procedure for reaching the judgment of value and the decision differs depending on which 'time' one finds oneself in. If one is affected by a strong inclination or by conflicting inclinations, it is precisely the negotiation of these inclinations that will lead one to a genuine judgment of value and a good decision. The rules for the discernment of spirits that Ignatius proposes for the first and second weeks of the *Exercises* have to do precisely with this 'second time' of election. They are guidelines for the negotiation of the affectivity in which *possible* values are apprehended. The one exception is the 'consolation without a cause,' which is the source of the first 'time' of election, in which we are placed by the grace of God in the condition of creative tension in which values can be truly apprehended by feelings in a manner that, because there are no further questions and one knows that such is the case, is analogous to reflective understanding in arriving at the truth.

The third time of election does not figure in these rules. When one is already in the condition of equilibrium of which Ignatius speaks when writing of the third 'time,' but is still not strongly inclined, one does not negotiate conflicting affective inclinations — there are none to negotiate. Instead one proceeds to the judgment of value and the decision through a process of rational weighing of the cons and pros of the various alternatives. One can do this precisely because one is already in the state of detachment and openness that is required for an authentic decision. When one is in that state of detachment, one can follow the lead of rational consciousness in moving toward one's decision. The third 'time' thus corresponds to Lonergan's discussion in chapter 18 of *Insight*, where behavior is moral precisely because one follows the lead of rational consciousness.

What, then, is the process of negotiating affectivity during the second 'time'? The various inclinations that one is experiencing are apprehensions of *possible* values in feelings. Such apprehensions are to decision what insights are to cognition. They are a dime a dozen, and the problem arises in figuring out which of them are genuine and which are illusory. One has to negotiate the feelings in which the possible values are apprehended, and so Ignatius counsels us to pay careful attention to every moment of an inclination, to watch its beginning, its entire process, and the end to which it leads. Only if all are good is the inclination to be assented to and followed. And what characterizes this 'good' in this context? I think it is precisely the finalistic tension of the dialectic of consciousness. This is the state one already finds oneself in in the third time of election, where one proceeds to decision by following the lead of rational consciousness. In the third time, one is to move to judgments of value and decision by reasoning. In the second time, therefore, one is to move to judgments of value and decision by following those inclinations that would lead one to the equilibrium of the integral dialectic of consciousness, and by rejecting those inclinations that lead one away from it.

If this interpretation is correct, the Ignatian counsel regarding the process of arriving at authentic decisions is remarkably comprehensive. At any time we either are or

are not abiding in the state of creative finalistic equilibrium in the authentic dialectic of consciousness. And if we
are, we are either experiencing strong affective inclinations
in the face of a decision or we are not. If we are experiencing strong inclinations in this state of genuineness, and if
they are those which Ignatius refers to as 'consolation without a cause,' there are no further questions. If we are not
experiencing strong inclinations, we are advised to follow
the lead of rational consciousness, weighing the cons and
pros of the various alternatives against the measure established by the Gospel. But if we are not in the state of equilibrium characteristic of the first and third 'times,' we are
advised to follow those inclinations that would lead us to
the integral dialectic of consciousness and to reject those
inclinations that would distort the tension of consciousness in either direction.

Moreover, the distortions can be related to the different states of the soul that figure in Ignatius's advice to
people in the second 'time': desolation, consolation, and,
by implication from the Ignatian text, false consolation.
The interplay among these states is complex, and I cannot
go into all the various forms that it may take. But I would
suggest that generally consolation is the state of dynamic
creative finalistic orientation that I have been calling the
integral dialectic of consciousness; desolation distorts this
dialectic in the direction of 'too little possibility'; and false
consolation apprehends as possible value what is not of
real value. The latter can either distort the dialectic of consciousness in the direction of 'too much possibility,' or, if
followed, lead one to the desolation of 'too little possibility.' (In the last analysis, this is not an either/or, for distortion in the direction of too much possibility will strengthen
the opposed principle, leading to either a righting of the
dynamic equilibrium or a manic-depressive oscillation of
consciousness from one distortion to the other.)

5   What is the affective apprehension of values that can be to judgments of value, not what insight is to judgments of fact, but what reflective understanding is to the latter judgments? Lonergan gives us at least two complementary indications of an answer to this question. The first is the value apprehension of an affectivity converted to love in the family, love in the community, and the love of God; as long as one is in love, one abides in self-transcendence, in the dynamic equilibrium of the dialectic of consciousness, as 'a successful way of life.'[42] The second has to do with the value apprehension of an affectivity in the dynamic state in which feelings respond to values, not in accord with just any scale of preference, but in accord with a scale of preference constituted by successive degrees of self-transcendence; the successively heightened tension of the consciousness of the genuine person responds to values in accord with the scale of values that Lonergan speaks of in *Method in Theology*. It is a normative scale of preference for measuring affective integrity: vital, social, cultural, personal, and religious values. When one is in such a dynamic state, and as long as one remains in it ('Abide in my love'), one's apprehension of values in feelings is to the judgment of value what reflective understanding is to the judgment of fact. But when one is not in such a state, one's apprehension of values is to the judgment of value what direct insight is to the judgment of fact; it is an apprehension of possible value, and it must be submitted to questions for deliberation in which one negotiates the affective apprehensions in the manner suggested by Ignatius in his rules for the second 'time' of election.

Now what I have been calling psychic conversion is an aid to this process of negotiation. It enables one to understand and work on one's affective state. Again, the interpretation of the dream and the analogous symbolic processes of Jung's 'active imagination' and Ira Progoff's various 'internal dialogues' are ways (though somewhat time-consuming!) of conducting this negotiation. They all involve associating affective states with imaginal representations, and negotiating the affective states by internal communication with the symbolic figures.

6   There are implications of this position for a reorientation of depth psychology. Lonergan has provided a heuristic structure of what it is to be 'well' psychologically. The lead in establishing this heuristic structure is not taken by the psyche, whose affective apprehensions may be either genuine or illusory. Precisely as psychic — that is, without reference to their connections with intentional consciousness — affective apprehensions contain no more of a criterion for distinguishing what is genuine from what is illusory than does sensation for distinguishing what is true from what is false. The lead is taken, rather, by intentionality, which unleashes the successive stages of self-transcendence that are the measure of the authenticity of affective response. On the other hand, Lonergan explicitly links affective responses with one's orientation in the world motivated by *values*. Feelings as intentional responses mediate between elemental symbolic representations and value orientation. Thus the various techniques of symbolic communication employed by depth psychology, beginning with dream interpretation, are reconceived as processes by which one either explicitly acknowledges or establishes in oneself a determinate orientation to the world of values. These techniques can be reinterpreted as steps toward the affective conversion through which one's apprehension of values in feelings moves from being to the judgment of value what insight is to the judgment of fact to being to the judgment of value what reflective understanding is to the judgment of fact.

7   There are also implications regarding the scale of values to which affectively converted subjects sponta-

neously respond. The integral dialectic of consciousness defines what is meant by 'personal value,' that is, 'the person in his self-transcendence, as loving and being loved, as originator of values in himself and in his milieu, as an inspiration and invitation to others to do likewise.'[43] This originating value is placed at the fourth level of the scale of values, corresponding to the fourth level of consciousness. Corresponding, respectively, to the third, second, and first levels of consciousness are cultural, social, and vital values. (The association of culture with reflection and of the good of order with intelligence can be documented as a consistent factor throughout Lonergan's works.) And religious values correspond to the fifth level of consciousness.[44] These relations may be considered from below and from above. From above, the higher levels are the condition of the possibility of successfully functioning schemes of recurrence at more basic levels. From below, questions emerging at more basic levels evoke the operations that will lead to consolidations at the higher levels.

Personal value is dialectical, precisely in the sense of the integral dialectic of consciousness which I am here arguing to be discoverable in Lonergan's writings; and so are at least what Lonergan calls cultural and social levels of value. The integrally dialectical quality of social values is a major emphasis in chapter 7 of *Insight*, where the linked but opposed principles to be preserved in creative tension with one another are vital intersubjectivity and practical intelligence. It is precisely in speaking of this 'dialectic of community' that Lonergan emphasizes what has become the major point of my interpretation: namely, that 'dialectic rests on the concrete unity of opposed principles; the dominance of *either* principle results in a distortion, and the distortion both weakens the dominance and strengthens the opposed principle *to restore an equilibrium*.'[45] The dialectic of community is rooted in the foundational dia-

lectic of the subject. Now, cultural value is intermediate
between personal value and social value, both from below
and from above. From below, problems at the level of social value pose questions that will be resolved only by proportionate changes at the level of cultural values. From
above, these cultural values are requisite for reversing the
cycle of decline at the social level: 'if men are to meet the
challenge set by major decline and its longer cycle, it will
be through their culture that they do so.'[46]

Can we speak of an as yet unrealized, and so still to
be evoked, integral dialectic at the level of culture analogous to the integral dialectics of the subject and of community? I have tried to do so, drawing on Eric Voegelin's
discussion of cosmological and anthropological symbolizations (read: constitutive meaning).[47] I cannot go into
details on this matter here; it is quite involved, and my
explorations in this area are still very tentative. But if there
is any validity to what I am saying, then we can understand historical process itself in terms of an 'analogy of
dialectic' obtaining among the relations of personal, cultural, and social values. More precisely, our understanding of these levels of value can enable us to contribute to
the reorientation of human science and, drawing on this
science, to derive the major *general* categories for a systematic theology that would understand Christian doctrines in the light of an understanding of history; and those
doctrines would express our understanding of religious
value, precisely in its relation to personal, cultural, and
social values.

This goal of a systematic theology that understands
Christian doctrines in the light of an understanding of history is a distant one. But perhaps this paper helps to indicate the sources of the categories for understanding history which I wish now to employ in a systematic understanding of Christian doctrine. The major problem that

some have found with these categories lies in my appropriation of the notion of dialectic from Lonergan's work. I have tried in this paper to indicate that there are grounds in Lonergan's work for understanding dialectic as I have. This understanding in no way conflicts with Lonergan's more usual use of the term 'dialectic' to indicate the method that advances positions and reverses counterpositions. As I have tried to suggest, the root of the counterpositions lies precisely in breaking the integral dialectic of consciousness.

8   In a systematics constructed in light of an understanding of history, the basic special categories would be derived from religiously differentiated consciousness and would ground contemporary theology's transposition of such metaphysical categories as could be systematically employed in medieval theology once the theorem of the supernatural entitative order had been developed. They will articulate the conditions of integral dialectics of the subject, culture, and community. At each of these levels of value, integrity is a function, not of either of the two constitutive principles of dialectic, but of a higher synthesis that is conditioned in the last analysis by religious values. The source of an integral dialectic of community lies in authentic cultural values proportionate to the dimensions of the social reality, and so today in some very definite sense in crossculturally constitutive meaning. But the source of genuine cultural values lies in a personal integrity itself conditioned by the grace of the universal willingness that is needed for the integral dialectic of the subject. This grace is the foundation of soteriological constitutive meaning. This in turn is the proximate condition for authentic cultural values; or in other words, the integral dialectic of cosmological and anthropological constitutive meaning.

Grace is thus the ultimate condition for the integrity of the three dialectics constitutive of historical process.

Hence, the articulation of the experience of grace constitutes a set of special categories in a theology that would mediate between a cultural matrix and the significance and role of Christian faith in that matrix. This is why an objectification of the dialectics constitutive of history enables the construction of a systematic theology that would understand Christian doctrine in the light of an understanding of human history.

In this way, too, we may approach an understanding of that realization of dialectic that has to do with contradictories, and so with the dialectical method that advances positions and reverses counterpositions. The basic positions are a function of the integral dialectic of consciousness, the basic counterpositions a function of the distortion or breaking of that dialectic. But the intellectual conversion articulated in the basic positions is itself a function of the religious conversion that establishes the integral dialectic of consciousness. The *radical* dialectic of contradictories concerns the reception or refusal of the grace of charity. Only the supernatural conjugate form of charity establishes consciousness in the creative tension of its integral dialectic. Once consciousness is established in that tension, one's knowing will be, and can be known to be, what one is brought to affirm it to be in the eleventh chapter of *Insight*. Unless one exists in the tension of the integral dialectic of consciousness, one will explicitly or implicitly fall into the knowing that is without understanding or the clinging to understanding that sacrifices knowing on the altar of immanentism, relativism, or idealism. The basic position on knowing is a function of the creative finalistic tension of the dialectic of the subject made possible by grace. This is how the personal values capable of deriving genuine cultural values come about, and these cultural values will be the condition for an integral dialectic of intersubjectivity and practical intelligence in the social order. From this basis in a theology of grace in history, I think, one can proceed to elaborate a systematic theology of other doctrines as well that would be a theological understanding of human history throughout.[48]

9   I close with one further comment that may help to clarify the relation between genetic and dialectical methods. At the end of his discussion of genuineness, Lonergan writes:

> Finally, there is the sanction of genuineness. To fail in genuineness is not to escape but only to displace the tension between limitation and transcendence. Such a displacement is the root of the dialectical phenomena of scotosis in the individual, of the bias of common sense, of basic philosophical differences, and of their prolongation in natural and human science, in morals and religion, in educational theory and history. But this issue takes us from genetic method to dialectic, and so the present discussion ends.[49]

'Dialectic' is used here in the sense of the method that studies and reverses distortions. By interpreting this passage in the light of the quotation from chapter 7 with which I began, we could say that genetic method in human science studies the integral dialectic of consciousness in the subject and its ramifications in culture and social order; and that dialectical method studies and reverses the distortions of this integral dialectic's tension between limitation and transcendence at these three levels of value.

Notes

1 Bernard Lonergan, *Insight* (see above, chapter 1, note 20) 243/ 268.

2 Ibid.

3 Ibid. 243-44/268.

4 Ibid. 244/ 268.

5 Ibid. 743/765.

6 See Bernard Lonergan, *Topics in Education* (see above, chapter 2, note 15) 145.

7 Lonergan, *Insight* 743-44/765.

8 For a contrary view, see Ronald McKinney, 'Lonergan's Notion of Dialectic,' *The Thomist* 46 (1982) 221-41.

9 Lonergan, *Insight* 244/268-69.

10 Ibid. 244/269.

11 Ibid.

12 Ibid.

13 Ibid. 217/242.

14 See Robert M. Doran, 'Dramatic Artistry in the Third Stage of Meaning,' chapter 7 in *Intentionality and Psyche*.

15 Lonergan, *Insight* 244/269.

16 Ibid. 218/243.

17 Ibid. 244/269.

[18] Ibid. 217/242.

[19] Ibid. 233/258.

[20] Ibid.

[21] Ibid.

[22] Ibid. 244/269.

[23] Ibid. xvii/11-12.

[24] Ibid. xxii/17.

[25] Ibid. xxviii/22.

[26] Ibid. 324-28/349-52.

[27] Ibid. 233/258.

[28] Ibid. 474/499.

[29] Ibid. 319/343.

[30] Ibid. 474-75/499.

[31] Ibid. 244/269.

[32] Ibid. 472-75/497-99.

[33] Ibid. 476/501.

[34] Bernard Lonergan, 'Natural Right and Historical Mindedness' (see above, chapter 2, note 9) 172-75.

[35] Ibid. 173.

[36] Lonergan, *Insight* 478/503.

[37] Ibid. 475/499.

38 Ibid. 191/214.

39 Ibid. 549/572.

40 Lonergan, 'Natural Right and Historical Mindedness' 179.

41 See Karl Rahner, 'The Theological Concept of Concupiscentia,' in *Theological Investigations*, vol. 1, trans. Cornelius Ernst (London: Darton, Longman & Todd, 1961) 347-82; for Rahner on gnoseological concupiscence see, for example, 'The Foundation of Belief Today,' in *Theological Investigations*, vol. 16, trans. David Moreland (New York: Crossroad), esp. 5-7.

42 Bernard Lonergan, 'A Post-Hegelian Philosophy of Religion,' in *A Third Collection* 208.

43 Bernard Lonergan, *Method in Theology* (see above, chapter 1, note 1) 32.

44 1993 note: In the paper 'Philosophy and the Religious Phenomenon,' discovered only after Lonergan's death, there is mention of six levels of consciousness; the four-leveled structure of intentional consciousness is open at either end: to a symbolic operator effecting the emergence of materials into consciousness in the first place, and to a level of being in love, beyond the fourth level. Religious love is one dimension of this highest level. See Bernard Lonergan, 'Philosophy and the Religious Phenomenon,' in *Method: Journal of Lonergan Studies* 12:2 (1994) 125-46.

45 Lonergan, *Insight* 233/258, emphasis added.

46 Ibid. 235/261.

47 See Eric Voegelin, *Israel and Revelation* (see above, chapter 1, note 8) 56.

48 1993 note: As will be clear from the final chapter in this book, I would now hold that a systematic theology must begin with the doc-

trine of God. The only preliminary matter to be treated is, not the theology of grace, but the religious experience that constitutes the horizon in which the doctrine of God can make sense.

[49] Lonergan, *Insight* 478/503.

5 Jung and Catholic Theology

The Catholic philosopher and theologian David Burrell has written, 'On balance Jung's work promises to prove as reliable a handmaid for doing theology today as more metaphysical schemes proved in the past. Every such interpretative scheme must be carefully monitored and critically employed, yet that defines the theologian's task.'[1]

I have often wondered whether the dialogue between Jung and Victor White, the Catholic theologian probably most in direct contact with Jung, would have proved more fruitful had White taken the 'turn to the subject' that Catholic theologians more attuned to Kantian and post-Kantian problems and modes of thought had undergone. The conversation between Jung and White might have gotten beyond the impasse it seems to have reached, for Jung clearly was firmly embedded in the philosophic tradition of the *anthropologische Wendung* of modern thought, and it was in the context of his appropriation of that tradition that he formulated his insights. Moreover, it was to that tradition that he thought himself to be contributing, complementing its concern with the subject as conscious knower and deliberate historical agent with his own apprehension of the elemental meanings that come to expression in the primordial symbols of the sensitive psyche. White, on the other hand, stood in that particular tradition of Thomist thought for which metaphysics was the basic science and metaphysical categories were primary and foundational. Could it be that the discussion between them, fruitful though it was and certainly generative of a personal friendship, could go no further than it did because the two men represented and stood within two quite distinct stages of meaning in the evolution of consciousness, because they had two quite distinct *loci* of data for foundational 'terms and relations' expressing the basic horizon within which all other matters would be discussed?

I offer this as a hermeneutical hypothesis, and propose to engage Jung from within the stage of meaning that was his own. There I will indicate some of the contributions Jung makes to Catholic theology, and the area in which Catholic theology would still beg to differ. The area of difference will be the same as that with which Victor White experienced difficulty, but perhaps posing the question from within a horizon similar to Jung's, at least in its affirmation of the subject as foundational, will enable, if not agreement, at least better understanding of the differences.

I   **The Turn to the Subject and Catholic Theology**

The cognate horizons are constituted by a common rejection of naive objectivism and by a concomitant affirmation of the constructive operations and states of the subject in the assembling of a world: by the insistence, if you want, that the subject pole and the object pole are isomorphic and equiprimordially constitutive dimensions of the worlds in which human beings live. Catholic theology long resisted the turn to the subject of modern philosophy because of a fear that it would lead inevitably to idealism, relativism, immanentism, and neglect of a cognitive opening upon the realm of absolute transcendence.[2] These suspicions have never completely disappeared from Catholic thought, despite the monumental efforts and achievements of such giants as Bernard Lonergan and Karl Rahner, in whose work the contributions to Catholic theology of the turn to the subject are overwhelmingly obvious. Irrational fear of the turn to the subject is being voiced with new stridency today by many Catholic neoconservatives. And it must be admitted that on the face of things the history of modern philosophic thought lends some support to these fears, in that the majority of modern philosophers who grant a constitutive function to the subject in the cognitive and existential construction of the world as objective pole of horizon have indeed not transcended idealism, unless it be by an appeal to faith that is as arbitrary as the objectivism of the conservatives. Until the middle of this century the dominant philosophic voices in Catholicism were united despite other differences by the conviction that Catholic thought had to provide a common front against the priority of the subject in the construction of a philosophy or a theology. A few, commonly referred to as transcendental Thomists, took modern philosophy seriously, and attempted to move beyond the Kantian impasse from within the framework established by an acceptance of the Kantian problematic.

One Catholic thinker frequently mentioned as belonging to this group was the late Bernard Lonergan. The classification is somewhat superficial, since there are real differences among these various thinkers. But Lonergan's critique of the antisubjective bias of the Catholic mainstream was sharp, even at times acerbic. Permit me to quote at length one representative example.

> ... one can so emphasize objective truth as to disregard or undermine the very conditions of its emergence and existence. In fact, if at the present time among Catholics there is discerned a widespread alienation from the dog-

mas of faith, this is not without a previous one-sidedness that so insisted on the objectivity of truth as to leave subjects and their needs out of account.

Symptomatic of such one-sidedness was the difficulty experienced by theologians from the days of Suarez, de Lugo, and Bañez, when confronted with the syllogism: What God has revealed is true. God has revealed the mysteries of faith. Therefore, the mysteries of faith are true. There is, perhaps, no need for me to explain why this syllogism was embarrassing, for it implies that the mysteries of faith were demonstrable conclusions. But the point I wish to make is that the syllogism contains an unnoticed fallacy, and the fallacy turns on an exaggerated view of the objectivity of truth. If one recalls that truth exists formally only in judgments and that judgments exist only in the mind, then the fallacy is easily pinned down. What God reveals is a truth in the mind of God and in the minds of believers, but it is not a truth in the minds of unbelievers; and to conclude that the mysteries of faith are truths in the mind of God or in the minds of believers in no way suggests that the mysteries are demonstrable. But this simple way out seems to have been missed by the theologians. They seem to have thought of truth as so objective as to get along without minds. Nor does such thinking seem to have been confined to theoretical accounts of the act of faith. The same insistence on objective truth and the same neglect of its subjective conditions informed the old catechetics, which the new catechetics is replac-

ing, and the old censorship, which insisted on
true propositions and little understood the need
to respect the dynamics of the advance toward
truth.[3]

Lonergan differs from most other Catholic thinkers
who took the turn to the subject, precisely in the radical
nature of his commitment to disclosing the dynamics of
the advance toward truth. While other Catholic thinkers
who took seriously the *anthropologische Wendung* tended to
begin with the Kantian epistemological question, What are
the conditions of valid knowing? Lonergan makes that
question consequent on the more radical question, What
am I doing when I am knowing? The latter is a question of
cognitive praxis or performance. It seeks an account, understanding, and affirmation of the actual concrete process one engages in on the way to the judgment, 'This is
(or is not) the case.' My own efforts to monitor but also
employ the work of Jung in Catholic theology are grounded
in Lonergan's answer to that question and to the subsequent epistemological question, and in other developments
in his thought that were possible only because of that answer. So I will devote a fair amount of attention to his
position.

2   A Dream and Its Meaning

I wrestled for nearly three years with the question,
How am I to integrate what Lonergan has taught me regarding the structure and dynamics of my cognitive and
decisional operations with the dimensions of the psyche I
had discovered through a Jungian maieutic of dreams and
feelings? I had been a student of Lonergan's writings from
the summer of 1967, and in 1972 began to discuss my dreams
with a psychologist of Jungian persuasion, Charles Gold-

smith. I realized that with Lonergan's help I had differentiated levels of conscious performance, and was convinced, as I still am today, that Lonergan brings one to an affirmation concerning oneself that is not subject to fundamental revision. But it was immediately clear when I began to explore the world of dreams that I was entering a dimension of interiority different from that with which Lonergan acquaints one. It too had its truth, and because it was a dimension of the same interiority as that whose cognitional and existential operations Lonergan had uncovered, I knew there had to be an intelligible connection. But I did not discover what this connection is until a dream provided me with the set of images needed for the emergence of insight. I was in Zürich at the time, attending lectures at the Jung Institute and attempting to write my doctoral dissertation on precisely this problem. I had written about twenty introductions to the dissertation, but as yet did not have the basic insight I needed to progress any further.

In the dream I am walking down a flight of stairs. The house bore a great deal of resemblance to the one in which I was living in Zürich, the Jesuit house from which the periodical *Orientierung* is published. I was nearing the first floor of the house, and intended to go down to the basement, when I met Bernard Lonergan coming up the stairs. He looked at me very intently, but also with a friendly look in his eyes, and said, 'If you really want to see some images, come with me!' He took me up the stairs, to the top floor of the house, and we entered a large room arranged as a movie theatre. We sat in two chairs centered in the room about three-quarters of the way back from the movie screen, and a motion picture began to appear on the screen. Lonergan was seated to my right, I to his left.

Lonergan met me between the first and second floors of the house. The house is interiority. At the threshold between the experience of presentations (the first floor) and insight (the second floor) there are constellated by the spirit of inquiry the images from which insight is emergent. The basement into which I had intended to go is the unconscious. The top floor to which Lonergan took me is the highest level of intentional consciousness, the existential level on which we perform the operations of deliberation, evaluation, and decision. Lonergan calls it the fourth level of consciousness. Between it and the second level, that of insight, there is a third level where we test our formulated insights, to judge whether they are true or false. The main point of the dream, then, is that the images emergent from the basement are to be admitted into consciousness by memory (first level), interpreted by understanding (second level), interpreted critically (third level), and used as materials for the deliberations and evaluations that culminate in the decisions through which we constitute the world and ourselves (fourth level). That Lonergan was to my right means that he had discovered the operations of consciousness. That I was to his left means that I was complementing his discovery with the exploration of what many psychologists call the unconscious. That we were centered in the room means that the taut balance of conscious intentionality and the sensitive psyche is not to be displaced in one direction or the other. And that the images that Lonergan had invited me to see appeared on a movie screen means that if one negotiates psychic images and feelings by bringing them up the various levels of consciousness, one gains an aesthetic distance from them that is not possible if one meets them in the basement, a distance that allows them to become materials for the construction of a work of art in the forging of one's self, the production, in Lonergan's words, of the first and only edition of oneself.[4]

The dream suggests, too, images needed for insight into a particular problem that was vexing me as I attempted

to work out the answer to my questions. For I was convinced that Jung's position on the reconciliation of good
and evil could not be squared with my own beliefs and
values. Locating a special relevance of the psyche's symbols for the operations of the fourth level of intentional
consciousness helped me to develop my position on these
matters. For at the fourth level of consciousness there is
encountered a problem of opposites quite other than that
which is represented by the relative positioning of Lonergan
and myself in the dream. The latter opposition is the creative tension of conscious intentionality and the sensitive
psyche. It is an opposition that can constitute an integral
dialectic of the subject, a dialectic of contraries. Quite distinct from it is the opposition that appears when I ask myself
whether I will affirm or deny this integral dialectic, whether
I will allow myself to be constituted as an integral dialectic
of conscious intentionality and the psyche or whether I
will allow this dialectic to be distorted by a displacement
of the tension in either direction, either to the 'right' or to
the 'left,' either to the exploits of a consciousness disasso-
ciated from the psyche or to the drift of a psyche not governed by the imperatives of authentic conscious performance. The opposition uncovered by such a question is
the opposition of good and evil. It is not to be resolved in
the same manner as is the opposition of conscious intentionality and the psyche. The latter opposition is resolved
by a choice of both intentionality and the psyche, precisely
in their creative tension with one another. Here was the
dimension in which Jung would complement Lonergan.
The problem of good and evil, however, is a problem of
choosing either this tense unity of intentionality and the
psyche (good) or allowing the creative tension to be displaced in the direction of either the proud spirit or the
directionless psyche (evil). The question of good and evil
constitutes a dialectic of contradictories. Here the choice

is not of both opposites, but of one or the other. But a choice of the good is a choice as well of the creative tension of the dialectic of contraries constituted by the opposition of conscious intentionality and the psyche. In such distinctions there appears, I believe, both the contribution that Jung can make to Catholic theology, and the precise place at which that theology must part ways with him. The contribution lies in the discovery of the psyche as creative counterpart to conscious intentionality in the forging of self and world as works of dramatic art. The discrepancy lies in the tendency in much of Jung's writing not to distinguish the dialectic of contraries constituted by intentionality and the psyche from the dialectic of contradictories constituted by good and evil, and so to encourage an integration of good and evil analogous to the integration of intentionality and the psyche.

It has been clear to me ever since the experiences narrated above that foundations for a science of the psyche are provided in Lonergan's differentiation of conscious intentionality. The dream itself provides images for such a conviction. And theological consequences of this discovery have become ever more obvious to me. For the integrity that theologians speak of when writing of the myth of the fall and the doctrine of original sin is the creative tension of the opposites involved in a dialectic of contraries; concupiscence is our tendency to displace such a tension in one direction or the other; sin is capitulation to that tendency; and the need for grace is the need for a set of habits and for actual inclinations both of which are beyond the resources of our native capacities. The basic categories of a theological anthropology can be derived precisely from the foundations established by integrating Lonergan's discovery of the structure of conscious intentionality with much of what Jung has disclosed about the sensitive psyche, its tendencies, and the meaning of its symbols.

3   **The Structure of Conscious
        Intentionality**

Having stated the psychic validation and evidence for my position, I will now proceed to relate as briefly as possible the foundations I find in Lonergan's analysis of conscious intentionality for a proper employment and monitoring of Jungian psychology in Catholic theology.

One may discern four stages in Lonergan's work on intentional consciousness. The first stage is directly concerned with the question, What am I doing when I am knowing? and with the subsequent questions, Why is doing that knowing? and What do I know when I do that? The other three stages build on his answer to those questions. Again, the second of these questions is the Kantian epistemological question seeking the conditions of valid knowing. But for Lonergan, prior to that question and grounding the manner in which one answers it is the more radical question of cognitive praxis itself: what actually occurs when one is involved in cognitive performance?

The question, What am I doing when I am knowing? is answered in the eleventh chapter of Lonergan's book *Insight*.[5] But the answer is a function of a rigorous phenomenology of cognitive operations carried out in the first ten chapters, and it takes the form of an invitation to the reader to ask himself or herself whether or not these operations occur in his or her own consciousness, and precisely in this set of relations. It is an invitation to self-appropriation. I cannot possibly summarize the details of the first ten chapters, and so must be content with a brief presentation of Lonergan's cognitional theory as the latter is proposed in chapter 11 of *Insight*.

In any paper that treats Jung and will probably be read by people more familiar with Jung than they are with Lonergan, it is crucial to emphasize from the outset that the term 'consciousness' does not mean the same thing for Lonergan as it does for Jung. This is not to take sides, saying that one is correct and the other erroneous in his use of this term, but simply to clarify the diverse meanings so as to avoid unnecessary confusion. Consciousness for Lonergan includes a great deal of what Jung and other psychiatrists would locate in the unconscious. For consciousness is not representation, perception, knowledge, but simply self-presence, whether or not the latter is subsequently objectified in clear and precise terms. Thus a great deal of what depth psychologists mean by 'the unconscious' would be, in Lonergan's vocabulary, conscious but not objectified, hidden in the obscurity of mere self-presence, unmediated by articulate self-understanding or even by explicit advertence at a more primordial experiential level.

With this understood, we can proceed to relate what Lonergan says about consciousness in the pivotal chapter of *Insight*. It is probably easiest to appeal to the reader's present experience of studying this paper. If the reader were at this precise moment experiencing only a set of black marks on white paper, if there were no understanding going on and no attempt to understand what I am writing, he or she would be operating only at what Lonergan calls the empirical level of consciousness. At this level, meaning is only potential. But in fact, more is going on. The reader is attempting to understand what I am trying to communicate. Operative, whether formulated or not, is the question, What is he talking about? This is a question for intelligence, and such questions constitute the initial stage of a level of consciousness distinct from mere experiencing, a level concerned with understanding. Such questions are essential if understanding is ever to emerge in the experiential flow. Under the impact of such questions, our experience is organized and patterned in such a way as to provide the proximate materials for insight or understanding. And our empirical consciousness, our pure self-presence, is itself modified as we attempt to understand, and again when we reach understanding. There is, then, a second level of consciousness whose concern is understanding. It presupposes and sublates the first, empirical level of presentations, and it comes to term as a second level of consciousness as we conceptualize and formulate what we have understood. But these formulations themselves prompt us to raise yet a further question, Is it true? This Lonergan calls a question for reflection, as distinct from a question for intelligence. Its concern is the truth of what we have understood and formulated. It promotes consciousness to a third level of awareness, the reasonable or rational level, and it leads to a grasp of the sufficiency or insufficiency of evidence for a prospective judgment, 'Yes, this is the case.'

The three levels of cognitive operations are unified by a pure question, which further constitutes what human consciousness is. Not only is consciousness pure self-presence but I am present to myself as an unrestrictedly open, if inarticulate, question. This question is for intelligibility, and then for truth. It will not be satisfied in any given instance short of the grasp of the sufficiency of the evidence that allows me to pronounce on any given issue, 'This is so.' If the evidence for such a judgment is not forthcoming or grasped, it is unreasonable for me to pass judgment on the issue under investigation. But if the evidence is forthcoming and is grasped as such, then it is equally unreasonable for me not to move to the act of judgment. On this account truth is intentionally independent of the subject, and in the affirmation of the truth on a given issue I reach a cognitive self-transcendence. Yet ontologically the same truth resides only in the subject.

Intentionally it goes completely beyond the subject, yet it does so only because ontologically the subject is capable of an intentional self-transcendence, of going beyond what he feels, what he imagines, what he thinks, what seems to him, to something utterly different, to what is so. Moreover, before the subject can attain the self-transcendence of truth, there is the slow and laborious process of conception, gestation, parturition. But teaching and learning, investigation, coming to understand, marshaling and weighing the evidence, these are not independent of the subject, of times and places, of psychological, social, historical conditions. The fruit of truth must grow and mature on the tree of the subject before it can be plucked and placed in its absolute realm.[6]

Lonergan poses as radical foundation of the rest of philosophy, and later in *Insight* of theology, the self-affirmation of the knower to which he invites his readers in chapter II of *Insight*. For any attempt to deny the judgment that I am a conscious unity whose operations unfold on the three levels of experience, understanding, and judgment is self-defeating, since such an attempt would appeal to a set of experiences that one claimed to understand, and would argue that one's understanding of these experiences is true or at least closer to the truth than the position that it is supposedly denying. Any denial of the foundational judgment contradicts performatively the cognitive content of the judgment itself. In this way, Lonergan maintains, a sure foundation can be established for the subsequent construction of a philosophy.

Lonergan's work subsequent to *Insight* disengaged three other foundational dimensions. First, there occurs

the affirmation that intentional consciousness is constituted by a fourth level that is beyond and sublates the three
levels that he invites one to affirm as true of oneself in
Insight. The fourth level of consciousness is the level on
which we apprehend possible and real values, deliberate,
evaluate, form judgments not of fact but of value, decide,
and carry out our decisions in action. It is a level on which
consciousness is existential, self-constitutive, and world-
constitutive, where 'constitution' is now understood not
in the purely cognitive sense of constructive understanding, but in the practical and historical sense of effecting
the actual structure of oneself as a good or evil person
through one's decisions and actions as these contribute to
the making of being through praxis. Next, there is an affirmation of falling in love and of the dynamic state of being
in love as the consummation of our conscious intentionality and the radical ground of consistent self-transcendence
in our knowing and our deciding. Love is spoken of by
Lonergan as a threefold reality: there is the love of intimacy in the family, the love of humanity in the civil community, and the love of God that constitutes the structure
of any genuine religious orientation. Finally, Lonergan
came more and more to emphasize in his late papers that
there is another vector in the intentional and structured
self-presence that is consciousness besides the upwardly
directed dynamism that most of his work emphasizes. The
other vector moves through consciousness from above
downward, and is actually prior to and ground of any upwardly moving creativity.

> ... there is development from above down-
> wards. There is the transformation of falling in
> love: the domestic love of the family; the hu-
> man love of one's tribe, one's city, one's coun-
> try, mankind; the divine love that orientates

man in his cosmos and expresses itself in his
worship. Where hatred only sees evil, love reveals values. At once it commands commitment
and joyfully carries it out, no matter what the
sacrifice involved. Where hatred reinforces bias,
love dissolves it, whether it be the bias of unconscious motivation, the bias of individual or
group egoism, or the bias of omnicompetent,
shortsighted common sense. Where hatred
plods around in ever narrower vicious circles,
love breaks the bonds of psychological and social determinisms with the conviction of faith
and the power of hope.[7]

I am aware that such a short exposition cannot possibly provide any reader unfamiliar with Lonergan with
the conviction, on which I will base the rest of my argument, that in these four steps Lonergan has succeeded in
grasping and articulating the essential structure of authentic
human consciousness, and in so doing has brought the
modern turn to the subject to a series of plateaus, all of
which lie beyond idealism, relativism, and subjectivism. I
can only ask the reader to accept that this is my position,
and to accept Lonergan's invitation to the exploration of
self that he proposes, asking oneself whether or not
Lonergan has arrived at a set of true and foundational judgments that represent a kind of watershed in the history of
the turn to the subject. What is important for my present
concern is that Lonergan's work does take seriously the
turn to the subject that represents also the tradition in
which Jung stood and to which Jung would make a contribution, and that Lonergan's achievement in this tradition
is the work precisely of a contemporary Catholic theologian, done for the sake of the development of a contemporary Catholic theology. Furthermore, it was Lonergan's

intention, in my mind largely fulfilled in his work, to uti-
lize his achievement of a kind of completion to the turn to
the subject as the foundation of a transposition into the
modern world of what is permanently valid in the Catholic tradition, and especially in the work of Thomas Aquinas.

4   Psychic Conversion

Lonergan formulates his judgments on the subject
precisely as foundational for theology, by stating that the
foundations of theology lie in the objectification of intellectual, moral, and religious *conversion*. It is precisely at
this point of conversion as foundation that I would locate
the significance of Jung. For, I believe, Lonergan's account
of conversion needs to be complemented precisely in the
area that Jung explored. Jung, perhaps most effectively of
all depth psychologists to date, serves to indicate what is
required to complete Lonergan's work on the subject, even
as Lonergan's work serves to reorient what from a Catholic standpoint cannot be accepted in Jung.

I have expressed the complement that a reoriented
depth psychology can offer to Lonergan's work by speaking of a fourth dimension of conversion. I call it psychic
conversion. Its closest Jungian counterpart would be what
Jung called 'the transcendent function.'[8] But I formulate
my understanding of it by drawing on a transposition that
Lonergan proposes, in the sixth chapter of *Insight*, of the
Freudian notion of the censor. Lonergan understands the
censor in the light of his notion of intentional consciousness. The censor is a particular orientation of intentionality
and imagination such that these are either open to the
reception into consciousness of the images needed for
insight and decision, or resistant to allowing these images
to make their way into conscious awareness. In the first
case the censor is constructive, in the second case
repressive. Lonergan writes of the censor:

Primarily, the censorship is constructive; it selects and arranges materials that emerge in consciousness in a perspective that gives rise to an insight; this positive activity has by implication a negative aspect, for other materials are left behind, and other perspectives are not brought to light; still, this negative aspect of positive activity does not introduce any arrangement or perspective into the unconscious demand functions of neural patterns and processes. In contrast, the aberration of the censorship is primarily repressive; its positive activity is to prevent the emergence into consciousness of perspectives that would give rise to unwanted insights; it introduces, so to speak, the exclusion of arrangements into the field of the unconscious; it dictates the manner in which neural demand functions are not to be met; and the negative aspect of its positive activity is the admission to consciousness of any materials in any other arrangement or perspective. Finally, both the censorship and its aberration differ from conscious advertence to a possible mode of behavior and conscious refusal to behave in that fashion. For the censorship and its aberration are operative prior to conscious advertence, and they regard directly not how we are to behave but what we are to understand. A refusal to behave in a given manner is not a refusal to understand; so far from preventing conscious advertence, the refusal intensifies it and makes its recurrence more likely; and, finally, while it is true that conscious refusal is connected with a cessation of the conscious advertence, still this connection rests, not on an obnubilation of intelligence, but on a shift of effort, interest, preoccupation. Accordingly, we are led to restrict the name 'repression' to the exercise of the aberrant censorship that is engaged in preventing insight.[9]

My initial insight regarding psychic conversion, however, as is obvious from the dream narrated above, had to do with the ulterior finality of the censorship, a finality beyond insight, one in the realm of decision and action . It was formulated in terms of the connections that Lonergan draws between feelings and values, on the one hand, and feelings and symbols, on the other hand. And it concluded that because of these connections, the ulterior meaning of the dream is constitutive and existential, not only cognitive. Nor does Lonergan's emphasis on insight in his treatment of the censorship imply a purely cognitive point of view or finality. For already he was clear on the relative place of insight in the structure of consciousness. While it arises on experience, insight is oriented to judgments of fact and of value and ultimately to decision and action. Thus my initial insight does not contradict the definition I was subsequently to give of psychic conversion: the transformation of the imaginative and affective component of the censor from a repressive to a constructive functioning in one's world constitution and self-constitution. The connection lies in the inextricable connection of feelings to the images that are allowed into consciousness. It is easier, says Lonergan, to suppress images than to suppress feelings. The feelings attached to a suppressed image will become detached from that image and attach themselves to other, more incongruous apprehensive contents. In this way the repressive activity of the censor is responsible for a cumulative fragmentation of the sensitive psyche. But these feelings have a more or less direct relation to our existential self-constitution as historical and world-constitutive agents, because of the intimate connection of feelings with values. Thus the ulterior finality of the censorship is with respect to the same fourth level of consciousness which emerged in my dream as the level from which the images emergent from the unconscious are to be negotiated.

On the relation of feelings to values, Lonergan writes:

> Feelings that are intentional responses regard two main classes of objects: on the one hand, the agreeable or disagreeable, the satisfying or dissatisfying; on the other hand, values, whether the ontic value of persons or the qualitative value of beauty, understanding, truth, virtuous acts, noble deeds. In general, response to value both carries us towards self-transcendence and selects an object for the sake of whom or of which we transcend ourselves. In contrast, response to the agreeable or disagreeable is ambiguous. What is agreeable may very well be what also is a true good. But it also happens that what is a true good may be disagreeable. Most good men have to accept unpleasant work, privations, pain, and their virtue is a matter of doing so without excessive self-centered lamentation.
>
> Not only do feelings respond to values. They do so in accord with some scale of preference. So we may distinguish vital, social, cultural, personal, and religious values in an ascending order. Vital values, such as health and strength, grace and vigor, normally are preferred to avoiding the work, privations, pains

involved in acquiring, maintaining, restoring them. Social values, such as the good of order which conditions the vital values of the whole community, have to be preferred to the vital values of individual members of the community. Cultural values do not exist without the underpinning of vital and social values, but nonetheless they rank higher. Not on bread alone doth man live. Over and above mere living and operating, men have to find a meaning and value in their living and operating. It is the function of culture to discover, express, validate, criticize, correct, develop, improve such meaning and value. Personal value is the person in his self-transcendence, as loving and being loved, as originator of values in himself and in his milieu, as an inspiration and invitation to others to do likewise. Religious values, finally are at the heart of the meaning and value of man's living and man's world.[10]

Again:

Intermediate between judgments of fact and judgments of value lie apprehensions of value. Such apprehensions are given in feelings. The feelings in question are not ... non-intentional states, trends, urges, that are related to efficient and final causes but not to objects. Again, they are not intentional responses to such objects as the agreeable or disagreeable, the pleasant or painful, the satisfying or dissatisfying. For, while these are objects, still they are ambiguous objects that may prove to be truly good or bad or only apparently good or bad. Apprehensions of value occur in a further category of intentional response which greets

either the ontic value of a person or the quali-
tative value of beauty, of understanding, of
truth, of noble deeds, of virtuous acts, of great
achievements. For we are so endowed that we
not only ask questions leading to self-transcendence, not only can recognize correct answers
constitutive of intentional self-transcendence,
but also respond with the stirring of our very
being when we glimpse the possibility or the
actuality of moral self-transcendence.[11]

My initial insight regarding psychic conversion was
to join this understanding of the connection between feelings and values with the relation that obtains between feelings and symbols. On the connection between feelings and
symbols, Lonergan writes that '[a] symbol is an image of a
real or imaginary object that evokes a feeling or is evoked
by a feeling.'[12] One's affective capacities, dispositions, and
habits can be ascertained by studying the symbols that
awaken determinate affects and by the affects that evoke
determinate symbols. The development or aberration of
feelings involves the transformation and transvaluation of
symbols. 'What before was moving no longer moves; what
before did not move now is moving. So the symbols themselves change to express the new affective capacities and
dispositions ... Inversely, symbols that do not submit to
transvaluation and transformation seem to point to a block
in development.'[13]

The primary function of symbols, Lonergan says, is
internal communication.[14] It is to the process of internal
communication, to associated images and feelings, memories and tendencies that one must appeal if one is going to
interpret and explain a symbol. In discussing the various
interpretive systems, Lonergan evinces a distinct sympathy for 'the existential approach that thinks of the dream,

not as the twilight of life, but as its dawn, the beginning of
the transition from impersonal existence to presence in
the world, to constitution of one's self in one's world.'[15]

These preliminaries are essential for understanding
what I mean by psychic conversion, and the manner in
which Lonergan's position on the subject establishes a
context for the employment and monitoring of depth-psychological systems, including Jung's. From the standpoint
of Lonergan's position on the subject, psychic conversion
involves an extension of the upwardly moving vector of
intentional consciousness as self-presence, an extension
not at the highest reaches of that vector but at its very
emergence as conscious finality. Very much like the transcendent function of Jung, it involves a transformation of
the censorship over images and concomitant feelings from
a repressive to a constructive functioning in one's development and self-constitution. But in reliance on Lonergan,
the meaning of this transformation is the effective emergence of the subject as a perceptive, insightful, reasonable,
and existentially responsible agent. Lonergan's position on
the subject enables a greater precision on psychic finality
than is presented in the depth-psychological systems
themselves. But the sublation into intentional consciousness of the images and tendencies of the psyche enriches
the perspective on the subject provided by intentionality
analysis, and enables a further self-appropriation beyond
the cognitive, moral, and religious dimensions that have
been specified and disclosed in Lonergan's work.

5   Employing and Monitoring Jung

It is within the framework established by these considerations that I would indicate the relevance of Jung's
work for a future Catholic theology grounded in the self-
appropriation of the cognitive, moral, religious, and psy-

chic dimensions of the very subject responsible for doing the theology in question. I will discuss five aspects of Jung's thought which I regard as positive contributions to the position on the subject foundational of theology, and a sixth aspect that such theology would submit to rather relentless criticism. The five positive contributions are: the finality of psychic process, the complexes, the notion of psychic wholeness, the archetypes, and the dialectic of matter and spirit. The complex sixth aspect, the one that needs to be reoriented, revolves around the notion of the self, particularly as it would involve an integration of the contradictory opposites of good and evil.

5.1   Psychic Finality

A complete encounter with depth psychology would have to begin not with Jung but with Freud. But Paul Ricoeur has, I believe, already presented an interpretation of Freud and a dialectical critique of his theory that are sufficient for our purposes.[16] The heart of Ricoeur's critique lies in his balancing of Freud's archeology of the subject with a teleology drawn largely from Hegel's *Phenomenology*. I have suggested that a more appropriate teleological counterpart to the Freudian archeology might be found in Jung, since Jung treats precisely the same dimensions of the subject as does Freud, and finds there, in addition to the reference ever backwards of everything psychic, a forward-looking aspect that characterizes the psyche itself as an upwardly if indeterminately directed dynamism constituting symbolic embodiments of an ever fuller elemental meaning. Especially since it is in a theory of the symbol that Ricoeur would meet the Freudian archeology with a corresponding teleology, his argument would only have been strengthened had he relied, not on Hegel, but on Jung for his argument.[17]

Such an evaluation of Jung, however, would affect the very theory of the symbol on which Ricoeur relies. For Ricoeur the self can be appropriated only by a detour through the symbolic objectifications of the human spirit writ large in the productions of culture. Even for his understanding of the symbol, then, Ricoeur turns not to the elemental productions of dreams but to cultural objectifications that have been distanced from the objectifying subject. The teleological dimensions of symbolism discovered in these objectifications are not for Ricoeur characteristic of our dreams, but only of so-called 'higher' symbolic forms.

> I suggest that we distinguish various levels of creativity of symbols ... At the lowest level we come upon sedimented symbolism: here we find various stereotyped and fragmented remains of symbols, symbols so commonplace and worn with use that they have nothing but a past. *This is the level of dream-symbolism,* and also of fairy tales and legends; here the work of symbolization is no longer operative. At a second level we come upon the symbols that function in everyday life; these are the symbols that are useful and are actually utilized, that have a past and a present, and that in the clockwork of a given society serve as a token for the nexus of social pacts; structural anthropology operates at this level. At a higher level come the prospective symbols; these are creations of meaning that take up the traditional symbols with their multiple significations and serve as the vehicles of new meanings. This creation of meaning reflects the living substrate of symbolism, a substrate that is not the result of social sedimentation ... This creation of mean-

ing is at the same time a recapture of archaic fantasies and a living interpretation of this fantasy substrate. *Dreams provide a key only for the symbolism of the first level;* the 'typical' dreams Freud appeals to in developing his theory of symbolism do not reveal the canonical form of symbols but merely their vestiges on the plane of sedimented expressions. The true task, therefore, is to grasp symbols in their creative moment, and not when they arrive at the end of their course and are revived in dreams, like stenographic grammalogues with their 'permanently fixed meaning.'[18]

Ricoeur has not correctly understood the meaning and function of dreams. Lonergan refers to a 'basic viewpoint' on dreams, as we have seen, represented in 'the existential approach that thinks of the dream, not as the twilight of life, but as its dawn, the beginning of the transition from impersonal existence to presence in the world, to constitution of one's self in one's world.'[19] Not only is the work of symbolization truly operative and effective in many dreams; it functions in the same manner as Ricoeur posits for his higher-level, prospective symbols: 'creations of meaning that take up the traditional symbols with their multiple significations and serve as the vehicle of new meanings.' Dream interpretation serves precisely 'to grasp symbols in their creative moment.' Many dreams are not just revivals of symbols that have arrived at the end of their course and so have a permanently fixed meaning, but transformations of energic compositions in precisely the manner and direction displayed in the dream symbol itself. Dream interpretation confirms, rather than proves an exception to, Ricoeur's penetrating analysis of the structure of the living symbol.

Jung could have strengthened Ricoeur's dialectic with Freud, then, since Jung finds at the level of elemental symbolic production precisely the prospective exploration of adult life that Ricoeur would say is characteristic of the genuine symbol. Without ever for once denying the causal approach insisted on by Freud, Jung complemented it with the teleological approach that would regard the symbol as pointing ahead to some generic goal, a goal that becomes specific only in the further unfolding of elemental symbolic process. This goal is revealed by the subsequent stages of the symbolic process itself as psychic wholeness. The oneiric symbolic expressions through whose interpretation a dimension of self-appropriation can occur have precisely the concrete mixed structure that Ricoeur described in his higher-level symbols. The opposed interpretive paths of psychoanalysis and phenomenology are reconciled with one another in the recognition of the living and creative symbol as an identity of regression and progression, of archeology and teleology, of repetition of the archaic and anticipatory exploration of adult life. But the concrete mixed texture of the living symbol is grounded in the participation of the energically constituted sensitive psyche itself in both the schemes of recurrence of the bodily organism and the dynamism of the spirit. This was recognized by Jung with a clarity that would have helped Ricoeur in his confrontation with Freudian archeology.

Nonetheless, while Jung grasped the mediate position of the psyche between organism and spirit,[20] his Kantian presuppositions prevented him, I believe, from accurately understanding the spirit pole of the dialectic of the subject. The context for a theological appropriation of Jung is set by the intentionality analysis that we summarized all too briefly above. Intentionality serves to specify more concretely precisely in what psychic teleology consists.

I begin my theological employment and monitoring of Jung, then, with the position that the general context for psychic self-appropriation is set by Lonergan's intentionality analysis. The data of human interiority are twofold. There are the data of intentionality, summarized above, and there are the data of the sensitive psyche: the stream of sensations, memories, images, emotions, conations, associations, bodily movements, and spontaneous intersubjective responses, and the symbolic integrations of these that are our dreams. The psychic stream undergoes changes with the performance of the operations of the spirit. One feels differently after one has understood from the way one felt before the emergence of insight. So too, one's dispositional immediacy is different after one has arrived at a judgment consequent on the grasp of sufficient evidence from one's 'self-taste' prior to such reflective understanding. Again, one's psychic experience is different upon the making of a decision from what it was when one was trying to decide on a course of action in a given situation. The psyche *is* endowed with a finality, as Jung recognized, but that finality is to be understood as an upwardly directed dynamism toward participation in the operations of inquiry and understanding, reflection and judgment, deliberation and decision, and in the dynamic state of being in love in the family, in the community, and with God. The psyche is a potential participant in the clarity of insight, the assurance of judgment, the peace of a good conscience, the joy and dynamism of love. This potential is reflected in the psyche's own sensitive experience, and will be manifest in our dreams. The psyche not only serves the spirit, in that we need its images if we are to understand anything, but it also participates in the spirit's very own life of understanding and world constitution and self-constitution. The intentionality studied by Lonergan and the psyche studied by Jung are distinct, though not separate, dimensions of consciousness. The psyche is to be understood within the context of self-appropriation established by Lonergan's intentionality analysis. The changes of psychic experience with various intentional operations manifest that the psyche is endowed with a finality to participation in the life of the spirit.

5.2 Complexes

The relation between the intentional spirit and the sensitive psyche, however, is a reciprocal one. If our intentional operations have a constitutive influence on the quality of our psychic life, it is also the case that the quality of our psychic life has a great deal to do with the ease and alacrity with which intentional operations are performed. There is, if you want, an affective self-transcendence that accompanies the spiritual self-transcendence of our operations of knowing, deciding, and loving, and that is strengthened by the authentic performance of these operations. But this affective self-transcendence is also a prerequisite if the sustained fidelity to the performance of these operations is to mark one's entire way of life. And as we know all too well, the movement of sensitive consciousness can interfere with the performance of intentional operations. There can be felt resistance to insight, manifest in the repressive exercise of the censorship; there can be a flight from understanding, a desire not to judge, a resistance to decision, a habitual lovelessness. There can be other desires and fears that affect to a greater or lesser extent the integrity of our operations at the different levels of intentional consciousness. There may be required a healing of the psychic blockages to authentic operations before the sustained performance of intentional operations in their normative pattern of inquiry and understanding, reflection and judgment, deliberation and decision can characterize our lives.

Intentionality analysis may very well provide the key to what constitutes authentic psychotherapy; but it remains that such therapy may have to occur before one's intentionality can be, not analyzed, but implemented in one's own world constitution and concomitant self-constitution.

Such therapy would be a matter of freeing the psychic energy bound up in what Jung called negative complexes, so that this energy is free to cooperate rather than interfere with the operations through which direction is to be found in the movement of life. Jung described a complex as 'the *image* of a certain psychic situation which is strongly accentuated emotionally and is, moreover, incompatible with the habitual attitude of consciousness. This image has powerful inner coherence, it has its own wholeness and, in addition, a relatively high degree of autonomy, so that it is subject to the control of the conscious mind to only a limited extent, and therefore behaves like an animated foreign body in the sphere of consciousness.'[21] But in the same paper Jung distinguished a negative from a purposeful aspect of complexes. Complexes usually function as compositions of inferior sensitivity, but their negative traits can be transformed if the ego assumes toward them the proper attitude. The key to the proper attitude is to regard the complex not only as symptom but also as symbol. The symptom points backward to causation, the symbol forward to the reorientation and balancing of conscious attitudes. Complexes are the structural units of the psyche as a whole. Each unit is constellated around a nuclear element, a focus of energy and content, value and meaning. These constitutive units of the psyche enjoy a relative independence from one another and from the conscious ego. Even the ego is a complex of energies and representations bearing on the familiar, everyday tasks, functions, and capacities of the individual. The healthy psyche is one in which the ego remains in contact with other complexes, preserving them from the dissociation from conscious awareness that grants them a second authority that thwarts the aims and objectives of the ego. And the key to this contact is to adopt a symbolic approach to the complex. As we have just emphasized, what Freud would explain causally in terms of dissociation or displacement Jung will retrieve by symbolic association. The retrieval is not a denial of the causal approach, but a sublation of it into a viewpoint that balances Freudian archeology with a teleological approach. And, we have argued, the finality of the psyche can be disengaged with greater precision if one views it as a tendency to participate in the ever higher organizations constituted by authentic intentional operations.

The structure of consciousness disengaged by Lonergan provides a helpful framework for the incorporation of the complex theory into a contemporary Catholic theology. The levels of intentional consciousness constitute what Lonergan calls a creative vector in consciousness. It moves, as it were, from below upwards. 'There is development from below upwards, from experience to growing understanding, from growing understanding to balanced judgment, from balanced judgment to fruitful courses of action, and from fruitful courses of action to the new situations that call forth further understanding, profounder judgment, richer courses of action.'[22] To the extent that one's consciousness proceeds smoothly and uninterruptedly from experience to insight, from insight to judgment, from judgment to decision, from decision to new experiences, insights, judgments, decisions, one is effecting a series of cumulative and progressive changes in the world and in oneself. Moreover, each successive level entails a further degree of self-transcendence. To move out of the stupor of the animal to the intelligence of the human being, one must transcend the merely sensitive desire for participation in the rhythms of the body, as well as the intricate subtleties of the flight from understanding. To move from insight to truth, from what might be so to what really is the case, one must move beyond the state of non-committal supposition and hypothesis constituted by the second level of consciousness, to the verification of one's suppositions and hypotheses constituting the third level. And to do the truth, either by bringing one's actions into harmony with what one knows or by the creative praxis of constituting the new world that should be but is not, calls for yet a further degree of self-transcendence. But the psyche has to participate in the self-transcending capacities of the spirit if one is to be able to perform these operations. And for that participation there may be required a depth-psychological discovery and healing of the affective obstructions to creativity. This depth-psychological maieutic will be an understanding and overcoming of negative complexes. But the negativity of the complexes receives specific meaning when the psyche is understood as the sensorium of the transcendence through which human beings constitute their world and, concomitantly, themselves.

What we have said is tantamount to a theological sublation of the complex theory into the theology of moral impotence and the need for grace. Autonomous psychic complexes that would prevent one from participating in the creative adventure of the human spirit are to be regarded always as victimized compositions of energy formed as a result of the violence done to one's psyche whether by significant others, oppressive social structures, or the misuse of one's own freedom and responsibility. Psychic spontaneity as such is never morally responsible for its own disorder. Disordered complexes are the victims of history. Victimization by others and self-victimization usually conspire with one another in the genesis of psychic disorder. The constitution and causation of psychic disorder will vary from person to person, so that no general, exhaustive, or exclusive mode of causation may be determined. But what counts is that the causation is always a matter of victimization.

The process of understanding and healing negative complexes will often take a person back to his or her earliest memories or beyond. But healing is conditioned by the adoption of a particular attitude on the part of the subject affected. We tend spontaneously to believe that we can adopt one of two postures to our own affective disorder. We can either repress it further, or entirely renounce moral responsibility in its regard. Repression constricts the emotional energy gathered in the complex, and eventually this energy will be explosive. Moral renunciation, though, is just a capitulation to the power of the energies constellated in the complex, and simply strengthens these energies, making it ever more difficult for one to move to a new position beyond the disorder. From a theological point of view, victimized complexes are the fruit of the sin of the world, a dimension of what the scholastics referred to as *peccatum originale originatum*. To the extent that one has freely conspired in their formation, they are also the fruit of personal sin. And the redemption of the energies bound up in these complexes must be effected, not by repression, nor by moral renunciation, but by a healing love that meets one at the same depth as the disorder. The victimized dimensions of ourselves will not be healed by judgment and condemnation, but only by mercy and forgiveness. Redemptive love must reach to the wound and even deeper, and must touch it in a manner contrary to the action that was responsible for the victimization.

There is, then, an alternative to repression and moral renunciation. But it, too, has its difficulties. The alternative is to participate in the compassion of a redemptive love in regard to our disordered affections. This means, first, recognizing that the complex is a victim of oneself or of history or of some combination of these, and ceasing to hate oneself for what one cannot help but feel. It means, next, adopting an attitude of compassion in regard to our affective disorder. It means, finally, allowing there to emerge from this recognition and compassion a willingness to cooperate with whatever redemptive forces are at hand to heal the disorder and transform the contorted and fragmented energies, even to consolidate these energies into psychic participation in the self-transcendent quest for direction in the movement of life.

The difficulty with this alternative is that it is impossible to implement unless there be some power from beyond ourselves to release us into the requisite posture. For to be compassionate toward the negative emotional forces that derail us from the direction to be found in the movement of life is to be intelligent, reasonable, and morally responsible in their regard, and this is precisely what we are rendered incapable of by reason of the force of these complexes. Again, adopting the alternative is a function of an affective self-transcendence that is not at our disposal precisely because of the power of the complex. Although the solution is clear, one is unable to avail oneself of it because the requisite willingness is lacking. And there is nothing one can do to provide oneself with that willingness. We can acknowledge the reasonableness of a certain manner of proceeding, and still be unable to act in accord with it. We are doomed to adopt toward the victimized complex one of the attitudes that will further victimize it. We cannot emerge from the vicious circle of disordered affective development. Let me add that moral impotence due to affective disorder is especially acute with regard to complexes rooted in one's earliest experiences, in experiences coincident with or preceding one's earliest memory. For these are often impossible to objectify in a way that illuminates us as to what we are negotiating.

If we are to reach a freedom to treat our emotional darkness with compassionate objectivity, that freedom must be given to us. We will not find it in the creative vector that moves from below upwards in consciousness. It must come from beyond the creative vector. In the final analysis it can come only from the reception of an unconditional love that puts to rest our efforts to constitute ourselves with inadequate resources. The love that can sustain the movement of the healing vector from above downwards in consciousness, moreover, is itself beyond *all* human capacity. All human beings are incapable of sustaining their own healing from victimization by the sin of the world, let alone the healing of another. Human love will simply further victimize unless it is itself free of the distortions and derailments of affectivity that are inevitable under the reign of sin. No human love will heal, unless it is itself participation in divine love. No human being can be the source of another's redemption from evil.

A human love, moreover, that would truly participate in divine love, and so that could mediate healing, must be able to be on the receiving end of the darkness of the one to whom it mediates the gift of redemptive love. Then the healing will be mediated precisely in and through the suffering of the one who loves. And one knows oneself to be sufficiently healed to be an instrument of divine love, only when one can endure precisely the same kind of suffering as that which caused one's own victimization, but without being destroyed by it again.

There is much more that could be written about the dynamics of healing. But this is not the place for such comments. My purpose is to emphasize aspects of Jungian psychology that can be employed in Catholic theology, and at this point I have tried only to show that the complex theory can provide help to the development in interiorly differentiated consciousness of a theology of moral impotence, sin, and the need for and gift of grace.

5.3   Psychic Wholeness

I think it safe to say that the notion of psychic wholeness was the guiding or heuristic principle of Jung's investigations. Fairly early in his career he began to question Freud's notion of displacement mechanisms for the distribution of an irreversibly sexual libido, in favor of a notion of the transformation of an originally indeterminate psychic energy. Psychic energy is finalistically oriented to an indeterminate goal of individuation, and is transformed in the lifelong process of specifying and moving toward that goal. The question of what psychic processes are seeking to become is therapeutically as important to him as the Freudian question of their origin. Central to this issue is the distinction of symptom from symbol.

> The fact that there are two distinct and mutually contradictory views eagerly advocated on either side concerning the meaning or meaninglessness of things shows that processes obviously exist which express no particular meaning, being in fact mere consequences, or symptoms; and that there are other processes which bear within them a hidden meaning, processes which are not merely derived from something but which seek to become something, and are therefore symbols. It is left to our discretion and our critical judgment to decide whether the thing we are dealing with is a symptom or a symbol.[23]

The psychic energy that undergoes symbolic transformations intends as its goal the condition of generalized equilibrium that characterizes the individuated person. Psychic energy functions in accord with the principle of the conservation of energy. But, whereas Freud employs this principle when speaking of repression and substitute formation, and whereas for both Freud and Jung the libido never leaves one structure to pass over into another without bringing the character of the old into the new, for Jung the character of the old is also transformed when it passes into the new. Thus, what for Freud would always signify Oedipal incestuous fantasy in a quite literal sense may very well for Jung symbolize something that invites and facilitates adult development. Energy is indeterminately distributed into various systems, and these systems change as energy becomes redistributed. The changes are manifest in the processes of symbolic transformation. Psychic development takes place because causes have been transformed into symbolic expressions of the way that lies ahead. The equivalent quantum of energy once invested in a cause can be given to the symbol that releases and empowers development. The process of symbolic transformation of energy is the 'unfolding of the original, potential wholeness.'[24] It gradually centralizes the personality around a midpoint, which is one of Jung's several meanings for the term 'the self.'

It is clear from what we have already said how closely Jung's view of the symbol coincides with Lonergan's. I would add to what I have already said of Lonergan's view only the religious dimension of affective integrity that he emphasizes.

> ... at the summit of the ascent from the initial infantile bundle of needs and clamors and gratifications, there are to be found the deep-set joy and solid peace, the power and the vigor, of being in love with God. In the measure that that summit is reached, then the supreme value is God, and other values are God's expression

of his love in this world, in its aspirations, and in its goal. In the measure that one's love of God is complete, then values are whatever one loves, and evils are whatever one hates so that, in Augustine's phrase, if one loves God, one may do as one pleases, *Ama Deum et fac quod vis.* Then affectivity is of a single piece. Further developments only fill out previous achievement. Lapses from grace are rarer and more quickly amended.[25]

In many ways, then, Jung's insights into the transformation of psychic energy through the catalytic agency of the symbolic process can be employed by theology to enrich our understanding of the effects of the love that meets us in our darkness and heals our contorted energies so as to make of us God's work of art.

5.4   The Archetypes

Jung's convictions regarding the extension of psychic depth beyond what is allowed for in Freud's theory of libido were greatly strengthened by his discovery of archaic images emergent from the dimensions of energic life that he came to call the collective unconscious. Certain symbolic combinations emerge from deeper and more 'impersonal' sources than are envisioned by a theory of personal repression. The strange, even numinous, effect of these images can be explained only by a dimension of psychic energy that enjoys a relative autonomy from the personal ego. Neither were these images repressed, since they were never conscious, nor can they be made conscious except in their own time. And when they are made conscious, the ego must adopt toward them a posture of respectful negotiation, since they are invested both with great potential for one's development and with destructive capacities.

There are, then, for Jung two dimensions to the psychic energy that is not invested in or constitutive of the ego complex: the personal unconscious and the collective unconscious.[26] I would correlate Jung's collective unconscious with an archetypal function characteristic of the orientation of sensitive consciousness to what Lonergan calls mystery. And I would recognize Jung as a major contributor to the restoration of this orientation to modern consciousness. Lonergan introduces his discussion of mystery with a discussion of 'the sense of the unknown.'

> ... our analysis forces us to recognize the paradoxical category of the 'known unknown.' For we have equated being with the objective of the pure desire to know, with what is to be known through the totality of intelligent and reasonable answers. But, in fact, our questions outnumber our answers, so that we know of an unknown through our unanswered questions.[27]

Our being, Lonergan says, involves both a succession of levels of higher integration, and a principle of correspondence between the systematizing forms on higher levels and what would otherwise remain coincidental manifolds on lower levels. '... these higher integrations on the organic, psychic, and intellectual levels are not static but dynamic systems; they are systems on the move; the higher integration is not only an integrator but also an operator; and if developments on different levels are not to conflict, there has to be a correspondence between their respective operators.'[28] The intellectual operator is the spirit of inquiry that heads us toward ever fuller and richer understanding. It is headed into the known unknown. But 'the principle of dynamic correspondence calls for a harmonious orientation on the psychic level, and from the nature of the case such an orientation would have to consist in some cosmic dimension, in some intimation of unplumbed depths, that accrued to man's feelings, emotions, sentiments.'[29]

The images that have to do with the sphere of the known unknown are named either mystery or myth, depending on whether they are promotive and reflective of the authentic orientation of the higher levels of consciousness to intelligibility, being, and the good or whether they obstruct this orientation or reflect a contradictory orientation. One's interpretation of these affect-laden images will be a function of one's position on the structure and objective of conscious dynamism. Our confrontation with the known unknown cannot be dodged.

> The detached and disinterested desire to know is unrestricted; it flings at us the name of obscurantists if we restrict it by allowing other desire to interfere with its proper unfolding; and while that unfolding can establish that our naturally possible knowledge is restricted, this restriction on possible attainment is not a restriction on the desire itself; on the contrary, the question whether attainment is in all cases possible presupposes the fact that in all cases attainment is desired. Moreover, this unrestricted openness of our intelligence and reasonableness not only is the concrete operator of our intellectual development but also is accompanied by a corresponding operator that deeply and powerfully holds our sensitive integrations open to transforming change.[30]

The 'profound disillusionment of modern man' and 'the focal point of his horror' is that

> He had hoped through knowledge to ensure a development that was always progress and never decline. He has discovered that the advance of human knowledge is ambivalent, that it places in man's hands stupendous power without necessarily adding proportionate wisdom and virtue, that the fact of advance and the evidence of power are not guarantees of truth, that myth is the permanent alternative to mystery and mystery is what his hybris rejected.[31]

I would argue that Lonergan's analysis of intentional consciousness provides the criterion for distinguishing in the realm of the archetypal what is mystery from what is myth. For the moment, though, I wish only to state that Jung's disclosure in a scientific psychology of the realm of the archetypal is consonant with developments in Catholic theology that would take their stand on the turn to the subject and make that turn foundational for doctrinal and systematic positions.

5.5   *The Dialectic of Spirit and Matter*

The energic potentialities for creativity that Jung named the archetypes are a function of an excess of psychic energy that no exclusively causal-reductive approach to the psyche can either theoretically understand or practically negotiate. They can be understood only in terms of a creative tension emergent from the opposed poles of matter and spirit.[32] In his late work, and especially in the programmatic essay of 1946, 'On the Nature of the Psyche,'

Jung emphasized that the similarity between the organizing activity of the archetypes and the regulating processes in the instincts is not to be understood in purely biological terms. 'In spite of or perhaps because of its affinity with instinct, the archetype represents the authentic element of spirit.'[33] In this sense, 'archetype and instinct are the most polar opposites imaginable,'[34] yet 'belong together as correspondences [and] subsist side by side as reflections in our own minds of the opposition that underlies all psychic energy.'[35]

Jung thus postulates two 'transcendental principles' that are quite distinct from each other, namely, instinct and spirit. For Jung they are transcendental in the Kantian sense of postulates needed to account for observable phenomena. Their tension sparks the energic transformation catalyzed in primordial images, whose purpose is to unite the opposites. As they are mediated with one another in the archetypal image, they cooperate with one another in pursuit of the goal of individuation. In the image, spirit is incarnate, and instinct acquires meaning. Jung calls these transcendental factors psychoid, in that they are known through their effects on the psyche and by analogy with the psyche, yet are autonomous from the psyche and not subject to the free disposal of the ego, as much psychic energy is. Archetypes-as-such are for Jung no longer psychic; only the archetypal images are. Archetypes-as-such are the transcendental factor of meaning in the instinct, determining psychic orientation. Instinct is called the psychic infrared, passing over into the physiology of the organism and merging with its chemical and physical conditions. Spirit is the psychic ultraviolet, a field exhibiting none of the peculiarities of the physiological yet also not to be regarded as psychic even if it manifests itself in psychic occurrences. The psychic image is the concrete synthesis, the unity-in-tension, of spirit and matter, of future and past, of teleology and archeology. The spirit-instinct polarity can be considered the most basic pair of opposites united by psychic process.[36]

In this same essay Jung formulates a very important insight whose logical consequences he unfortunately did not develop. Mentioning it at this point will provide us with a natural transition to the sixth element in Jung's thought which I want do discuss, the area in which theologians will (or should) have the most difficulty with Jung. In my treatment of this sixth point, I will mention as well the profound theological significance of the matter-spirit dialectic as Jung conceives it.

The insight to which I refer has to do with the moral significance of the spirit-instinct polarity. The contrariety in itself, he says, has no moral significance, insofar as 'instinct is not in itself bad any more than spirit is good. Both can be both.'[37] What does possess moral significance is the process of the reconciliation or mediation of the opposite poles. The inclination of psychic process to one extreme or the other is symptomatic of a one-sidedness that is characteristic of Western modernity and that must be overcome by the realization of that inferior part of the personality that Jung calls the shadow. The growing awareness of the shadow is not merely an intellectual problem, but 'has far more the meaning of a suffering and a passion that implicate the whole man.'[38] Such a confrontation 'is an *ethical* problem of the first magnitude, the urgency of which is felt only by people who find themselves faced with the need to assimilate the unconscious and integrate their personalities.'[39] Most people still do not find themselves in such a situation.[40]

5.6   The Self and the Problem of Evil

Had Jung drawn the logical consequences of what he says in the essay 'On the Nature of the Psyche' regarding the problem of evil, he would have distinguished two kinds of problems of opposites, and thus two kinds of dialectical processes constitutive of individuation. The first I call a dialectic of contraries, and the second a dialectic of contradictories. Lonergan says there is a dialectic if '(1) there is an aggregate of events of a determinate character, (2) the events may be traced to either or both of two principles, (3) the principles are opposed yet bound together, and (4) they are modified by the changes that successively result from them.'[41]

In his talk of instinct and spirit, or matter and spirit, Jung is speaking of one kind of opposition, whereas the opposition of good and evil is of quite another kind. This is admitted by Jung himself in the passage just cited: 'Instinct is not in itself bad any more than spirit is good. Both can be both.' The drama of the incarnation of spirit in matter through the evolution of matter into consciousness is the arena of the mystery of good and evil. The mystery is experienced in the sensitive psyche, which *feels* the tension of matter and spirit since it participates in both. What is good is the achievement of a creative tension of spirit and matter; what is evil is the displacement of this tension *in either direction*. Good and evil are not among the opposites to be reconciled in the process of the reconciliation of spirit and matter. Rather, good and evil qualify the process itself. Jung is not consistent in implementing the insight formulated in 'On the Nature of the Psyche,' and the inconsistency leads to a major confusion in his thought and to a dangerous set of recommendations communicated through Jungian therapy by those who are themselves immersed in the confusion. Good and evil are not yet another instance of reconcilable poles in the process of individuation. Here is the principal area in which Jung's work needs to be monitored critically by the theologian.

Jung's genuine contributions to a correct understanding of the dialectic of contraries between matter and spirit

must not be overlooked, however. The creative tension of
matter and spirit as felt by the psyche living in their 'in-
between' is precisely what theology has meant by the state
of integrity. Our tendency to displace this tension in either
direction is what is meant by concupiscence. Our capitulation to this tendency is sin. Our inability to maintain the
tension in its integrity on the basis of our own resources is
our need for grace. And habits that do consolidate us in a
relatively firm hold on the creative tension are the fruit of
grace. Jung has made a major contribution, willy-nilly, to
a theology of sin and grace that would take its stand on the
interiorly differentiated consciousness made possible by
the turn to the subject. Theology can turn to Jung for a
great deal of illumination on many of the central doctrines
of Christian faith, and especially for categories to express
the meaning of these doctrines in terms set by the modern
exigence for the clarification of subjectivity.

Nonetheless, the theological comments just made
illustrate the distinction that theology will draw between
the dialectic of spirit and matter, on the one hand, and the
dialectic of good and evil, on the other hand. Resolution
of the dialectic of spirit and matter is a matter of both-
and. Resolution of the dialectic of good and evil is a matter of either-or. And the either-or is specified by the both-
and of the dialectic of spirit and matter: either the creative
tension of spirit and matter or the displacement of this
tension in one direction or another. The potential is present
in Jung's work for moving into the realm of transcendence
in which the drama of personal integrity is ultimately decided. Jung himself comes more and more to regard the
background of psychic events reflective of the drama not
as a body of contents that can be controlled by the conscious ego. He acknowledges an ineffable ground of psychic occurrences that ultimately is independent of the ego's
judgment and decision — a darkness beyond adequate

categorization, incommensurable to the understanding of a finite intelligence, inaccessible to conscious comprehension and correction. This darkness is for Jung not absurdity but inaccessible light, invested with a significance incommensurable with the paltry, flickering light of ego consciousness. The ego is a participant in a mystery of existence that lies beyond our powers of rational comprehension and control. The ego can submit to the mystery in reverence, and this constitutes both its responsibility and its highest achievement. The submission is painful, a succession of dark nights. But if the ego refuses to submit it fails to be a bearer of the mystery of existence. This refusal is sin as the demonic, the sin of a prideful self-assertion that insists on caging the incomprehensible and boundless mystery of God within the narrow confines of the self.

Nonetheless, the realm of absolute transcendence, alone equal to the drama of individuation, remains beyond Jung's horizon. It is compacted into a world-immanent noumenal background to phenomenal or empirical reality. This noumenal background is conceptualized in Jung's various late treatments of the self. We must conclude our discussion, then, with an interpretation and critique of Jung's position on the self.

Jung calls the archetype of the self 'the archetype which it is most important for modern man to understand.'[42] The self is for Jung endowed with a twofold empiricality. It is initially empirical in that it is anticipated by the psyche in the form of spontaneous or autonomous symbols of unity, totality, and centeredness, such as the quaternity and the mandala. The significance of such symbols is attested by history as well as by empirical psychology. Wholeness is an objective factor that confronts the subject independently of the ego. Its value is higher than that of other archetypes. The self, then, is empirical also in the fuller sense of the experience of the 'bounded infinity' of the individuating psyche, that is, the experience of the progressive reconciliation of the opposites of matter and spirit through the transforming power of archetypal images. The intellect can understand the symbols of the self without the individual being changed by them, but this is not the sense in which Jung speaks of the importance of understanding the self. He is speaking of an understanding permeated by feeling, by valuation, an understanding that is empirically rooted not just in an anticipation, but in the always asymptotic realization of the process of individuation. And for such an understanding one must have a prior lived acceptance of the unconscious, of the shadow, of the contrasexuality and bisexuality of the subject. For these are aspects of the totality of the self. And it is these aspects that 'modern man' is least willing to accept. Only when value and feeling inform the judgment passed on their meaning is the subject *affected* by the process of integrating that meaning.

Why did Jung say that the self is the archetype most important for 'modern man' to understand? There is a change occurring in the psychic situation of the 'Christian aeon,' a change that is crystallized and captured in the notion of the self, which contains a potential contribution to the birth of a 'new religion' in our time. Jung placed synchronistic stock in the fact that, astrologically speaking, the symbol of Pisces is the representation of two thousand years of Christian development, and the emergent symbol of the Age of Aquarius is the *Anthropos*. This change symbolizes an alteration in the Christ image, which up to now has been inadequate to the task of liberating the 'true man.' So, too, in the East the Buddha image has proven unable to protect traditional culture against the invasion of materialistic and totalitarian ideologies. These images, says Jung, are too spiritualistically one-sided to be able to represent human wholeness adequately. They are 'lacking in darkness and in bodily and material reality.'[43] The medieval alchemists perceived this, and sought to free from matter a divine Anthropos, 'an image of man in which good and evil, spirit and matter, were genuinely united and through which not only man but also all of nature would be made whole.'[44]

> At bottom it is the image of man in the Aquarian Age which is being formed in the collective unconscious. The astrological image of the Aquarian period is an image of man which, according to Jung, represents the Anthropos as an image of the Self, or of the greater inner personality which lives in every human being and in the collective psyche ... The task of man in the Aquarian Age will be to become conscious of his larger inner presence, the Anthropos, and to give the utmost care to the unconscious and to nature.[45]

Jung's book *Aion* discusses the relations between the traditional Christ image and the natural symbols of wholeness or the self. His investigation 'seeks, with the help of Christian, Gnostic, and alchemical symbols of the self, to throw light on the change of psychic situation within the "Christian aeon."'[46] The volume interprets where we stand historically today as participants in what Jung read to be a major transformation occurring in our time.

Symbols of unity and totality stand for Jung at the highest point on the scale of objective values, because they cannot be distinguished from the image of God in the human soul. They are invested with such value because they are symbols of order that occur principally in times of psychic disorientation and reorientation. They bind and subdue the lawless powers of fragmentation and darkness, and they depict or create an order that transforms the chaos into a cosmos.

How are these symbols related to the image of Christ? Jung is preoccupied by the saturation of Christian tradition with vague premonitions of the conflict of Christ and the Antichrist. He finds contemporary parallels to this conflict in 'the dechristianization of our world, the Luciferian development of science and technology, and the frightful material and moral destruction left behind by the second World War.'[47] Christ is still the living myth of our culture, 'our culture hero, who, regardless of historical existence, embodies the myth of the divine Primordial Man.'[48] It is Christ who occupies the center of the Christian mandala, and it is he whose kingdom is the pearl of great price, the treasure buried in the field, the grain of mustard, the heavenly city. Christ, then, has represented for Christians the archetype of the self, the true image of God after whose likeness we are made. But for almost all theologians, pastors, and faithful in both the Roman Catholic and the Protestant traditions, the image of God in us has not resided in the 'corporeal man,' but in the invisible, incorporeal, incorrupt, immortal rational soul. Jung is convinced that 'the original Christian conception of the *imago Dei* embodied in Christ meant an all-embracing totality that even includes the animal side of man.'[49] Originally the recognition of the archetype of wholeness in the Christ image restored a primal state of oneness with the spontaneous God image in the human psyche. But the Christ image very early came to lack wholeness, since there was excluded from it the dark side of things. Everything dark was turned into a diabolical opponent of the God image. Christ became a symbol of the heroic ego rather than of the self. The figure of the redeemer became onesidedly bright. The dark side of the human totality became ascribed to the Antichrist, the devil, evil. But, says Jung,

... the psychological concept of the self, in part derived from our knowledge of the whole man, but for the rest depicting itself spontaneously in the products of the unconscious as an archetypal quaternity bound together by inner antinomies, cannot omit the shadow that belongs to the light figure, for without it this figure lacks body and humanity. In the empirical self, light and shadow form a paradoxical unity. In the Christian concept, on the other hand, the archetype is hopelessly split into two irreconcilable halves, leading ultimately to a metaphysical dualism.[50]

The dogmatic figure of Christ was made so sublime and spotless that all else turned dark beside it. It became so onesidedly perfect that it demanded a psychic complement to restore the balance. This complement is found not in the Christ image but in the image of Satan as the Antichrist, which now came to be the archetypal image of matter and instinct, just as Christ came to supply the archetypal image of spirit.

It was through reflections such as this that Jung came to include good and evil among the opposites to be reconciled with one another in the process of individuation. And it is at this point that the Christian theologian must part from Jung. The departure will involve four steps. First, the *imago Dei* that human subjects are is to be located in human cognitional processes, in the procession of inner words of conception and judgment from acts of understanding, and in the procession of acts of love from the inner word. Second, the body participates in the transformation of the person into an *imago Dei*, and this participation is sensitively experienced in the psyche and imaginally reflected in the psyche's symbols when the psyche has become, by God's grace, a sensorium of transcendence. Third, the self that is thus constituted as an *imago Dei* is both integrator and operator of its own developmental processes. As integrator, it is adequately symbolized in the mandala. But to cling to the mandala and the integration it represents when the process of development presents one with further questions for understanding and truth or for value — and it is in the procession of inner words from insight and reflective understanding that the *imago Dei* resides in us — is to refuse the self-transcendence through which we continue to find authentic direction in the movement of life. Finally, the one-sided choice of the self as integrator over the self as operator of further development can become in the extreme a self-enclosure that not only would lock one in an epistemological idealism, but also would represent a refusal of the absolute or vertical self-transcendence toward the mystery of God that is our authentic destiny.

I cannot here develop the first of these points, due to the limitations of this paper. I would simply recall the psychological analogies for approaching an understanding of the mystery of the Trinity that are found in the works of Augustine and especially of Aquinas.[51] These still represent the high point in Christian reflection on the *imago Dei* in the human subject. On the second point, perhaps enough has been said already. The symbols that emerge from the psyche in our dreams of the morning are both reflective of the selves we have become and anticipatory of the adventures yet to come in the quest for direction in the movement of life. As reflective of what we have become, they will represent a bodily participation in the life of the human spirit. They will be invested with the beauty that is the splendor of truth. But as anticipatory of what is yet to come, they will be symbolic of the self as operator of further development. The mandala may well be a symbol of the self as integrating what one has become. It is not an adequate symbol of the self as operator of a higher integration. The theologian monitoring Jung will not negate, but will relativize, the symbol of the mandala.

With this comment we come to the third and fourth points of an adequate critique of these farther reaches of Jungian thought. As I began this paper by narrating and interpreting a dream of my own, perhaps I can close by interpreting a dream of Jung's. I wager that this interpretation will contain a more effective elucidation of my meaning than would further discursive argumentation.

The dream which I wish to interpret is narrated in Jung's autobiographical reflections. It begins with Jung's father fetching from a shelf a heavy folio volume of the Bible bound in a fishskin. He opens the Bible to the Pentateuch and begins to deliver a profound interpretation of a certain passage. His interpretation, Jung admits, 'was so intelligent and learned that we in our stupidity could not follow it.'[52] The 'we' to whom Jung refers are Jung himself and two other psychiatrists. In the next scene Jung's father takes him alone into a house which Jung's father says is haunted, and where loud noises were being uttered by the inhabitants. The house had thick walls. Jung and his father climbed a narrow staircase to the second floor. There, Jung says,

> ... a strange sight presented itself: a large hall which was the exact replica of the *divan-i-kaas* (council hall) of Sultan Akbar at Fatehpur Sikri. It was a high, circular room with a gallery running along the wall, from which four bridges led to a basin-shaped center. The basin rested upon a huge column and formed the sultan's round seat. From this elevated place he spoke to his councilors and philosophers, who sat

along the walls in the gallery. The whole was a gigantic mandala. It corresponded precisely to the real *divan-i-kaas*.

In the dream I suddenly saw that from the center a steep flight of stairs ascended to a spot high up on the wall — which no longer corresponded to reality. At the top of the stairs was a small door, and my father said, 'Now I will lead you into the highest presence.' Then he knelt down and touched his forehead to the floor. I imitated him, likewise kneeling, with great emotion. For some reason I could not bring my forehead quite down to the floor — there was perhaps a millimeter to spare. But at least I had made the gesture with him. Suddenly I knew — perhaps my father had told me — that the upper door led to a solitary chamber where lived Uriah, King David's general, whom David had shamefully betrayed for the sake of his wife Bathsheba, by commanding his soldiers to abandon Uriah in the face of the enemy.[53]

Jung states that it was probably the Book of Genesis that his father was interpreting in the dream. For Jung the fishskin is a symbol of the muteness and unconsciousness of fish. His father did not succeed in communicating his message, Jung says, because of the stupidity and malice of Jung and his companions. Uriah is a guiltless victim, a prefiguration of Christ. The significance of Uriah means Jung's own mission to speak publicly about 'the ambivalence of the God-image in the Old Testament.' Uriah also prefigures the loss of Jung's wife in death. 'These were the things that awaited me, hidden in the unconscious. I had to submit to this fate, and ought really to have touched my forehead to the floor, so that my submission would be complete. But something prevented me from doing so entirely, and kept me just a millimeter away.'[54] The result prefigured by the dream was the book *Answer to Job*, the one book Jung said he would not revise.

I will risk an interpretation of this dream that runs counter to Jung's. His father is trying to communicate something important to him and his psychiatrist colleagues. 'It dealt with something extremely important which fascinated him.'[55] But none of them can understand what his father is trying to say. The fishskin is a symbol, not of mute unconscious stupidity, but of salvation. It is the *Ichthus*. Jung's father is communicating the biblical message of salvation from God. The passage his father is interpreting, if indeed it was from Genesis as Jung seems to think, is allusive to *God's* 'answer to Job,' 'Where were you when I laid the foundations of the earth?' (Job 38.4). The dream does prefigure the writing of *Answer to Job*, but as a message not to write that book. Jung's father is communicating to Jung and to psychiatry the invitation to acknowledge a transcendent exigence, and to integrate the exigence with their knowledge of the archetypal sense of the unknown which they have discovered. Jung and his friends cannot understand the message. The second part of the dream is a further attempt to communicate the same message. The alternative to accepting the message is the haunted house, the occult realm where people try to achieve a position beyond all opposites, including even the contradictory opposites of good and evil. This is the Great Round as something to be transcended, the mandala as symbol of an integration, yes, but of a temporary integration that must be gone beyond. It is the self chosen by the ego as supreme principle, but understood by Jung's father as something to be transcended in adoration of the Highest Presence. Even the fact that the invitation occurs on the second floor may be significant, for the second floor may be the second level of consciousness, the level of one's own ideas, the level which an idealist cannot transcend. Jung will not submit to the invitation to transcend the self. The symbol of such transcendence is the mystery of innocent suffering represented in Uriah. Jung does not submit to the relentless transformation of the integrator, the perfect mandala that becomes demonic when it is apotheosized, and the result is seen in the religious posture of Jung's alternative answer to Job, where the problem of evil is radically the problem not of human beings, but of God. The meaning of the dream is not archetypal but anagogic, not natural but supernatural, not simply psychological but religious. Jung is invited to rethink the position that was to come to expression in *Answer to Job*. He refused, and the dream catalyzed that refusal, appropriated it at the sensitive level of Jung's consciousness.

This is in no way to deny the positive significance of the mandala as a symbol of integration. It simply adds to this emphasis the insistence on the relentless transformation of the integrator by the operator of consciousness as a notion of being, a notion of the good, and a notion of transcendent mystery.

The essential theological critique and monitoring of Jung will lie in a distinction of different kinds of opposites, and of different ways of negotiating the respective conflicts. There are opposites that are contraries. Such are matter and spirit, consciousness and the unconscious, the masculine and feminine dimensions of the psyche, the ego and the personal shadow as victim of social and personal history. Between such opposites there can be established a dialectical integration, a creative tension that constitutes personal integrity. But there are also opposites that are contradictories. Western epistemology has for two millennia formulated the opposition of the true and the false in the principle of contradiction. An analogous opposition of contradictories is that of good and evil. A dialectic of contradictories cannot be resolved by integration, only by choice. And the choice bears precisely on the negotiation of the various dialectics of contraries: either their dialectical and creative tension, or their dissociation and the consequent distortion of their relations with one another. The integral dialectic of contraries is good, while its distortion is evil.

With these comments I must bring this lengthy essay to a close. I have tried to argue that Jung's work can prove of enormous benefit to a Catholic theology that takes its stand on interiorly differentiated consciousness, since Jung helps us disengage in self-appropriation a dimension of our interiority that, first, is not made explicit in the writings of theologians who have taken the turn to the subject, and, second, is a necessary and inevitable complement to the dimensions that these theologians have tried to disengage. But I have argued, too, that the dimensions uncovered by such a thinker as Lonergan set the context for the psychic self-appropriation that Jung renders available. If that latter and crucial point is accepted, then one is able to reverse the elements of Jungian thought that are theologically not acceptable. These aspects have to do almost entirely with the implications of Jung's later writings on the self, the Christ image, the problem of evil, and the image of God in the self. These unacceptable dimensions can be reversed through the distinction of a dialectic of contraries from a dialectic of contradictories, the specification of quite different ways of negotiating the distinct dialectics, and the insistence that the correct way of negotiating the dialectic of contradictories is at the same time the key to the appropriate reconciliation of those contrary opposites whose harmonious functioning is the immanent intelligibility of personal integrity and authenticity.

Notes

1 David Burrell, *Exercises in Religious Understanding* (South Bend, IN: University of Notre Dame Press, 1974) 232.

2 For a thorough presentation of such an interpretation of modern philosophy, see Cornelio Fabro, *God in Exile, Modern Atheism: A Study of the Internal Dynamic of Modern Atheism, from Its Roots in the Cartesian Cogito to the Present Day*, trans. and ed. Arthur Gibson (Westminster, MD: Newman Press, 1968).

3 Bernard Lonergan, 'The Subject,' in *A Second Collection*, ed. Bernard J. Tyrrell and William F.J. Ryan (London: Darton, Longman & Todd, 1974) 71-72.

4 Ibid. 83.

5 Bernard Lonergan, *Insight* (see above, chapter 1, note 20).

6 Lonergan, 'The Subject' 70-71.

7 Bernard Lonergan, 'Healing and Creating in History' (see above, chapter 3, note 7) 106.

8 C.G. Jung, 'The Transcendent Function,' in *The Structure and Dynamics of the Psyche*, trans. R.F.C. Hull, vol. 8 in The Collected Works of C.G. Jung, Bollingen Series XX (Princeton: Princeton University Press, 1969) 67-91.

9 Lonergan, *Insight* 192-93/216.

10 Bernard Lonergan, *Method in Theology* (see above, chapter 1, note 1) 31-32.

11 Ibid. 37-38.

12 Ibid. 64.

13 Ibid. 66.

[14] Ibid. 66-67.

[15] Ibid. 69.

[16] Paul Ricoeur, *Freud and Philosophy*, trans. Denis Savage (New Haven: Yale University Press, 1970).

[17] See Robert M. Doran, *Subject and Psyche* (see above, chapter 1, note 11) chapter 3.

[18] Ricoeur, *Freud and Philosophy* 504-506, emphasis added.

[19] Lonergan, *Method in Theology* 69.

[20] See C.G. Jung, 'On the Nature of the Psyche,' in *The Structure and Dynamics of the Psyche* (see above, note 8) 159-234.

[21] C.G. Jung, 'A Review of the Complex Theory' in *The Structure and Dynamics of the Psyche* (see above, note 8) 96.

[22] Lonergan, 'Healing and Creating in History' 106.

[23] C.G. Jung, *Psychological Types*, trans. R.F.C. Hull, vol. 6 in The Collected Works of C.G. Jung, Bollingen Series XX (Princeton: Princeton University Press, 1971) 478.

[24] C.G. Jung, 'On the Psychology of the Unconscious,' in *Two Essays on Analytical Psychology*, trans. R.F.C. Hull, vol. 7 in The Collected Works of C.G. Jung, Bollingen Series XX (Princeton: Princeton University Press, 1966) 110.

[25] Lonergan, *Method in Theology* 39.

[26] See, for example, C.G. Jung, *Psychological Types* 485.

[27] Lonergan, *Insight* 531-32/555.

[28] Ibid. 532/555.

[29] Ibid.

30 Ibid. 546/569-70.

31 Ibid. 549/572.

32 See C.G. Jung, 'On Psychic Energy,' in *The Structure and Dynamics of the Psyche* (see above, note 8) 26.

33 C.G. Jung, 'On the Nature of the Psyche' 206.

34 Ibid.

35 Ibid.

36 See ibid. 207.

37 Ibid. 206.

38 Ibid. 208.

39 Ibid.

40 See ibid. 208-209.

41 Lonergan, *Insight* 217/242.

42 C.G. Jung, *Aion: Researches into the Phenomenology of the Self*, trans. R.F.C. Hull, vol. 9ii in The Collected Works of C.G. Jung, Bollingen Series XX (Princeton: Princeton University Press, 1968) 266.

43 Marie-Louise von Franz, *C.G. Jung: His Myth in Our Time* (New York: C.G. Jung Foundation, 1975) 135.

44 Ibid. 136. Notice the equation of good/evil with spirit/matter. This is precisely the problem.

45 Ibid.

46 Jung, *Aion* ix.

47 Ibid. 36.

[48] Ibid.

[49] Ibid. 41.

[50] Ibid. 42.

[51] See Bernard Lonergan, *Verbum:Word and Idea in Aquinas,* ed. David Burrell (Notre Dame: University of Notre Dame Press, 1967).

[52] C.G. Jung, *Memories, Dreams, Reflections* (see above, chapter 1, note 24) 218.

[53] Ibid. 218-19.

[54] Ibid. 219-20.

[55] Ibid. 218.

Part Two

Cultural Dimensions of Foundations

6 Theological Grounds for a World-Cultural Humanity

My efforts over the past eight years have been devoted to trying to establish that the intentionality analysis of Bernard Lonergan renders possible a reorientation of the science of depth psychology. I have argued in addition, and as a consequence of this first conviction, that the change in the human subject that results from bringing the differentiated operations of conscious intentionality to bear upon human psychic sensitivity constitutes a dimension of conversion. I have called this psychic conversion.[1] I have tried to integrate psychic conversion with the intellectual, moral, and religious conversions whose objectification constitutes the theological functional specialty 'foundations.'[2] My work has thus been devoted to the two functional specialties of communications and foundations: communications, insofar as the objectification of the conversions can ground a reorientation and integration of the human sciences;[3] and foundations, insofar as the particular human science to which I have addressed myself studies a dimension of that same human interiority whose differentiations and conversions constitute the foundational reality of theology. If the application of the differentiated operations of intentionality to the states of the human psyche represents the psychic conversion that I have tried to articulate, then this articulation constitutes a dimension of theological foundations. Such has been my argument.

In the present paper I wish to speak briefly to these same two concerns. But I have an ulterior purpose. For I am convinced that the implementation of the theological method that is provided us in Lonergan's extraordinary and indeed improbable set of achievements[4] must take the form not only of a new statement of Christian doctrines and of a new systematic understanding of the divinely originated solution to the problem of evil, but also of a reorientation of the human sciences through the interdisciplinary collaboration of human subjects whose self-understanding is mediated by the same intellectual, psychic, moral, and religious self-appropriation that would inform, originate, and ground the new doctrinal and systematic theologies. This interdisciplinary collaboration will be essential even for work in the functional specialties of doctrines and systematics as these are conceived by Lonergan.

Philip McShane, in his book *The Shaping of the Foundations*, says: 'Without the personal labor involved in arriving at one's own adequate general theological categories, ... sets of special categories relative to religious interiority, authenticity, and redemptive history may well emerge, but they run the danger of being a new nominalism.'[5] General theological categories are categories that theology shares with other disciplines.[6] The theological nominalism indicted by McShane would presume that Christian experience and development occur independently of the secular experience of persons and communities, and so can be spoken of without reference to the objects of other intellectual and scientific activity, to psychological and social reality, and to political and economic transactions. It is especially to psychological reality that I have addressed myself. But even here I have been developing not so much general theological categories as transcendental considerations that would guide the generation of the general categories. These latter must be derived in an interdisciplinary collaborative effort of psychologists, psychiatrists, neurophysiologists, biochemists, biophysicists, and so on. Again, I am indebted to Professor McShane for his constant reminder that I not so address myself to the concerns of psychology as to imply that this hard scientific labor can be dispensed with now that we are equipped with adequate heuristic grounds. Far from dispensing with this labor, I wish to insist that it represents an indispensable element for implementing Lonergan's method, even as that method is pertinent to constructing a new theology *in oratione recta* that addresses itself to the present and to the future. An interdisciplinary reorientation of the human sciences on the basis of Lonergan's theological foundations represents one dimension of the functional specialty 'communications.'

It is my purpose in this paper, then, to situate this interdisciplinary collaboration within the dialectic of history that sets the concrete conditions of our responsibility for the future of humanity. Such collaboration will be a dimension of the superstructure of a global effort to create a humane crosscultural alternative to the various social, political, and economic monstrosities that are the systemic structural objectifications and agents of inauthenticity with which we must come to terms in these latter stages of the longer cycle of decline. I wish to speak of this global effort and of the pertinence of Lonergan's work to its concerns. In doing so, I will try, finally, to suggest how the collaborative scientific and scholarly praxis that is grounded in theological foundations can have far-reaching ramifications and implications even for the everyday transactions that constitute the infrastructure of our global social, cultural, and economic life.[7]

I   The Reorientation of Depth Psychology

The contributions of Lonergan to the reorientation of depth psychology are both clear and momentous. The higher viewpoint on the human subject that emerges in his own disengagement of the distinct quality and privileged position of existential responsibility as both grounding and sublating cognitive authenticity opens us heuristically upon the possibility of what Eric Voegelin has called a psychology of orientations.[8] We can now envision the possibility of elaborating a psychology that would order the entire stream of our sensations, memories, images, emotions, conations, bodily movements, associations, and spontaneous responses to persons and situations, and so the whole of our sensitive psychic undertow — order it in accord with the participation of the human sensitive psyche in the normative order of the search for direction in the movement of life. This order is disengaged in Lonergan's thematization of the creative vector of human consciousness and in his more recent anticipation of a discernment of the healing vector within that same consciousness.[9] Such a psychology would be sharply contrasted with the various psychologies of passional motivation that have dominated the modern academic psychological milieu, and that, says Voegelin, could understand without remainder only a certain pneumopathological type of person. These psychologies of motivation acknowledge no higher order of values than the social value of the good of order. Even their contribution to the pursuit of social order calls for a cynical manipulation of more elementary passions. What is missing from the grounding of such psychologies is an understanding of the self-transcendent objectives of human intentionality, objectives whose pursuit is the condition of the possibility of human psychic flourishing. Consequently these psychologies consider what are in fact autonomous religious, personal, and cultural values to be at best purely particular values, and in some instances particular values of the sort that threaten the social control that motivates the pragmatic engineers of our political and social Leviathans.

The elements in Lonergan's work that I have drawn upon to ground a reorientation of depth psychology are sufficiently well-known that I can simply list them here. They include: the differentiation of intentional from nonintentional feelings;[10] the differentiation within intentional feelings of responses to value from responses to mere satisfactions;[11] the further differentiation within responses to values of various degrees of affective self-transcendence isomorphic with an objective scale of values in which religious, personal, and cultural values condition the possibility of a sustained pursuit of justice in the social order and so of an equitable distribution of particular goods;[12] the establishment of the normative order of intentionality as a grid for the existential discernment of affective self-transcendence;[13] conversely, the use of affective self-transcendence as a criterion for discerning whether one is indeed being attentive, intelligent, reasonable, responsible, and loving; the reciprocal relationship between feelings and symbols and between affective development and symbolic transformation;[14] and the at least implicit acknowledgment of an aesthetic base in the normative order of intentionality for the character of a person's religious, moral, and indeed even cognitive authenticity.[15] On the basis of these elements I have attempted to generate the further methodological notions of second immediacy,[16] the imaginal,[17] and psychic conversion,[18] to establish the distinction of three orders of elemental symbolism — the personal, the archetypal, and the anagogic[19] — and on the basis of this distinction to engage in an ongoing dialectic with Jungian archetypal psychology.[20]

Recently I have discovered that Lonergan's paper on healing and creating in history suggests a model for understanding the transformation of the aesthetic quality of our religious, moral, and cognitive being,[21] and that the far-reaching explanatory potentials of his talk of limitation and transcendence in the discussion of genuineness that appears in *Insight*[22] can become the basis of a psychology of religious discernment. The various operations that constitute the creative vector in human consciousness are permeated by feelings. To the extent that these feelings are not congruent with the self-transcendent objectives of their corresponding operations, to the extent that one does not *desire* meaning, truth, the real, the good, and attunement with a world-transcendent God whose Word and Love are incarnate in Christ Jesus, to that extent these *operations* of conscious intentionality are inhibited from reaching their objectives. The automatisms and complexes of our psychic sensitivity interfere with the spontaneous unfolding of the normative order of the search for direction in the movement of life. The universal willingness that can initiate and sustain schemes of recurrence that would meet the problems set by decline must originate elsewhere than in the development from below upwards of our intentional capacities.[23] The absolutely supernatural conjugate form of charity, of the gift of God's love, however it is mediated through the universal instrumentality of all proportionate being,[24] is radically a healing of the convulsive aesthetic undertow whose spontaneous energic compositions and distributions propel us to displace in one direction or another the tension of limitation and transcendence whose cognitive and existential acknowledgment would constitute our genuineness. A displacement in the direction of limitation heads in the limit to a state of psychotic depression, while a displacement in the direction of transcendence heads to schizophrenic inflation. But we can be anywhere on the continuum toward one or the other of these pathological disintegrations, and we can even oscillate from one displacement to the other in manic-depressive inconsistencies. The internal time consciousness that constitutes the sensitive psyche and its imaginal productions must be converted to a taut participation in the intentions of being and the good that are not bounded by the horizon of time. Only a transparent grounding in God, only being in love in an unrestricted fashion, can unify the otherwise Protean commingling of opposites that results from the fact that our interiority is both spiritual and psychic. A third-stage-of-meaning[25] conversion of affectivity to such participation in the normativity of the intentional quest is a fruit of what I am calling psychic conversion. In psychic conversion the story structured by memory and anticipation, the story of the creative tension of limitation and transcendence, of its various displacements and its continual reestablishment in the gift of God's forgiving love, is not only healed but also appropriated with something approaching explanatory precision. Elaborations of the model of limitation and transcendence thus permit a reinterpretation and reformulation of both the axial and the Christian traditions of discernment. Much of my current research is devoted to developing such a psychology of discernment.

2   Psychic Conversion

The explanatory self-appropriation of the story structured by the creative tension of limitation and transcendence, particularly as that story is told in the trustworthy elemental symbolizations of one's dreams, constitutes a defensive scheme of recurrence around the advances of the human spirit attained in Lonergan's objectification of the normative order of the search for direction in the move-

ment of life. We know from *Insight* that a scheme or a series of ranges of schemes of recurrence that have already
emerged within the concrete universe whose immanent
intelligibility is an emergent probability can place around
itself a defensive scheme that increases the probability of
its survival.[26] The psychic conversion that I have labored
to effect in myself, to understand, and to articulate brings
the pulsing flow of psychic sensitivity forward to a share in
the self-transparency of the subject achieved in Lonergan's
transcendental method. In this way it offers one both affective and symbolic indications of the likelihood of the
genuineness or inauthenticity of one's present cognitive,
moral, and religious stance: affective indications, in that
the tension of limitation and transcendence is *felt* by a sensitive psyche that mediates between the relatively fixed
schemes of recurrence of the material organism and the
spiritual intentionality whose objective is unrestricted by
the space and time that are the field or matter or potency
in which emergent probability is the immanent form or
intelligibility;[27] symbolic indications, in that the energic
complexes that constitute these mediating psychic affects
are both expressed and transformed in the spontaneous
elemental symbolizations of our dreams.[28] Through the
appropriation of these affective and symbolic indications,
a defensive scheme is placed around the advances in self-
transcendence that accrue from the self-appropriation of
one's cognitive, moral, and religious exigences. In this sense
psychic conversion is foundational. Since it unifies the
normative order of inquiry with our psychic sensitivity, it
provides a dimension, not so much of the materials to be
integrated in the rest of human knowledge, including theological knowledge, as of the integrating structure of the
subjects who will articulate an explicit semantics of the
real.

In *Psychic Conversion and Theological Foundations*, I
propose that a methodical psychology grounded in self-

appropriation would be a transcendental aesthetics, that is, an explicit integration through self-appropriation of our intention of the beautiful with our notions of the intelligible, the true, the real, and the good. The integration of psychic and neural energy into the normative unfolding of the pure question of the human spirit completes, I believe, the therapeutic intention of Lonergan's transcendental method to effect a mediated return to immediacy on the part of the self-appropriating cognitive and existential agent.[29] A further retrieval of the medieval heritage in the mode of interiority would substantiate this claim. For the medievals did not limit the transcendental field to the intelligible, the true, the real, and the good. They included also the beautiful, the objective of the aesthetic intentionality of the sensitive psyche. Sensitive consciousness is itself intentional, and its intentionality is not obliterated or displaced, but rather sublated, by any genuine intention of meaning, of truth, and of the human good. As there is a transcendental notion of the intelligible, of the true, of the real, of the good, so there is a transcendental notion of the beautiful. It resides in our sensitive consciousness as the latter participates in the intentionality of the other transcendental notions. As the other transcendental notions are revealed in the unfolding of the normative order of inquiry, so the notion of the beautiful resides in the intentional feelings that give to the intention of meaning, the reflective grasp of truth, and the existential discernment of values their momentum, their drive, their satisfaction, and their specifically human drama. One's story is a matter of the satisfaction or frustration of one's desire for meaning, truth, reality, and genuinely ordered values. That the story is human is a function of the specifically differentiating normative order of inquiry, the source of transcendence. But that it is a story at all is perhaps a function of the transcendental notion of the beautiful that resides in a sensitive consciousness that cannot be left behind or displaced in any genuine human exercise of intelligence, rationality, and deliberation, but that is the very condition of the genuineness that lies in a creative tension of limitation and transcendence.

3   Toward a World-Cultural Humanity

As with everything else in the transcendental method that establishes the third stage of meaning, so too the retrieval through self-appropriation of the intention of the beautiful is not an end in itself. Lonergan speaks in *Insight* not simply of conceiving and affirming the integral heuristic structure of proportionate being, but also of implementing it, and of doing so in such a way as to effect 'a transformation and an integration of the sciences and of the myriad instances of common sense.'[30] Moreover, there can be found in the development of Lonergan's thought a movement from speaking of the cognitional-theoretic foundations of this implementation, as in *Insight*, to proposing a set of theological foundations for an interdisciplinary reorientation of the human sciences, as in *Method in Theology*: theological foundations that include the cognitional-theoretic positions of *Insight* within a higher viewpoint that is explicit in its articulation of positions on the moral and religious as well as on the cognitive subject.[31] In *Insight*, the disclosive and transformative praxis of constructing an explicit semantics of the real is a function of implementing the three basic philosophic positions inherent in cognitional theory: the positions on knowing, being, and objectivity.[32] The development that appears in *Method in Theology* expands the list of basic positions, so that the foundations of the transforming and integrating activity that Lonergan has in mind when he speaks now of integrated studies are not simply philosophic but properly theological foundations. The intellectual conversion that articulates itself into the three basic positions of *Insight* is itself grounded in a moral conversion, and this moral conversion follows upon a religious conversion.[33] The modality of psychic conversion that is to be included as a dimension of these theological foundations follows upon intellectual conversion and enables the self-appropriation of moral and religious conversion.[34]

Now to speak of the theological foundations of a transformation and an integration of the sciences and of the myriad instances of common sense is to imply a new synthesis of faith and culture. It is also to indicate both the superstructural component of this new historical synthesis — the transformation and integration of the sciences — and its infrastructural component — the transformation and integration of the myriad instances of common sense. And to speak of a movement from philosophic foundations to theological foundations that include but sublate the philosophic is to suggest a distinction between the integral heuristic structure of proportionate being and the transcendental notion of value: a distinction that is not afforded us in *Insight* but that is present both in *Method in Theology's* disengagement of the fourth level of consciousness and in the affirmation that appears in the same book that, while the structure of judgments of value is identical with that of judgments of fact, the respective contents or meaning of such judgments differ from one case to the other.[35] Thus it is that one can approve of what does not exist and disapprove of what does. This recognition of the distinctness of the existential dimensions of foundations from the cognitive dimensions established in *Insight* grounds a further distinction between the real human world as it is and the good human world as it is to be brought into being. This good human world is in the limit a new historical synthesis of faith and culture. I call it a world-cultural humanity. I locate its superstructural component in the interdisciplinary collaboration that, grounded in theological foundations, would intend a transformation and an integration especially of the human sciences, and its infrastructural component in the transformation and integration of the myriad instances of common sense through a further implementation of the same theological foundations.

The term 'world-cultural humanity' is borrowed from Lewis Mumford's book *The Transformations of Man.*[36] After tracing in descriptive fashion some of the major cultural forms that have constituted what Eric Voegelin would call the substance of history,[37] Mumford raises the question of where we go from here. What may we anticipate? What ideal types may we use to help us describe our contemporary options? He proposes two dialectically alternative courses that confront us today on a cosmopolitan scale. The first he calls post-historic humanity, and the second world-cultural humanity. His argument is to the effect that, short of a global transformation of human consciousness and of cultural values similar in its impact to the various localized axial differentiations of the order of reason and of the world-transcendent measure of human integrity that occurred in the millennium 500 B.C.E. - 500 C.E., humanity is condemning itself — and here I use other terminology than that employed by Mumford — to a cumulative and irreversible determination of its neurophysiology, memory, imagination, intelligence, and existential praxis in inflexible schemes of recurrence fixed by neural, psychic, social, economic, political, conceptual, and linguistic determinisms. The alternative to this post-historic humanity is suggested in the contrary ideal type of a world-cultural humanity that is grounded in a self-understanding of human subjects that can so mediate the differentiations of consciousness achieved in the past as to bring them forward to a new and crosscultural unity rooted in an explicit appropriation of the common and so transcendental constituents of human genuineness.

Mumford's ideal types are precise enough to evoke in us the same persuasion that some, including myself, have arrived at by studying and pondering and being changed by the work of Bernard Lonergan: namely, that we are challenged by the unfolding course of intelligent emergent probability to an agency that would mediate a new axial development in human consciousness, that new control of meaning grounded in interiorly differentiated consciousness that Lonergan has called the third stage of meaning.[38] For the appropriation of the transcultural roots of human genuineness that would ground a world-cultural humanity is precisely what is rendered possible by the transcendental or generalized empirical method that gives us what Lonergan calls theological foundations. What Mumford's ideal type of a world-cultural humanity enables us to envision in an imaginative form that can stir the affective momentum and drive of our intentional operations is a global community grounded in analogously realized attainments of the human genuineness that Lonergan enables at least superstructural practitioners to appropriate through interiorly differentiated consciousness. This global community would be an emerging alternative, especially to the principal agents in today's world of a posthistoric humanity: namely, to the two escalating and competing totalitarianisms that lie in an overly centralized and bureaucratic form of socialism such as is paradigmatically manifested in the Soviet bloc, on the one hand, and in the correspondingly monolithic network of transnational corporations that has assumed effective control of the capitalist world and of many of the developing nations of the Third World, on the other hand.[39] The anticipation of a world-cultural community that is not a homogenization of

cultural differences but a grounding of crosscultural enrichment in interiorly differentiated consciousness envi-
sions the formation of a humane alternative to our present
and seemingly exhaustive options between a state-con-
trolled monopoly and a monopoly-controlled state,[40] both
of which violate on the level of systemic social-structural
objectifications the law of the tension of limitation and
transcendence that constitutes the intrinsic intelligibility
of all genuine development in this concrete universe of
proportionate being.

The interdisciplinary effort at a transformation and
reorientation of the human sciences that would constitute
the superstructural component of a world-cultural community would go forward simultaneously on several fronts.
Its intention would be, I believe, to redirect the scientific
understanding of humanity in accord with the constituents of genuineness that are mediated by the differentiation of intentional and psychic interiority, and especially
in accord with the law of limitation and transcendence that
is intrinsic to all genuine personal and social development.
I have argued that the reorientation of depth psychology is
part of the very foundations of this implementation of
Lonergan's method in the human sciences. But the implementation must extend (1) to a reorientation of the social,
anthropological, and political sciences, under the guiding
orientation of an intention to ground crosscultural understanding and cooperation in the transcendental constituents of human genuineness in all cultures; and (2) to a
reorientation of the science of economics in accord with
the same vision of crosscultural communication and enrichment. We can only be grateful that Lonergan is presently turning his attention to a transformation of economic
knowledge that — if I am understanding it correctly —
would have economic transactions embody the law of limitation and transcendence whose progressive articulation

is simultaneously a promotion of genuine human development.

As we come into possession of this law through interiorly differentiated consciousness, we will find its transformative impact also upon the myriad instances of common sense.

The original experience of the search for direction in the movement of life is variously differentiated or compacted in the different cultural communities whose sets of meanings and values constitute the substance of our history. Eric Voegelin has distinguished three modes of symbolization through which cultures have expressed their self-understanding: the cosmological, the anthropological, and the soteriological.[41] I will try to understand these modes of symbolization in accord with the law of limitation and transcendence, will imply the relevance of psychic conversion to an integration of the truth of these various modes, and will indicate the pertinence of Lonergan's work not only for the transformation and integration of the sciences but also for the development of the common sense of a world-cultural community.

In terms of Lonergan's differentiations of the constituents of human genuineness, we might say that cultures that exist under the forms of cosmological symbolization, where the prime analogate for the cultural order lies in the rhythms and processes of nonhuman nature, have not differentiated the theoretic and world-transcendent realms of meaning, to say nothing of the interior, scholarly, and soteriological realms, from the compactness of the aesthetic and ecological sensitivities that inform their common sense. Due to their non-differentiation, especially of theory and of world-transcendent reality, these cultures effectively displace the tension of limitation and transcendence in the direction of limitation, and so they are effectively prevented from assuming responsible control over the future course of their history by reason of a too compact identification with the schemes of recurrence operative in nonhuman nature. But there is an abiding truth in the cosmological symbolizations of preaxial cultures. While it is true that for these cultures today to remain under the dominance of cosmological symbolization is for them to become the easy prey of the competing and escalating totalitarianisms that, left unchecked, would institute a post-historic humanity, it is no less true that the abiding truth of cosmological symbolization must be mediated through interiorly differentiated consciousness to a crosscultural community that would counteract the contrary displacement in the direction of transcendence that characterizes the exploits of the competing and escalating totalitarianisms. The characteristic features of cosmological symbolization, as these are disengaged by such scholars as Voegelin and Mircea Eliade, bear striking resemblances to what the psychologist Carl Gustav Jung has called the archetypal symbols of the collective unconscious. While I have emphasized in my own work that Jung fails to distinguish these archetypal symbols from the anagogic symbolizations that both give rise to and express a transcendent and then a soteriological differentiation of consciousness, it can in no wise be denied that Jung has provided us with the principal instrument for mediating through interiorly differentiated consciousness the ecological exigences for creative tension with the schemes of recurrence of nonhuman nature that, however compactly, form the truth of the cosmological mentality. The recovery through what I have called psychic conversion of these archetypal expressions of the exigence for a balanced relation between nature and culture will mediate to an emerging crosscultural community, among other things, an ecological differentiation of consciousness that will preserve and yet transform by sublation the abiding truth of the cosmological societies.

Lonergan's mediation of intellectual conversion, on the other hand, is, I believe, at least in part a disengagement through interiorly differentiated consciousness of the axial insights into the order of the soul as the measure of the integrity of a society, and of the world-transcendent measure of the order of the soul itself, that came to expression in anthropological symbolization. And a further mediation of the substance of history through interiorly differentiated consciousness is present in Lonergan's paper on healing and creating in history. For this paper enables us to distinguish between the eros of an interiority that is well-ordered because of its attunement in ultimate concern with the world-transcendent measure of integrity and the charity of a person who has been healed by the gracious initiative of this world-transcendent measure in one's own regard. A soteriological differentiation is thus implicitly distinguished from the differentiation of world-transcendent Being. This further differentiation, however, does not displace but only radicalizes the tension of limitation and transcendence that is established to the extent that one is grounded in God. The soteriological truth adds to the anthropological insights, disengaged in a new fashion through intellectual conversion, several differentiating characteristics.

First, the world-transcendent ground and ultimate referent of the original experience of the search for direction in the movement of life is now known, not simply as the source of a movement in our hearts and minds through which we are inclined to attunement with God, but as the agent of startlingly new developments in history through which God establishes a saving partnership with God's people.

Secondly, the anthropological differentiations represented noetic advances that, however much they may originally have been grounded in revelatory experience,

were easily attributed to the immanently generated advances of human knowledge that constitute the ordinary
development of this knowledge; and the power of truth
regarding the normative order of inquiry led the culture
that was built on an analogy with the well-ordered soul to
regard its own order as normative and permanent for other
cultures as well; but if the measure of the order of the
community finds its root in the astonishing interventions
of a God who not only raises up prophets and brings down
kings, but humbles himself unto death on a cross to re-
deem the people from bondage, then no established human order can be regarded either as permanent or as invested with the normativity that would license it to deal
with other orders on its own terms alone.

Thirdly, the anthropological truth placed such a pre-
mium on human integrity in the search for direction in
the movement of life that it established an aristocratic notion of human worth and of human community. But the
soteriological surprise that in fact does meet the anthropological eros, but in such a manner as to be a scandal and
a stumbling block to the soul that comforts itself on its
disengagement of the normative order of attunement to
the measure of integrity, acknowledges that the poor and
the enslaved are those whom God favors as most God's
own, in fact whom God intervenes not only to save but to
make into the very instruments of salvation for others and
even for their aristocratic oppressors. Until one has acknowledged in one's own person the same victimization
and helplessness that is objectified in the historical bondage of the oppressed, one cannot inherit the reign of God.

Fourthly, a shift is thus introduced in the tradition
of discernment, which indeed has its origins in the pre-
Christian disengagement of the order of attunement with
God. Under anthropological self-understanding, discernment is a matter of discriminating those inclinations that

draw us to attunement with the world-transcendent measure of integrity from those inclinations that draw us away from such attunement. Under soteriological self-understanding, the detachment that is the precondition of anthropological discernment is sublated into a participation in the law of the cross that the Word of God has assumed and revealed as the most complete embodiment of attunement with the measure of integrity under the concrete conditions of a history distorted by the social and personal surd that we know as sin.

Exclusively soteriological symbolization, however, contains an inherent danger that was perhaps first manifested in the Christian variants of Gnosticism, but that can also work its way into the community that would assume the vocation of building a humane crosscultural alternative to the escalating totalitarianisms. Lonergan alludes to this danger when he speaks of the healing vector without the creative vector as a soul without a body.[42] Eric Voegelin points to it in his talk of the modern Gnosticisms,[43] with their metastatic understanding of human history. An exclusive reliance on soteriological self-understanding would repudiate the truth of anthropological symbolization, a truth that is mediated in explanatory fashion in Lonergan's articulation of transcendental method. Such a repudiation would neglect the exigences for integrity that characterize what Lonergan has called the creative vector in human consciousness. Despite the fact that these exigences cannot be fulfilled in an unbiased and undistorted fashion except to the extent that we are healed by the saving love that moves from above downwards in human consciousness, a neglect of these exigences shortchanges the demand for radical integrity that is inherent in the covenant that is God's partnership with God's people.

Here too we find, I believe, the acute pertinence of
Lonergan's work for the concerns that have come to expression in the various theologies of liberation and in political theology, concerns that also obviously lie behind my
own vision of a crosscultural community committed to
schemes of recurrence that provide a genuine alternative
to the deculturation that would head in the limit to a post-
historic form of human existence. The history of ancient
Israel is ample witness to the fact that a culture need not
have reached the noetic disengagement of individual integrity in order to be visited by soteriological truth. And it
surely has been a mistake in missionary endeavors to insist on the anthropological disengagements as somehow
essential for Christian evangelization. But a theology of
liberation that would revert to a denigration of the integrity of the individual as the measure of cultural values and
of cultural values as the condition of a just social order —
and by no means do I want to imply that this is the case
with all such theologies[44] — would be guilty of a regression within the history of soteriological self-understanding itself. It is true that such self-understanding originally
emerged, not out of anthropological differentiations, but
as a leap beyond the compactness of cosmological symbolization. Thus soteriological self-understanding only
gradually differentiated the radical significance of individual
integrity, whereas anthropological truth was constituted
by this differentiation. In soteriological history individuation moved into the light only against the backdrop of
social apostasy. The community informed by soteriological
self-understanding learned only gradually the truth that
the integrity of a community is measured by the integrity
of the individuals who compose it. But this constitutes no
warrant for us to repeat the failures that gave rise to this
insight. The denigration of the significance of cognitive
and existential integrity that would display itself in a too

easy marriage with Marxist analysis and praxis would not only relegate to oblivion the Christian tradition of contemplation through a disparagement of the spirituality of the individual; this loss of attunement with the God who is not only the objective of our longings but the saving partner under whose protection we walk humbly but upright through life would become an agent by default of that final collapse of all intellectual and existential synthesis that is our distinct contemporary option.

4   Conclusion

Lonergan's mediation of the transcultural constituents of integrity has provided me with the conviction that a humane global alternative to the escalating totalitarianisms is a distinct possibility that has already emerged in the course of the unfolding of intelligent emergent probability. But, lest we ourselves violate the law of limitation and transcendence, let us keep in mind that axial transformations of consciousness and of culture take centuries to establish schemes of recurrence with a high probability of survival. The foundations of a world-cultural humanity have already been laid in Lonergan's disengagement of the crosscultural exigences of human intentionality and, I believe, in the work of Carl Gustav Jung and others to identify the crosscultural symbolic indicators of the participation of psychic sensitivity in, or of its derailment from, the normative order of the search for direction in the movement of life. But we still must be concerned with the probability of survival for the already emergent schemes of recurrence grounded in self-appropriation. I take great comfort in this regard from Jung's suggestion that the formation of a stable crosscultural community grounded in the elements of transcendental subjectivity that are in part differentiated in his work would take 600 years.[45] We stand today at the very beginning of a quite new venture in the history of the human community: a venture whose urgency is established by the dreadfulness of the alternatives that are inevitable if we do not assume our responsibility for transforming and integrating both the sciences and the myriad instances of common sense. But we will not witness in our own lifetimes the results of our efforts to consolidate the already emergent foundations and to begin to build upon them. I would hope only that my own disengagement of a psychic conversion as a defensive circle around Lonergan's differentiation of the exigences of human authenticity helps to increase the probability of the survival of the third stage of meaning that comes to expression in his work. But for all of us the universal willingness of agapic consciousness that must inform our labors if they are to be truly detached and disinterested and so in harmony with the normative order of inquiry is the work of the healing vector that moves, not from below upwards in human consciousness, but from above downwards. This specification applies as well to the superstructural labor of transformative interdisciplinary praxis as it does to the infrastructural reorientation of our everyday dramatic intersubjectivity. In either set of instances, the law of the healing vector, moreover, is the law of the cross, and the criterion of discernment is a taut affective balance of limitation and transcendence that is only radicalized when we discover that attunement with the world-transcendent measure of our own noetic and existential integrity is embodied in the cross and resurrection of Jesus as the pattern that this world-transcendent measure assumed in becoming human flesh.

I experience a real inadequacy in expressing my admiration and gratitude for Fr. Lonergan's work and for the encouragement that he has provided me over the past seven years. But I hope that the foregoing remarks are some small indication of the tasks that he has enabled me to assume and to anticipate.

Notes

[1] See Robert M. Doran, *Subject and Psyche* (see above, chapter i, note 11); *Psychic Conversion and Theological Foundations* (see above, chapter i, note 9); 'Psychic Conversion,' (see above, chapter i, note 12); 'Subject, Psyche, and Theology's Foundations' (see above, chapter i, note 13); 'The Theologian's Psyche: Notes toward a Reconstruction of Depth Psychology' (see above, chapter i, note 26); 'Aesthetic Subjectivity and Generalized Empirical Method' (see above, chapter i, note 27); 'Jungian Psychology and Lonergan's Foundations: A Methodological Proposal' (see above, chapter i, note 32); 'Dramatic Artistry in the Third Stage of Meaning' (see above, chapter i, note 28).

[2] Bernard Lonergan, *Method in Theology* (see above, chapter i, note 1) chapter 11.

[3] Ibid. 364-67.

[4] Improbable in the sense that the dimension that Michael Polanyi said would remain always tacit has been objectified. See John V. Apczynski, 'Integrative Theology: A Polanyian Proposal for Theological Foundations,' *Theological Studies* 40:1 (1979) 23-43.

[5] Philip McShane, *The Shaping of the Foundations: Being at Home in the Transcendental Method* (Washington, D.C.: University Press of America, 1976) 19.

[6] Lonergan, *Method in Theology* 281-88.

[7] On cultural infrastructure and suprastructure, see Bernard Lonergan, 'Belief: Today's Issue,' in *A Second Collection* (see above, chapter 5, note 3) especially pp. 91-97.

[8] Eric Voegelin, *The New Science of Politics* (see above, chapter i, note 31) 186.

⁹ On the two vectors, see Bernard Lonergan, 'Healing and Creating in History,' (see above, chapter 3, note 7). Most of Lonergan's work, of course, is concerned with objectifying the creative vector.

¹⁰ Lonergan, *Method in Theology* 30-31.

¹¹ Ibid. 31.

¹² Ibid. 31-32.

¹³ Ibid. 33-34.

¹⁴ Ibid. 64-69.

¹⁵ Ibid. 31-32.

¹⁶ Doran, *Subject and Psyche*, chapter 2.

¹⁷ Ibid. chapter 4.

¹⁸ Ibid. chapter 5.

¹⁹ Doran, 'Aesthetic Subjectivity and Generalized Empirical Method.'

²⁰ In addition to the articles mentioned in footnote 1, see Robert M. Doran, 'Psyche, Evil, and Grace' (see above, chapter 1, note 35); 'Jungian Psychology and Christian Spirituality' (see above, chapter 1, note 33); 'Primary Process and the "Spiritual Unconscious"' (see above, chapter 1, note 30); and 'Christ and the Psyche' (see above, chapter 1, note 22).

²¹ See Doran, 'Jungian Psychology and Christian Spirituality: I.'

²² Bernard Lonergan, *Insight* (see above, chapter 1, note 20) 472-79/497-504.

²³ On universal willingness, ibid. 623-24/646-47.

24 On the absolutely supernatural conjugate form of charity, ibid. 698-700/720-22, 726/748-49; 741/762-63. On universal instrumentality, Bernard Lonergan, *Grace and Freedom: Operative Grace in the Thought of St. Thomas Aquinas*, ed. J. Patout Burns (London: Darton, Longman & Todd, 1971) 80-84.

25 On the third stage of meaning, Lonergan, *Method in Theology* 93-96.

26 '... schemes might be complemented by defensive circles, so that if some event F tended to upset the scheme, there would be some such sequence of conditions as "If F occurs, then G occurs; if G occurs, then H occurs; if H occurs, then F is eliminated." Lonergan, *Insight* 118/141. On the probability of emergence, the probability of survival, and the role of defensive circles in survival, ibid. 121/144.

27 Ibid. 170-72/194-95.

28 See Doran, 'Dramatic Artistry in the Third Stage of Meaning.'

29 See Doran, *Subject and Psyche*, chapter 2.

30 Lonergan, *Insight* 396/421.

31 Chapter 2 of my book *Psychic Conversion and Theological Foundations* is devoted to establishing this interpretation of Lonergan's development.

32 Lonergan, *Insight* 387-88/413.

33 'Bernard Lonergan Responds,' in *Foundations of Theology*, ed. Philip McShane (South Bend, IN: University of Notre Dame Press, 1972) 233-34.

34 As with all aspects of genuineness, psychic conversion is analogously realized. I am speaking of psychic self-appropriation.

35 Lonergan, *Method in Theology* 37.

[36] Lewis Mumford, *The Transformations of Man* (see above, chapter 1, note 6).

[37] Voegelin, *The New Science of Politics* 78.

[38] I have presented my interpretation of Lonergan to this effect in Chapter 1 of *Subject and Psyche*.

[39] 1993 note: See above, chapter 1, note 5.

[40] Matthew Lamb, *History, Method, and Theology* (Missoula: Scholars Press, 1978) 49.

[41] Eric Voegelin, *Israel and Revelation* (see above, chapter 1, note 8) 56.

[42] Lonergan, 'Healing and Creating in History' 107.

[43] See, for example, his book *The New Science of Politics*.

[44] But see Alfredo Fierro, *The Militant Gospel: A Critical Introduction to Political Theologies* (Maryknoll, NY: Orbis, 1977).

[45] See Max Zeller, 'The Task of the Analyst,' *Psychological Perspectives* 6:1 (1975) 75. See also my article 'Aesthetics and the Opposites' (See above, chapter 1, note 27).

7   Suffering Servanthood and the Scale of Values

This paper is an expanded and revised version of a class lecture that I was invited to give to Jesuit students preparing for presbyteral ordination at Regis College in Toronto. In this lecture I was to speak to the question, How are we to relate the social justice and cultural mission of the priest to the priest's 'cultic-theological' role? I decided from the outset that in place of the expression 'cultic-theological role' I would speak of the priest's prophetic, sacramental, and pastoral ministry. My decision was based on two considerations. First, there is no intrinsic theological role for the priest. There is, to be sure, a religious role, conferred by the sacrament of orders. But theology and religion are distinct, and while one may be called by God to be a theologian, no sacrament confirms or confers such a call. Second, there is an ambiguity to the conception of the priest's cultic role which I was determined to clarify in the course of the lecture. I regarded the clarification as of great importance, because I was and remain convinced that many students preparing for presbyteral ministry today are responding to the crisis in the priesthood by taking cover behind a hieratic persona that has been transcended once and for all not only in the sacrifice of Jesus but even in Israelite revelation itself, in the vision of the suffering servant in Deutero-Isaiah (Isaiah 42.1-9; 49.1-6; 50.4-11; 52.13-53.12). My decision to speak of the prophetic, sacramental, and pastoral ministry of the priest was confirmed by the discovery that the Second Vatican Council has deliberately chosen a consistent way of speaking of the ministry of the church and of episcopal and presbyteral service: the Council speaks of the three-fold ministry of teaching (prophetic), sanctifying (sacramental), and shepherding (pastoral).

I chose, moreover, to address the topic from the standpoint of a systematic theologian. That is to say, I chose to relate *theologically* the social justice and cultural mission of the priest and the priest's prophetic, sacramental, and pastoral role. The alternative would have been a more immediately practical presentation that would have treated specific instances and problems: questions of running for political office, for example, or of active participation in armed revolutionary struggles, or of civil disobedience, etc., etc., etc. I reasoned that, while such questions may be foremost in many people's minds and may even have been what the students had in mind when asking me to address the topic, the primary question in this regard at the present time is one of the appropriate mentality. Until that mentality becomes a part of the *sensus fidelium* — and it surely is not that yet — these more practical questions cannot be treated in more than a coincidental and usually inconsistent fashion. We can be intelligently practical only if we know what our goals are, then determine general policies, and finally devise and implement procedures in concrete situations. When the requisite mentality has not yet been appropriated, a community will generally tend to fasten upon procedural questions, and so will act more on expediency or impulse than on the basis of what it has consciously chosen. It should come as no surprise that the appropriate mentality is not part of the *sensus fidelium*. To my knowledge, the document 'Justice in the World' prepared by the 1971 Synod of Bishops, is the first official

Roman declaration to affirm that the promotion of justice is a constitutive element in evangelization: not a byproduct, not a happy result, but an intrinsic formal component, so that there is no authentic evangelization process that is not dynamically structured in such a way as to foster the transformation of unjust social structures and distorted cultural values. Quite simply, it takes more than eleven years for the church to assimilate such an insight in such a way that the relevant patterns of proceeding are inscribed not only in the minds and hearts but also in the bones and molecules of those responsible for ministry. In such a situation it is the theologian's responsibility to offer what he or she judges to be requisite constitutive dimensions in the mentality that has yet to emerge in a consolidated public fashion in the church.

Two elements of the work that I am presently engaged in are here offered as such constitutive dimensions. The first has to do with the model of the church as the community of the suffering servant in history. With reference to the concrete question of presbyteral ministry, those ordained to such ministry, as they enter ever more deeply into the mystery of the suffering servant of God as this vision of the prophet that we call Deutero-Isaiah is fulfilled and transcended in Christ crucified and raised, will find the unity of the social justice and cultural mission of the priest and the priest's prophetic-sacramental-pastoral role emerging as the fruit of their growth in Christ. But the second element is equally important from both a theological and a ministerial point of view. What is it concretely to exercise the ministry of the suffering servant in history? It is to work for the establishment of the integral scale of values or, what comes to the same thing, the establishment of the appropriate relation between the social infrastructure and the cultural superstructure of society. My paper, then, is divided into two parts: first, church and priest as servant; and second, the social and cultural situation of ecclesial ministry in general and of presbyteral ministry in particular. From a methodological point of view, the paper may be regarded as an exercise, first, in foundations, insofar as the two parts are involved in generating, respectively, special and general categories; and second, in systematics, insofar as these categories are employed in the theoretical work of understanding ecclesial and presbyteral ministry.

I   The Community of the Suffering Servant

We do not know what the future will bring, culturally, politically, economically, technologically, socially, religiously. We know what some of the horrible possibilities are, and we even feel that some of them might be imminent. Our sense of apprehension is supported by the analyses of numerous experts. Among these possibilities are total war, worldwide economic depression, increasing violations of the most basic human rights, the casting into oblivion of the cultural and civilizational achievements of various groups of men and women, the competition of escalating imperialistic systems that always border on totalitarianism, the anarchy of sensitive spontaneity unable to tolerate totalitarian control, or perhaps simply the abiding absurdity of a global situation whose clearest and maybe sole intelligible feature lies in 'an equilibrium of economic pressures and a balance of national powers.'[1]

In the face of such a situation at least two things are required. In Hannah Arendt's words, we must 'discover the hidden mechanics by which all traditional elements of our political and spiritual world were dissolved into a conglomeration where everything seems to have lost specific value, and has become unrecognizable for human comprehension, unusable for human purpose.'[2] And we must 'develop a new guarantee which can be found only in a new political principle, in a new law on earth, whose validity this time must comprehend the whole of humanity while its power must remain strictly limited, rooted in and controlled by newly defined territorial entities.'[3] The first of these tasks must be performed both historically and structurally. My effort will be structural, because that is where I judge that I may be capable of making some contribution, and also because such an approach may enable us to understand as well something of what a new guarantee, a new political principle, a new law on earth might be. Ultimately, it can be only the law of the cross,[4] but only as this law is realized in the concrete mission of establishing the integral scale of values in human relations.

In my most recent work I have been principally engaged in elaborating a structural understanding of the situation that is addressed by a contemporary Christian systematic theology. I find that situation to be global, since almost every regional cultural matrix is principally defined by the planetary structural conditions of our time. Moreover, I start from the fact that the world is torn and broken by the ambitions of competing and escalating imperialistic systems that border always on becoming or promoting totalitarianisms and counter-totalitarianisms. And I propose that a theology that mediates between a cultural matrix and the significance and role of the Christian religion within that matrix not only addresses one situation but also evokes another one, in and through its mediating task. Such a theology evokes proximately the community of the church, which is to serve as a catalytic agent for an alternative situation in the world. And remotely such a theology evokes that alternative world situation as well, through the prophetic, sacramental, and pastoral ministry of the church. The theologian's ultimate interest lies in the alternative situation in the world, but his or her proximate attention is to the church as catalytic agent of that alternative world situation: the church that cooperates with God in working out *God's* solution to the problem of evil.

The alternative situation in the world I imagine and envision as consisting in a global network of communities living in accord with another scale of values than that which has given rise to the imperialistic systems. The mission of the church is to be a catalytic agent for the formation of a global network of human communities living in accord with an integral scale of values. And the mission of the presbyter, through prophetic, sacramental, and pastoral ministry, is to lead the church in being a leaven for this new law on earth, this new political principle of limited power and newly defined territorial entities. The church has a ministry to the world, a mission to serve the emergence of a new law, and the presbyteral office has the mission of leading the church in the exercise of this ministry to the world. The church will be a catalytic agent of a world-cultural humanity by itself becoming a global network of communities of Christian witness, Christian fellowship, and Christian service in the constitution of a renewed and transformed global community. Its catalytic agency will be sacramental, in that the church is to be the sign and instrument both of the reconciling and healing grace of Christ and of the unity of humankind in its catholicity and cultural diversity. The church is to be the incarnational sacrament of Christ, and the eschatological sacrament of the world, neither wavering nor being crushed until true justice is established on earth (Isaiah 42.4).

The more I reflect on the sacramental-catalytic agency of the church in our world, the more the paradigm of the church as the community of the suffering servant becomes for me the dominant model. The church is to be the Body of the Christ who fulfills and transcends the vision of Deutero-Isaiah regarding the servant of God. It is to be the incarnational sacrament of Christ to and for the world, by embodying in its members and communities and ministries the pattern of the servant's redemptive and representative suffering. And it is to be the eschatological sacrament of the world by being a catalytic agent of integrity among the nations. Its agency consists in nothing more nor less than its fidelity to the integral scale of values. The church is to be a global network of communities of witness, fellowship, and service, embodying the vocation of the suffering servant of God, in accord with the 'just and mysterious law of the cross,' filling up in the bodies of its members what is lacking in the sufferings of Christ, until the islands have received and rejoiced in his law. And the presbyteral ministry is conferred by ordination as an office of prophetic, sacramental, and pastoral leadership vis-à-vis this sacramental-catalytic mission and ministry of the church to the world.

Why have I focused on the paradigm of the suffering servant of God in order to understand the church and especially the presbyteral ministry? We know that the sacrifice of Christ fulfills and transcends all the priesthoods and ritual sacrifices of the Old Testament and of paganism. But the Old Testament also transcends its own notions of priesthood in the exodus of Israel from Israel[5] symbolized in the vision of the suffering servant. The Old Testament understanding of priesthood is brought to fulfillment in the songs of the servant of God. The history of Israel contains and exhibits several modalities of priesthood. Moses exercised a priestly office when he offered sacrifices to God in the name of the whole people. The heads of families and of tribes exercised similar functions which later developed into the priesthood of the king. The Levites, of whom we usually think when we consider priesthood in the Old Testament, served the cult and the law in an official capacity within the Israelite community. But with the prophets, with their recognition of the universality and enormity of sin, the awareness developed that perfect worship would be brought about only in the last days, when through God's own agency full glory would be given to God and full access had to God on the part of the people. The cultic, ritual, and sacrificial priesthood of the Levites is recognized by the prophets as insufficient. It cannot do what it set out to do; it cannot open access to God, nor achieve expiation for sin, nor deliver reconciliation between God and the community. Jeremiah and Ezekiel show some awareness that in their own personhood and in its historical agency they are themselves taking on the sin of the people, voluntarily accepting it and suffering it, and that through this suffering fidelity they are anticipating a new covenant. But in Deutero-Isaiah we are provided with the vision of the sole just one, the innocent one who takes on himself the iniquities of all and wins healing for all precisely by doing so. The servant is exercising a priestly ministry in a way that succeeds. 'Ours were the suffering he bore, ours the sorrows he carried ... He was pierced through for our faults, crushed for our sins. On him lies a punishment that brings us peace, and through his wounds we are healed' (Isaiah 53.4-5). Redemption comes to the people, not through the cultic, ritual sacrifices of the Levites, but through the historical suffering of the just one who voluntarily accepts the pain and suffering accruing from the vicissitudes of history and offers himself as a sacrifice for sin. The priestly ministry is brought to its fulfillment in his historically imposed and voluntarily accepted suffering.

The New Testament acknowledges Jesus as the fulfillment of the vision of the suffering servant. It is not through ritual and cultic action, but through his suffering in history, that the sole just one opens access to God. The ritual, liturgical, and cultic element of Old Testament priesthood is transformed by, included in, and transcended by the vision of the servant even in the Old Testament itself; but in the one New Testament writing that focuses explicitly on Christ's priesthood, the letter to the Hebrews, this priesthood is understood as the fulfillment in history of the redemptive mission of the servant. Only in this writing is *hiereus* used of Christ, but even so his priesthood is understood in terms not of the Levitical priesthood, but of the offering of the suffering servant.

> This is what he said, on coming into the world: You who wanted no sacrifice or oblation, pre-pared a body for me. You took no pleasure in holocausts or sacrifices for sin; then I said, just as I was commanded in the scroll of the book, "God, here I am! I am coming to obey your will." Notice that he says first: You did not want what the Law lays down as the things to be offered, that is: the sacrifices, the oblations, the holocausts and the sacrifices for sin, and you took no pleasure in them; and then he says: Here I am! I am coming to obey your will. He is abolishing the first sort to replace it with the second. And this will was for us to be made holy by the offering of his body made once and for all by Jesus Christ. (Hebrews 10.5-10)

Immediately prior to this passage is a quotation from the fourth servant song: 'So Christ, too, offers himself only once *to take the faults of many on himself* (Hebrews 9.28).

It is in line with such an understanding of Christ's priesthood that we must understand the priesthood of the church and of the presbyter within the church. The church is a priestly people in that it fills up what is lacking in the sufferings of Christ, offering itself together with Christ in the midst of the pain and suffering of the world, voluntarily taking upon itself this suffering so as to cooperate with God's work in Jesus for the redemption of the world. And the presbyter, through the prophetic, sacramental and pastoral ministry, is to lead and guide the church precisely in this priestly ministry, so that the church can truly be the leaven for the new law on earth by its own participation in the mystery of Christ, the suffering servant of God.

I said earlier that I was convinced that as those ordained to the presbyteral ministry within the church enter ever more deeply into the mystery of the servant as this vision is fulfilled and transcended in Christ crucified and raised, they will find the unity of the social justice and cultural mission of the priest and the priest's prophetic-sacramental-pastoral role emerging as the fruit of their growth in Christ. The social and cultural meaning of the suffering servant of God, the servant's role in bringing, if you want, a new political principle, a new law, whose validity is global and whose power is limited because rooted in and controlled by territorial entities other than nations, states, and empires, is suggested by Eric Voegelin's interpretation of the significance of the servant songs. For Voegelin the vision of the suffering servant is at once the culmination of Old Testament revelation and the completion of the transimperial form of existence that this revelation introduces into history. His interpretation is suggestive of the profound political implications of a model of ecclesial and presbyteral ministry based on the servant songs.

Voegelin summarizes the main points of his *Israel and Revelation* in the following words:

> From the imperial order in cosmological form emerged, through the Mosaic leap in being, the Chosen People in historical form. The meaning of existence in the present under God was

differentiated from the rhythmic attunement to divine-cosmic order through the cult of the empire. The theopolity, supplemented by kingship for survival in pragmatic history, however, still suffered under the compactness of its order. The order of the spirit had not yet differentiated from the order of the people's institutions and mores. First, in his attempt to clarify the mystery of the tension, Isaiah split the time of history into the compactly unregenerate present, and a quite as compactly transfigured future, of the concrete society. Through Jeremiah this unregenerate present then gained its existential meaning, in as much as the prophet's participation in divine suffering became the omphalos of Israelite order beyond the concrete society. And through Deutero-Isaiah, finally, there emerged from existential suffering the experience of redemption in the present, right here and now. The movement that we called the Exodus of Israel from itself, the movement from the order of the concrete society toward the order of redemption was thus completed. The term 'completion' must be properly understood. It means that the order of being has revealed its mystery of redemption as the flower of suffering. It does not mean, however, that the vision of the mystery is the reality of redemption in history: The participation of man in divine suffering has yet to encounter the participation of God in human suffering.[6]

The prophets, from the middle of the eight century B.C.E. to the fall of Jerusalem in 586, attempted to come

to grips with Israel's defection from the true order disclosed in the Sinaitic revelation. They expected disaster as
punishment for this defection, and they called for a return
to the law of God. But as the disaster drew closer, their
expectation that the institutions and mores of the concrete
society would and could be reformed gave way to a belief
in a total transformation of order that would occur after
the present concrete society had been swallowed up by a
catastrophe. Isaiah responded to this new expectation by
forming his own group of disciples as the remnant of Israel beyond the present concrete society, entrusting to them
the secret of true order that was to be publicly revealed
only in the indeterminate future when God's spirit would
descend on the remnant's ruler. A century later, Jeremiah
became aware that existence in society under God, which
was the whole point of the Sinaitic revelation, was not to
assume the concrete form of a small Israelite theopolity
surrounded by mighty empires. Jeremiah expanded his
prophetic concern beyond Israel to include the whole Near
Eastern world. Israel remained the holy center, but the
society under God was to embrace the nations. Since both
Israel and the nations were in a state of disorder, the center of order contracted into the person of the prophet
Jeremiah. Both Isaiah and Jeremiah depart from a vision
of the order of the concrete Israelite society toward an indeterminate goal. Isaiah's departure is temporal, Jeremiah's
spatial. In either case one can no longer say of which concrete society the prophets are speaking when they imagine
the carrier of true order, or just what kind of order the
society will have when it is transfigured by the new covenant written on hearts of flesh. The *terminus ad quem* of
the prophetic vision is no longer a concrete society with a
clearly recognizable order, for there are problems of order
that extend beyond the existence of a concrete society and
its institutions, and there will always be a gulf between

true order and the order realized concretely by any society. The existence of a concrete society in a definite form will not resolve the question of order in history. No chosen people in any concrete historical form can ever be the ultimate center of the true order of humankind.

Deutero-Isaiah is the prophet who lived through the anguished anticipation of Israel's final exodus: now an exodus not of migration from Chaldean civilization nor from Egyptian bondage, but from Israel itself as a society organized for national purposes under God in the midst of other imperial civilizations. Each exodus represents a step in the movement away from cosmological imperial civilization to society in history under God. In the writing of Deutero-Isaiah, Voegelin discovers a progression of experience and symbolization from the expectation of a concrete order of an Israel restored by Cyrus to the mystery of the exodus from concrete order itself that is symbolized by the suffering servant. The original message of Deutero-Isaiah, building upon the heritage left him by his predecessors, emphasizes salvation in a manner that no longer hinges on the fulfillment of the law, and so that no longer views salvation as the alternative to suffering. Neither salvation nor suffering has disappeared from the message, but they are no longer alternatives. God is now revealing God's own self as the redeemer, and the appeal of the prophet is simply that the people accept God as such. Israel has been forgiven, and so in a definite way the question of conduct is now in the past. The concern now is not with the order of life under the covenant of the law, but with the order under the redeemer God. The Servant embodies that order, and so is the covenant to the people, the light to the nations. Redemption is revealed as the fruit of suffering, *right here and now*. This is the new dispensation. Even the Exodus from Egypt is unimportant in comparison with the 'new things' that God is doing.

Concretely the 'new' consists proximately in the liberation from the Babylonian exile. But these events of power politics are understood as a revelational epoch, because in them the reality of God and of God's power over the flesh are being revealed in a way that brings redemption from the false gods of empire. Above the vicissitudes of empire 'the word of our God shall stand forever' (Isaiah 40.8). With this insight God is revealed as the God of all humankind. And since Israel as a concrete society has perished with the empires, 'the Israel that rises from the storm that has blown over all of mankind is no longer the self-contained Chosen People but the people to whom the revelation has come first to be communicated to the nations. It has to emigrate from its own concrete order just as the empire peoples had to emigrate from theirs. The new Israel is the covenant and light to the nations (42.6), the Servant of Yahweh through whom God will make his salvation reach to the end of the earth (49.6).'[7]

The servant's task is to spread the news of redemption from Israel to the nations. His task is to be carried out not under the conditions of a complete dissolution of the empires in which man apes God, but under those of a succession of concretely realized imperial ambitions. The task 'will bring ridicule, humiliation, persecution, and suffering to the men who undertake it under such unauspicious circumstances.'[8] The servant becomes 'a new type in the history of order, a type created by the prophet in Israel and for Israel, to be figured by others until the task is accomplished.'[9] His task will be completed only when everyone becomes a disciple of God, as the servant is. He will execute his mission by obedience in adversity, not rebelling or turning back, nor being confounded by ill-treatment of his person. 'Trusting in God will he continue to speak with a disciple's tongue what he has been taught by God.'[10] And finally the people will come to believe the unbelievable tale of representative suffering, and when they do so they will know the completion of liberation from the order of empire. 'The Servant who suffers many a death to live, who is humiliated to be exalted, who bears the guilt of many to see them saved as his offspring, is the King above the kings, the representative of divine above imperial order. And the history of Israel as the people under God is consummated in the vision of the unknown genius, for as the representative sufferer Israel has gone beyond itself and become the light of salvation to mankind.'[11] An abiding preoccupation with the servant is manifest in Acts 8. 'The Ethiopian eunuch of the queen, sitting on his cart and reading Isaiah, ponders on the passage: "Like a sheep he was led away to the slaughter." He inquires of Philip: "Tell me, of whom is the prophet speaking? of himself, or of someone else?" Then Philip began, reports the historian of the Apostles, and starting from this passage he told him the good news about Jesus.'[12]

Our vision of the church in the midst of the vicissitudes of empire in our own day is one of a global network of communities of Christian witness, Christian fellowship, and Christian service to humanity that would embody under any possible, probable, or actual conditions of the present and future the vocation of the suffering servant of God in accord with the just and mysterious law of the cross. Such a network of communities is informed by the divinely originated solution to the mystery of evil, the solution that 'will be not only a renovation of will that matches intellectual detachment and aspiration, not only a new and higher collaboration of intellects through faith in God, but also a mystery that is at once symbol of the uncomprehended and sign of what is grasped and psychic force that sweeps living human bodies, linked in charity, to the joyful, courageous, wholehearted, yet intelligently controlled performance of the tasks set by a world order in which the problem of evil is not suppressed but transcended.'[13] To mediate this solution theologically with our contemporary global cultural matrix is simultaneously to evoke an alternative situation: the liberation of humanity from the vicissitudes of imperial order and disorder, through fidelity to the integral scale of values through which a new law is brought to the earth, a law whose validity extends to everybody, whose power is strictly limited, and whose concrete embodiment consists in newly defined territorial entities in the constant process of renovation and revitalization through the outpouring of the Spirit of God upon all flesh.

2   Culture and Society

What concretely does it mean for the church to exercise the ministry of the suffering servant in our day? What does it mean for the presbyter to lead the church in this mission through prophetic word, sacramental action, and pastoral care?

2.1   The Dimensions of Society

The question is social and cultural. It addresses the structure of disintegration and evokes the structure of integrity. It asks about the structural mechanics of dissolution, and it anticipates the organic structure of a socially redemptive process.

I will use the word 'society' according to the convention employed by David Tracy, for whom it is a broad generic term that encompasses several more specific dimensions. Tracy lists three such components: the technoeconomic order, the polity, and culture.[14] While we do indeed speak of a technoeconomic order that is concerned with the organization and allocation of goods and services and the occupational and stratificational systems of the society, we have learned from Karl Marx that technological institutions (the 'forces of production') should be differentiated from the economic system (the 'relations of production'). Moreover, it seems that we should add one further dimension, one to which Marx was not sufficiently sensitive and whose neglect decisively amputates his understanding of the structure of society: intersubjective spontaneity, primordial human intersubjectivity. This dimension will never be comprehended by understanding the relations established among technology, economic systems, politics, and cultural meanings and values. It is the primordial base of human community. When understood in general terms it seems, as Lonergan says, almost 'too obvious to be discussed or criticized, too closely linked with more elementary processes to be distinguished sharply from them.' Lonergan describes it as follows:

> The bond of mother and child, man and wife, father and son, reaches into a past of ancestors to give meaning and cohesion to the clan or tribe or nation. A sense of belonging together provides the dynamic premise for common enterprise, for mutual aid and succor, for the sympathy that augments joys and divides sorrows. Even after civilization is attained, intersubjective community survives in the family with its circle of relatives and its accretion of friends, in customs and folkways, in basic arts and crafts and skills, in language and song and dance, and most concretely of all in the inner psychology and radiating influence of women. Nor is the abiding significance and efficacy of the intersubjective overlooked when motley states name themselves nations, when

constitutions are attributed to founding fathers,
when image and symbol, anthem and assem-
bly, emotion and sentiment are invoked to im-
part an elemental vigor and pitch to the vast
and cold technological, economic, and political structures of human invention and convention. Finally, as intersubjective community precedes civilization and underpins it, so also it
remains when civilization suffers disintegration
and decay.[15]

When intersubjectivity is understood in less general
terms, however, we can see quite clearly its importance for
the structure of society. For it is the cohesive bond of groups
that are formed on the basis of common interests,
convictions, tasks, problems. It binds one group together
and divides it from another group. It is the most basic of
all social dimensions.

Society, then, is composed of five elements:
intersubjective spontaneity, technological institutions, the
economic system, the political order, and culture. We have
just discussed intersubjective spontaneity. Technology is
rooted in the insight that the recurrent desires of individuals and groups can be met in a recurrent way through the
formation of capital. Technology at its roots, I believe, is
the system and set of instruments, including human labor
power, involved in the formation of capital, for the sake of
meeting in a recurrent fashion the recurrent desires for
consumer goods on the part of the intersubjective groups
of a society. The economic system is 'some procedure that
sets the balance between the production of consumer goods
and new capital formation, some method that settles what
quantities of what goods and services are to be supplied,
some device for assigning tasks to individuals and for dis-
tributing among them the common product.'[16] The politi-

cal order meets problems that arise because of the difficulty of achieving effective agreement among the various intersubjective groups regarding the allocation and distribution of the products of the economic system and the technological institutions. It is a public bond that extends beyond family and intimate associations, and so beyond intersubjective spontaneity, through which a society forms and implements its notions of justice and legitimate power.[17] Culture is the operative set of meanings and values that govern a society's way of life. In Clifford Geertz's words, it is 'an historically transmitted pattern of meanings embodied in symbols, a system of inherited conceptions expressed in symbolic forms by means of which men communicate, perpetuate and develop their knowledge about and attitudes toward life.'[18] Culture is the clue to the ethos (tone, character, quality of life, style) of a society, and to its comprehensive ideas of order or its worldview. It sets the horizon within which the specific problems of political agreement are to be resolved.

The more complex a society, the more differentiated these dimensions will and must be. But the essential question about any concrete contemporary society has to do with how these five elements are related to one another in that society. And an even more basic question is, Is there a general or heuristic formula that specifies how these elements *should* be related to one another? If there is, we can provide a structural analysis of the mechanics of disintegration and a structural formula for the new law on earth that, given the fact that there will always be a gulf between true order and the order realized concretely by any society, it is the mission of the community of the suffering servant perseveringly to mediate to the nations.

2.2   Some Principles of Social and Cultural Analysis

2.2.1 The Individual and Society.

I begin with two assumptions that emerged in the course of my psychological work, but that have proven to be equally determinative of my emerging position on social and cultural issues.

First, the deepest desire of the human person is so to forge the materials of his or her own life as to make of one's world, one's relations with others, and concomitantly of oneself, a work of art.

Second, this desire is fulfilled to the extent that persons discover and follow, step by step, the direction that is to be found, but that also can be missed, in the movement of life.

These basic assumptions mean that the health or distortion of a society is to be weighed against the measure of human dramatic artistry in community. The process of the development or maldevelopment of the person as a dramatic artist and that of the progress or decline of a society are to be understood mutually. The key to dramatic artistry lies in what Lonergan refers to as 'the challenge of history,' that is, 'progressively to restrict the realm of chance or fate or destiny and progressively to enlarge the realm of conscious grasp and deliberate choice.'[19] In this regard Lonergan's understanding of individual and social process coincides with that of the Brazilian educator Paulo Freire, for whom liberation is primarily deliverance from fatalism. By 'chance or fate or destiny' Lonergan is referring to the psychological and social determinisms that, as he says elsewhere,[20] can be broken only by the conviction of faith, the power of hope, and the joy and sacrifice of love. In *Method in Theology*, the equivalent condition is one of participating freely in a process that is at once individual and social, and that consists in the making of humanity: in its advance in authenticity, in the flowering of human affectivity, and in the direction of human labor to ends that are really worth while.

Against this background, we may state the relation of personal and social development as follows:

(1) the desire to make of one's life a work of art by discovering and following the direction to be found in the movement of life is facilitated to the extent that the social conditions that stimulate personal change allow for and foster the use of one's understanding and the exercise of one's freedom so that one participates in the process of the human good; and this desire is impeded to the extent that these factors of understanding and freedom are restricted by the mechanisms of psychological conditioning, social absurdity, and in the limit totalitarian control;

(2) these societies will successfully meet the challenge of history, avoiding and overcoming the grip of conditioning, bias, and control, to the extent that the persons who compose them are exercising intelligence and freedom in genuinely forging a work of art as they constitute their world, their relations with others, and concomitantly themselves;

(3) this is not a vicious circle, for the process of society has a certain dominance over that of the individual, who is born into and raised in and stimulated by the already given social situation; the situations that stimulate and condition the factors within the person that are responsible for his or her development are constituted by the culture, the polity, the economic system, the technological institutions, and the habits of sensitive spontaneity that prevail in the person's society, whether these be in the process of progress or of decline;[21] and

(4) conditions of cultural, political, and general social decline pose a special problem: how is the decline to be reversed if the development of individuals is so inti-

mately conditioned by the situations of the society? Revolution is no automatic guarantee, for perhaps the problem is not simply one of an unjust economic and political system. Perhaps these are symptoms of a miscarriage of the relations that should obtain among all five of the elements constitutive of society. Perhaps the revolutionaries are themselves the victim of this more inclusive miscarriage. Perhaps the problem lies deeper than can be met by a revolution: in general rather than group bias. Moreover, it is not sufficient, though it is true, to say that social conditioning does not necessarily mean social determinism. This is too easy a way out of the problem, one employed by reactionaries as they offer their bromides to the poor, counseling them to raise themselves out of poverty by industry and initiative. The advice overlooks the problem of statistical probabilities: as social situations deteriorate, the probability rises that persons will not be provided the atmosphere in which they will even be stimulated to authentic development. In the limit, we may envision, as Lewis Mumford does, a post-historic situation in which the probabilities of development in genuine dramatic artistry are so infinitesimally low that, for all practical purposes, history has come to an end, and human beings become as programmed by social and neural patterns as is a colony of ants.[22] Thus Hannah Arendt can speak of our uncertainty of 'what will happen once the authentic mass man takes over ... He will have more in common with the meticulous, calculated correctness of Himmler than with the hysterical fanaticism of Hitler':[23] of Himmler, who once spoke of 'the new type of man who under no circumstances will ever do "a thing for its own sake."'[24]

The problem of decline can be reversed only by the formation of a creative minority within the society in question: a minority which grasps what is going forward, understands its roots, anticipates its ever more disastrous consequences, and decides both to resist it and to offer an alternative to it.

2.2.2 Practicality and Artistry.

One of the principles of the reversal, of resistance and of the alternative way of life, is that practicality in originating and developing capital and technology, the economy and the state, must be subordinated to the construction of the human world, of human relations, and of human subjects as works of art. This subordination takes place through bringing human practicality into a taut balance with the demands of primordial intersubjectivity. The delicately nuanced process emanating from these two factors, which will always be in tension with one another, constitutes human artistry in the social forging of the human world. If either of these principles plays too dominant a role, out of balance with the other, the society suffers decline. When practicality is exercised without concern for spontaneous community, the intersubjective base of the community is destroyed and people become rootless. When the intersubjective base is overly emphasized, particularly in its group ethos, those practical insights that might indeed be conducive to meeting a society's real problems but that call for the sacrifice of narrow group or class interests are neglected. Social progress is, in part, the harmonious unfolding of the changes that result from each of these linked but opposed principles of change: the taut balance of practicality and spontaneity. This is one constituent element of dramatic artistry on the social scene.

2.2.3 The Scale of Values.

The balance of practicality and artistry has to do primarily with the exercise of human intelligence, which must be stretched beyond the confines of practical common sense and become alert to other considerations as well. But meeting the challenge of history demands not only the exercise of intelligence but also an orientation of human freedom, without which even the proper exercise of intelligence is impossible. Let us consider the following passage from Machiavelli's *The Prince*, a passage employed several years ago in a paper by Fred Lawrence on political theology. Let us use it as a point of departure for treating the question of the appropriate orientation of human freedom.

> Many have imagined republics and principalities which have never been seen or known to exist in reality; for how we live is so far removed from how we ought to live, that he who abandons what is done for what ought to be done will rather learn to bring about his own ruin than his preservation. A man who wishes to make a profession of goodness in everything must necessarily come to grief among so many who are not good. Therefore it is necessary for a prince who wishes to maintain himself to learn how not to be good, and to use this knowledge and not use it according to the necessity of the case.[25]

Until the final sentence of this passage, Machiavelli and the suffering servant would be in agreement. But at this point the servant would say: therefore it is necessary for one who no longer cares whether he can maintain himself to learn how to be good in everything and to use this knowledge in every case.

The passage from Machiavelli recommends the sacrifice of integrity for expediency. And the point of the required orientation of freedom that we envision is precisely that one must take one's stand, not on expediency but on integrity. What does this mean? By answering this question I believe that we can understand the appropriate relations among the five elements of society.

I have been greatly helped in this regard by reflecting on the implications of what Lonergan has called the scale of values, and by trying to disengage the relations that obtain among the various levels of this scale.

> [W]e may distinguish vital, social, cultural, personal, and religious values in an ascending order. Vital values, such as health and strength, grace and vigor, normally are preferred to avoiding the work, privations, pains involved in acquiring, maintaining, restoring them. Social values, such as the good of order which conditions the vital values of the whole community, have to be preferred to the vital values of individual members of the community. Cultural values do not exist without the underpinning of vital and social values, but none the less they rank higher. Not on bread alone doth man live. Over and above mere living and operating, men have to find a meaning and value in their living and operating. It is the function of culture to discover, express, validate, criticize, correct, develop, improve such meaning and value. Personal value is the person in his self-transcendence, as loving and being loved, as originator of values in himself and in his milieu, as an inspiration and invitation to others to do likewise. Religious values, finally, are at the heart of the meaning and value of man's living and man's world.[26]

2.2.3.1   Infrastructure and Superstructure

I want to begin my comments on the scale of values by addressing a problem originally introduced by Marx. It has to do with the infrastructure and the superstructure of a society.

With Marx I will hold that any concrete society is composed of an infrastructure of concrete everyday transactions and a superstructure of meanings and values that govern these transactions or that reflect them. For Marx, the infrastructure is constituted by the forces and relations of production, that is, by technology and the economic system, as these provide the material frames of reference that confine our powers of projective consciousness. Forces of production fall into the two classes of labor power and the 'objective' means of production. These are the material foundation of all human existence and expression. The economic relations of production distort these forces and render them destructive by stipulating the material use values that it is their function to make — those that sustain or increase profits for the ruling class — and the mode of operation of the productive forces themselves — riveted division of labor, exhaustion of natural resources, inefficient use of productive forces. These relations of production are the proprietary connections between the forces of production and their owners. The essential and defining principle of the economic structure is the law of surplus labor: the few extract payment from the many in the form of surplus labor in exchange for the means of subsistence. The infrastructure is constituted by a complex relation between forces and relations of production: the economic structure fetters the forces of production until these are ready to burst the bonds, at which point the conditions for revolution have been prepared.

For Marx the superstructure is constituted by the legal and political institutions of society, by ideology, and by the forms of social consciousness. Law and politics are a sanctioned and coercive regulator of the economic relations of production, a conscious construction that arises upon already existing antagonisms between the ruling class and the workers and that regulates these antagonisms in the interests of the ruling class. They are a reflex of the economic base, an indispensable defense mechanism that provides a mask covering over the real situation of the relations of production and that enforces this situation by any means found necessary. Ideology consists of the various articulated forms of social self-understanding whereby society formulates publicly effective conceptions that influence people's apprehension of themselves. Most ideology employs empty generalities rather than determinate categories, endows its principal illusory categories with self-subsisting powers of motion, validates the established social order and invalidates what challenges it, is tied to the past in its language and referents, and clothes existing economic relations in an illusorily attractive guise. Its whole purpose is to conceal the real relations of production, class divisions, and laws of exchange prevailing in the society and to rationalize the legal and political aspect of the superstructure, thus ensuring society's inaction with regard to changing the underlying economic base. And forms of social consciousness are the presupposed principles behind ideological formulations, governing them much in the same way as Kant's a priori forms are said to govern determinate categories, though unlike Kantian forms these are socially acquired.

Infrastructure and superstructure for Marx are related by the laws of economic and technological determinism. The economic base determines the superstructure insofar as it imposes work constraints and leisure constraints on individuals, selects out all superstructural phenomena that do not comply with the economic structure, and introduces the content of the economic structure into superstructural phenomena, as in ideology and the forms of social consciousness. Technological determinism, however, necessitates that the economic order so correspond with the stage of development of the productive forces that a certain level of this development will impel the class struggle that, through superstructural changes, will burst the economic structure asunder. The forces of production may be fettered by the economic structure, but only so long as such fettering does not involve relinquishing or forfeiting an established productive stage in a permanent and qualitatively significant way.[27]

My evaluation of Marx's position, if I have correctly understood it, is that he presents an analysis of what in fact can happen when individual, group, and general bias hold sway, but that he has fallen victim to general bias in elevating these facts into laws; that, because his analysis is based on an artificial intersubjective ground, it displaces the tension of limitation and transcendence;[28] and that this displacement is only accentuated in the dominant Marxist tradition of state socialism. The fact that an identical structural deviation occurs in both capitalism and state socialism — and John McMurtry has argued this to my satisfaction[29] — is an argument for an identical root, one that lies in neither economic system as such but in the general bias that allowed both systems to emerge. As Alvin W. Gouldner has argued, Marx focused on the defective consciousness of bourgeois society and on the transformation of the capitalist infrastructure that determines bourgeois consciousness, but he did not analyze with sufficient clarity the kind of society that would strengthen and extend the role of consciousness and reason in life.[30]

An alternative position on the infrastructure and superstructure of society might help to delineate such a society, and to give flesh and bone to our earlier employment of the special categories derived from the Isaianic vision of the suffering servant and his mission in the world. What would it be to bring a new law on earth in our time, what would it be neither to waver nor be crushed until true justice is established on the earth? Perhaps we can answer these questions by presenting, with the help of Lonergan's scale of values, an alternative to the Marxist position on the infrastructure and superstructure of society.

I will maintain, then, that an integral society's infrastructure would be constituted by the dialectical unfolding of the tension of spontaneous intersubjectivity (for the most part, the principle of limitation) with the technological, economic, *and legal-political* institutions of the society. Note that the legal and political institutions are an element of the infrastructure of an integral society, not of the superstructure. The latter is the realm of the determinants of publicly shared and effective meanings and values, and so of culture, of the operative assumptions of meaning and value informing the way of life of the infrastructure. The infrastructure, moreover, will be healthy or diseased depending on whether the tension of the process emergent from the two principles of social change — intersubjective spontaneity and social order — is preserved in a state of taut balance or whether one or other of these principles has gotten the upper hand in determining the course of social process.

Let us relate these considerations of infrastructure and superstructure to the levels of value given by Lonergan. The infrastructure of any concrete society is constituted by the concrete realization of vital and social values in that society, whether that realization be healthy or diseased. The values that constitute culture, again whether healthy or diseased, make up the superstructure.[31]

What about personal and religious values? They lie beyond the three levels of value that constitute the public formation of the superstructure and infrastructure of the society, in the realm of personal decision and orientation. As Voegelin said when discussing the servant, there are problems of order that extend beyond the existence of a concrete society and its institutions. But these values do not constitute a merely private realm of existence without relevance to the cultural superstructure and the social and vital infrastructure of the society. Quite to the contrary, they are the ultimate determinants of cultural integrity, of social progress, of the appropriate relation among the five elements that constitute society, and so of the equitable distribution of vital goods. And the relations among the five levels of value help us to see how this is the case.

2.2.3.2   *Healing and Creating in History: A New*
            Application

In discussing these relations, let us begin with the level of personal values. The person as a self-transcendent originator of values in self and world, the person in his or her integrity, does not exist, is in fact an impossibility, without the gift of God's grace. Thus religious values are the condition of the possibility of personal integrity. Moving next to the level of cultural values, genuine cultural values arise from the pursuit of the beautiful in story and song, ritual and dance, literature and art; from the pursuit of the intelligible in science and scholarship and reflection on life; and from the pursuit of the true in philosophy and theology. Now these pursuits are integral only to the extent that they are carried on by persons of moral and intellectual integrity. Thus personal values are the condition of the possibility of the actual and recurrent functioning of genuine cultural values as the public determinants of meaning and value in a society. Next let us move to the values of the social order, to political organization, economic relations, and technological developments. These are good to the extent that they are formed and implemented in dia-

lectical tension with the legitimate demands of spontaneous intersubjectivity. To that extent they will embody genuine cultural values: values emergent from the pursuit of
the beautiful, the intelligible, and the true. Cultural values, through which the meanings that we live by are discovered, expressed, validated, criticized, developed, and
improved, are thus the condition of the possibility of a social
order that is really worth while. Finally, vital values are
available to the community only to the extent that the social
order is just, and so a just social order is the condition of
the possibility of the equitable distribution of vital values.

Notice what has happened in this analysis. The higher
reaches of the scale of values determine the realization of
the more basic levels: no personal integrity without divine
grace; no cultural values without personal integrity; no just
social order without genuine cultural values; and no vital
values for the whole community without a just social order.

Is there also a relation that obtains the other way
around, from below upwards? While the movement from
above downwards is the movement of conditioning, or even
of healing, that from below upwards is the movement of
differentiation and so of creativity. The basic principle here
is the following: problems in the effective and recurrent
realization of more basic levels of value, especially when
they reach the point of the breakdown of previously functioning schemes, can be solved only by a new differentiation of higher levels of value. The newly differentiated
higher-level values will in turn determine the effective realization of the more basic levels.

Thus: problems in the effective distribution of vital
values to the whole community can be solved by new technological developments, new economic relations, and new
forms of political organization at the level of social values.
But such new social relations can become effectively recurrent only if a change occurs in the cultural values that

determine the community's way of life. This change must
be commensurate with the demands of the social order.
The differentiation of more inclusive and refined cultural
sensitivities, however, calls for a deepening perception, and
perhaps a conversion, of persons in their constitution of
the world, their relations with one another, and themselves
as works of art. And a more sustained pursuit of self-transcendent living is impossible without the continuing transformation of the person that is the work of God's grace at
the core of one's being, and so without the ever further
refinement of religiously differentiated consciousness.

These points enable us to say something further
about the relations that prevail among the elements that
constitute the infrastructure itself: intersubjective spontaneity, technology, the economy, and politics. We have already said that the infrastructure is constituted by the tension of spontaneous intersubjectivity with the technological, economic, and political institutions of a society. So
our main question now is about the relations among technology, the economy, and politics. What will that relation
be when the cultural and social orders are healthy?[32]

The key to answering this question, it seems to me,
has to do with the function of politics. When the integral
scale of values is overruled, legal and political institutions
become the lowest rung of a mendacious superstructure
erected for the preservation of a distorted economic infrastructure, whether capitalist or socialist. The integral scale
of values is neglected when integrity in the creation of a
work of dramatic art gives way to practical expediency.
Then egoistic and group interests predominate in determining the relation of the levels of value and the relation
of the five elements constitutive of society. The first level
of value to suffer, the first element of society to disinte-
grate, is culture. The public determinants of meaning and
value that would arise from the pursuit of the beautiful,

the intelligible, and the true are evacuated from the social scene. They retreat into the margins of society, or become the tools of economic interests. Legal and political institutions take the place of culture as the sources of the public meanings and values governing the society's way of life. And these institutions are themselves now determined by economic interests, so that the meanings and values that govern the way of the society become ultimately economic. Legal and political institutions should be devised to bring about the effective unfolding of a social process arising from the tension of intersubjective groups with technological and economic institutions. Instead these institutions become the instruments of economic interests and distort the process of society in accord with those interests. The function of politics is twisted into an ideological defense mechanism for the interests of social groups. What it should be is the institution whereby the whole society can be persuaded by rational arguments and symbolic example to exist and change in the tension of vital spontaneity and social organization. But when the tension is upset by the predominance of economic expediency, the political slips out of the infrastructure and begins to usurp more and more the functions of culture, becoming a mendacious but quite public determinant of the meanings and values informing the way of life of the society. Then the social order becomes less and less the product of people who have been educated in the pursuit of beauty, intelligibility, and truth; it is the product of a distorted aesthetic consciousness, a perverted intelligence, and an uncritical rationality. Morality and religion follow suit, retreating into the margins of society and becoming merely private concerns. As personal values are thus amputated, the good is rendered inefficacious in the structuring of the cultural and social order. And religious values are either explicitly denied and even forbidden in the public cultural domain, or they are twisted into perverse supports for the distorted culture and society, as in American civil religion.

The key to avoiding these distortions is the reverence that is to be paid to culture that keeps it from becoming proximately practical and expedient. The art and the literature, the narrative and song, the ritual and dance, the science and scholarship, the philosophy and theology, the theater and broadcasting, the journalism and history, the school and university, the personal depth and public opinion[33] that take their stand on integrity and so that generate meanings and values to inform the society's way of life as emergent from the integral pursuit of the beautiful, the intelligible, the true, and the good — these are the proximate sources of infrastructural and general social flourishing. Genuine politics would mediate cultural values to the social infrastructure. It would persuade the infrastructure to a balance of spontaneity and order in keeping with genuine cultural values.

2.2.3.3   *Imperialism*

We said earlier that the actual situation addressed by a contemporary systematic theology is characterized primarily by competing imperialistic systems always bordering on the brink of totalitarianism. The root of imperialism lies in the subordination of the political to economic interests. Yet the first to formulate such a distorted relation between economics and politics, Marx, did not speak of imperialism, and the capitalism of his day was not imperialistic. Hannah Arendt dates the beginning of economic imperialism in the mid-1880s. It is characterized by an economic reality that Marx's theory neither accounts for nor anticipates. Marx anticipated that technological institutions, including human labor power, would become too large and complex and differentiated for economic units of ownership to control. At this point, the conditions for revolution prevail, and economic ownership of the forces of production can slip into new hands that are more complex and organized and that can control the complexity of the forces of production. It can move from private to public ownership. What Marx did not anticipate is that economic units of ownership could become too large and too complex to correspond in a rational fashion with technological institutions, including human labor power, and with the tension between the social order and the intersubjective spontaneity of the groups constituting the society. What happens when that becomes the case, of course, is not revolution but economic imperialism: the extension of the power of economic ownership beyond the society in which it originated, and the exploitation of the forces of production of other societies for the sake of meeting one's own economic interests. Such is the core of imperialism, which is at its roots an economic phenomenon.

2.2.3.4   Global Cultural Values

Two final points must be made with regard to the scale of values. They follow quite smoothly out of what we have already seen.

First, we must address the global nature of the distortions that constitute the situation of the world today. The disease in the relations of the levels of value and in the relations of the elements of society is not confined to a given society. It is global, primarily because of imperialism and its effects. The disease is planetary, and the remedy lies in a properly conceived and responsibly implemented world-cultural alternative. We are already intuitively aware of the global dimensions of the problem. What I want to do is to ground that intuition in the scale of values.

As we have seen, the effective realization of the higher levels of value is the condition of the possibility of the recurrent realization of the more basic levels. But there is also the relation from below upwards, the relation of differentiation and creativity. The maldistribution of particu-

lar goods raises the question that will lead to a more differentiated articulation and even a dramatic transformation of technological, economic, and political institutions.
The need for such a transformation raises the question of
a change in the operative meanings and values that determine the society's way of life. This change may demand a
transformation of persons to a more comprehensive integrity. And this moral and intellectual conversion may depend for its stability on a deeper religious life.

In our contemporary situation, the problem of the
equitable distribution of particular goods, of the recurrent
realization of the most vital human values meeting the most
vital human needs, is clearly global. Facing the problem
demands that we work out and implement a global economic order enabling the operation of technological institutions on a more regional level to meet the demands of
vital spontaneity; and that we create globally effective political institutions embodying the conceptions and exercising the power implied in our notions of global justice.
We will not be able or willing to create globally effective
technological, economic, and political institutions unless
we differentiate public determinants of meaning and value
that regard primarily not the way of life of our regionally
defined and circumscribed societies but the global community of men and women, and so unless our cultural values
are themselves somehow crosscultural. Next, we cannot meet
the challenge of generating crosscultural meanings and values without doing violence to our own cultural roots, unless
we differentiate the crosscultural constituents of human integrity through a new science of human interiority. Generating this science takes a certain kind of moral commitment to
the future of humanity that demands the sacrifice of more
immediate satisfactions. And living from and on the basis of
such a commitment calls for a deepening of the religious
lives of the men and women called to that enterprise.

Again: The breakdown of the distribution of particular goods evokes the question that enables and demands a new differentiation of the social order and so of technology and economics. Today this new order must be global, for the breakdown is global. The breakdown of the good of order evokes the questions that call forth a more differentiated set of cultural meanings and values. Today these must emerge from crosscultural communication and development if they are to effect the global social institutions that are needed to meet the global problem of vital values. Problems regarding the crosscultural integration of previously more regional cultural values evoke the questions that force more exacting discussion of personal integrity and its crosscultural constituents. And the recurring sense of our own incapacity for sustained autonomous integrity, which is only heightened by such explorations as these, sets in motion the pure question that is in effect our supplication for an ever more refined and purified religious orientation. This religious orientation will ground the personal integrity needed for the collaboration that will establish genuine cultural values for a global human community. These values will affect the infrastructure through the political specialization of common sense, whose function it is to persuade the community to the needed economic and technological changes that can meet the demands of the intersubjective groups of a global humanity for the satisfaction of their most vital needs.

2.2.3.5   *The Preferential Option for the Poor*

My final point has to do with the same structure, and unfolds another of its implications. My argument in effect constitutes a defense, perhaps even a grounding, from the standpoint of a transcendental anthropology, for the insight of liberation theologians regarding the hermeneutically privileged position for theology of the most grievously oppressed peoples of our globe, and regarding the

preferential option for the poor that must govern the
church's exercise of all of its ministry. The situation that I
have attempted to portray is one affected by the distortions of the integral scale of values, disrupting the relation
between the social infrastructure and the cultural superstructure that would obtain if subjects in community were
faithful to the task of dramatic artistry. Culture has either
retreated into an ivory tower or has been made proximately
practical. The political takes the place of culture in the
superstructure, becoming the principal conscious determinant of the public meanings and values of the society.
Politics is diverted from its authentic task of mediating
cultural values to the economic and technological structures so as to forge them in line with the demands of dramatically artistic living. The economic system has been
diverted from its proper task of regulating technological
structures so as recurrently to provide the whole community with the materials to be forged into a work of art. The
economic system has become instead the preserve of the
advantaged. The consequence is a massive oppression of
the disadvantaged that has become global, just as the reach
of economic imperialism has become global. From below
upwards, then, it is global injustice that most basically structures the situation in which we find ourselves, and that
provides the final criterion for the adequacy of any
alternative. Consequently, if the new cultural values that
are generated are not endowed with the capacity for evoking a global horizon for economic justice, they are not the
cultural values demanded by the situation that confronts
us today.

3   Conclusion

Much could and eventually must be said about the
constitution of the needed cultural values. Space permits

me only to refer the reader to the suggestions that I have previously made regarding the integration of the cosmological, anthropological, and soteriological insights of various human cultures of the past.[34] Let me conclude with the simple reminder that the church, commissioned as it is to be the bearer of soteriological truth, will be faithful to its commission only to the extent that it embodies in its members, its communities, and its ministries the law of the cross through which the servant of God fills up in his or her own body what is lacking in the sufferings of Christ, neither wavering nor being crushed until true justice is established on the earth. Such is the priestly vocation of the church, and such alone is the fulfillment of authentic presbyteral ministry. The divine and only solution to the mystery of evil will never cease to encounter 'men clear-sighted enough to grasp that the issue is between God and man, logical enough to grant that intelligence and reason are orientated toward God, ruthless enough to summon to their aid the dark forces of passion and of violence.'[35]

> By force and by law he was taken; would any-
> one plead his cause? Yes, he was torn away from
> the land of the living; for our faults struck down
> in death. They gave him a grave with the wicked,
> a tomb with the rich, though he had done no
> wrong and there had been no perjury in his
> mouth. God has been pleased to crush him with
> suffering. If he offers his life in atonement, he
> shall see his heirs, he shall have a long life, and
> through him what God wishes will be done.
> His soul's anguish over, he shall see the light
> and be content. By his sufferings shall my
> servant justify many, taking their faults on him-
> self. Hence I will grant whole hordes for his
> tribute, he shall divide the spoil with the mighty,
> for surrendering himself to death and letting

himself be taken for a sinner, while he was bearing the faults of many and praying all the time for sinners. (Isaiah 53.8-12)

Notes

[1] Bernard Lonergan, *Insight* (see above, chapter 1, note 20) 229/254.

[2] Hannah Arendt, *The Origins of Totalitarianism* (New York: Harcourt, Brace, Jovanovich, 1972) viii.

[3] Ibid. ix.

[4] Bernard Lonergan, *De Verbo Incarnato* (see above, chapter 1, note 25) 552-93.

[5] Eric Voegelin, *Israel and Revelation* (see above, chapter 1, note 8) 491.

[6] Ibid. 501.

[7] Ibid. 506.

[8] Ibid. 507.

[9] Ibid.

[10] Ibid. 512.

[11] Ibid. 515.

[12] Ibid.

[13] Lonergan, *Insight* 723-24/744-45.

[14] David Tracy, *The Analogical Imagination* (New York: Crossroad, 1981) 6-14.

15 Lonergan, *Insight* 212/237-38.

16 Ibid. 208/234.

17 Tracy, *The Analogical Imagination* 7.

18 Clifford Geertz, *The Interpretation of Cultures* (New York: Basic Books, 1973) 89.

19 Lonergan, *Insight* 228/253.

20 Bernard Lonergan, 'Healing and Creating in History' (see above, chapter 3, note 7) 106.

21 See Lonergan, *Insight* 218/243.

22 Lewis Mumford, *The Transformations of Man* (see above, chapter 1, note 6) 120-36.

23 Arendt, *The Origins of Totalitarianism* 327.

24 Ibid. 322.

25 Quoted in Fred Lawrence, 'Political Theology and "The Longer Cycle of Decline," *Lonergan Workshop* 1, ed. Fred Lawrence (Scholars Press, 1978) 239.

26 Bernard Lonergan, *Method in Theology* (see above, chapter 1, note 1) 31-32.

27 My understanding of Marx has been greatly influenced by John McMurtry, *The Structure of Marx's World-view* (Princeton, NJ: Princeton University Press, 1978).

28 See Lonergan, *Insight* 472-75/497-99.

29 See McMurtry, *The Structure of Marx's World-view* 171-87.

30 Alvin W. Gouldner, *The Dialectic of Ideology and Technology: The Origins, Grammar, and Future of Ideology* (New York: Seabury, 1976) 15-16.

^{31} 1993 note: I subsequently modified this position, to include the everyday level of cultural values in the infrastructure. It is the reflective level of cultural values that constitutes the superstructure.

^{32} Note the importance of putting the question this way. When one starts with diseased entities, one risks erecting facts into laws, as Marx did with society and Freud with the psyche.

^{33} See Lonergan, *Insight* 241/266.

^{34} See Robert M. Doran, 'Theological Grounds for a World-cultural Humanity' (above, chapter 6).

^{35} Lonergan, *Insight* 729/750.

8 Theology's Situation: Questions to Eric Voegelin

I do not consider myself an expert in the thought of Eric Voegelin. But I have found myself deeply enriched, instructed, and challenged by many of his writings, especially the four presently available volumes of *Order and History*.[1] In the present paper, however, I hope not so much to specify the precise influence of Voegelin on my own work as to outline the development of that work to date and to employ that outline as a point of departure for dialogue with Voegelin and his students. The positive influence that Voegelin's work has had on my own will be apparent in the outline.

My work to date is a series of preliminary investigations anticipating a contemporary systematic theology. These prior investigations have not yet come to an end, but the general contours are already apparent. The work is an exercise in the theological functional specialty 'foundations.'[2] It offers a heuristic structure for understanding three distinct but interrelated dialectical processes constitutive of the situation which a systematic theology addresses, where that situation is in general a matter of the dialectic of authenticity and inauthenticity. These processes are the dialectic of the subject, the dialectic of community, and the dialectic of culture. Each process is a dialectic because it is an unfolding of linked but opposed principles of change.[3] But the overall dialectic of authenticity and inauthenticity is a dialectic of contradictories: it is resolved only by a choice between alternatives. And the dialectics of the subject, of community, and of culture are dialectics of contraries: both poles must be affirmed, each in its proper place. In a dialectic of contraries, the condition of the possibility of an *integral* dialectic lies in a third principle that stands above the two principles internally constitutive of the dialectic. The distortion of the dialectic of contraries through the ascendancy of one of its two internally constitutive principles is rooted in the maldevelopment or breakdown of this third, synthetic principle, and results in inauthenticity, as contradictory to the authenticity constituted by the integral dialectic of contraries.

Thus the dialectic of the subject is internally constituted by the two principles of neural demand functions and dramatically patterned intelligence,[4] and the condition of its integrity is an adequate and in the last analysis universal antecedent willingness.[5] The dialectic of community is internally constituted by spontaneous intersubjectivity and practical intelligence,[6] and the condition of its integrity is culture.[7] And the dialectic of culture itself is internally constituted by cosmological and anthropological basic assumptions of meaning and value informing given ways of life, and the condition of its integrity is a differentiated soteriological vector that moves from above downwards in human consciousness.[8] Each dialectic of contraries is an instance of the tension of limitation and transcendence constitutive of all genuine development in the universe.[9] Neural demand functions, spontaneous intersubjectivity, and cosmological insights are the principles of limitation in the respective dialectics of the subject, community, and culture; and dramatically patterned intelligence, practical intelligence, and the anthropological principle are the respective principles of transcendence. Willingness, culture, and the soteriological differentiation of consciousness are higher syntheses conditioning the possibility of integrity in the respective dialectics of contraries. The dialectic of contradictories has ultimately to do with the integrity or disintegration of these higher syntheses.

The situation to be addressed by any systematic theology mediating not *in oratione obliqua* from the past into the present but *in oratione recta* from the present into the future is constituted by the actually functioning relations among these dialectics. The dialectic of culture, moreover, operates on two levels: a spontaneous level of everyday transactions, which this dialectic shares with the dialectics of the subject and of society, and a reflexive level of scholarly and scientific objectification, which reflects, among other things, on all three everyday dialectics. From a normative point of view, the everyday functioning of the three dialectics in their relations with one another constitutes the infrastructure of the situation, and the reflexive objectifications the superstructure. When this relationship of infrastructure and superstructure is upset, the situation is distorted. For then something that belongs in the infrastructure usurps the prerogatives of the superstructural level of culture.

Theology is superstructural. Through the use of special theological categories, it mediates the meanings and values constitutive of Christian witness, fellowship, and service with the (sometimes dialectically reoriented) general categories that theology shares with other superstructural disciplines.[10] The mediation is a matter not of correlation, as erroneously presupposed by many contemporary theological methodologies,[11] but of creative systematic construction. It is conducted in an atmosphere of interdisciplinary collaboration. It is governed by foundational reflection on converted interiority. And it heads toward a basic science of humanity, of which theology is but a part, and which is concerned not only with the understanding, but also with the making, of history.[12] The foundations of the mediation lie in interiorly differentiated consciousness, which is the source of the derivation and purification especially of the general categories but also, when extended to include religious and Christian self-appropriation, of the special categories.[13]

The first phase of my work was concerned with the dialectic of the subject. I have recently completed the initial stage of a study of the dialectic of community, and am only beginning to work out the dynamics of the dialectic of culture. It is with this third dialectic that the work of Eric Voegelin may prove to be most provocative of insight. But his writings have helped me to understand better what I was doing in my work on the dialectic of the subject, and have posed the central problem with which I had to deal in my reflections on the dialectic of community.

1   The Dialectic of the Subject

My work on the dialectic of the subject, I realized after reading Voegelin, is geared to providing among other things the basis for what he calls a psychology of orientations as opposed to a psychology of passional motivations. A psychology of orientations is 'a science of the healthy psyche, in the Platonic sense, in which the order of the soul is created by transcendental orientation.' A psychology of passional motivation is a 'science of the disoriented psyche which must be ordered by a balance of motivations.' It is incomplete, 'in so far as it deals only with a certain pneumopathological type of man.'[14] More precisely, I have attempted to articulate the reorienting influence of the intentionality analysis of Bernard Lonergan on the science of the sensitive psyche, and then to argue that this reoriented science — reoriented from a psychology of motivations to a psychology of orientations — complements the intentionality analysis from which it is derived, by providing a further dimension of interiorly differentiated consciousness. Such an articulation implies, I believe, a differentiation of the Greek *psyche*, employed interchangeably by Voegelin as 'soul' or 'psyche,' into transcendentally oriented intentionality and the sensitive psyche.

The basis for the reorientation of the science of the psyche I found in the recognition by Lonergan in his post-1965 writings of the existence and indeed primacy of a fourth level of intentional consciousness that is distinct from the three levels uncovered in the cognitional analysis of *Insight*. Existential consciousness governs the authenticity of the empirical, intellectual, and rational levels of consciousness, and sublates them into its own concern for world-constitutive and self-constitutive praxis. The fourth level of consciousness is a notion of value. It intends the human good, which is a concrete process, at once individual and social, and which consists in the making of human history, the flowering of human authenticity, the fulfillment of human affectivity, and the direction of human labor to a good of order and to particular goods that are really and not just apparently worth while.[15] These potential values are apprehended in intentional feelings,[16] which themselves function in a relationship of reciprocal evocation with symbols: 'A symbol is an image of a real or imaginary object that evokes a feeling or is evoked by a feeling.'[17] Existential self-appropriation, the understanding, knowledge, and self-conscious orientation of the subject as a deliberating, evaluating, deciding subject can, I concluded, be greatly aided by employing these relations among symbols, feelings, and values, and so by using one's spontaneously produced symbolic manifestations as a clue to insight into the intentional feelings that themselves are revelatory of one's spontaneous preferential scale of values.[18]

The scale of values is determined in accord with a criterion of self-transcendence.

> Not only do feelings respond to values. They do so in accord with some scale of preference. So we may distinguish vital, social, cultural, personal, and religious values in an ascending order. Vital values, such as health and strength, grace and vigor, normally are preferred to avoiding the work, privations, pains involved in acquiring, maintaining, restoring them. Social values, such as the good of order which conditions the vital values of the whole community, have to be preferred to the vital values of individual members of the community. Cultural values do not exist without the underpinning of vital and social values, but none the less they rank higher. Not on bread alone doth man live. Over and above mere living and operating men have to find a meaning and value in their living and operating. It is the function of culture to discover, express, validate, criticize, correct, develop, improve such meaning and value. Personal value is the person in his self-transcendence, as loving and being loved, as originator of values in himself and in his milieu, as an inspiration and invitation to others to do likewise. Religious values, finally, are at the heart of the meaning and value of man's living and man's world.[19]

A psychic conversion that establishes a working commerce between neural demand functions and dramatically patterned intentional consciousness can enable a subject intent on existential self-knowledge to ascertain, and to participate in guiding and orienting, the development of his or her spontaneous scale of value preferences.[20]

The commerce of neural demand functions and intentional consciousness is dialectical, where a dialectic is conceived as 'a concrete unfolding of linked but opposed principles of change.'[21] Dramatically patterned imagination and intelligence operate preconsciously in the selection of images for insight, and of their concomitant affects. They function as a censorship over neural demands for psychic representations. The censorship can be either constructive or repressive. It is constructive if it

> ... selects and arranges materials that emerge in consciousness in a perspective that gives rise to an insight; this positive activity has by implication a negative aspect, for other materials are left behind, and other perspectives are not brought to light; still, this negative aspect of positive activity does not introduce any arrangement or perspective into the unconscious demand functions of neural patterns and processes.[22]

The censorship is repressive if

> ... its positive activity is to prevent the emergence into consciousness of perspectives that would give rise to unwanted insights; it introduces, so to speak, the exclusion of arrangements into the field of the unconscious; it dictates the manner in which neural demand functions are not to be met; and the negative aspect of its positive activity is the admission to consciousness of any materials in any other arrangement or perspective.[23]

The dialectic is described as follows:

The contents and affects emerging into consciousness provide the requisite aggregate of events of a determinate kind; these events originate from two principles, namely, neural demand functions and the exercise of the constructive or repressive censorship; the two principles are linked as patterned and patterning; they are opposed inasmuch as the censorship not only constructs but also represses, and again inasmuch as a misguided censorship results in neglected neural demands forcing their way into consciousness; finally, change is cumulative, for the orientation of the censorship at any time and the neural demands to be met both depend on the past history of the stream of consciousness.[24]

Voegelin has called our attention to the need of developing a vocabulary for understanding, not psychopathology, but pneumopathology: 'spiritual disease has never been made the object of systematic inquiry and no suitable vocabulary has been developed for its description.'[25] In this regard, the instructive point about the heuristic structure that Lonergan offers for understanding and appropriating psychic processes lies in the dialectical relationship of neural demand functions and dramatically oriented *intentionality* at the ground of the events that constitute the experience of the sensitive psyche. The key issue is what one *wants*. There is an aberration of understanding resultant upon the love of darkness. The issue is one of *willingness*, which is more radically a spiritual orientation than it is a psychic state of affairs.

Effective freedom itself has to be won. The key point is to reach a willingness to persuade oneself and to submit to the persuasion of others. For then one can be persuaded to a universal willingness; so one becomes antecedently willing to learn all there is to be learnt about willing and learning and about the enlargement of one's freedom from external constraints and psychoneural interferences. But to reach the universal willingness that matches the unrestricted desire to know is indeed a high achievement, for it consists not in the mere recognition of an ideal norm but in the adoption of an attitude towards the universe of being, not in the adoption of an affective attitude that would desire but not perform but in the adoption of an effective attitude in which performance matches aspiration.[26]

Within such a perspective, psychotherapy should be conceived regulatively as the enlargement of one's effective freedom from the psychoneural interferences that block one's performance as a self-transcending attentive, intelligent, rational, and morally responsible person. Real therapy of the psyche, then, is an extension of an ever greater antecedent willingness into the domain of the neural demand functions themselves. The movement of conversion to willingness is a movement from above downwards in consciousness,[27] and so is radically a therapy of pneumopathology before it becomes one of psychopathology. Moreover, the science of the sensitive psyche must be grounded in an explanatory objectification of the exigences of the notions of intelligibility, truth, being, and value that constitute the perennial and transcultural structure of the human spirit. In this regard at least, then, my attempts to date to reorient the science of depth psychology on the basis of Lonergan's intentionality analysis are also attempts to meet Voegelin's call for 'a science of the healthy psyche, … in which the order of the soul is created by transcendental orientation.'

That transcendental orientation, of course, is for Voegelin ultimately the orientation to the divine ground. My own reliance on Lonergan is in accord with this insistence. 'There is to human inquiry an unrestricted demand for intelligibility. There is to human judgment a demand for the unconditioned. There is to human deliberation a criterion that criticizes every finite good. So it is … that man can reach basic fulfillment, peace, joy, only by moving beyond the realms of common sense, theory, and interiority and into the realm in which God is known and loved.'[28] The sensitive psyche participates in the dynamism of transcendentally oriented intentionality.

In my efforts to articulate the function of the psyche as what Voegelin would call a sensorium of transcendence,[29] I have engaged in a fundamental critique of Jungian archetypal psychology, arguing principally that Jung's notion of archetypal symbols suffers from the same limitations that Voegelin finds characteristic of the cosmological symbolization to which the archetypes in fact correspond. 'Not much is really clear beyond the experience of participation and the quaternarian structure of the field of being, and such partial clearness tends to generate confusion rather than order, as is bound to happen when variegated materials are classified under too few heads.'[30] In fact, Jungian immanentism clouds even the experience of participation in being, incurs the danger of the inflated self-assertion that, I fear, is the ultimate meaning of Jung's work, and reduces the cosmological quaternarian field (gods and humans, world and society) to a matter of the self-enclosed psychological functions of thinking, feeling, sensation, and intuition. Jung is correct in disengaging a dimension of transpersonal symbolization which he calls archetypal, a dimension not accounted for in Freudian psychoanalysis. But transpersonal symbolization is itself twofold. Archetypal symbols — a term to which I assign a less inclusive connotation than does Jung — are taken from nature and imitate nature, thus manifesting the participation of psyche and organism in cosmic rhythms and processes, and providing access to the retrieval through interiorly differentiated consciousness of the partial truth of the cosmological societies. Anagogic symbols, however, even when taken from nature as in some eschatological symbolizations, manifest either the anthropological principle that our transcendental orientation to the divine is the measure of the order of the soul, and the order of the soul the measure of society,[31] or the soteriological truth of existence in Christ Jesus, existence redeemed from the distorted dialectic of the subject and invited then to participate in the redemptive law of the cross. (The latter truth, I believe, is not sufficiently differentiated by Voegelin from the anthropological principle that reached its first clear articulation in Greek philosophy. We will see more of this later, when we discuss the dialectic of culture. For the moment, it is sufficient to indicate that the antecedent willingness that is the condition of the possibility of an integral dialectic of the subject is a fruit of this soteriological vector in human consciousness, whether this soteriological vector be expressly acknowledged as such or not.)

There is one further aspect of Voegelin's thought that will prove helpful to me in any future work that I do on the dialectic of the subject. It emerges most clearly in 'The Beginning of the Beginning,' and it has to do with the dialectic — for Voegelin, paradox — of consciousness as at once intentionality and luminosity.[32] It is this dialectic (of contraries) that in a way lies at the origin of my attempts to complement Lonergan's work with an articulation of psychic conversion. These attempts began with a question regarding the relations between the later Heidegger and the early Lonergan. I have not yet reflected enough on Voegelin's thoughts regarding this dialectic of consciousness to say more than that I suspect that psychic conversion and Lonergan's intellectual conversion might represent the means of retrieving, respectively, and in interiorly differentiated consciousness, Voegelin's consciousness as luminosity and his consciousness as intentionality. Voegelin's insistence on consciousness as luminosity represents, I believe, a valuable complement to Lonergan's analysis of intentionality; but students of Voegelin who desire greater precision on consciousness as intentionality should turn to Lonergan, whose objectification of this dimension of consciousness is unparalleled in accuracy, clarity and explanatory power, and, incidentally, bears remarkable resemblances to Voegelin's retrieval of the classic experience of reason.[33]

2   The Dialectic of Community

'Society' is a generic term embracing five interrelated elements: spontaneous intersubjectivity, technological institutions, an economic structure, the polity, and culture. Culture has two levels: the everyday and the reflexive. The source of technological institutions, the economic structure, and the polity lies in practical intelligence. The actually functioning relations among these elements determine the health or pathology of a society. As my work on the dialectic of the subject was concerned with the constitution of the healthy psyche, so my reflections on the dialectic of society have an equally normative purpose, and so are geared toward a regulative and heuristic understanding of the constitution of a healthy society. The work on the dialectic of the subject was a matter of implementing Lonergan's transcendental method so that it grounds a reoriented science of psychic sensitivity; that on the dialectic of community implements the same method to ground a reoriented science, or set of sciences, of society. The dialectic of community, as we learn from Lonergan, is internally constituted by the two linked but opposed principles of human intersubjectivity and the commonsense practicality that is responsible for technological institutions, the economic structure, and the legal and political arrangements of a society. The dialectic is integral when the changes resulting from these two principles take account of and keep pace with one another. It is distorted to the extent that either principle gains the ascendancy in the determination of these changes. The condition of an integral dialectic of community lies in neither principle itself but in culture: infrastructurally, in the meanings and values that inform everyday transactions, and superstructurally, in the reflexive objectifications of these meanings and values in the various human sciences, in philosophy, and in theology. The integrity of culture, in turn, is grounded in the 'dimension of consciousness' that Lonergan calls cosmopolis: a dimension that is 'neither class nor state, that stands above all their claims, that cuts them down to size, that is founded on the native detachment and disinterestedness of every intelligence, that commands man's first allegiance, that implements itself primarily through that allegiance, that is too universal to be bribed, too impalpable to be forced, too effective to be ignored.'[34] From such a 'dimension of consciousness, a heightened grasp of historical origins, a discovery of historical responsibilities,' there can emerge 'an art and a literature, a theatre and a broadcasting, a journalism and a history, a school and a university, a personal depth and a public opinion, that through appreciation and criticism give men of common sense the opportunity and help they need and desire to correct the general bias of their common sense.'[35] For that general bias is the radical source especially of the distortions of the integral dialectic of community that prevail in the current situation.

General bias distorts the dialectic of intersubjectivity and practicality in the direction of practicality. It is more radically disintegrative of society than is the group bias that displaces the dialectic in the direction of intersubjectivity, for it generates a longer cycle of decline. The cycle promoted by group bias generates its own reversal more quickly, for the practical ideas excluded or mutilated by powerful groups are championed later by the disadvantaged, whose sentiments 'can be crystallized into militant force by the crusading of a reformer or a revolutionary,'[36] while the reversal of the cycle generated primarily by general bias depends on implementing 'ideas to which all groups are rendered indifferent'[37] by the pretensions of practical shortsightedness to the imperious omnicompetence of instrumentalized rationality. Such ideas include those 'that suppose a long view or that set up higher integrations or that involve the solution of intricate and disputed issues,'[38] and so that demand the subordination of common sense to a higher specialization of human intelligence. That higher specialization, which is at once theological, philosophic, and human-scientific, is grounded in 'the discovery, the logical expansion, and the recognition of the principle that intelligence contains its own immanent norms and that these norms are equipped with sanctions which man does not have to invent or impose.'[39] This principle is implemented on the superstructural level of culture by developing an empirical, critical, and normative human science, where 'empirical' includes preeminently taking account of the data of consciousness, and on the everyday level in the cultural values that would sustain and support the integral dialectic of intelligence and intersubjectivity. Cosmopolis has a responsibility for the integrity of culture on both levels. It fails to meet this responsibility on the superstructural level to the extent that it sanctions the subordination of human science to the biased intelligence of those that produced the presently available data. It fails on the everyday level if it does not resist the deterioration of culture into 'a factor within the technological, economic, political process, ... a tool that serve[s] palpably useful ends'; and to the extent that it does not promote culture as 'an independent factor that passes a detached yet effective judgment upon capital formation and technology, upon economy and polity.'[40]

The relations among the constitutive elements of society can be further understood, I have found, if we reflect in more detail on the scale of values mentioned in the previous section. The levels of value are related to each other in a number of ways. Among these sets of relations I would posit two that are particularly germane to the present discussion: a relation of differentiation and creativity that obtains from below upwards, and a relation of conditioning and enablement that obtains from above downwards. From below, problems in the recurrent realization of values at a lower level can frequently be solved only by the creation of new arrangements at a higher level. Thus, a breakdown of the equitable distribution of vital values to the whole community can at times be solved only by the creation at the level of social values of new technological realities, or by the adjustment of the economic system, or by a change at the level of law or politics. Moreover, it may be the case that the changes demanded at this level of social values are so extensive as to demand the differentiation and implementation of transformed cultural values, at either the everyday or the reflexive level of culture, or at both. These changes may themselves be so demanding as to require a conversion to greater personal integrity on the part of persons who would be originating values. And personal integrity cannot be sustained without the effective operation of and cooperation with divine grace, and so without a deepening and more pervasive religious conversion.

These relations of creativity and differentiation from below upwards obviously imply a set of relations of conditioning and enablement from above downwards. Religious values condition the possibility of personal integrity. Personal integrity conditions the possibility of a culture that neither retreats into an ivory tower nor capitulates to imperious practicality. Such a culture conditions the possibility of the integral dialectic of community in the establishment of the good of order. And this dialectic conditions the possibility of the effective and recurrent distribution of vital values to the whole community. Within the dialectic of community itself, moreover, the elements emergent from commonsense practicality — technology, the economy, and the polity — are related in a similar fashion. The problem of a recurrent realization of particular goods evokes technology or capital formation, technology evokes the economy, and the economy evokes the polity;[41] but technology is for the sake of meeting recurrent vital desires, the economy is for the sake of the effective functioning of the technological system, and politics is for the sake of the integral dialectic between economic and technological arrangements, on the one hand, and intersubjective spontaneity on the other hand.

The position just enunciated differs on several counts from the Marxist one. First, Marx located the basic dialectic of society as a dialectic ultimately of contradictions within practicality — namely, between technology (the forces of production) and the economy (the relations of production), whereas Lonergan has articulated it as a dialectic of contraries between practicality and intersubjectivity. Second, this difference implies a subordination of practicality to the dramatic constitution of the human world as a work of art. Third, this subordination implies the possibility of genuine and autonomous integrity at the level of culture, and the responsibility of culture for the integrity of the dialectic of community. Fourth, the legal and political domains constitute an element of the infrastructure, not of the superstructure of society. The superstructure is constituted by the reflexive level of culture. When the normative scale of values is respected, culture is not an ideological domain created for the conscious but mendacious representation of the underlying conflict between forces and relations of production, but is a pursuit of the meanings and values that, among other things, will develop the human capacities by which the integral dialectic of community can be preserved or restored. The genuine function of politics is not to guarantee, by ideology, the capitulation of practical intelligence to group ethos or of speculative intelligence to instrumental practicality, but, on the contrary, to persuade individuals and groups to subordinate and adapt their vital spontaneities to genuinely practical ideas and to persuade the proponents of these ideas to respect the legitimate demands of individual and group spontaneity. Finally, and most radically, my position differs from the Marxist one in the role it assigns to the possibility and significance of personal integrity sustained and deepened by God's grace.

The relations that I have posited among the levels of value may be employed, I believe, as a means of understanding and discussing some of the problems that arise in contemporary political philosophy. These problems, in turn, force a further clarification of the integrity of the scale of values itself. In both of these areas, moreover, questions for dialogue with Eric Voegelin arise.

Liberal democratic and Marxist political philosophies share in common one structural feature that is illuminated

by the scale of values: in them there is found either a neg-
ligence of or a skepticism regarding the autonomy of religious, personal, and cultural values, and so a tendency to
collapse the effectively operative scale into the two more
basic levels of social and vital values. When this neglect
affects the actual workings of a liberal or Marxist society,
legal and political institutions slip out of the infrastructure
and become the lowest rung, as it were, of a mendacious
superstructural edifice erected for the sake of preserving a
distorted dialectic of community in which intersubjectivity
is neglected in its autonomous capacity as a formative principle of society and is twisted through group bias into becoming an ally of a practicality distorted by general bias.
Legal and political dimensions of society are then determined by economic relations rather than devised to effect
the unfolding of an integral dialectic between these relations and intersubjective groups. Politics should be the
infrastructural institution whereby the whole community
can be persuaded by rational argument and symbolic example to exist and change in the tension of the opposites
of vital spontaneity and practical ideation and decision.
Under the dominance of a group bias conscripted by general bias, however, it becomes rather an instrument of the
distortion of the dialectic through a displacement of that
tension. Slipping out of the infrastructure, it becomes a
mendacious determinant of the meanings and values that
inform the way of life of segments of the community. Thus
it usurps the prerogatives of culture. The public determinants of meaning and value that would arise from the pursuit of the beautiful, the intelligible, the true, and the good
are evacuated from the cultural scene. They retreat into
the margins of society. The effective culture becomes merely
an instrument of distorted practicality. The superstructure
becomes a surd when the political specialization, defaulting on its legitimate and necessary infrastructural func-

tion, invades the domain of culture. Genuine culture surrenders its function of autonomously determining the
meanings and values that, through political integrity, would
otherwise govern the economy and the institutions of technology as dialectical counterparts of spontaneous
intersubjectivity. The meanings and values that govern the
way of life of the society become nothing more than the
projections of a distorted social dialectic. As culture retreats, morality and religion follow suit. The good, which
is the objective that guides and orders the pursuit of the
true, the intelligible, and the beautiful, is rendered inefficacious in the structuring of the cultural and social order.
Religious values are either explicitly denied and even forbidden in the public domain, as in some Marxist states, or
twisted into perverse supports for the distorted culture and
society, as in American civil religion. The entire structure
is upset by the derailment of the political, a derailment
rooted in the loss of the tension between practicality and
intersubjectivity which it is the responsibility of culture to
inform and of politics to implement. Only the integrity of
a culture that refuses to become proximately practical and
expedient, yet that insists on remaining on the scene, can
prevent such distortions from taking place.

If this is the upshot of liberal and Marxist political
philosophies, classically inspired political philosophies,
while they stress the integrity of culture and at times, as
with Voegelin, of the personal and religious levels of values
as well, exhibit a problem contrary to that of the liberal
and Marxist positions: namely, a truncation or relative
neglect of the two more basic levels of value. Their acknowledgment of questions of distributive justice and the
economic order is by and large negative: they criticize with
great acumen the pretensions of liberal and Marxist ideologies to promote the just social order to which they claim
to be devoted; but they neglect the extent to which their

own oversight of the constitutive function of vital and social values in the entire scale of values can render the classical tradition susceptible to an unwitting conscription by
default or retreat into especially the liberal distortions of
the dialectic of community. More precisely, while classically inspired political philosophies correctly affirm that
the social order is a derivative of operative cultural values
and that the latter are conditioned by personal integrity or
the lack thereof, and thus while they display a sensitivity
to the relations that obtain from above downwards among
the levels of value, they do not recognize that the relations
from below upwards may call for more than a reaffirmation of the cultural values of the classical tradition. Perhaps these values, however necessary they may be, must
today be sublated into an entirely new horizon that institutes a quite novel set of cultural values commensurate
with the dimensions of the social problem.

The crucial link in the scale of values vis-à-vis the
difficulties contained in both liberal and Marxist political
philosophies, on the one hand, and in classically inspired
political philosophies, on the other hand, has to do with
the relations of reflexively objectified culture, that is, of
the superstructure, to the entire infrastructure of everyday
cultural values, politics, the economy, technology, and
spontaneous intersubjectivity. The opposed tendencies
manifest that the relations of religious, personal, and cultural values among themselves and the relations between
social and vital values are easier to grasp and affirm than
are either the relations of the three higher levels to the two
more basic levels or the relations within culture itself between the superstructure and the everyday. A political
philosophy must be created which, while maintaining the
permanent validity of the classical tradition, sublates this
tradition into a higher synthesis characterized as well by a
concern for the questions, though not the solutions, of
liberalism and Marxism.

The distortions instituted by liberalism and Marxism provide the very conditions for developing such a philosophy. For, precisely as a result of the skewed dialectic of community sponsored by the competing and escalating imperialisms of late capitalism and state socialism, these distortions are now global, and in a systemic fashion. The relations from below upwards among the levels of value begin with a global maldistribution of vital goods that can be rectified only by a new global network of if-then relationships at the levels of technological institutions, economic systems, and political relations. The need for a globally accepted social order can be met only if crossculturally generated cultural values are established to insure the integrity of the social dialectic on a global scale. These values must be elaborated by cosmopolitan collaboration at the superstructural level, but they must be effective as well at the everyday level of culture. The means for elaborating them lie in the appropriation, philosophic reference specification, and integration of the various regionally inherited cultural values that constitute the human heritage. Such an enormous task of cosmopolitan collaboration, however, will depend for its integrity on the appropriation through interiorly differentiated consciousness of the transcultural psychic and intentional constituents of authentic human participation in the search for direction in the movement of life. And this transformation at the level of personal value will itself depend upon both the clarification and the enrichment of authentic religiosity that is demanded if the entire task is to succeed. Central to this development will be dialogue and cooperation among the major religions of the world.

The link between superstructure and infrastructure, and that between cultural values in general and the social order, are reestablished in such a perspective. The global nature of the contemporary exigence for social order calls for the development of a new set of cultural values as the condition of the possibility of a just social order, where justice is a function of the integral dialectic of spontaneous intersubjectivity and practical intelligence. When the social order becomes global, cultural values must become world-cultural, if minds and hearts are to be equal to the tasks set by the conditions of global technological, economic, and political interdependence. A problem at a lower level of value is not to be met simply by mere restructuring at that level nor even by a retrieval of traditional cultural values unmediated by attention to the concrete infrastructural realities that set the context of the problem in the first place.

It is important at this point to distinguish our anticipations of a world-cultural humanity from the various tendencies that for Voegelin constitute the modern gnosticisms. Whether they be intellectual or political in nature, the gnosticisms immanentize the teleological and axiological components of Christian hope.[42] Immanentizing the teleological constitutes progressivism, immanentizing the axiological constitutes secular utopianism, and immanentizing both constitutes the activist mysticism deriving from Comte and Marx. As we will see in more detail in the next section, our anticipation of a world-cultural network of communities not only does not immanentize Christian eschatology, but takes its stand on the world-transcendent objective of Christian hope. Moreover, while the gnosticisms tend to reflect a less differentiated spirituality than that which can be discovered in the classical and Christian sources of Western civilization, our anticipation of an ecumenic consciousness entails the advancing differentiation brought about by intellectual and psychic self-appropriation. Finally, while the gnosticisms are meant to become mass movements, our anticipation recognizes the difference between the fuller realization of ecumenic consciousness in cosmopolitan explanatory self-appropriation and the everyday post-interiority transformations brought about by successful communication on the part of the cosmopolitan minority, and sharply distinguishes its own vision of a global network of communities living in accord with the integral scale of values from the mass movements catalyzed by the *libido dominandi*.

Nonetheless, one critical comment regarding Voegelin's understanding of the modern gnosticisms is in order. He says:

> No matter to which of the three variants of immanentization the movements belong, the attempt to create a new world is common to all. This endeavor can be meaningfully undertaken only if the constitution of being can in fact be altered by man. The world, however, remains as it is given to us, and it is not within man's power to change its structure.[43]

While we have reason for dissatisfaction with the world in which we live, nonetheless, says Voegelin, besides attributing our dissatisfaction to the intrinsic drawbacks of the situation, 'it is likewise possible to assume that the order of being as it is given to us men (wherever its origin is to be sought) is good and that it is we human beings who are inadequate.'[44]

Surely a distinction is in order here, one that would advance the positions and reverse the counterpositions in the modern gnosticisms. From the ontology implicit in many of the modern gnosticisms can be drawn the insight that is constitutive of modern historical consciousness in general: the human world, mediated and constituted by meaning and motived by value, is the product of human insights, judgments, and decisions. Human praxis *is* constitutive of being: not originatively creative of its elemental structure, but responsibly constitutive of the character of the human world as good or evil. The real human world as it is and the good human world as it ought to be are not coincident. In the world mediated by meaning, the notions of being and of value are not coincident. Surely the movement from the real human world as it is to the good human world as it ought to be is grounded in a transformation of ourselves; but self-constitution is coincident with world constitution. A philosophy of world-constitutive praxis need not violate the order of the soul masterfully disengaged in Voegelin's retrieval of classical sources. The conversion positions on praxis characteristic of classically inspired political philosophies and the world-transformation positions present but counterpositionally formulated in the modern gnosticisms can be integrated with one another by forcing the meaning of the integral scale of values as a guide to authentic praxis itself. The implications of this will be most evident in the exigence that emerges for the development of crossculturally generated cultural values to inform a global social order constituted by the integral dialectic of community.

3   The Dialectic of Culture

In this section I am merely stating in very rudimentary and hypothetical fashion a quite recent insight that emerged from several years of considering what Voegelin has written about cosmological, anthropological, and (to a far less extensive degree) soteriological symbolizations of the experience of order. The insight is this: as there is a dialectic of the subject between neural demands and dramatically patterned intentional consciousness, a dialectic whose principle of integrity lies in a universal antecedent willingness, and as there is a dialectic of community between intersubjectivity and practicality, with its synthetic principle in culture, so there is a dialectic of culture itself between cosmological and anthropological insights, with its synthetic principle of integrity lying in the soteriological vector, which comes to maximal clarity in Christian revelation, and which it is the function of theology at any given time and place to mediate with the prevailing cultural matrix so as to promote the integrity of the dialectic of culture. Moreover, this soteriological vector is the source of the universal willingness and of the integral culture that are the principles of integrity, respectively, for the dialectics of the subject and of community.

In *Israel and Revelation* Voegelin enunciates a set of three principles that he uses to understand and relate the experiences and symbolizations of order that appear in the course of human history. These three principles are:

(1)   The nature of man is constant.

(2)   The range of human experience is always present in the fullness of its dimensions.

(3)   The structure of the range varies from compactness to differentiation.[45]

Following Voegelin let us call the range of experience that is always fully present but never fully differentiated the search for direction in the movement of life; 'life is experienced as man's participation in a movement with a direction to be found or missed.'[46] And let us risk the judgment that the participatory quality of the experience constitutes consciousness as luminosity, and the search for direction consciousness as intentionality.

Not only is life experienced as a movement with a direction that can be found or missed. In addition, everything depends on finding the direction and following it, each step of the way. This nuclear element of all experience is at the base of culture. Cultural order and the self-understanding informing it are a function of the search

and of the incremental answers to it arrived at in the course
of history. No matter how compact or differentiated an
individual's consciousness or a culture's self-understanding may be, the ordering symbols that express the meaning of a way of life are always a function of this 'original
experience' of consciousness.

The structure of the range of this experience, Voegelin
says, varies from compactness to differentiation. Compact
cosmological symbolizations find the paradigm of order
in the cosmic rhythms. This order is analogously realized
first in the society, and social order provides the framework determining individual rectitude. Cultures minimally
or maximally informed by a differentiation of insight and
rational reflection from the sensitive flow, on the other hand,
have expressed the experience of life in either incipient or
highly developed philosophies. Then the aspired-to world-
transcendent measure of integrity is the standard for the
integrity of the individual, and the well-attuned individual
measures the integrity of the society. Such is the basic
structure of anthropological truth.

There is a basic and ineradicable tension between
cosmological and anthropological truth. It is another instance of the dialectical tension of limitation and transcendence. An anticipatory and purely descriptive understanding of this tension may be arrived at by distinguishing the
different experiences of time that permeate the two ways
of experiencing and understanding the participatory engagement in the movement of life. It would seem that cosmological truth is rooted in the affective and so biologically based sympathy of the human organism with the
rhythms and processes of nonhuman nature, whereas anthropological differentiations are implicitly or thematically
constitutive of history as a process involving the contribution of human insight, reflection, and deliberation. From
a purely descriptive point of view, the difference appears

to be one between cyclical and linear time. If we start from the present ecological crisis generated by the technologies of societies whose scientific expertise is ultimately dependent on the theoretic differentiation of a Western variant of the anthropological breakthrough — however sharply modern science differs from classicist ideals — we see that, while Western cultures have pursued scientific and technological expertise to such an extent as to lose affective sympathy with the rhythms and processes of nature, less technologically advanced cultures, while maintaining this affective sympathy, have succumbed too massively to the rhythms and processes with which they feel themselves to be in harmony. The ecological crisis is due, it seems, to our allowing the apparent linearity of humanly constituted history to play fast and loose with the apparent cycles of nature, and to interfere with them in a cavalier fashion that introduces a fourth, mechanomorphic process of experience and symbolization. Cultures, on the other hand, that have not undergone the axial transformation of theoretic differentiation, have allowed the rhythms of their own cultural lives to be determined too exclusively by the affective sympathy they enjoy with the cycles of nature, so that their experience, if not interfered with by alien expansionism, is nonlinear and to that extent ahistorical. Because the only linearity they experience is due to alien intrusion, their sense of historical self-constitution is more negative than positive: it is radically a sense of the destruction of their own culture, an experience of their victimization by cultures affected by a contrary distortion of the dialectic of community.

In actual fact, nonhuman nature is not strictly speaking cyclical, nor is history precisely linear. If nonhuman nature were cyclical, it would display no emergence of novelty. And if history were strictly linear we could not account for the conditioning of later events by the potentialities inherent in earlier events. The whole concrete universe is informed by an intelligibility that Lonergan calls emergent probability. In nonhuman nature as well as in human history there are neither cycles nor linear sequences of ever new events, but schemes of recurrence that have a certain probability of emergence and a quite distinct probability of survival.[47] Nonetheless, the emergence and survival of schemes of recurrence in nonhuman nature differ from the emergence and survival of schemes of recurrence that can be changed by the execution of free decisions based on new insights. What we are dealing with here is a difference not between cyclical and linear time but between different probabilities of emergence and survival due to the presence or absence of human intelligence, rationality, and decision.

When a culture is in affective sympathy with the relatively fixed schemes of recurrence in nonhuman nature, it displays a profound respect and even reverence for the exigences of those schemes and regards them as exhibiting something like a sacred order. Care will then be taken not to violate these exigences, a care that has to be described as religious. But the same culture is liable to be burdened with a fatalistic conception of its own historical life. It will regard human society as subordinate to the same schemes of recurrence or, it appears, cycles, that inform the process of the cosmos. The capacity of insight and decision to change society and history by introducing new schemes of recurrence into a distinctly human and so intelligent emergent probability, is liable to be overlooked. Such an oversight, of course, today makes such a culture an easy prey for domination by those of a different persuasion, who do acknowledge and employ practical insight and decision in their capacity to change the course of history. Particularly is this the case if the historically-minded group is insensitive to the affective sympathies of the cosmological culture with the rhythms and processes of nature. Cultures and peoples with an affective ecological sympathy with nature thus tend to a mythical or magical view of human affairs, seeing themselves as massively subordinate to and reliant on cosmic powers for the determination of their destinies. Their distrust in or ignorance of the power of insight and freedom to change the course of human events is exploited by expansionist imperialist ambitions of whatever variety. In fact, the clash of mentalities and cultures is a conflict between a way of life too closely identified with nonhuman schemes of recurrence, on the one hand, and an inflated self-constitutive process too sharply divorced from these schemes of recurrence, on the other hand. In the cosmological societies we find a displacing of the tension of limitation and transcendence in the direction of limitation, and in the technologically advanced societies a displacement of the same tension in the direction of transcendence. Contrary distortions of the integral dialectic of community confront one another under these circumstances.

The acknowledgment of the power of understanding and freedom to change both history and nature is a constitutive feature of the rise and success of modern science. Yet that very process is itself dependent on a theoretic differentiation of consciousness that long antedates the modern scientific revolution, however different classical ideals of science may be from modern objectives. In this sense it may legitimately be asked if the distortion of the integral dialectic of society in the direction of transcendence that is characteristic of technologically advanced societies is not rooted in an inherent danger immanent in the anthropological breakthrough itself. The cosmological tendency to identify too closely and in the last analysis fatalistically with the rhythms and processes of nonhuman nature is, I believe, readily intelligible due to the human organism's radical participation in precisely those schemes of recurrence and the human sensitive psyche's radical participation in the human organism. What is not so clear is why the mechanomorphic distortion of the same dialectic in the direction of transcendence is rooted in an exclusivism of anthropological truth to at least the same extent that the cosmological distortion is grounded in the fatalistic temptation inherent in cosmological truth. If we consider this question we will be able to understand why the integrity of the dialectic of culture can be grounded neither in cosmological truth alone nor in anthropological truth alone, but in some third process of experience, insight, symbolization, conceptualization, reflection, judgment, deliberation, and decision that we will call soteriological, and that grounds the integrity of the dialectic of cosmological and anthropological truth.

What we must try to understand is why anthropological truth without cosmological truth is apt to become *eventually* mechanomorphic distortion, and so to promote a relatively post-historic mode of existence counterbalancing the relatively prehistoric existence of the cosmological societies. Historical existence is normatively constituted by an integral dialectic of limitation and transcendence. But the prehistoric distortion of that dialectic is more readily intelligible than the post-historic. What is it about anthropological truth itself that renders it susceptible to mechanomorphic derailment, and so to a reversal of the axial advances achieved in the anthropological breakthrough? What is the internal flaw constitutive of this breakthrough that, unless guarded against by a set of defensive circles, lessens its probability of survival? Why is this diminishing probability of survival not to be understood as a reversion to cosmological cycles, as Voegelin seems to suppose,[48] but as a fall into post-historic mechanomorphism? Finally, why is it the case that *only* 'a society in existence under God is in historical form,'[49] and what does this realization say about the crucial significance of the soteriological vector with respect not only to the cosmological form of existence — this Voegelin begins to explicate quite profoundly in *Israel and Revelation* — but also to the anthropological?

The key to the potential derailment of the anthropological breakthrough is to be found, I believe, in the fate of 'the myth' and the subsequent loss of the experience not so much of consciousness as intentionality but of consciousness as luminosity, not so much of the search for direction but of the movement in which life participates and in which intentional consciousness searches for, finds, and misses direction. Voegelin has displayed the sensitivity of Plato to the fate of the myth, and so the fate of the sensitive symbolizing psyche and its energic compositions and distributions, under the impact of the anthropological breakthrough to the order of the soul as the measure of society and to the world-transcendent ground as the measure of the order of the soul. But that sensitivity is precarious, and with its loss or neglect there arises the forgetfulness of the divine measure exhibited even by the sophistic antagonists of Plato's Socrates. The myth is the permanent transcendental guarantee of consciousness as luminosity, as the experience of participation in the movement of life, as a demand for attunement with what is lasting in being. And consciousness as luminosity is the permanent transcendental guarantee of the *obligation* of consciousness as intentionality to find the direction *in* the movement of life. The loss of the myth is the loss of the consciousness of the 'It-reality'[50] within which intentionality is authentically oriented by the intention of intelligibility, truth, and goodness to the 'Thing-reality' partially constituted by world-constitutive praxis. The loss of the myth is the source of the derailment of intentional consciousness by general bias into the immanentization of the modern gnosticisms.

In *Psychic Conversion and Theological Foundations* I
tried to show that the neglect of the sensitive psyche, which
I am here arguing to be the source of the participatory
luminosity displayed in the myth, is as radically responsible for the longer cycle of decline as is the derailment of
intelligence into the shortsighted omnicompetence displayed by Lonergan as the general bias of commonsense
practicality; and I explained the foundational role of a transcendental aesthetic in the constitution of the self-appropriation of what I now, following Voegelin, would call consciousness as luminosity. In fact the anthropological breakthrough resulted, in Plato, in a transformation of the myth;
in parallel fashion, the generalized empirical method that
results from the self-appropriation of consciousness as intentionality is required for an accurate self-appropriation
of consciousness as luminosity: psychic analysis depends
for its integrity on intentionality analysis. But, as I have
argued from the beginning of my project, intentionality
analysis must be complemented by psychic analysis. The
self-appropriation of rational self-consciousness makes
possible, but also requires, 'a new Christian philosophy ...
of mythical symbols ... that would make intelligible ... the
myth as an objective language for the expression of a transcendental irruption, more adequate and exact as an instrument of expression than any rational system of symbols.'[51] The anthropological breakthrough to the differentiation of insight and reason from the sensitive flow and of
explanation from description is so powerful that it could
result in a more or less grave neglect of the constitutive
contribution of the sensitive flow itself, a neglect in the
understanding of existence that will lead to the loss of consciousness as luminosity and to the truncation of consciousness as intentionality into the instrumental manipulation
of Thing-reality within a horizon no longer constituted by
the experience of participation in It-reality. Voegelin's Plato,

of course, did not succumb to this danger. But was he tempted to it?[52] For there is inherent in the axial differentiation a tendency to forget its partiality, and to reject rather than sublate and transform that from which the new clarifications are differentiated. *Contra* Voegelin, then, may we not root the modern gnosticisms more profoundly in a potential derailment in the anthropological breakthrough than in a supposed ambiguity in the Christian symbols and promise of salvation? In fact, I wonder whether Voegelin does not himself imply as much when he writes:

> Philosophy and Christianity have endowed man with the stature that enables him, with historical effectiveness, to play the role of rational contemplator and pragmatic master of a nature which has lost its demonic terrors. With equal historical effectiveness, however, limits were placed on human grandeur; for *Christianity* [emphasis added] has concentrated demonism into the permanent danger of a fall from the spirit — that is man's only by the grace of God — into the autonomy of his own self, from the *amor Dei* into the *amor sui*. The insight that man in his mere humanity, without *fides caritate formata*, is demonic nothingness has been brought by Christianity to the ultimate border of clarity which by tradition is called revelation.[53]

The substantiating of this position will demand a more explanatory presentation of the differentiation of the soteriological from the anthropological either than appears in Voegelin's work or than I am prepared to offer at present. The incipient soteriology of Voegelin is with respect to deliverance from cosmological-imperial existence. A simi-

lar study of the soteriological in relation to the anthropological reaching for the divine ground remains to be done.
And when it is done, it must show the influence of the
soteriological on the integrity of the cosmological-anthro-
pological tension that constitutes the dialectic of culture.
Such a study would begin, I believe, not with culture itself, but with the person as originating value. There it would
show the soteriological as the condition of the possibility
of the integral dialectic of the subject between neural demand functions and dramatically patterned intentional
consciousness, and so between the two radical sources,
respectively, of cosmological and anthropological truth.
And because the integrity of culture itself is the condition
of the possibility of the integral dialectic of community,
the soteriological dimension of participation in the movement of life is the radical source of the integrity of all three
of the dialectics that we have discussed in this paper,
grounding the integral dialectic first of the subject (personal value), then of culture (cultural value), and finally of
community (social value). This would make of Christian
foundational and systematic theology a more comprehensive and exact form of reflection on this participation than
is the philosophy that articulates the eros for the divine
ground. And yet the Christian theologian can perhaps find
no better source in the contemporary scene for an
understanding of, and a challenge to, a life of authentic
reflection on the experience of participation in a movement that has a direction that can either be found or missed,
than is offered in the rich meditations that have been shared
with us by Eric Voegelin.

Notes

1 For volume 1, see above, chapter 1, note 8. Volume 2, *The World of the Polis*, and volume 3, *Plato and Aristotle* were published by Louisiana State University Press in 1957, and volume 4, *The Ecumenic Age*, in 1974. An uncompleted fifth volume, *In Search of Order*, was published posthumously in 1987, after the first publication of the present paper.

2 See Bernard Lonergan, *Method in Theology* (see above, chapter 1, note 1) chapter 11.

3 Bernard Lonergan, *Insight* (see above, chapter 1, note 20) 217/242.

4 Ibid. 189-96/212-20.

5 Ibid. 598/621-22, 610-11/633-35, 623-24/646-47.

6 Ibid. 214-18/239-44.

7 Ibid. 236-38/261-63.

8 See Eric Voegelin, *Israel and Revelation* (see above, chapter 1, note 8) 56, and Bernard Lonergan, 'Healing and Creating in History' (see above, chapter 3, note 7).

9 Lonergan, *Insight* 472-75/497-99.

10 Lonergan, *Method in Theology* 281-93.

11 For a critique of the method of correlation, see Fred Lawrence, 'Method and Theology as Hermeneutical,' in *Creativity and Method* (see above, chapter 1, note 10) 79-104.

12 Lonergan, *Insight* 227/252, 233-34/258-59.

13 Lonergan, *Method in Theology* 292-93.

14 Eric Voegelin, *The New Science of Politics* (see above, chapter 1, note 31) 186.

[15] Lonergan, *Method in Theology* 52.

[16] Ibid. 30-34.

[17] Ibid. 64.

[18] See Robert M. Doran, *Subject and Psyche* (see above, chapter 1, note 11), chapter 1.

[19] Lonergan, *Method in Theology* 31-32.

[20] See Doran, *Subject and Psyche* passim, and *Psychic Conversion and Theological Foundations* (see above, chapter 1, note 9) passim.

[21] Lonergan, *Insight* 217/242.

[22] Ibid. 192/216.

[23] Ibid.

[24] Ibid. 217/242-43.

[25] Eric Voegelin, *From Enlightenment to Revolution*, ed. John Hallowell (Durham, NC: Duke University Press, 1975) 263.

[26] Lonergan, *Insight* 623-24/646-47.

[27] See Lonergan, 'Healing and Creating in History.'

[28] Lonergan, *Method in Theology* 83-84.

[29] Voegelin, *The New Science of Politics* 52.

[30] Voegelin, *Israel and Revelation* 3.

[31] See Voegelin, *The New Science of Politics* 66-70.

[32] See Eric Voegelin, 'The Beginning of the Beginning,' chapter 1 in the posthumously published *In Search of Order* 12-47.

[33] See Eric Voegelin, 'Reason: The Classic Experience,' *The Southern Review* 10 (1974) 237-64.

[34] Lonergan, *Insight* 238/263.

[35] Ibid. 241/266.

[36] Ibid. 225/250.

[37] Ibid. 226/252.

[38] Ibid. 228/253.

[39] Ibid. 234/259.

[40] Ibid. 237/262.

[41] Ibid. 208-209/232-34.

[42] Eric Voegelin, *Science, Politics and Gnosticism* (South Bend, IN: Gateway, 1968) 99-100.

[43] Ibid. 100.

[44] Ibid. 86-87.

[45] Voegelin, *Israel and Revelation* 60.

[46] Eric Voegelin, 'The Gospel and Culture,' in *Jesus and Man's Hope*, ed. D.C. Miller and D.Y. Hadidian (Pittsburgh: Pittsburgh Theological Seminary, 1971) 63.

[47] See Lonergan, *Insight,* chapter 4.

[48] Voegelin, *Israel and Revelation* 126-33.

[49] Ibid. 132.

[50] See Voegelin, 'The Beginning of the Beginning.'

[51] Voegelin, *From Enlightenment to Revolution* 22.

[52] See Voegelin, *Plato and Aristotle* 133.

[53] Voegelin, *The New Science of Politics* 78-79.

9   Bernard Lonergan: An Appreciation

A thorough introduction to the thought of Bernard Lonergan would occupy several volumes. Moreover, such a work cannot be written for a number of years, since many of Lonergan's writings are as yet unpublished, important notes and fragments are still to be made available and in some instances still to be deciphered, and some of his lectures are still to be edited from tape in a publishable form. But already it is clear that the work of few if any other twentieth-century thinkers has a comparable range of implications for various fields or a comparable importance for the future of thought and indeed of human living. It can reasonably be argued that Lonergan penetrates more directly and swiftly to the heart of the matter than do most, if any, other contemporary figures.

That 'heart of the matter' is, for the early Lonergan, the act of human understanding, and for the later Lonergan, the events that constitute intellectual, moral, and religious conversion. Lonergan says on the opening page of his first great book, *Insight*, that to grasp the act of understanding 'in its conditions, its working, and its results is to confer a basic yet startling unity on the whole field of human inquiry and human opinion.'[1] And at the turning point of a later great book, *Method in Theology*, he writes that 'the basic idea of the method we are trying to develop takes its stand on discovering what human authenticity is and showing how to appeal to it.'[2]

Lonergan's work is formidable. Most of his readers find *Insight* an enormously difficult work. The mastery of this one book alone would be, for most of us, the task of a lifetime. The book cannot adequately be taught in one semester, not even in an entire year, even to the most talented and advanced doctoral students. Only a series of seminars over several years, such as have been devoted occasionally to Hegel's *Phenomenology*, could begin to do it justice. Many readers are easily discouraged especially by the opening five chapters, with their exploration of the nature of understanding in mathematics and contemporary physics. And if they breathe a sigh of relief when the more familiar terrain of common sense begins to be discussed in the sixth chapter, it is not long before another kind of challenge is posed, an existential invitation to the major personal transformation that is Lonergan's primary intention in all of his work. The transformation is to an authentic personhood or subjectivity, whose intellectual, moral, and religious constituents are explored with rigorous consistency and ever more comprehensive inclusiveness as he moves from an account of understanding to a position on judgment, then to an analysis of the constituents of responsible choice, and finally to a description of religious love.

Preceding *Insight* Lonergan wrote two ground-breaking, perhaps definitive, interpretations of Aquinas,[3] and following *Insight* he worked out a theology of the Incarnate Word and the Trinity,[4] moved ever so slowly and carefully to a theological method that, if implemented, will entail the complete reconstruction of Catholic theology,[5] and returned to earlier work elaborating a macroeconomic theory whose implications, many believe, are as important for economics as his earlier work is for philosophy and theology.[6] His unpublished papers and as yet unedited lectures delivered over a period of some twenty-five years only add to the list of materials to be studied by anyone who would reach up to the mind of a genius and bring that mind to bear on the problems of our day.[7]

Fortunately, I have been asked to write an introduction, not to Lonergan, but to a book of essays on Lonergan. It is the burden of these essays, and not of my introduction, to explore in some detail the contribution that Lonergan makes to the solution of various pressing questions, especially in theology. The present volume is intended to meet the need for an interim introduction to Lonergan's work that would begin to point to its implications for theology, and that would show the central importance of the invitation to transformation and self-appropriation that is the unifying theme throughout his work. That leaves me free to devote my attention to a matter that is perhaps more elusive, but that will probably attract increasing attention over the next years and decades as others begin to reap the rich harvest of Lonergan's work. What sort of commitment lies behind this monumental achievement? What values motivated Lonergan? What atmosphere would he promote in the academy, the church, and the wider society?[8] Why did he undertake to do what he did? What were his fundamental convictions?

What I will say in response to these questions I discovered first by reading Lonergan's works, and only later confirmed during the years when I was privileged to know him personally. But the items that I single out in response to these questions are what drew me to Lonergan in the first place. And they are perhaps even more important today than they were at the time I first encountered his work. I will mention three interrelated items: tradition and modernity in thinking, the promotion of a 'perhaps not too numerous center' in the church,[9] and the detachment of a long-range point of view in society, a 'withdrawal from practicality to save practicality.'[10] The three are related in

that they are analogous embodiments in Lonergan's own
life and thought of the creative tension that constitutes for
him the immanent intelligibility of human genuineness or
authenticity.[11]

I   Tradition and Modernity

A former student of mine, who has continued to read
Lonergan for many years after he was first introduced to
Insight, recently commented to me, after having read a
collection of some of Lonergan's later writings,[12] that these
papers show a remarkably sane and balanced attitude toward modernity. Lonergan's attitude contrasted with my
former student's own preconciliar Catholic upbringing,
with its fear of modern developments and its long-stand-
ing rejection of modern methods of inquiry. But I remarked
in response that Lonergan's critical and discerning respect
for modern advances — a respect at least partly rooted in
his love of mathematics and science — is balanced by an
equally pervasive, if also equally critical, reverence for the
best in the classical intellectual tradition of the West — for
Plato and Aristotle, Augustine and Aquinas, the Greek
breakthrough to theory, and the medieval synthesis of faith
and reason. Here is a mind, one of the few I have encountered, that is *equally* at home in both the old and the new,[13]
and equally critical of both.

To illustrate this, I need only turn to the book of
essays that my friend had been reading. It manifests both
ever deepening interpretations of Aristotle and Aquinas
and a penetrating and appreciative reflection on the emerging religious consciousness of our time, both an affirmation of the Nicene and Chalcedonian doctrines regarding
Christ and a reinterpretation of those doctrines in terms
of Lonergan's own transformation of the modern notion
of the subject, both a retrieval of the Aristotelian notion of

praxis and a commitment to the socially transformative overcoming of contemporary alienation and determinism. The list could go on and on. In fact, almost all of Lonergan's published writings can be filtered through the hermeneutic grid of his respectful attention to, learning from, and critical reorientation of both tradition and modernity.

Behind this balanced and comprehensive attitude there lies a profound reverence for the life of the mind, the spirit of inquiry, the desire to understand, wherever and under whatever circumstances human questioning is exercised. Yet this reverence is neither uncritical nor atemporal. It combines with perhaps the most lucid understanding yet achieved of the actual workings of the inquiring mind, to enable an appreciation of classical and modern thinkers that sorts out what is to be brought forward from what is to be reoriented or left behind. And it acknowledges with pinpoint accuracy how a priori structures develop with historical advances in understanding. The calculus, for example, originated at a precise and easily identifiable time in the history of modern mathematical inquiry; but differential equations are now a dimension of the physicist's heuristic anticipations 'from above' of the immanent intelligibility of the data investigated 'from below.'[14]

Working hand in hand with this respect for the life of inquiry at any time and place is a commitment to honor the charge of Pope Leo XIII's encyclical on the revival of Thomist studies, *Aeterni Patris*: a commitment, in the Pope's own words, *vetera novis augere et perficere*, to augment and complete the old with the new. To my knowledge, Lonergan first cites the Pope's mandate in a latter to his Jesuit Provincial in 1935, and he adds, 'I take him at his word.'[15] He mentions the encyclical again in the last of his *verbum* articles, where he explains what he was about as follows:

My purpose has been the Leonine purpose,
vetera novis augere et perficere, though with this
modality that I believed the basic task still to
be the determination of what the *vetera* really
were.[16]

A third mention of the same papal challenge appears
at the very end of *Insight,* where the determination of what
the *vetera* really were has given way to a methodological
anticipation of what the *nova* could be. Neither the scholarly research that establishes texts nor the intellectual penetration that reaches to the development of another
thinker's mind and to its motives and causes is sufficient.

After spending years reaching up to the mind
of Aquinas, I came to a twofold conclusion. On
the one hand, that reaching had changed me
profoundly. On the other hand, that change was
the essential benefit. For not only did it make
me capable of grasping what, in the light of my
conclusions, the *vetera* really were, but also it
opened challenging vistas on what the *nova*
could be.[17]

2   The Not Too Numerous Center

Mention of a papal encyclical and of the commitment that it inspired in the mind and heart of a modern
thinker is an obvious springboard to my next topic,
Lonergan's attitude toward the church and its *aggiornamento.*

Lonergan was a *peritus* at the Second Vatican Council. He was named by Pope Paul VI as an original member
of the International Theological Commission. He served
other special Vatican commissions, including the Secre-

tariat for Non-Believers. But I think it accurate to say that his main ecclesial concern after the Second Vatican Council was with the depth, both religious and intellectual, to which the church must penetrate if it is to realize 'Pope John's Intention.'[18] That depth is manifest in the centrality of the notion of authenticity in all of his writings bearing on *aggiornamento*.[19] But it is clear, too, in his reflections on the forces within the church that would militate against a real renewal.

> There is bound to be formed a solid right that is determined to live in a world that no longer exists. There is bound to be formed a scattered left, captivated by now this and now that new possibility. But what will count is a perhaps not numerous center, big enough to be at home in both the old and the new, painstaking enough to work out one by one the transitions to be made, strong enough to refuse half measures and insist on complete solutions even though it has to wait.[20]

If the scattered left dominated some aspects of the church's life during the first twenty years following the Council, it is no secret that the solid right is flexing its muscles today. Lonergan understood the difficulty as a crisis of culture, and referred to the problematic mentality of the right as 'classicism.' If he was distressed by the 'scattered left,' he also was fearful of the 'solid right.' For if he could describe himself as 'a Roman Catholic with quite conservative views on religious and church doctrines,'[21] he also could write the following about 'the shabby shell of Catholicism':

There are two ways in which the unity of the
faith may be conceived. On classicist assumptions there is just one culture. That one culture
is not attained by the simple faithful, the people,
the natives, the barbarians. None the less, career
is always open to talent. One enters upon such
a career by diligent study of the ancient Latin
and Greek authors. One pursues such a career
by learning Scholastic philosophy and theology. One aims at high office by becoming profi-
cient in canon law. One succeeds by winning the
approbation and favor of the right personages.
Within this set-up the unity of faith is a matter of
everyone subscribing to the correct formulae.[22]

The other way of conceiving the unity of faith is to find
the 'real root and ground of unity' in 'being in love with
God — the fact that God's love has flooded our inmost
hearts through the Holy Spirit he has given us (Romans
5.5).'[23] Then one will find the function of church doctrines
to lie within the function of Christian witness. And

the witness is to the mysteries revealed by God
and, for Catholics, infallibly declared by the
church. The meaning of such declarations lies
beyond the vicissitudes of human historical
process. But the context, within which such
meaning is grasped, and so the manner, in
which such meaning is expressed, vary both
with cultural differences and with the measure
in which human consciousness is differentiated.[24]

The essential, again, is the human authenticity that begins
with the acceptance of the gift of God's love that 'consti-

tutes religious conversion and leads to moral and even intellectual conversion.'[25] And this authenticity, ever precarious, is twofold:

> There is the minor authenticity or unauthenticity of the subject with respect to the tradition that nourishes him. There is the major authenticity that justifies or condemns the tradition itself. In the first case there is passed a human judgment on subjects. In the second case history and, ultimately, divine providence pass judgment on traditions ... [T]he unauthenticity of individuals becomes the unauthenticity of a tradition. Then, in the measure a subject takes the tradition, as it stands, for his standard, in that measure he can do no more than authentically realize unauthenticity.[26]

It is not simply with the tradition, then, but with the authenticity of the tradition that Lonergan was concerned,[27] and more precisely with the communication of an authentic religious tradition in the pluralistic context of modern culture. Essential to this communication is the distinction between classicist and modern notions of culture, and the clean break that the church must make with classicism, so as to become 'all to all.'[28] On the difficulties attendant on this challenge, Lonergan wrote, in words that comprise aspects of his campaign against both the solid right and the scattered left:

> On the one hand, it demands a many-sided development in those that govern or teach. On the other hand, every achievement is apt to be challenged by those that fail to achieve. People with little notion of modern scholarship can

urge that attending to the literary genre of biblical writings is just a fraudulent device for rejecting the plain meaning of scripture. Those with no taste for systematic meaning will keep repeating that it is better to feel compunction than to define it, even if those that attempt definition insist that one can hardly define what one does not experience. Those, finally, whose consciousness is unmitigated by any tincture of systematic meaning, will be unable to grasp the meaning of such dogmas as Nicea and they may gaily leap to the conclusion that what has no meaning for them is just meaningless.[29]

It was against 'the real menace to unity of faith' that Lonergan struggled, against 'the absence of intellectual or moral or religious conversion.'[30] And it was in the interest of promoting those conversions of mind and heart that he made his extraordinary contribution to the differentiation of consciousness through the process of self-appropriation. For with sufficient differentiation of consciousness, one can exercise a pluralism of communications without falling prey to the threefold peril of a distinct kind of pluralism resulting from lack of conversion, a peril that Lonergan described as follows:

First, when the absence of conversion occurs in those that govern the church or teach in its name. Secondly, when, as at present, there is going forward in the church a movement out of classicist and into modern culture. Thirdly, when persons with partially differentiated consciousness not only do not understand one another but also so extol system or method or scholarship or interiority or slightly advanced prayer as to set aside achievement and block development in the other four.[31]

3   The Long-range Point of View

The extraordinary balance that Lonergan's mind reached between fidelity to tradition and respect for modernity, between fidelity to doctrine and the promotion of responsible pluralism, is a function, I think, of what perhaps more than anything else characterizes both his own mode of thinking and the cognitive authenticity that he would encourage in others: his approach to practicality or praxis.

The seventh chapter of *Insight* is our main source of data on this facet of Lonergan's thinking and mentality. This complex text, I have come to believe, is a fairly sustained and quite subtle reorientation of Marx. It was this chapter that first persuaded me I had encountered not only a brilliant mind, but also a thinker with a message of profound importance for our time. But the practical upshot of Lonergan's work was already indicated in the preface to *Insight*. One quotation will suffice to show what Lonergan thought to be the ulterior finality of what he was about.

Insight into insight brings to light the cumulative process of progress. For concrete situations give rise to insights which issue into policies and courses of action. Action transforms the existing situation to give rise to further insights, better policies, more effective courses of action. It follows that if insight occurs, it keeps recurring; and at each recurrence knowledge develops, action increases its scope, and situations improve.

Similarly, insight into oversight reveals the cumulative process of decline. For the flight from understanding blocks the insights that concrete situations demand. There follow unintelligent policies and inept courses of action. The situation deteriorates to demand still further insights, and as they are blocked, policies become more unintelligent and action more inept. What is worse, the deteriorating situation seems to provide the uncritical, biased mind with factual evidence in which the bias is claimed to be verified. So in ever increasing measure intelligence comes to be regarded as irrelevant to practical living. Human activity settles down to a decadent routine, and initiative becomes the privilege of violence.[32]

Lonergan told me in several conversations during the year before he died that the chapters on common sense (6 and 7) and on judgment (9 and 10) were the first chapters of *Insight* that he wrote, that they contained what he most wanted to say, and that it was in order to substantiate his point in these chapters that he wrote the first five, which treat of insight in mathematics and modern science.[33] What he most wanted to say, then, included preeminently a position on the role of human intelligence in history and society, and on the relation of intelligence to social and cultural progress and decline, especially in view of the distinct dangers confronting human society today.

Lonergan's concern with these questions can be traced back at least to the same 1935 letter to his Jesuit Provincial in which he mentions Pope Leo XIII's *Aeterni Patris*. Indeed, the charge *vetera novis augere et perficere* is there appealed to, precisely in order to explain his 'excursion into the metaphysic of history.' He admitted the 'enormity' of the influence of Hegel and Marx on his position on history, but maintained that his own position, already drafted, would go quite beyond them. 'It takes the "objective and inevitable laws" of economics, of psychology (environment, tradition) and of progress (material, intellectual; automatic up to a point, then either deliberate and planned or the end of a civilization) to find the higher synthesis of these laws in the mystical Body.'[34] Between the lines one can read the basic sketch of what later would become a quite thorough position on the structure of history.

The reorientation of Marx that Lonergan's position entails locates the basic social dialectic, not between forces and relations of production, but between practical common sense as it erects technological, economic, and political structures, on the one hand, and vital intersubjectivity, on the other hand. The political dimension of society is located, not in the superstructure, as in Marx, but in the infrastructure. The superstructure is constituted by the reflective, objectifying dimension of culture that steps back from everyday practicality and exercises critical, dialectical, and normative judgment on the workings of practical common sense. The forces that militate against a harmonious or integral dialectic of practicality with intersubjectivity — individual, group, and general bias — are examined, and the stress is laid on the distorting influence of the general bias against long-term consequences, ultimate issues, and theoretical questions.

Of this analysis, Lonergan wrote many years later that it was worked out on the model of a threefold approximation. He used the analogy of Newton's planetary theory to explain what he meant.

Newton's planetary theory had a first approximation in the first law of motion: bodies move in a straight line with constant velocity unless some force intervenes. There was a second approximation when the addition of the law of gravity between the sun and the planet yielded an elliptical orbit for the planet. A third approximation was reached when the influence of the gravity of the planets on one another is taken into account to reveal the perturbed ellipses in which the planets actually move. The point to this model is, of course, that in the intellectual construction of reality it is not any of the earlier stages of the construction but only the final product that actually exists. Planets do not move in straight lines nor in properly elliptical orbits; but these conceptions are needed to arrive at the perturbed ellipses in which they actually do move.

In my rather theological analysis of human history, my first approximation was the assumption that men always do what is intelligent and reasonable, and its implication was an ever increasing progress. The second approximation was the radical inverse insight that men can be biased, and so unintelligent and unreasonable in their choices and decisions. The third approximation was the redemptive process resulting from God's gift of his grace to individuals and from the manifestation of his love in Christ Jesus.[35]

A later expansion and refinement of the theory appears in Lonergan's paper 'Natural Right and Historical Mindedness.'[36] There the 'dialectic of history' is set forth under six headings. First, human meaning develops in human collaboration. Second, there is a succession of plateaus on which expansions of meaning occur: the development of common sense or practical intelligence; the specialization of intelligence in theory; and the move to interiority and method. Third, there are quite specific ideals proper to the third plateau, which was the one on which Lonergan himself was working. These ideals are

> such self-awareness, such self-understanding, such self-knowledge, as to grasp the similarities and the differences of common sense, science, and history, to grasp the foundations of these three in interiority ... and, beyond all knowledge of knowledge, to give also knowledge of affectivity in its threefold manifestation of love in the family, loyalty in the community, and faith in God

and

> such self-transcendence as includes an intellectual, a moral, and an affective conversion. As intellectual, this conversion draws a sharp distinction between the world of immediacy and the world mediated by meaning, between the criteria appropriate to operations in the former and, on the other hand, the criteria appropriate to operations in the latter. Next, as moral, it acknowledges a distinction between satisfactions and values, and it is committed to values even where they conflict with satisfactions. Finally, as affective, it is commitment to love in the home, loyalty in the community, faith in the destiny of man.[37]

Fourth, there is needed a critique, in the light of the first three headings, of what our past has made us. Fifth, ambiguity arises 'when first-plateau minds live in a second-plateau context of meaning, or when first- and second-plateau minds find themselves in a third-plateau context.'[38] And sixth, beyond all dialectic, there is the dialogue in which this ambiguity can be resolved.

> Dialectic describes concrete process in which intelligence and obtuseness, reasonableness and silliness, responsibility and sin, love and hatred commingle and conflict. But the very people that investigate the dialectic of history also are part of that dialectic and even in their investigating represent its contradictories. To their work too the dialectic is to be applied.
>
> But it can be more helpful, especially when oppositions are less radical, for the investigators to move beyond dialectic to dialogue, to transpose issues from a conflict of statements to an encounter of persons. For every person is an embodiment of natural right. Every person can reveal to any other his natural propensity to seek understanding, to judge reasonably, to evaluate fairly, to be open to friendship. While the dialectic of history coldly relates our conflicts, dialogue adds the principle that prompts us to cure them, the natural right that is the inmost core of our being.[39]

If Lonergan here mentions 'natural right,' it is, I believe, in order to relate his position to that of Leo Strauss and his followers.[40] The latter position, for all its acumen in retrieving the tradition of classical political philosophy, both remains on the second plateau, and is unable to adopt a balanced attitude toward modernity. But Lonergan's third plateau, which would recover and integrate the advances toward which modernity has been moving, at the same time does not reflect modernity's rejection of the classical tradition. The move to interiority enables the recovery and reorientation of the *vetera* and their integration with a critically reoriented set of *nova*. For modernity, no less than the classical tradition, moves on the second plateau. The 'second stage of meaning' comes to its term, perhaps, in Hegel. The advance to a third plateau grounded in the self-appropriation of interiority is required if humanity is not to fall victim to the series of ever less comprehensive syntheses that today threaten civilization with destruction.

There is to be distinguished in the structure of human history, then, a shorter cycle and a longer cycle. The distinction marks another contrast with Marxist analysis. The shorter cycle turns on the ascendancies to power of various groups or nations and their subsequent replacement by other groups who champion the rights of the previously downtrodden. The longer cycle cuts through all such reversals of power, to reveal a sustained decline that results from the neglect by all groups of long-term consequences, ultimate issues, and theoretical questions. It is to responsibility for the longer cycle that Lonergan would call his readers. And it is the awareness of this responsibility that again enables him to strike such a delicate balance in his thinking. The balance is not only between the old and the new, the classical and the modern, but also between the political 'right' and 'left,' 'conservative' and 'liberal,' liberal and Marxist. In historical thinking, Lonergan reaches and invites to a higher synthesis of the liberal thesis and the Marxist antithesis[41] in a philosophy of history that accounts for both and moves beyond them by criticizing their defects.

Lonergan's historical and political thinking has yet
to be appreciated to the same extent as have other dimensions of his work. But in many ways it represents what
may be the most important aspect of his remarkable
achievement. A case can be made that his entire life's work
may be understood from and organized around the six
points that I summarized above on the dialectic of history.
If that summary seems more obscure than the rest of what
I have written here, perhaps it is because his thought in
the area of a philosophy and theology of history is so comprehensive and far-reaching. But with this excuse I must
end this section, for any further explication would make
my introduction far lengthier than it should be.

4   Conclusion

I close by reflecting on a strange phenomenon that
perhaps has not escaped the attention of some readers.
Lonergan's thought meets with an intensity of emotional
response that, it seems, is more vehement than that given
to the work of most other thinkers. This is true both of
those who accept his work and of those who reject it. While
the reasons for opposition to Lonergan's work are no doubt
multiform and complex, I suggest that they may be partly
due to the extraordinary balance that I have tried to focus
on here.

In other words, if one finds oneself firmly planted on
one side or the other of the various dichotomies that
Lonergan manages to transcend by a higher synthesis, if
one belongs to one or other of the various groups that
achieve ascendancy and then are supplanted in the shorter
cycle, whether in the academy, the church, or the wider
society, will one not resent and reject a thought that would
relativize one's own position by sublating it into a higher
viewpoint, a viewpoint that brings forward what is to be

brought forward and leaves behind what is to be left behind? Lonergan's thought meets with resistance from the advocates of both the old and the new, the right and the left, the reactionary, the liberal, and the Marxist. And the resistance is not due to the fact that, transcending these oppositions, he stands for nothing at all, but is rather the manifestation of an all too human tendency to oppose moving beyond the limitations of one's own position, especially when the achievement and maintenance of that position have already cost one dearly in terms of the politics of everyday living.

Perhaps this represents as well as anything the point that I have been trying to make. Lonergan is an important and indeed vitally significant thinker precisely because he does invite us all beyond the narrow confines of less inclusive viewpoints to the achievement of a horizon capable of meeting responsibly the immense problems of academy, church, and society with which we are confronted in our day. This is not to say that he has given us the last word, so that all we need do is make our own some Lonerganian 'system.' He comments any number of times in *Insight* that his own account of the processes constitutive of human knowledge will and must be improved upon in the light of further advances of human understanding. It is more accurate to say that he has given us a first word, a foundational word on which even the improvements and nuances that are required can be built. So I close by expressing my own persuasion that, if one wants to find one's way amidst the welter of conflicting opinions with which we are confronted today, one can do no better than to spend years reaching up to the mind of Bernard Lonergan before one sets out on one's own. As Lonergan's own reaching up to the mind of Aquinas changed him profoundly, and as that change was the most important thing, so reaching up to the mind of Lonergan will transform our own approach to every serious issue with which we attempt to come to terms; and precisely that transformation will be the most important ingredient that we can bring to the resolution of the issues with which we must be concerned today.

Notes

[1] Bernard Lonergan, *Insight* (see above, chapter 1, note 20) ix/4.

[2] Bernard Lonergan, *Method in Theology* (see above, chapter 1, note 1) 254.

[3] Bernard Lonergan, *Grace and Freedom* (see above, chapter 6, note 24); *Verbum* (see above, chapter 5, note 51).

[4] Bernard Lonergan, *De constitutione Christi ontologica et psychologica* (Rome: Gregorian University Press, 1964); *De Verbo incarnato* (see above, chapter 1, note 25); *De Deo trino* (Rome: Gregorian University Press, 1964).

[5] Lonergan, *Method in Theology*.

[6] Bernard Lonergan, *Essay in Circulation Analysis*, to be published as volume 15 in Collected Works of Bernard Lonergan (Toronto: University of Toronto Press).

[7] Cf. Lonergan: '... it is only through a personal appropriation of one's own rational self-consciousness that one can hope to reach the mind of Aquinas, and once that mind is reached, then it is difficult not to import his compelling genius to the problems of this later day.' *Insight* 748/770.

[8] On the academy, the church, and the wider society as theological 'publics,' see David Tracy, *The Analogical Imagination* (see above, chapter 7, note 14).

[9] Bernard Lonergan, 'Dimensions of Meaning,' in *Collection*, vol. 4 in Collected Works of Bernard Lonergan, ed. Frederick E. Crowe and Robert M. Doran (Toronto: University of Toronto Press, 1988) 245.

[10] Lonergan, *Insight* 241/266.

[11] See ibid. 474-79/499-504.

[12] Bernard Lonergan, *A Third Collection* (see above, chapter 2, note 9).

[13] See 'Dimensions of Meaning' 245.

[14] See Lonergan, *Insight* 38-39/62-64.

[15] Bernard Lonergan, Letter to Very Reverend Henry Keane, S.J., available in the archives of the Lonergan Research Institute, Toronto.

[16] Lonergan, *Verbum* 215.

[17] Lonergan, *Insight* 748/769.

[18] Bernard Lonergan, 'Pope John's Intention,' in *A Third Collection* 224-38.

[19] See, for example, Bernard Lonergan, '*Existenz* and *Aggiornamento*, in *Collection* 222-31; 'The Response of the Jesuit as Priest and Apostle in the Modern World,' in *A Second Collection* (see above, chapter 5, note 3) 165-87.

[20] Lonergan, 'Dimensions of Meaning' 245.

[21] Lonergan, *Method in Theology* 332.

[22] Ibid. 326-27.

[23] Ibid. 327.

[24] Ibid.

[25] Ibid.

[26] Ibid. 80.

[27] 1993 note: This (among other things, such as the notion of being and the specification of authenticity in terms of self-transcen-

dence) differentiates Lonergan's talk of authenticity from that of Martin Heidegger. Recent discoveries have given grounds for arguing that Heidegger's appeal to authenticity is an arbitrary call to allegiance to what in fact became one of the most evil political regimes in human history. See Victor Farías, *Heidegger and Nazism*, ed. Joseph Margolis and Tom Rockmore, trans. Paul Burrell and Gabriel R. Ricci (Philadelphia: Temple University Press, 1989) and Hugo Ott, *Martin Heidegger: A Political Life*, trans. Allan Blunden (London: Harper Collins, 1993).

28 Lonergan, *Method in Theology* 329.

29 Ibid. 329-30.

30 Ibid. 330.

31 Ibid.

32 Lonergan, *Insight* xiv/8.

33 On one occasion, Lonergan said, 'Chapters 6 through 9' and on another occasion, 'Chapters 7 through 10.' Thus it may be that he included in this account the important and difficult chapter 8 on 'Things.'

34 Letter to Henry Keane.

35 Bernard Lonergan, '*Insight* Revisited,' in *A Second Collection* 271-72.

36 Bernard Lonergan, 'Natural Right and Historical Mindedness,' in *A Third Collection* 169-83, esp. 176-83.

37 Ibid. 179.

38 Ibid. 181.

39 Ibid. 182.

40 See Leo Strauss, *Natural Right and History* (Chicago: University of Chicago Press, 1953).

41 Lonergan, *Insight* 241/266.

10 Common Ground

I am honored to have been asked to write the foreword to this important volume. It is my belief that the
essays presented here not only signal what are emerging as
the central themes in a new period of Lonergan studies —
community, dialogue, otherness, mediation, plurality —
but also will significantly advance the discussion of these
issues.

I have been asked by the editors to limit my comments to the question, How does Bernard Lonergan's work
provide a common ground? With my first complete reading of Lonergan's *Insight* in 1967, I was convinced that he
had gone a long way toward meeting one of the aims he
expressed in the preface to that book, namely, to seek a
common ground on which people 'of intelligence' might
meet. What I did not know then, of course, was how much
more desperate the exigence for such an open space for
dialogue would become in the latter third of the twentieth
century. The fragmentation of knowledge that Lonergan
describes so eloquently at the end of chapter 16 of *Insight*
has, it would seem, grown only more acute, and with it the
potential for ideological stalemates, mutual recriminations
of all sorts, and the denial through silence of the very
existence of those with views other than our own. Nor are
such crises limited to the rarefied atmosphere of the
academy. As Lonergan argues persuasively in chapter 7 of
Insight, wherever the possibility of independent inquiry and

open communication has been stifled, the seeds of totalitarianism have already been sown.

It may be, though, as some of Lonergan's musings on our age encourage us to hope, that the intensity of the crisis of meaning that affects us is also in part a function of the fact that something very new, something with enormous positive potential, is occurring in history. I regard the paper 'Natural Right and Historical Mindedness' as presenting Lonergan's most developed presentation of the issue of the dialectic of history, a topic that he kept coming back to for over forty years preceding this late statement of its contours. In this paper historical process is understood radically in terms of the advance and dissemination of meaning; and we stand at the very beginning of a new stage or plateau in that process. Earlier plateaus involved, first, the development of practical intelligence and ideas, and second, the differentiation of consciousness that occurs when people acquire habits of mathematics, science, and philosophy. But today concern has shifted from meanings to acts of meaning, from products to source. And the Babel of our day may be a function of more or less complete success in moving onto this new plateau — and of course of the strident survival in our midst of minds and hearts that will not make this move at all. From this perspective Lonergan's search for a common ground can be clarified as a progressive and cumulative effort to articulate a normative source of meaning, and so to express the horizon that those who have entered onto the new plateau might share if that horizon could be adequately thematized. From this perspective, too, the major moments in the development of Lonergan's own thinking can be viewed as successive increments in the clearing of the common ground. For, it turns out, the book that I first read in 1967 was only the beginning of Lonergan's articulation of the new plateau's horizon.

What I propose to do, ever so briefly, in this foreword, then, is to highlight these major moments, in the hope that this developmental overview might provide some context, immanent to Lonergan's own writings, for the encounters in the space Lonergan has cleared that are the topic or at least the objective of most of the essays assembled in this volume.

Insight is, of course, the basic breakthrough, for it is there that the common ground emerges, not as a set of contents of cognitive acts, but as a basic group of operations that constitute all human beings as knowers. The central operation emphasized is insight itself, the act of understanding. Its structure, Lonergan tells us, is always and everywhere the same. He is convinced (and elsewhere argues persuasively) that Aristotle and Aquinas grasped basic features of insight that their late medieval and modern interpreters overlooked. But even if these interpreters had not neglected insight, their articulation, like Aquinas's, would have been for the most part metaphysical, not psychological, and that is not the kind of radical recovery of insight that Lonergan advances in this book.

Rather, he begins by appropriating the modes of modern scientific understanding and by offering a generalized heuristic discussion of what is common to the myriad instances of common sense and common nonsense. From these he moves us step by step closer to his goal of a common ground. In the course of the book we are presented with and asked to appropriate at least the following kinds of insight: the direct insight that grasps intelligibility in the presentations of sense and imagination, whether in science or in common sense; the inverse insight that grasps that, in a sense, there is no intelligibility to be grasped; the identifying insight that discovers a unity-identity-whole in data; the reflective insight that ascertains that the conditions for a prospective judgment have (or have not) been fulfilled; the introspective insight that grasps intelligibility in the data of consciousness; the basic philosophic insights that articulate the structure of knowing, the meaning of 'being,' and the elements of objectivity; the metaphysical insights that work out the implications of a basic isomorphism between knowing and known, that acknowledge that the truly known is being, and so that greet being as intrinsically intelligible; the genetic insights that specify the operators of development; the dialectical insights that press for coherence between performance and content and so reverse what is incoherent with the basic positions on knowing, being, and objectivity; the practical insights that size up situations and, when moral, grasp what possibly it would be good for one to do; the limit insights that grasp one's own incapacity for sustained development on the basis of one's own resources; the religious insights that discern the gift of a higher integration; the theological insights that employ analogies to ground a few stuttering words about transcendent mystery.

But with all of this, the point is missed entirely if one concentrates exclusively on the content of these insights. The only common ground of all of these insights is that they are insights, acts of understanding. And this is a common ground whether they all occur in one subject or in many. In the one subject it is a common ground whence there can be derived, through a metaphysics, the integration of the known. In many subjects, it is a common ground for communication and collaboration. The fact that we all understand, and so share the common dynamic that the early chapters of the book unfold, is, when affirmed, the basic and radical move onto the common ground. And the fact that we are asked not only to acknowledge that common ground but also to appropriate it by relating insight to its antecedent conditions and its results in human knowing and living marks that new and common ground as also a new plateau. The beginning of Lonergan's articulation of what in *Insight* is called the common ground, which he later would call the normative source of meaning, has begun with insight into insight.

But this insight is also an owning, an appropriation, a claim upon a natural right, and the acknowledgment of a task, a responsibility, an imperative. All of these different types of insights occur in a common field named consciousness or self-presence — the subject as subject. This field can never be fully objectified, since the subject doing the objectifying is always and inescapably beyond the subject being objectified. This is important. Lonergan's variety of a 'turn to the subject' is not a turn to the subject as object of some controlling 'inner look.' The field in which the turn occurs, consciousness, is not perception, representation, or knowledge (except in the limited sense that *experience* is knowledge as presentation of data). It is rather the field of the awareness of self, the self-taste (Hopkins), that accompanies all conscious acts and states. The objectification of it that is possible can occur only through a humbling and purifying heightening of awareness itself, a heightening that enables not only an attending to, and insight into the relations of, the successive operations and states that occur in the unfolding of conscious dynamism, but also a personal judgment that this is what I am and a decision to be faithful to it.

Moreover, *Insight* discloses other operations besides those of experience of data of sense and of consciousness and insight into those data. The link between these two levels of consciousness is the question for intelligence: What? Why? How often? etc. And the insight itself is productive of the 'inner word' or set of concepts that, when formulated in language, prompts a further question, this time for critical reflection: Is it so? This question is satisfied by the reflective insight that (1) grasps that the conditions for a judgment are or are not fulfilled, (2) grounds the inner word of yes or no, and so (3) results in judgment. Holding the entire process together is the desire to know, which is spontaneous and unrestricted but not automatic. While it is never satisfied on any issue until the yes or no of reasonable judgment is reached, and while it then resumes the process by turning to other questions, its governance of conscious performance can be blocked by bias. And so Lonergan's uncovering of the various forms of bias is a further disclosure of the common ground, but this time of its darker elements.

Furthermore, in *Insight* Lonergan made an initial move toward clarifying what he would only later acknowledge as a distinct level of consciousness, that of decision, so that the language that *Insight* will use for the clearing of the common ground is 'the self-appropriation of one's rational self-consciousness.' And before he turns to decision and ethics, Lonergan draws out the implications of the self-affirmation of the empirically, intelligently, and rationally conscious knowing subject by outlining an integral heuristic structure of the *known*, a metaphysics, that constitutes a brilliant beginning upon overcoming the fragmentation of knowledge.

With the eventual recognition that decision names a fourth level of activity beyond those constituting us as knowers, Lonergan gradually shifts the language for the common ground from 'rational self-consciousness' to 'intentionality.' The normative source of meaning consists of more than the acts of meaning that in *Insight* are called formal (conceptualization) and full (judgment). Meaning is effective and constitutive, and grounding its constitutive function is the world constitution and self-constitution, the making of being, that occurs in the existential moments in which we realize that it is up to ourselves to decide individually and communally what we are going to make of ourselves. Lonergan's later reflections on these moments, for example in *Method in Theology* (1972), go far beyond the limited and somewhat limiting analysis of decision in *Insight*, even as they preserve the latter's essential grasp of the utter contingency of decision and action in relation to the knowledge that precedes it.

One of the new emphases, which will become increasingly important as we move toward Lonergan's most complete statement on the normative source of meaning in 'Natural Right and Historical Mindedness,' is the role now accorded to feelings. Potential values are apprehended in intentional feelings, that is, in those feelings that respond to an apprehended object or course of action. The process of deliberation that follows is one in which a person ascertains whether the possible value thus apprehended is truly or only apparently good. The truly good, while it may also be immediately satisfying, is not discerned on the basis of that criterion, for what is satisfying may also not be a genuine value. The truly good, rather, carries us to transcend ourselves, and on that basis Lonergan suggests a normative scale of values that, I believe, is of utmost importance for historical understanding and action: values are vital, social, cultural, personal, and religious, in an ascending order of self-transcendence, and the levels of value are related in a complex fashion. Thus, to focus only on the areas most important in the present volume, the collaborative and communicative process of open and honest conversation about what is most significant for human living is itself a cultural value, perhaps the central cultural value. But it arises upon and is conditioned by the infrastructural foundation of the social institutions that either encourage its occurrence or, in Habermas's terms, more or less systematically distort communication; it depends upon the authenticity of the persons who engage in it and so on the extent and solidity of the processes of conversion they have undergone; and to the extent that it is effective it changes both these persons in their capacity as originating personal value and the social institutions that constitute part of its infrastructural base.

With the acknowledgment of decision as a distinct level of what he came to call intentional consciousness, Lonergan moved to the articulation of a far richer notion of the human good than the purely cognitional foundations of *Insight* permitted. I cannot here go into its elaborate structure, but will simply indicate that the grounds for its unfolding lie at least in part in the integration that deliberation effects of the knowing that *Insight* differentiated and of the feeling that is acknowledged in the later works as a distinct element in the normative source of meaning or common ground of communication and collaboration.

To this point, then, the common ground, when appropriated, is a distinct plateau consisting of four levels of intentional consciousness — in shorthand, experience, understanding, judgment, and decision — and of the feelings that are the mass and momentum of intentional consciousness and that must be submitted to a self-appropriation analogous to that which Lonergan's analysis of intentionality enables with respect to operations.

The next step in the clearing of the common ground or the ascent to a new plateau is the revelation and appropriation of love as the supreme instance of personal value and the highest confluence of intentional operation with feeling. This theme emerges with particular poignancy in the late essays published in *A Third Collection* (1985). Love is total commitment, whether in intimacy, in the family, in interpersonal relations, in the civic community, or in relationship with transcendent mystery. It can be so powerful as to dismantle previous horizons, reveal new values that one could not previously have apprehended, and start one on a whole new course of living, transform one into a new creation. Its working, then, is often strangely independent of the upwardly moving creative dynamism that proceeds through knowledge to decision. However much it is sometimes preceded by knowledge of the beloved, it is always something that happens to us. We fall in love. And it need not always be preceded by knowledge, especially when our falling in love is initiated by, and has as its term, a transcendent mystery that we do not and cannot apprehend.

Love's movement through the common ground, the field of consciousness, is inverse to the movement that has preoccupied us to this point. It first reveals values in their splendor and efficacy, and transvalues our values as it shapes a new horizon. It then discloses, among values, the value of truth, and so strengthens us in the pursuit of intelligibility and truth through our cognitive operations. And, usually ever so slowly, it transforms our very sensitive, dramatic, and intersubjective spontaneity, so that body joins psyche and spirit in one total loving commitment, one complete yes to existence in the cosmos and to our negotiated and discerned place within it.

It is my view, though, that the most important moment or step in Lonergan's clearing of a common ground on which all men and women could, if they so wish, meet was formulated only after all of the above elements had been worked out in his major writings. In some of the essays that he wrote in the last ten years of his life, many of which, again, are contained in *A Third Collection* (1985), he portrays this four-tiered structure of intentional consciousness and concomitant feeling as *open on both ends*, open to what he variously calls (1) a tidal movement that precedes waking experience on one end and that goes beyond responsible decision on the other end, or (2) the passionateness of being that is the very upwardly and indeterminately directed universal dynamism that in *Insight* he called fi-

nality. Most significant of all is the assertion that the normative source of meaning consists of more than intentional
operations. It lies in an entire ongoing process of self-transcendence that embraces the levels of intentional operations in a more inclusive whole. Underpinning the subject
as experientially, intelligently, rationally, morally conscious
is a symbolic operator that through image and affect coor-
dinates neural process with the goals of intentionality. Accompanying that same subject, as we have seen, is the mass
and momentum of feeling. And going beyond that subject
is an operator of interpersonal relations, total commitment,
and religious love. The latter elements are now located,
not on the fourth level of intentional consciousness, but
on a level or even levels beyond what intentionality analysis alone can disclose. And the former ingredients introduce a most elemental level of consciousness that can be
called, at least tentatively, primordial psychic process.

My own way of articulating this development is as
follows: if intentional consciousness, at least in its dramatic
pattern of operations, can be called the search for direction in the movement of life, then this tidal wave or passionateness of being that underpins, accompanies, and
overarches intentional operations is the very movement of
life itself. It too calls for negotiation, as did the intentional
operations whose working and interrelations Lonergan
discloses. But negotiating the operations is distinct from
negotiating the movement, however much each negotiation has to be attentive, intelligent, reasonable, and responsible. The normative source of meaning is, in the last
analysis, more than intelligence and more than intentional
operations. It is the dialectical interplay of these with an
autonomous but related movement of life that begins before intentional operations in neural processes and psychic imagery and affect, and that reaches beyond intentional operations in a total being-in-love in families, in

communities, and with God. The entire ongoing process of self-transcendence that is the normative source of meaning is more than intentional operations, and this 'more' is what Lonergan pointed to and began to articulate towards the end of his life. It is also what I have attempted to articulate in the notion of psychic conversion, a notion which Lonergan assured me in personal correspondence is a 'necessary complement' to his own work.

And so we end, not with a fully cleared field for common ground, but with a further task to which Lonergan pointed but which he did not complete. His own achievement, from this perspective, can be viewed as fulfilling his modest claim of providing an operational analysis that is not subject to radical revision, however much it may be further refined. That in itself is the secure movement onto a new plateau. It remains for us who have been brought to ourselves in a most intimate way by his writings now to make our home on this new plateau. Being at home on the plateau to which Lonergan brought us will happen to us as we negotiate the tidal movement of life by employing the very operations that he taught us to acknowledge, discriminate, claim as our own, and relate to one another. Eventually, while we may still limit intentional operations to four levels of consciousness, we will have to acknowledge in all at least six levels on which we are present to ourselves. For we will have to add an underpinning in elemental psychic process and an overarching context of a total commitment of being-in-love. We will also need to disengage distinct operators for these further levels. And we will need to be far more attentive to the feelings that accompany our intentional operations and function as a kind of moral criterion of their dramatic integrity or authenticity. In building a home, as in constructing a ship (to borrow another image from the preface to *Insight*), one has to go all the way. It is to

Lonergan's undying credit that he never claimed, at any step in the process that I have outlined here, that he had gone the whole way. Always there was, and, I hope, always there will be, a next step. If I have called attention to Lonergan's own pointing to the present next step, it is not to imply that taking it will finally bring us the whole way. For one thing, there is no possible mediation of totality — this is the very meaning of the move to the new plateau; for another thing, there can be a totality of mediation only asymptotically; and for a third thing, even on that mediation we have only begun. May this volume not only analyze, but also encourage and release, the communication that will enable many hands together to build a common home on the new plateau.

**Cosmopolis and the Situation:
A Preface to Systematics and
Communications**

My paper suggests an interpretation and application
of the meaning of cosmopolis[1] in the context of a generalized heuristic approach to situational analysis for direct
theological discourse, that is, for the second phase of theology, which mediates from the present into the future. I
have presented much of this material in lectures elsewhere,
but I have chosen to repeat the material here, though in a
somewhat modified form, for several reasons. In the first
place, I have not yet had a chance for the kind of feedback
on this material that I desire before I move on into other
territory. Secondly, the next step in my endeavors is to
begin the actual task of constructing a contemporary systematic theology in the context established by this situational analysis; and I am simply not ready to present anything along these lines at the present Workshop. Thirdly,
most of my presentations at previous Boston College
Lonergan Workshops have involved various articulations
of and refinements on my notion of psychic conversion;
questions have arisen as to the social and cultural significance of this notion; and it is my hope that the present
review of my work on theology's contemporary situation
may at least begin to provide an answer to these questions.
Finally, the theme of the present Workshop deals with communications; and while my analysis of the situations to be

addressed and evoked by the second phase of theology has
been conducted primarily with an eye to systematics, it
would be at least as relevant to methodological reflection
on and actual performance of work in the functional specialty 'communications,' where, if my analysis is correct,
much work will have to be done on the part of those whose
development has brought them to interiorly differentiated
consciousness, to create in the broader milieu of the
infrastructural level of culture what I would call a post-
interiority mentality: that is, a mentality informed by the
commonsense communication of insights first arrived at
through the specialization of intelligence in the self-appropriation of human interiority.

1   **Introduction**

I begin with some commonplace observations. A
theology that is empirical and historically minded will
mediate the significance of Christian faith with a contemporary cultural matrix. In fact, all theology performs this
function, but only an age characterized by historical consciousness will undertake this responsibility with explicit
awareness of the fact that this is what it is doing. Such a
theology, then, will not strive to achieve the one complete
and permanent systematic understanding of what Christians hold to be true and value as good, but will be content
to acknowledge that its own systematic understanding of
reality in the light of Christ will be but one entry, as it
were, in a series of ongoing systems: an entry that is continuous with past achievements but also open to future
developments. Such a theology, then, will not start from
scratch each time it attempts the constructive work of systematic understanding, but will learn from, retain, and
incorporate into its own construction the genuine achievements of the past. If these achievements were attained

within a classicist framework, and moreover, in a context that gave a priority to theory and so in a context in which the theoretic differentiation of consciousness predominated, their basic terms and relations will be expressed in metaphysical categories. These categories will have to become derivative in any theology that is constructed in an age of historical mindedness. The basic terms and relations will have to be generated on the basis of the self-appropriation of the operations of the intelligent, reasonable, and responsible human subject.

These observations are by now commonplace among those of us who have attempted as best we can to make our own the directives offered by Bernard Lonergan regarding the procedures and tasks of contemporary theology. What I wish to stress is the implication following from these directives, to the effect that even a *systematic* theology constructed on the basis of interiorly differentiated and historically minded consciousness will address one situation, and, as mediating to this situation the significance of Christian faith, will evoke another situation that approximates more closely than the prevailing one to the conditions that would hold sway when the reign of God in human affairs is the primary factor in the intelligibility of the situation. A historically minded theology, as it mediates between a cultural matrix and the role and significance of Christian faith within that cultural matrix, addresses one situation in such a way as to evoke an alternative situation. Even systematic theology, then, must be self-consciously understood as praxis: praxis not simply as cognitive performance, and so as a kind of doing, but praxis as transformative catalytic agency in historical process.

If this is the case, at least three matters of great importance force themselves upon the individual theologian and upon the community of theological investigators. First, historically transformative praxis may not become practi-

cal in the narrow and immediate sense that is subjected to
such a convincing and devastating critique in Lonergan's
pages on general bias.[2] That is to say, it cannot succumb
to the major surrender of intelligence that, while retaining
the empirical function of intelligence, neglects and even
repudiates its critical, dialectical, and normative capacities.[3] Such a capitulation, I would maintain, along with
the neglect of general categories, constitutes the major
deficiency in much of what passes for systematic theology
today. Second, such a theology must be equipped with an
understanding of the structural features of the situation
that it is addressing and of the situation that it would evoke.
And third, this understanding of the respective situations
must be informed by a generalized heuristic anticipation
of *any* situation, if it is not to become bogged down in the
details of mere description that, however significant they
may be for the construction of a systematic theology and
even more for the various tasks of communications, will
unfailingly direct theological reflection along the narrow
lines of biased and shortsighted practicality unless they
are organized by a sufficiently critical, normative, and dialectical heuristic device that would keep everything in its
proper place. The main thrust of my paper, as of my recent work, is to offer rudimentary elements of such a heuristic device in such a way as to offer for systematic theology in particular, and second-phase theology in general, a
contribution that would help them fulfill the indispensable responsibilities of cosmopolis. In what sense is theology praxis, historical world-constitutive and world-trans-
formative agency? That is the question that has occupied
my attention.

Thus I offer the affirmation that theology is ministry. By this I mean that its mediation with a prevailing
cultural matrix of the meanings held as true by Christian
believers and of the values acknowledged as good by the

Christian community contributes to the constitutive meaning of Christian witness, fellowship, and service in the contemporary situation. Such witness, fellowship, and service, when authentic, are transformative of the situation. They are exercised with respect to the situation as it is, but they evoke an alternative situation that more closely approximates the reign of God. As informing the constitutive meaning of Christian living, theology is an intellectual ministry to the church. And since the church has a redemptive function to perform in human history, the theology that partly informs its constitutive meaning is also a dimension of the church's ministry in the world. I have no hesitation in maintaining that all genuine Christian theology, even the most theoretical, philosophically informed systematic theology, has a radically pastoral, prophetic, and kerygmatic intent, purpose, and import. Theology exists to evoke the church as a community of witness, fellowship, and service with a disclosive and transformative role to play with respect to the prevailing situation. Theology performs this function precisely by mediating the significance and role of Christian faith with the prevailing cultural matrix.

If this is correct, then one dimension of the ministry of theology to the church will consist in providing the church with a heuristic device for specifying the structural determinants of the prevailing cultural matrix. Such a device, I would maintain, is at least implicitly operative in every theology in the mode of direct discourse, that is, in all second-phase theological reflection. But it is not sufficient that this device remain implicit, for one of the reasons for conflict and antagonism among various theologies lies precisely in their different heuristic anticipations, their different assumptions, as to the structure of the situation which the theology is addressing and the structure of the situation being evoked. No resolution of these conflicts is satisfactory except on the basis of rendering explicit the manner in which the respective theologies conceive the prevailing and the desirable, that is, normative structures of the situations with which they are concerned.

It is precisely at this point that the first and radical options are taken, determining whether the theology in question will represent a major surrender of intelligence or whether it will insist on embodying not only the empirical, but also the critical, dialectical, and normative capacities of human intelligence. Will the theology in question be a matter of cosmopolitan intellectual collaboration, or will it be a contribution to the series of ever less comprehensive syntheses that constitute decline? The radical option in terms of which this question will be answered is already taken when the theology forms its assumptions as to the structure of the situations to be addressed and evoked in direct theological discourse. What is the structure of the reign of God? This, in special theological categories, is the first question to be answered by a theology in direct discourse in an age of historical consciousness, and so by a theology that would address one situation only to evoke an alternative situation. A theology that mediates between a cultural matrix and the significance and role of Christian faith in that matrix has as its first systematic task the elaboration of the structural intelligibility of the cultural matrix itself. This elaboration, as not only empirical but also critical, dialectical, and normative, will concern not only the prevailing cultural matrix but also the alternative matrix evoked by theological mediation. Foundationally speaking, then, the theology must be equipped with an adequate heuristic device for the specification of the structural determinants of both situations. The adequacy of this heuristic device will ultimately determine the communicative competence, to use Habermas's term, of the theology in question; and even the term 'competence' is used here in a sense that is not only empirical, but also critical, dialectical, and normative.

It is with questions such as these in mind that I have recently attempted an account of 'the situation.' My efforts have been to provide an adequate heuristic device, based on my understanding of chapter 7 of *Insight*, for the determination of *any* situation to be addressed and *any* situation to be evoked by a theology in direct discourse. Let me now state as briefly and as clearly as I can the conclusions to which I have come. I intend that this analysis be used as a dialectical instrument for the critical analysis of various endeavors at direct theological discourse, as a way of determining what these theologies conceive themselves as doing, how they conceive theological praxis, what they have set as their ultimate agenda, and in the last analysis how faithful they are to the Gospel which they claim to be mediating with the contemporary cultural matrix. For I intend this analysis to be at least the beginning of an attempt to specify the general and special categories in terms of which the reign of God in human affairs is to be understood. In terms of the theme of the present workshop, 'Understanding and Communication,' my claim is that the first indispensable requirement for adequate communication is an understanding of the situation that one is addressing and of the situation that one would evoke. My efforts have been to specify a heuristic device for adequate situational understanding.

2   A Situational Heuristic

The principal categories that I have arrived at in these efforts are *the analogy of dialectic* and the *integral scale of values*. It is in terms of these categories that a crucial question of a contemporary systematic theology is to be answered: what is the reign of God in human affairs? This question is crucial precisely because of the role of theology in an age of historical consciousness. Such a theology exists primarily to provide the constitutive meaning in terms of which the ecclesial community would evoke in its cultural matrix a closer approximation to the reign of God.

2.1   The Analogy of Dialectic

'The analogy of dialectic' refers to three distinct but intimately related dialectical processes: the dialectic of community, the dialectic of the subject, and the dialectic of culture. The manner in which these three processes are related to one another is specified in terms of my understanding of the integral scale of values.

The student of Lonergan is already familiar with the notions of the dialectic of community and the dialectic of the subject, and with the general notion of a scale of values based on the degree of self-transcendence to which we are carried by the various objects of our aspirations. 'The dialectic of culture' is my own construction, but it is derived by analogy with the dialectics of community and of the subject as these are set forth by Lonergan. Thus I arrive at the notion of the analogy of dialectic, where the prime analogate is the conscious dialectic of limitation and transcendence that constitutes the immanent intelligibility of all genuine human development. The notion of the *integral* scale of values is arrived at by attempting to answer the question as to how the three dialectics are related to one another. My answer is in terms of the relations that can be found to obtain among the various levels of value already suggested by Lonergan.[4]

The first step in understanding what I mean by the analogy of dialectic consists in differentiating between a dialectic of contraries and a dialectic of contradictories. While I am not prepared to take a stand on the full position of Ronald McKinney concerning the interpretation of Lonergan's use of the term 'dialectic,'[5] I do agree with him at least to this extent, that the term 'dialectic' is used quite differently in *Insight*'s discussion of the dialectics of the subject and of community from the way in which *Method in Theology* specifies dialectic as having to do with the concrete, the dynamic, and the *contradictory*. For the constitutive elements of the dialectics of the subject and of community, as these are presented in *Insight*, while they are indeed concrete and dynamic, are not contradictory. In fact, to conceive them as contradictory is to invite precisely the distortions of these dialectics that promote personal and historical decline. The constitutive elements of these dialectics are contraries, not contradictories. The dialectics are integral to the extent that they are 'a concrete unfolding of linked but opposed principles of change.'[6] The respective dialectics, then, are not a matter of either/or, as would be the case in a dialectic of contradictories, but of both/and. The changes emergent from the dialectic must flow from both of the constitutive elements, each in its appropriate relation to the other. The dialectic of contradictories comes into play with respect to the entirety of the dialectic of contraries: *either* the integral dialectic of contraries *or* its distortion through the transformation of a dialectic of contraries into a dialectic of contradictories opting for only one of the constitutive elements at the expense of the other.

The constitutive elements of the dialectic of the subject are neural demands for psychic integration and conscious representation, on the one hand, and the censorship over these demands exercised by dramatically patterned intelligence and imagination, on the other hand. The constitutive elements of the dialectic of community are spontaneous intersubjectivity and practical intelligence. To these two dialectics of contraries I have added a third, the dialectic of culture. It is internally constituted by cosmological and anthropological constitutive meaning: two distinct and contrary sets of insights regarding the direction that can be found and missed in the movement of life. The dialectics are analogous in that (1) each is an instance of the conscious tension of limitation and transcendence; (2) each is a dialectic of contraries, in that the processes of personal, cultural, and social change represent the more or less integral or distorted unfolding emergent from both of the constitutive principles of change in the respective dialectic; (3) each dialectic is integral to the extent that the relevant processes of change are a function of the harmonious interaction of *both* of the internally constitutive principles of the dialectic; and (4) each dialectic is distorted to the extent that the changes are a function of one of the internally constitutive principles at the expense, or to the exclusion, of the other.

Two other characteristics of the *analogy* of dialectic must be specified. First, in each case the integrity of the dialectic is not a function of one or other of its internally constitutive principles, but of a third element beyond these; and it is in terms of that third element that we locate for the first time the distinctly *theological* significance of the analogy of dialectic. Thus, the integral dialectic of neural demands and the censorship is a function of divinely infused charity, and also of faith and hope and of the other virtues insofar as the acts that proceed from them are a function of grace, of the created communication of the divine nature through which our actions are meritorious of eternal life with God. The integral dialectic of cosmological and anthropological constitutive meaning is a function of soteriological constitutive meaning, of the outer word. And the integral dialectic of spontaneous intersubjectivity and practical intelligence is a function of genuine cultural values, of the integrity of the dialectic of culture.

Second, at the level of this third factor of higher synthesis for each of the dialectics of contraries, there *is* operative a dialectic of contradictories: either the life of charity or some blend or other of the biases; either soteriological constitutive meaning or derailment into either the cosmological myth or the mechanomorphic deaxialization of the anthropological breakthrough of our classical forebears; either authentic cultural values or the distorted constitutive meanings resulting from deculturation.

2.2 An Intellectual Fundamental Option

The relations among the three dialectics of contraries are specified in terms of the integral scale of values. The discussion of the integral scale of values is perhaps best introduced by asking the question, Which of the three dialectics of contraries is the foundational one? If the three dialectics can be understood as specifying the immanent intelligibility of the historical process, then the question becomes, Which of them is the radical foundation of this intelligibility? This way of introducing the question of the integral scale of values has the merit, I believe, of inviting the disclosure of one's radical intellectual fundamental option. In this way it aids the theologian in the critical, dialectical, and normative exercise of intelligence in specifying the structural determinants of the situations to be addressed or evoked by his or her theology and in locating the positional or counterpositional characteristics of other contemporary attempts at direct theological discourse. The reasons for this claim should be apparent, but it is well to spell them out in some detail, since from this elaboration it will become apparent what characteristics are essential in a theology that would be a contribution to the cosmopolitan intellectual collaboration through which decline is to be reversed and progress promoted, and so in what sense the present efforts do in fact fulfill, however rudimentarily, some of the requirements of cosmopolis.

It would perhaps be helpful at this point to locate our reflections within the context of a particular interpretation of the *intellectual* milieu in which theology is to perform its present task of praxis-oriented mediation. For in addition to being ecclesial reflection and ultimately practical in intent and purpose, theology is also to be a fully intellectual enterprise, and so must assume its agenda partly from the intellectual context of its contemporary milieu. On this point I offer the following reflections.

In 'The Future of Thomism,'[7] Lonergan describes the task that he set for himself as one of effecting five bold transpositions from the medieval context, transpositions that are needed, he says, if a contemporary Thomism is to be able to understand, assimilate, penetrate, and transform modern culture. The five transpositions, all related to one another, are: from logic to method; from a classicist to a modern notion of science; from the metaphysics of the soul to the self-appropriation of the subject; from an apprehension of men and women in terms of human nature to an understanding of men and women through human history; and from first principles to transcendental method.

In much contemporary literature, just less than two decades after Lonergan wrote this understanding of the task that he was attempting to perform, we read much talk of the end of modern culture and the beginnings of a postmodern era. If there is any substance to such talk, it would mean that mediating Lonergan's achievements with modern culture is a matter, not of direct discourse, but of *oratio obliqua*, mediating from the past into the present, and that the direct discourse that mediates from the present into the future addresses a different context even from the one which occupied Lonergan just a few years ago. The new context grows out of the previous one, out of its achievements as well as its shortcomings, and so the indirect discourse that mediates Lonergan with modernity is not irrelevant to the direct discourse that would mediate his work with postmodernity. Yet the contemporary task of those who have learned from him is qualified somewhat differently from the task with which he was occupied for so many years.

If one attends to the language in which talk of a postmodern development is expressed, one will find that two of the transpositions of Thomist thought specified by Lonergan will be particularly relevant to the movement from modern to postmodern culture. These two are the transposition from the metaphysics of the soul to the self-appropriation of the subject, and the transposition from the apprehension of men and women in terms of human nature to an understanding of men and women through human history. For postmodern language speaks of the death of the subject and the end of history, and it does so in a way that casts great doubt on the claims of modern culture to have brought about a turn to the subject and a definitive emergence of historical consciousness. In this sense the *oratio obliqua* that would mediate Lonergan's achievements with modern culture becomes important in helping us understand the shortcomings of the modern preoccupations with subjectivity and history. In other words, the thesis that I would propose is that the talk of postmodern authors concerning the end of subjectivity and history is possible only because the modern turns to the subject and to historical consciousness were radically flawed. The indirect discourse that would mediate Lonergan with modernity would then become pertinent for the postmodern context in pointing to the possibility of another option within this context besides the drastic and ultimately nihilistic one proposed by postmodern authors. For this indirect discourse would achieve, by reason of its dialectical encounter with modern subjectivity and historical consciousness, the definitive fulfillment of the turn to the subject and to history, and so the beginnings of a new stage of meaning that is genuinely postmodern, but not in the nihilistic sense in which that term is so often used today. The postmodern context becomes, not one of a fated acceptance of absurdity as the final word, but one of an option between, on the one hand, the dissolution of the subject, the end of history, the celebration of the derisory, the cynical, the senseless, and, on the other hand, the self-appropriation of the subject in the fullness of the proportions reached by Lonergan, and the definitive establishment of historical consciousness on foundations that transcend the inevitability of a final relativism. Either option is postmodern. Posing the option forces upon us the question of where we go from here, in a way that compels choice and that lays bare the radical sources of the alternatives.

Moreover, it is possible to broaden the choice that is ours by including among the alternatives a third possibility that, like the other two, would acknowledge the failure of modernity, but would then revert to a classicist mentality as the only recourse. This third alternative, best represented in the conscientious work of Leo Strauss and his followers, is understandable, important, influential, certainly to be preferred to the nihilistic option, but also, I believe, ultimately futile. We may speak, at any rate, of a threefold set of alternatives constituting a postmodern option: nihilism, a new classicism, and a new stage of meaning grounded in the self-appropriation of the subject.

For the moment, primarily for the sake of greater clarity in speaking of the postmodern option, I will limit myself to a discussion of the alternatives of nihilism and self-appropriation. I do this despite the fact that I have far more sympathy for the neoclassicist position than for the nihilistic one. The postmodern option can then be specified more accurately as a choice between two possibilities at each of three of the levels of value specified by Lonergan. At the level of personal value, the choice is between self-appropriation and the dissolution of the subject. The postmodern proclamation of the death of the subject is not, I believe, simply a piece of existential or political rhetoric; nor is it intended as a bit of descriptive cultural criticism metaphorically delineating a felt atmosphere that would have to be *explained* in more precise and less poetic terms. Rather, it names quite directly a process of ever less comprehensive syntheses in both the cognitive and existential orders, due to the breakdown of the schemes of recurrence of the self-transcending operations of the human subject, a series of events or occurrences in the process of human history whose immanent intelligibility is an intelligent emergent probability. It names the ultimate upshot of the longer cycle of decline: the end of insight, rational reflection and judgment, and creative world-constitutive responsibility as historical agency.

At the level of cultural values, the option becomes one between the promotion of a transcultural stage of meaning rooted in the self-appropriation of the equally transcultural roots of human integrity, on the one hand, and the end of history as what Eric Voegelin might call a form of order, on the other hand.

And at the level of social values, the option is between the emergence of a global network of alternative communities intent on the right way to live, on the one hand, and the homogeneous and universal, that is, totalitarian, state, on the other hand.

In case anyone is inclined to regard my proposed alternative as too stark a reading of the contemporary situation, let me refer briefly to a book that has influenced my position. The clearest and most forthright instances of postmodern consciousness, as the word is being used here, are, I believe, still to be found in French philosophy, political thought, human science, and literary criticism from roughly 1960 to the present. But the influence of these currents of thought on the teaching especially of literature but also of philosophy throughout North America today is enough to persuade me that the series of movements and debates involved here is more than a merely localized phenomenon. One contemporary French philosopher, Vincent Descombes, has interpreted the movement of recent French philosophy as a passage from the generation (1930-1960) characterized by the influence of 'the three H's' — Hegel, Husserl, and Heidegger — to the generation (from 1960 on) dominated by the three masters of suspicion — Marx, Nietzsche, and Freud. In addition, Descombes has offered the interesting and convincing thesis that one can find the very roots of the second generation in the event that launched the first on its course, despite the fact that the second generation is characterized negatively by its polemic against the first. That event, or series of events, lies in Alexandre Kojève's lectures on Hegel's *Phenomenology of Spirit* delivered at the Ecole Pratique des Hautes Etudes from 1933 to 1939.[8] According to Descombes, the resurgence of French philosophical interest in Hegel during the 1930s was due in part, in Merleau-Ponty's words, to Hegel's potential for giving 'a *truth* above and beyond divergent points of view ... a new classicism, an organic civilization, while maintaining the sharpest sense of subjectivity.'[9] This potential was rooted, in turn, in the way in which Hegel seemed to provide (again in Merleau-Ponty's words) an exploration of the irrational and an integration of it into an expanded reason: what Merleau-Ponty rightly called 'the task of our century.'[10] But Kojève's interpretation of the Hegelian expansion of reason is precisely *not* an

understanding of reason's ability to gain sway in such areas as 'history and its violence, existence and its contingency, the unconscious and its stratagems,'[11] and so is not
an extension of reason into areas previously outside its
scope. Kojève sees rather a metamorphosis of reason into
its opposite, into madness as the passage to wisdom. Allow me, please, a fairly lengthy quotation from Descombes,
in order to capture the flavor of the mentality that calls
itself postmodern:

> Far from emphasizing the reasonable and con-
> ciliatory side of Hegel's thought, [Kojève's]
> reading dwells on its paradoxical, excessive,
> violent and, above all, sanguinary features ...
> His commentary on the *Phenomenology of Mind*
> presents it as an account of universal history in
> which bloody strife — and not 'reason' — is
> responsible for the progress of events towards
> the happy conclusion ... This explains why we
> find, among the most assiduous followers of
> Kojève's course, the very figures who were to
> supply most of the ammunition for the [later]
> 'generalized anti-Hegelianism' ... In the ver-
> sion advanced by Kojève, Hegel's thought pre-
> sents a number of features that might well at-
> tract a Nietzschean. It contains an element of
> risk and adventure; it endangers the thinker's
> very person, his *identity*; it reaches out beyond
> the generally accepted measure of good and
> evil ... There is little doubt that what so held
> the attention of Kojève's listeners was his abil-
> ity to compromise philosophy — in the sense
> that we speak of 'compromising acquaintan-
> ces' — by forcing it to traverse areas of exist-
> ence on which it had not impinged until then:

political cynicism, the virtue of massacre and violence, and, in a global way, *the unreasonable origins of reason*. Through Kojève's gift of eloquence, these aspects of Hegel's work, which had long been treated as the regrettable side of his philosophy, now came to be seen as the measure of its value. Reality is a fight to the death between men for ludicrous stakes ... and any philosophy that neglects this essential fact is an idealistic mystification. In brutal terms, this was Kojève's teaching.

Kojève bequeathed to his listeners a *terrorist conception of history*. The motif of Terror recurs in each successive debate up to the present day.[12]

Whether Kojève is correctly interpreting Hegel is subject to debate. But that his own evaluation of the Hegelian text-as-interpreted is itself an entry into the most destructive, indeed demonic, form of madness is in my view beyond question. On this reading, then, we might say that a so-called postmodern consciousness begins with the explicit acceptance, at the superstructural level of culture itself, of madness as the path to wisdom. Let us listen to Descombes as he describes some of the perduring influences in French thought of Kojève's lectures, and as we do so let us think of events in twentieth-century history far beyond the world of French philosophy. First, then:

The doctrine of *praxis* lacks all means of orienting or of judging action. It maintains that the idealist's ideal is a mystification now, but that it will have a meaning in the future. Meanwhile, then, a 'morality of realism,' drawn from experience, will have to suffice as grounds for action. It will not, therefore, be possible to look to philosophy for a rule of action. No *idea* can direct the philosopher of praxis in his actions, except the idea that he must act. Action becomes completely indeterminate. The revolt against idealist abstraction gives rise only to an *abstract* apologia for action and violence. The resolution is there to act against ills in general, but in a specific situation — and all situations are specific — the same set of premises can justify any decision whatsoever.[13]

Again:

Dialectical philosophy can now be defined as the thinking which identifies desire with pure negativity, and sees in it not only a negation, but a negation of the negation [where the first negation characterizes all action as labor and struggle, and the second names the overcoming of labor and struggle in the complete taming of nature and the definitive establishment of the homogeneous state.][14]

Again:

The final scene in this humanist version of the Hegelian dialectic provides us also with its principle. The last episode in the narrative of the story is understood as corresponding to a final stage in human history itself, beyond which there are to be no further developments. Kojève never failed to insist, provocatively enough, on the startling consequences of this thesis. History is at an end, and we enter now into its aftermath.[15]

Again:

In a philosophy of action, or of history, man is defined by the fact that he acts and

changes the course of things. If history is at an
end, nothing remains to be done. But an idle
man is no longer a man. As the threshold of
post-history is crossed, humanity disappears
while at the same time the reign of frivolity
begins, the reign of play, of derision (for hence-
forth nothing that might be done would have
the slightest meaning.[16]

But:

History was only concluded in theory, as
an idea, with precisely the *idea* (remaining to
be achieved, most likely, with terrorist methods) of a 'homogeneous State' — an expression which for [Kojève] could apply as much
to Hegel's reasonable State as to Marx's class-
less society. In order for this idea to become a
global reality, a little more time was required,
just long enough in which to act — an action
which would correspond to the wars and revo-
lutions in which we were mobilized.[17]

The context for implementing Lonergan's already
achieved transpositions, I submit, is now precisely one
constituted by the necessity of choosing between, on the
one hand, the anticipation of a post-historic homogeneous
State incrementally moved toward by terrorist and counter-
terrorist violence, and on the other hand, the anticipation
of what Merleau-Ponty described as a *truth* above and beyond divergent points of view, a truth that, while preserving the sharpest sense of subjectivity, provides access to a
new organic civilization on a transcultural or world-cultural basis. And the basic question on which this choice
depends is that concerning the issues raised by the masters of suspicion: is reason to be expanded so as responsibly to negotiate psychological (Freud), social (Marx), and

cultural-as-cosmological (Nietzsche) determinisms, or is it to be metamorphized into madness as the passage to wisdom? The three masters of suspicion raise, respectively, the question regarding each of the three dialectical processes which, in their interrelation with one another, constitute the intelligible core of the historical process.

In terms of the previous question as to which of the three dialectics is foundational, a question whose answer, I said, betrays a radical intellectual fundamental option, we might indicate the following: if one answers 'the dialectic of community,' one implicitly joins hands with Marx and his disciples, that is, with one of the current varieties of the nihilistic option, since cultural and personal values become here at best a function of the social infrastructure; if one answers 'the dialectic of culture,' one risks a classicist or at least premodern view of a given culture as normative; and so, if one wants to avoid both nihilism and classicism, one must hold that the foundational set of processes responsible for the intelligibility or absurdity of history lies in the dialectic of the subject. The authenticity or inauthenticity of subjects grounds the authenticity or inauthenticity of cultural traditions. And the authenticity or inauthenticity of cultural traditions grounds the integrity or disarray of the social order.

2.3   The Integral Scale of Values

The latter two sentences already imply a position on what constitutes the integrity of the scale of values. This position must be delineated more carefully. My usual way into this material has been through a more careful analysis of the dialectic of community and of the conditions of its integrity, as these are explicated by Lonergan. Let me, then, review this material once again in the present context.

There is an 'original' or primordial experience of the subject-as-subject, which forms the foundational reality for the various reflections that I have done in an attempt to complement and especially implement Lonergan's thought. In reliance on Eric Voegelin, I call this original experience the search for direction in the movement of life. The movement as such is experienced in the sensitive psyche. The search for and discovery of direction are conducted by intentional consciousness raising and answering questions for understanding, reflection, and deliberation. In proportion to one's success in finding the direction that can also be missed or lost, one so forges the materials that constitute the movement of life as to make of one's world, one's relations with others, and oneself a work of dramatic art.

Society provides the context for the project of dramatic artistry, and the latter project changes the social context for better or for worse. From my interpretation of chapter 7 of *Insight*, I find society to consist of five interrelated aspects or dimensions: primordial intersubjectivity; the technological institutions whose primary function is the formation of capital; the economic system; the political order; and culture. I find, too, that culture is understood by Lonergan to consist of two dimensions. There is the everyday level of meanings and values informing a given way of life; and there is a reflexive or superstructural level of scientific, scholarly, philosophical, and theological objectifications.

We said above that the dialectic of community is the concrete unfolding of the changes resulting from the tension of spontaneous intersubjectivity and practical intelligence. Now, practical intelligence is the source of three of the constitutive elements of society: technology, the economic system, and the political order. The integrity or distortion of the dialectic is a function of culture: proximately, of the everyday level, and remotely of the superstructural level. The infrastructure of society is constituted by spontaneous intersubjectivity, technology, economic relations, politics, and the everyday level of culture. The reflexive level of culture constitutes the society's superstructure. Culture at both levels is the condition of the possibility of the integrity of the dialectic of spontaneous intersubjectivity with the technological, economic, and political institutions created by practical intelligence. The integrity of the dialectic 'rests on the concrete unity of opposed principles [intersubjectivity and practical intelligence]; the dominance of either principle results in a distortion, and the distortion both weakens the dominance and strengthens the opposed principle to restore an equilibrium.'[18] It is the function of the dimension of consciousness that Lonergan calls cosmopolis to inform an intellectual collaboration at the superstructural level of culture that would assume responsibility for the dialectic of community, by attending to the cultural meanings and values that are operative at *both* the infrastructural and the superstructural level of culture. Authentic cultural values, truly operative and *correct* assumptions about the right way to live, constitute the higher synthesis upon which the integrity of the dialectic of community depends, whereas the breakdown of the dialectic of community is due to the breakdown of culture, either because culture has been 'forced into an ivory tower of ineffectualness by the social surd' or because it has 'capitulate[d] to its absurdity' by becoming narrowly practical or exclusively instrumental.[19]

The analysis of society presented in *Insight* is buttressed by reflection on the scale of values that Lonergan proposes in *Method in Theology*. Reflection on the scale of values, especially in the light of Lonergan's analysis of progress and decline in chapter 7 of *Insight*, reveals that, among the various relations that obtain among the levels of value, two are of special moment for a generalized heuristic anticipation of the situations to be addressed and evoked by a theology *in oratione recta*. First, there is the set of relations from above downwards. Higher levels of value condition the schemes of recurrence of more basic levels. Thus, God's grace is the condition of sustained personal integrity; such integrity is the condition of recurrently operative cultural values; authentic cultural values at both the infrastructural and superstructural levels condition the integrity of the dialectic of community that is the constitutive structure of social values; and the integral dialectic of community conditions the possibility of the equitable distribution of vital goods to the whole community, assuring liberation not only from hunger and misery but also from servitude and personal degradation, hopelessness and meaninglessness. Conversely, there is the set of relations that obtain from below upwards. Let us call them relations of differentiation and creativity. Thus, problems at the level of the recurrent distribution of vital goods can be met only by a realignment of the dialectic of community (new technological institutions, economic relations, political relations, or a new adaptation of sensitive intersubjectivity to practical necessity); this realignment demands changes in constitutive meaning, and so new cultural values at the infrastructural level of culture; the development of these cultural values may require superstructural reflection in the germane disciplines; in either case, changes in constitutive meaning may be so radical as to call for personal conversion or at least for a quite significant deepening and extension of one's present orientation; and the latter changes in turn are in need of God's grace.

Now the realities constitutive not only of the level of social values but also of the levels of cultural and personal values are revealed by our analysis to be dialectical processes, where the respective dialectics are understood in accord with our position on the analogy of dialectic spelled out above. When this position is joined with what we have just said about the relations that obtain among the levels of value, we find that the dialectic of culture is the condition of the possibility of an integral dialectic of community; and that an integral dialectic of subjects is the condition of the possibility of the integral dialectic of culture. The foundational dialectic is thus the dialectic of the subject.

3 Cosmopolis Today

One step remains to be taken before the situations to be addressed and evoked by a theology in direct discourse mediating from the present into the future are adequately conceived at least to get us started. That step involves a further implication of our analysis of the integral scale of values. The question that prompts us to take this step has to do with the application to the present situation of the entire analysis to this point. In other words, can the heuristic anticipation of theology's situations be further extended so as to provide the proximate clue that enables sufficient objectification of the current situation so that our theology will genuinely mediate between a cultural matrix and the significance and role of Christian faith within that matrix? The answer to this question arises from grasping an implication of our analysis of the relations from below upwards among the levels of value.

That implication is to the effect that the proportions of the relevant synthesis at higher levels required to meet the problem of schemes of recurrence at the more basic levels are set by the difficulties at the more basic levels themselves. And today the problem of the effective distribution of vital goods is markedly global in nature. Its solution will call for new social-infrastuctural relations on a global scale. The socioeconomic relations and political realities that constitute a globally interdependent commonwealth will demand for their realignment the generation of cultural values that are somehow crosscultural. The culture that is adequate to the proportions of a globally interdependent technological, economic, and political order in dialectical relationship with a crosscultural intersubjectivity is at best emergent in our present situation. A theology that would mediate in direct discourse from the present into the future at this juncture in human history will be mediating what Christians believe as true and value as good, not with a relatively stable set of cultural meanings and values, but with an emergent set required to meet the exigences of the present social order. Second-phase theology today will be participating in the very emergence of a new cultural matrix. It will be forging the very materials of constitutive meaning required for the emergence of a legitimate alternative to the present situation. What will be the constitutive meaning of the global network of alternative communities, catalyzed in part by ecclesial ministry but extending far beyond the formal boundaries of any church community, that will constitute the world-cultural humanity for which cosmopolis must opt in the face of the post-historic threat of contemporary nihilism? Theology is in the position today of contributing to the emergence of a new and decidedly global cultural matrix, by its very mediation to a cultural matrix of the significance and role of Christian faith. Second-phase theology, mediating from the present into the future, must conceive its task somewhat along these lines if it is to meet its responsibility to the church and to the world.

Limitations of space permit me to offer only a few suggestions along the lines of an answer to this question. I said above that the integral dialectic of culture is constituted by the tense interplay of cosmological and anthropological constitutive meaning, under the higher synthesis provided by soteriological constitutive meaning. The

suggestions offered here constitute but a brief amplifica-
tion of this assertion. But they are offered as a contribution to answering the question of what qualities are desirable in the categories employed by a theology mediating
in direct discourse from the present into the future. We
know already from Lonergan that these categories are to
be as transcultural as the self-appropriation of the
transcultural constituents of converted subjectivity will
permit. Among these constituents is the conscious dialectic of limitation and transcendence, and it is from this that
my suggestion derives whatever force it may have.

If my assertion regarding the structure of the dialectic of culture is correct, then the integrity of a human culture is a function of the concrete unfolding of cosmological and anthropological insight and truth, and the
inauthenticity of a human culture is a function of a breakdown of this integral unfolding due to the displacement of
the tension in favor of one or other pole of the dialectic.

A generalized account of research into cosmological
symbolizations would reveal, I trust, that in these symbolizations the experience of life as a movement with a direction that can be found, but also missed or lost, is projected
onto the cosmic rhythms, where the paradigm of order is
discovered. The movement proceeds from the order of the
cosmos, first to the society, and then to the individual. In
other words, the order of the cosmos prescribes the social
order, and the order of society dictates the constitution of
individual rectitude. Anthropological insight reverses this
movement, in that, since the measure of integrity is acknowledged to lie beyond the cosmos and so to be world-
transcendent, it provides the standard of integrity first for
the individual; and the well-ordered attunement of the individual to the world-transcendent measure of integrity
measures the integrity of the society.

The integrity of the dialectic of culture is the function, not of either of its internally constitutive poles, and

so not of cosmological nor of anthropological constitutive meaning, but of soteriological insight and truth. Now, it is precisely soteriological insight and truth that theology in direct discourse is to mediate to the prevailing constitutive meaning of a cultural matrix. Cosmological constitutive meaning, when exclusive of anthropological insight and truth, binds the schemes of recurrence of individual and social development too stringently to the schemes of recurrence of nonhuman nature; cosmological consciousness thus is prone to succumbing massively to a fatalism that seems inscribed in cosmic rhythms; and cosmological cultures all too easily become the prey of forces whose exclusively instrumental rationality has released consciousness from cosmic fatalism but at the expense of ecological participation in nature. Anthropological constitutive meaning exclusive of cosmological insight and truth is insensitive to its biologically based, rhythmic participation in nonhuman nature. Given a loss or disappearance of its original revelatory experience of being drawn beyond the cosmos for its standard of integrity, it becomes increasingly a matter of exclusively instrumental rationality. Lacking the pole of limitation that would be provided by its tense unity with cosmological constitutive meaning, it gives way to imperialistic ambitions, where imperialism is understood with Joseph Schumpeter as the objectless disposition on the part of a state or other macrosystem to unlimited forcible expansion.[20] The end result is the homogeneous state hailed by Kojève as the death of the subject and the end of history.

My suggestions for theology as cosmopolis, then, lead to the hope that a theology mediating in direct discourse from the present into the future will display the soteriological significance of the divinely originated solution to the mystery of evil with respect to both cosmological fatalism and the mechanomorphic distortion of anthropological insight and truth. The integral dialectic of culture, of cosmological and anthropological constitutive meaning under the higher synthesis of a soteriological differentiation of consciousness, could provide the ecumenically available set of meanings and values that are needed to inform the social infrastructure of a global network of communities alternative to the imperialistic distortions of the dialectic of community. Again, because such a set of cultural meanings and values is not yet constitutive of a stable cultural matrix, theology's task of mediation in direct discourse will itself be constitutive of the cultural values of a world-cultural humanity.

With these suggestions, I must close. The stage is set now to move to the actual work of systematic theology. I enter on this task with trepidation, for it is tempting to remain forever at the level of foundational refinement. I have no doubt that I have much more foundational reflection to do. But I will have to do it *ambulando*. I know, too, that my attempts at a contemporary systematic theology will be inadequate, and will be transcended, better sooner rather than later, by more adequate efforts than my own. Yet there surely is an awareness in the Lonergan community that it is time to begin the task of systematic theology, however rudimentary present efforts will shortly appear to be. What my work on the situations to be addressed and evoked by a contemporary systematic theology has provided is the hypothesis that the analogy of dialectic and the integral scale of values can provide the core intelligibilities or focal meanings of a systematics that is at once ecclesial reflection, rigorous system, and praxis-oriented mediation of constitutive meaning. Only the execution of the systematic task will verify whether that hypothesis is correct.

Notes

[1] See Bernard Lonergan, *Insight* (see above, chapter 1, note 20) 238-42/263-67.

[2] Ibid. 225-42/250-67.

[3] Ibid. 230-32/255-57.

[4] Bernard Lonergan, *Method in Theology* (see above, chapter 1, note 1) 31-32.

[5] See Ronald McKinney, 'Lonergan's Notion of Dialectic' (see above, chapter 4, note 8).

[6] Lonergan, *Insight* 217/242.

[7] Bernard Lonergan, 'The Future of Thomism,' in *A Second Collection* (see above, chapter 5, note 3) 43-53.

[8] See Vincent Descombes, *Modern French Philosophy*, trans. L. Scott-Fox and J.M. Harding (Cambridge: Cambridge University Press, 1980); Alexandre Kojève, *Introduction to the Reading of Hegel*, trans. James H. Nicholls, Jr., ed. Allan Bloom (New York: Basic Books, 1969).

[9] Quoted in Descombes, *Modern French Philosophy* 11.

[10] Quoted ibid.

[11] Ibid. 13.

[12] Ibid. 13-14.

[13] Ibid. 18-19.

[14] Ibid. 26.

[15] Ibid. 27.

[16] Ibid. 31.

[17] Ibid. 32.

[18] Lonergan, *Insight* 233/258.

[19] Ibid. 237/262.

[20] Joseph Schumpeter, *Imperialism/Social Classes: Two Essays*, trans. Heinz Norden (New York: New American Library, 1951) 6.

12   Education for Cosmopolis

This paper is a greatly revised version of a lecture that I delivered first at Loyola University in New Orleans in 1978 and then at the 1979 Lonergan Workshop at Boston College. The revision derives from subsequent and fuller reflection on the situations addressed and evoked by a contemporary Christian systematic theology. A summary of the results of this reflection is given in the first part of the paper. It is followed by a description of the development of intelligent, rational, and existential consciousness that would be required to meet this situation. Then the plausibility crisis of the contemporary academy is discussed in the light of the educational ideals proposed in the preceding section. The paper concludes with a proposal for a four-year liberal curriculum oriented to the development needed to meet the situation. This final section may serve more either as a regulative ideal or as the starting point for a discussion than as a set of practical prescriptions that could readily be implemented just as they stand.

1   The Situation

In the second chapter of *Method in Theology*, Lonergan offers us a scale of values whose ascending order, it seems, is determined by the degree of self-transcendence to which we are carried at each level.

... We may distinguish vital, social, cultural, personal, and religious values in an ascending order. Vital values, such as health and strength, grace and vigor, normally are preferred to avoiding the work, privations, pains involved in acquiring, maintaining, restoring them. Social values, such as the good of order which conditions the vital values of the whole community, have to be preferred to the vital values of individual members of the community. Cultural values do not exist without the underpinning of vital and social values, but none the less they rank higher. Not on bread alone doth man live. Over and above mere living and operating, men have to find a meaning and value in their living and operating. It is the function of culture to discover, express, validate, criticize, correct, develop, improve such meaning and value. Personal value is the person in his self-transcendence, as loving and being loved, as originator of values in himself and in his milieu, as an inspiration and invitation to others to do likewise. Religious values, finally, are at the heart of the meaning and value of man's living and man's world.[1]

The situation that would be addressed by a contemporary Christian systematic theology, as well as the anticipated situation which such a theology would evoke, can be understood best by disengaging some of the relations that obtain among the levels of value, and by employing this disengagement to understand (1) the breakdown of the integrity of human valuation that characterizes the present situation and (2) the integrity itself that would constitute the situation to be evoked.

Among the relations that obtain in the scale of values we may specify a relation from below upwards of differentiation and creativity and a relation from above downwards of conditioning and enablement. Thus a problem in the recurrent realization or effective distribution of vital values may give rise to the questions that, if pursued, would lead to new technological, economic, and political institutions at the level of social values. For these institutions to be promotive of a good of order that is truly worth while, they must respect the two principles of change that constitute the integral dialectic of community: the spontaneity of human intersubjectivity and the practical agency that is responsible for the maintenance and transformation of the organization of human affairs.[2] If *Method in Theology* states the function of culture to be one of discovering, expressing, validating, criticizing, correcting, developing, and improving the meanings and values that inform a given way of life, *Insight* makes it clear that the ulterior purpose of such refinements lies in the integrity of the dialectic of community.[3] More concretely, the development and implementation of new technological, economic, and political institutions may prove to be impossible short of a transformation of the cultural values informing a society's way of life. Culture functions at the two levels of everyday transactions and reflexive, superstructural objectification.[4] But for it to function with integrity at either level there is required the integrity of self-transcending persons originating values in themselves and their milieu, and inspiring and inviting others to do likewise. And sustained personal integrity is impossible without a living relationship of partnership and love with the absolutely transcendent source and goal of the human exigence for true meaning and real goodness, and so without the effective realization of religious values.

This relationship of differentiation and creativity from below upwards in the scale of values obviously implies a relationship of conditioning and enablement from above downwards. Religious values condition the possibility of personal integrity. Personal integrity conditions the possibility of the integrity of culture at both the superstructural and the infrastructural levels. The integrity of culture conditions the possibility of a social order that exists and functions in accord with the integral dialectic of community. And only such a social order renders possible the effectively recurrent distribution of vital values to the whole community.

The situation that a contemporary systematic theology would address, which in the present paper is considered also as the situation within which liberal education takes place, must be thought of in global terms. For the problem of the effective distribution of vital values is a global one, to be solved only by the creation and development of political, economic, and technological structures constructed from within such a global perspective. Such a solution is impossible without the crosscultural generation of such cultural values as could initiate, promote, and maintain the integral dialectic of community, and this in a global network of communities that would provide a genuine alternative to globally pervasive distortions of the scale of values. Such crosscultural communication will break down without the discovery and implementation of the crosscultural constituents of personal integrity that lie in the transcendental imperatives constituting the levels of human consciousness and in the refined affectivity necessary to be faithful to these imperatives. Finally, the implementation of these imperatives by truly attentive, intelligent, reasonable, responsible, and loving subjects in community demands their cooperation with God in working out, not our solution, but God's, to our problem of evil: a cooperation that, given the global context of the present situation, would be furthered by the dialogue of world religions.[5]

The principal agents of the global distortions of the scale of values are the various representatives of centralized state socialism that take their inspiration from one or other interpretation of Marx, and the network of disintegration spawned by multinational corporational capitalism. The structure of the distortions operative in Marxist states parallels that found in capitalist societies.[6] And the conflict between these two imperialistic networks is as productive of disintegration as are the distortions themselves that constitute each system of imperial ambition taken singly. The situation within which a liberal education today would take place, then, may be characterized largely in terms of global distortions of the integral scale of values, due in great measure to the exploits of competing and escalating imperial ambitions. A liberal education would be oriented to mediating the *cultural values* constitutive of an anticipated alternative situation in which the integrity of the scale of values would be the effectively operative norm of procedure.

2   Cosmopolis

2.1   The Problem

There is at least one problem in our articulation of the relations among the various levels of value that needs further treatment. Its contours become clear if we reflect on two opposed tendencies in contemporary political philosophy. Liberal democratic and Marxist political philosophies may be considered together, insofar as they reveal either a neglect of, or a skepticism regarding the autonomy of, religious, personal, and cultural values, and a tendency to collapse at least the effectively operative scale into the two more basic levels of vital and social values. Political philosophies which draw their inspiration from the classical tradition, on the other hand, emphasize the upper reaches of the scale of values but tend to neglect the more basic everyday-cultural and especially the social and vital values. In either case what is missed is the conditioning link between the superstructure and the infrastructure of society. Thus classically inspired political philosophies maintain a conversion position regarding praxis, whereas liberal and especially Marxist orientations stress social-structural transformation; and each praxis position is suspicious of the other. The relations among religious, personal, and cultural values and the relations between social and vital values are easier to grasp and assent to than is the relation of the three higher levels to the two more basic levels. If our position on the scale of values is to be accepted, then, we must establish that the relation that obtains between authentic cultural values and justice in the social order is every bit as firm as those that hold between other levels of value.

Our position regarding the levels of value and their relations is a component in a philosophy of world-constitutive praxis. From this perspective we may discern a blind spot in classically inspired political philosophies. Correcting this inadequacy may enable us to solve the larger problem of grasping the firm relation of conditioning and enablement that must obtain between the superstructure and the infrastructure of a healthy society. For, while classically inspired political philosophies *do* affirm correctly that the social order is a derivative of cultural values, they neglect to ascertain that breakdowns in the social order may signal a demand for more than simply a reaffirmation and reappropriation of the cultural values of the classical tradition. The latter values, while by and large valid, especially when retrieved by such a sensitive thinker as Eric Voegelin,[7] may have to be sublated into an entirely new horizon that institutes a quite novel set of cultural values commensurate with the dimensions of the social problem. This becomes particularly the challenge when the social order is a *global* network of 'if-then' relationships. The global nature of our contemporary social order calls for the development of a new set of cultural values as the condition of the possibility of a just global social order. This new set of cultural values must be crossculturally generated and must consist in a higher synthesis of the various regionally delimited cultural traditions participating in the institution of a crosscultural community. Moreover, applying the same principle of creativity and differentiation from below upwards among the levels of value, a major transformation at the level of personal value, a transformation measured by the proportions set by the task of the crosscultural generation of cultural values, will be required, in the form of the self-appropriation of the invariant and so crosscultural constituents of human integrity. And this personal transformation will call for a reconstitution of religious experience itself in the form of a willingness that is not only universal, in the sense in which Lonergan employs this term,[8] but explicitly and thematically ecumenic in its orientation toward the emergence, promotion, and survival of a world-cultural communitarian alternative to the distortions of the dialectic of community emergent from the agents of imperialism. These creative differentiations at the levels of cultural, personal, and religious values set the context for a concrete discussion and application of the higher viewpoint that Lonergan calls cosmopolis.[9] This higher viewpoint defines the objective of an adequate contemporary liberal education.

Lonergan speaks of a divinely originated solution to the mystery of evil, a solution informed by the following

three components: (1) 'a renovation of will that matches
intellectual detachment and aspiration'; (2) 'a new and
higher collaboration of intellects through faith in God';
and (3) 'a mystery that is at once symbol of the
uncomprehended and sign of what is grasped and psychic
force that sweeps living human bodies, linked in charity,
to the joyful, courageous, wholehearted, yet intelligently
controlled performance of the tasks set by a world order in
which the problem of evil is not suppressed but transcended.'[10] Our concern at present is primarily with the
new and higher collaboration of intellects through faith in
God, that is, with a religiously and theologically transformed cosmopolis.[11] The mystery of evil confronts us today in part in the spectre of a post-historic humanity[12] as
the limit or end result of the series of ever less comprehensive syntheses in the understanding and organization of
human affairs: a series that is rooted in the exclusively
instrumentalized rationality emergent from the general bias
of common sense.[13] Cosmopolis provides the corrective
to general bias; but, as a higher viewpoint in the mind, it is
dependent upon an actual higher integration in the being
of those informed by it, upon a universal willingness that
renders possible the effective freedom to collaborate in the
institution of a world-cultural humanity.

We must analyze the general characteristics of this
cosmopolitan collaboration before applying our understanding of cosmopolis to the current situation with its
invitation to, and indeed exigence for, the crosscultural
generation of the cultural values of a global communitarian
alternative to imperialism.

2.2   *The General Features of Cosmopolis*

Cosmopolis is a development of intelligence that
grounds a collaborative enterprise of subjects committed

to understanding, affirming, and implementing the integral dialectic of community. We can perhaps best move to an understanding of the dialectic of community if we begin by differentiating the several components of society.

I follow David Tracy in employing the term 'society' as a broad generic term encompassing several more specific dimensions. But while Tracy differentiates society into the three components of the technoeconomic order, the polity, and culture,[14] I find it more exact, first, to accept from Karl Marx a distinction of technological institutions (Marx's 'forces of production') from the economic system (Marx's 'relations of production'), to add with Lonergan yet another dimension, that of intersubjective spontaneity or primordial human intersubjectivity,[15] and to distinguish two dimensions to culture: the everyday and the reflexive. Society, then, consists of the five dimensions of spontaneous intersubjectivity, technological institutions, the economic system, the legal and political domain, and culture, where culture is a matter of both everyday meanings and values and reflexive objectifications of everyday transactions. The actually functioning dialectic of community is constituted by the relations that obtain among these components of society. The dialectic is integral when the relations are sound, and distorted when they are awry. The issue, then, is one of determining the constitution of sound relations among these dimensions of society.

Now the progress or decline of a society is to be understood in relation to the development or maldevelopment of the person as a dramatic artist.[16] We may interpret the relations in the following way: first, the desire to make of one's life, one's relations with others, and one's world a work of art, by discovering and following in freedom the direction to be found in the movement of life, is more readily fulfilled to the extent that the social conditions that stimulate personal change allow for and foster the use and development of intelligence and the exercise of freedom, and is subject to frustration to the extent that the factors of understanding and freedom are restricted by the mechanisms of psychological conditioning, social absurdity, and in the limit totalitarian control; second, a society will transcend the grip of chance or fate or destiny, of conditioning, bias, and control, to the extent that the persons who compose it are exercising intelligence and freedom in genuinely forging a work of art as they constitute their world, their relations with others, and concomitantly themselves; third, this is not a vicious circle, for the process of society has a certain dominance over that of the individual, who is born into, raised in, and stimulated by the already given social situation: the culture, the polity, the economic realities, the technological institutions, and the habits of sensitive spontaneity that prevail in the person's society; and fourth, conditions of cultural, political, and general social decline pose a special problem: how is the decline to be reversed if the development of the individuals who might initiate and promote the reversal is so intimately conditioned by social realities? Only the formation of a creative minority that grasps what is going forward, understands its roots, anticipates its consequences, and decides to resist it and to offer an alternative, seems to be adequate to the realities of major decline. And the roots of such decline lie in the perversion of intelligence, the neglect of the sensitive psyche, and the misuse of freedom that all are involved in what Lonergan calls general bias.

Effective resistance, then, demands the development of the intellectual, psychic, and moral capacities that can meet the decline at its roots. Lonergan's project of the self-appropriation of rational self-consciousness is in the interests of precisely such a development. Cosmopolis is Lonergan's term for the relevant development especially of intelligence. Its commitment is to the understanding and implementation of the integral dialectic of community.

The integral dialectic of community is a function of a taut balance between two linked but opposed principles of change: spontaneous intersubjectivity and the practical intelligence that institutes a good of social order. Practical intelligence is responsible for three of the dimensions of society: technology, the economic system, and the political order. The relation of these dimensions with spontaneous intersubjectivity is a function proximately of the everyday, and remotely of the reflexive, level of culture. The infrastructure of a healthy society is constituted by the dimensions of intersubjectivity, practicality, and the everyday level of culture. The reflexive level of culture constitutes the society's superstructure. The condition of the possibility of the integrity of the dialectic between spontaneous intersubjectivity and the technological, economic, and political arrangements instituted by practical intelligence is culture, in both its everyday and its reflexive components. A cosmopolitan intelligence thus assumes as its responsibility the integrity of culture in both of its dimensions. Its principal task lies in the transformation and integration of the sciences and scholarly disciplines that constitute the reflexive level of culture. But it must envision as well a transformation and integration of the myriad instances of common sense. Cosmopolitan intelligence, then, will inform an intellectual collaboration that assumes the integrity of culture as its principal responsibility and that implements this responsibility through a reorientation especially of the human sciences and of commonsense practicality, so as to promote in society and history an integral dialectic between spontaneous intersubjectivity and the practical constitution of technological, economic, and political institutions.

The reorientation of the sciences will be grounded in a *new* science that disengages the constitutive features of integral intelligence, rationality, and responsibility, and that reorients, I believe, first of all the science of the sensitive psyche and of the unconscious on the basis of its appropriation of intellectual, rational, and moral genuineness.[17] The reorientation of common sense would emerge as a post-interiority mentality influenced by the reorientation of culture promoted by the science of interiority. Cosmopolis, then, assumes responsibility for the integrity of culture by devoting itself to three interrelated functions: the elaboration of a science of human interiority; the consequent reorientation of the human sciences; and the reorientation of the everyday level of culture through the promotion and development of a post-interiority mentality at the level of common sense. The central notion in the reorientation of human science will be, I believe, the tension of limitation and transcendence,[18] which at the level of the dialectic of the subject obtains in the relations between neural demand functions and the censorship,[19] and at the level of the dialectic of community in the relations between spontaneous intersubjectivity and practical intelligence. Every instance of an integral dialectic of limitation and transcendence depends on a synthesis that stands above either pole. Thus, the dialectic of intersubjectivity and practicality depends on culture, and that of psychic spontaneity and dramatic intelligence on universal willingness; and so the grounds of reorienting human science in accord with that tension lie in an appropriation of that tension itself in the psychic and intellectual conversions constitutive of the science of interiority. The intellectual collaboration instituted by cosmopolitan intelligence thus

> ... stands on a basic analysis of the compound-in-tension that is man; it confronts problems

of which men are aware; it invites the vast potentialities and pent-up energies of our time to contribute to their solution by developing an art and a literature, a theatre and a broadcasting, a journalism and a history, a school and a university, a personal depth and a public opinion, that through appreciation and criticism give men of common sense the opportunity and help they need and desire to correct the general bias of their common sense.[20]

2.3 Cosmopolis Today

We remarked earlier that the dialectic of political philosophies — at least of liberal and Marxist philosophies, on the one hand, and classically inspired positions on the other — could be resolved by strengthening the link between cultural and social values; for this is the point at which all of these philosophies depart from a position consistent with the integral dialectic of community. And we suggested that this link can be strengthened by correcting a blind spot in the classically inspired political philosophies. These philosophies correctly maintain that the social order is a derivative of cultural values. But they do not grasp the isomorphism that is demanded between the proportions of the social problem and the differentiated inclusiveness demanded of the cultural values that would meet it. The global nature of the contemporary problem of social order calls for a crossculturally generated set of cultural values that consists in a higher synthesis of various regionally defined cultural traditions. This ecumenic set of cultural values will depend on the self-appropriation of the transcultural intentional and psychic constituents of human integrity, and thus on as thorough a retrieval as possible of (1) the prehistoric rhythms of psychic process,

(2) the history-constituting operations of autonomous intentionality, and (3) the tension of limitation and transcendence, of psyche and intentionality, that constitutes the integral dialectic of the subject, and that is the core of authentic personal values.

The regionally defined cultural traditions that would constitute the heritage of a world-cultural humanity may, for purposes of clarity, be differentiated into cosmological, anthropological, and soteriological variants.[21] The task of cosmopolis today is to generate a set of cultural values that is a function of the integration of these three distinct disclosures regarding the direction to be found in the movement of life. More precisely, it seems that the basic dialectic here is between cosmological and anthropological truth, and the integrity of the dialectic is a function of the soteriological vector that moves from above downwards in human consciousness.

The cosmological societies regard the recurrent events of nature, often linked with intracosmic divinities, as what from a more differentiated perspective may be called the prime analogate of order. The order of reality moves from nature to society, and from society to the individual. Thus a society is invested with integrity to the extent that its order is a participation in and reenactment or embodiment of the cosmic order; and the individual is invested with integrity if he or she takes one's allotted place in a society whose order is dictated by cosmic process.

In the anthropological symbolizations the order of being undergoes a dramatic shift, so dramatic that it is spoken of by Karl Jaspers and others as axial.[22] The measure of order now becomes a world-transcendent divine reality, and order in society arises from that divine reality's attracting force within the minds and hearts of individuals. The society then takes on integrity to the extent that it is composed of persons of integrity, where personal integrity is a matter of responding to those inclinations that draw one to attunement with the world-transcendent ground of order, and of rejecting those inclinations that draw one away from such attunement. The relationship between individual and society is shifted from what it was in the cosmological societies. There the society was patterned after the cosmos, and the individual after the society. The cosmos was the measure of integrity for the society, and the society the measure of integrity for the individual. In the anthropological societies the divinity is the measure of the integrity of the individual, and the attuned individual the measure of the integrity of the society.

An integral world-cultural community would be informed by the dialectic of cosmological and anthropological truth. Not only is each mode of symbolization an expression of insights attained in humanity's search for direction in the movement of life. The cosmological mode is not simply superseded by the anthropological. It retains its validity in areas not covered by the anthropological differentiation: a validity that once again is being acknowledged in the development of an ecological sensitivity to the limits imposed by nature on human exploitation, domination, and control. Human individuals and cultures share an irreplaceable partnership in being with nonhuman nature, a partnership expressed in cosmological modes of symbolization, a partnership, finally, whose loss generates falsehood in human self-understanding and alienation in world constitution and self-constitution. The truth of this partnership is still available in the spontaneous psychic symbols that Jung calls archetypal: symbols taken from nature and imitating nature and so expressing our intimate participation in the schemes of recurrence of the material cosmos. The anthropological differentiation, on the other hand, is a recognition of certain dimensions of the truth about humanity that the cosmological or archetypal horizon is too compact to encompass. Our native capacity for transcendence is world-transcendent. As such it is differentiated in Greece by philosophy and in the Orient by the praxis of affective detachment. Voegelin conjectures that it takes a cultural crisis to awaken this recognition, which can arise when cosmologically ordered societies break down and so lose trust in cosmic order as a measure of integrity. Then the human soul ordered by attunement to the unseen measure becomes the criterion, sometimes even the model, of a social order rightly attuned to the sacred order of being. The integrity of the soul measures the integrity of the society, and God measures the integrity of the soul. Our participation in the rhythms and processes of nonhuman nature remains intact, but it is no longer the ultimate source of the integrity of our partnership in being and so no longer the measure of the rightness of our search for direction in the movement of life.

The integral dialectic of cosmological and anthropological truth joins the dialectic of the subject between neural demands and the censorship and the dialectic of community between spontaneous intersubjectivity and practicality as an instance of the tension of limitation and transcendence that characterizes all genuine development in the concrete universe of being. The source of the integrity of the dialectic of the subject lies in neither of its two poles taken singly but in universal willingness. The source of the integrity of the dialectic of community lies not in intersubjectivity nor in practicality but in culture. So too, the source of the integrity of the dialectic of cosmological and anthropological truth — let us call it the dialectic of culture — lies in neither of its two poles taken singly and in independence of the other, but in the transformative soteriological vector in consciousness whose differentiation constitutes in part the disclosive element in the events of divine revelation in Israel and Christianity.

Anthropological differentiation displays the emergence of the individual ego, its dissociation from the collective identifications of the cosmologically ordered societies. These collective identifications are twofold: the identification of the individual with the people and the identification of the people with the cosmos. These two forms of non-individuation can be understood in an interiorly differentiated mode in terms of Jung's notions, respectively, of collective consciousness and the collective unconscious. They still threaten the individuation of the person, but that threat is now acknowledged as an impediment to order rather than as the source of order. The individual is expected to differentiate between self and group and to assume personal responsibility for his or her own insights, judgments, and decisions. We are further expected to differentiate the agency of these intentional operations from the cosmic energic connections that link the human body to the nonhuman universe and that make archetypal symbolism such a perennial human phenomenon. Archetypal symbols are hindrances to individuation, however, only if one identifies with them or regards them as ultimate. They facilitate individuation if negotiated by an intelligence, rationality, and existential freedom that is distinct from the energic sources out of which these symbols arise. Anthropological truth is the source of the differentiation of such intelligence, rationality, and freedom. But cosmological truth preserves a place in the unfolding of integral development due to the abiding validity of the archetypal. An analysis of the soteriological vector would show its therapeutic efficacy vis-à-vis a displacement in either direction of the tension between cosmological rootedness and anthropological emancipation. A displacement toward the cosmological dehistoricizes our participation in being by linking us too compactly with the schemes of recurrence of nonhuman nature. A displacement toward the anthropological results in a loss of the myth as a constitutive feature of human self-understanding, and so in a sacrifice of consciousness as participatory luminosity to consciousness as world-constitutive intentionality. At its extreme, this displacement immanentizes the world-transcendent measure. It usurps the prerogatives of divinity. Ultimately it sacrifices the agency of the individual responsible for his or her own questions, insights, judgments, and decisions to the instruments of a potentially totalitarian power. Such a power absorbs personal responsibility into a new form of collectivism, one modeled now not on the cosmos but on the efficiently functioning machine, and objectifies its aspiration in social structures that invade the total fabric of human life like a creeping cancer.

In my most recent work, I have been attempting to develop an argument that it will be the role of a constructive contemporary systematic theology to disclose the therapeutic function of the soteriological vector vis-à-vis cosmological and anthropological displacements, and so the conditioning function of religious values on the integral dialectic of culture. Such a theology would function as a constitutive element in a cosmopolitan education. But our subject at the moment is not theology but education itself: the education that would mediate the integrity of culture to a situation that calls for a world-cultural integration of the dialectic of cosmological and anthropological truth as the condition of the possibility of a global order that is in harmony with the integral dialectic of community, and thus promotive of the equitable distribution of vital values to the whole human community.

3   The Academy: A Crisis of Plausibility

In *Psychic Conversion and Theological Foundations* I called attention to the way in which the potential plateau of intellectual synthesis achieved particularly in the work of Aquinas never became a consolidated basis for the further differentiating advances effected through the discoveries and methods of modern science, modern historical scholarship, and the two phases of the philosophic Enlightenment regarding, first, cognitive interiority, and then, world-constitutive praxis. The breakdown of the medieval synthesis was due largely to its employment of the Aristotelian notion of science as true and certain knowledge of the universal and necessary[23] and to the intellectual disasters consequent upon Scotistic conceptualism.[24] These inherent weaknesses at the heart of scholasticism prevented it from grounding a higher *existential* synthesis from which the speculative synthesis of Aquinas could be both integrated into a base of world-constitutive agency and internally criticized in dialectic with modern advances in science, history, and philosophy. The result of the conceptualistic derailment of the medieval achievement is the series of ever less comprehensive syntheses in cognitive and existential praxis that Lonergan calls the longer cycle of decline.[25] The scale of values has been operatively reduced to the objects of sensitive desires and to the social order whose purpose it is to assure the recurrent satisfaction of such desires. The surrender of our orientation to religious, personal, and cultural values in the face of the demands of shortsighted practicality results as well in a disharmonious and nonsequential, incongruous and nonrhythmic distortion of the flow of our sensations, memories, images, emotions, conations, associations, bodily movements, and spontaneous intersubjective responses, in a dissociation of the complexes of our psychic energy, and so in a sequence of ever less comprehensive syntheses in personal living.[26]

A genuine liberal education must be concerned with reversing this decline in the dialectics of the subject and of community. The distorted dialectics today manifest principally a displacement of the tension of limitation and transcendence in the direction of transcendence. Ironically, the neglect of limitation unduly limits the genuine transcendence of the human spirit, thus reducing the operative scale of values to a practical conspiracy between the levels of vital and social values. A contemporary liberal education would include an interpretive reconstruction of the historical constructions of the human spirit, of the intentional and psychic orientations out of which these constructions arose, and of the world opened up in front of these constructions. But it would engage its participants as well in the cumulative construction of a critical and normative human science that enables us to mediate not only from the past into the present but more radically and foundationally from the present into the future, on the basis of a thoroughgoing appropriation of the psychic and intentional roots of the tension of limitation and transcendence. Both mediations must occur in the context of a fundamental critique of the present situation as a resultant of the distorted dialectics of the subject, community, and culture. And both must be grounded in an explanatory self-appropriation of the tension of limitation and transcendence through the psychic and intellectual conversions that constitute the science of interiority. The appropriation of cultural acquisitions must not be merely a fusion of conversational horizons, much less a function of commonsense eclecticism,[27] but an evaluative or dialectical hermeneutic that, while allowing no past achievements to be forgotten, pushes them relentlessly to the transformations through which they can assume their appropriate place in the integral constitution of a global network of communities capable of providing an alternative to the distortions of the dialectic of community. The mediation from the present into the future, which is partly grounded in the appropriation, integration, and transformation of cultural acquisitions, is an implementation of the exigences generated by what, following others, we will call the second phase of the Enlightenment: exigences not only to clarify but also to effect the integrity of our cognitive and existential praxis.

The question of academic integrity is a question of fidelity to the normative scale of values as the source of an intellectual focus. An academy not so focused is guilty on a massive institutional scale of the major surrender of intelligence that is the principal agent of the longer cycle of decline.[28] Such an academy capitulates to one of two aberrations: either the ideological ruse that defines excellence in terms of proficiency within a distorted dialectic of community, or the escape of culture into the ivory tower of ever more dilletantish conceptualistic glass-bead games. In either case the academy is contributing only to the perpetuation of schemes of recurrence that are victimizing history. Authentic intellectual praxis in the contemporary situation involves the reorientation of common sense and science.[29] That reorientation today involves not only the liberation of dramatic intersubjectivity and of the practical organization of human affairs from the biases that have generated distortions in the dialectics of subjects, community, and culture; not only the purging from science of confused notions regarding reality, objectivity, knowledge, and value; not only a methodical integration of science derived from and grounded in an affirmation of the structure and implications of normative intentionality; but also the global perspective that would promote a human science and a common sense capable of informing the way of life of a crosscultural network of communities devoted to the integral dialectics of subjects, community, and culture. Structural conditions currently affecting the academy both internally and in its external relations with the economic and governmental institutions of the wider society, however, severely frustrate such an intellectual vocation.

My articulation of an internal critique of the academy has been aided by recent papers by Frederick Lawrence. The modern philosophic differentiation of consciousness has advanced to the recognition of the primacy of authentic praxis — both cognitive and existential — over theory. Lawrence finds a turning point from a first to a second phase of the Enlightenment in Kant's second *Critique*, where the emphasis of modern philosophy shifts from the cognitional activities and claims that preoccupied philosophers from Descartes to Kant's *Critique of Pure Reason*, and begins to center around 'faith, will, conscience, decision, action.'[30] With this shift there arises a question about the normative significance and limits of the first phase of the Enlightenment. This question emerges as the modern philosophic differentiation moves from interiority as cognitive and technical to interiority as constitutive and practical, as rationally and humanely constituting human history. The second phase of the Enlightenment is related to the concerns of what Lonergan calls dialectic and foundations, where the issues of cognitive, moral, religious, and psychological *integrity* are the matter under investigation, and where, as Lawrence puts it elsewhere, there ensues a painstaking elaboration and refinement of the assumptions which shape and frame our view of the main issues of living, the ultimate grounds for preferring one way of life to another, and so the basic alternative standards of political judgment.[31] Lawrence draws on Leo Strauss to argue that 'the trajectory of political thought stretching in one wave from Machiavelli through Hobbes, Locke, Smith, and in a second wave from Rousseau through Kant, Hegel, and Marx is rooted in the Machiavellian option to, in Lonergan's formulation, "develop 'realist' views in which theory is adjusted to practice and practice means whatever happens to be done."[32] But from the standpoint of the concern of the second phase of the Enlightenment to mediate theory and praxis, science's concern for utility so championed by the first phase, its demand for autonomy from philosophy, and its exclusion of questions that cannot be resolved by appeal to observation and experiment simply lend plausibility to 'the Machiavellian argument that true answers to the questions how we ought to live are so far removed from how we do in fact live as to be practically or politically irrelevant.'[33] On the grounds of the first phase of the Enlightenment alone, as Lawrence shows, politics and morality are completely separated from one another, human ends are privatized, and the common good gives way as the *raison d'être* of the political order to the purely private vital values of the protection and security of the individual; science itself is manipulatively derailed to serve what Bacon called 'the relief of man's estate;' and so knowledge is placed at the service of power; and even Marx, who criticized the bourgeois politics of the first phase of the Enlightenment, never suggested a motivation for revolution other than the maximation of satisfactions, and so failed to transcend the primacy of 'economic man' characteristic of the first wave of modern political thought and of bourgeois politics in general. The result, says Lawrence, is that 'in both liberal and communist political thought, the classical political orientation which judged the desire for wealth, glory, and freedom to do what one pleased utterly subordinate to the requirements of the good life is turned upside down. The political order is governed strictly in the light of the standards of security, comfort, and disoriented freedom.'[34]

For our purposes here, this means that to the extent that the academy remains an institution after the mold of the first phase of the Enlightenment, it operates on the assumption that education can proceed without a governing concern for a series of profound transformations in the presuppositions that shape and frame our view of the main issues of life, in the ultimate grounds for preferring one way of life to another, and so in the basic alternative standards of political judgment and choice; knowledge remains in the service of the relief of the human estate in the realms of security, comfort, and disoriented freedom; and curricula and methodologies neglect the normative exigences of inquiry and rather treat as normative the facts as they are. To that extent the academy is little more than a finishing school for agents of the longer cycle of decline.

The academy's neglect of the transformative issues of the second phase of the Enlightenment is due not only to its acceptance of an outmoded scientistic methodology, however, but also and perhaps more radically to the wider society's interest in preserving such an epistemology intact. The economic and governmental agencies that support the academy's existence either reject the concerns of the second phase of the Enlightenment or at least do not encourage that they be brought to bear on the unfolding and constitution of the public domain. The academy is not a promising environment for the intellectual vocation of cosmopolitan inquiry, when that inquiry is oriented to reversing the very distortions that keep the academy functioning. The task of developing within the academy the grounds for a cosmopolitan cognitive and existential synthesis that meets the surd of contemporary history at its roots will be a formidable one.

4   A Proposed Liberal Curriculum

Nonetheless, we must dream. I conclude, then, by proposing a liberal curriculum to serve as a point of departure for a discussion that would promote the agency required for cosmopolitan collaboration in the face of the longer cycle of decline. There are two aspects to this curriculum: a hermeneutic and a foundational aspect. The

hermeneutic aspect would be guided by an approach somewhat along the lines of the Great Books tradition; but the
core of the total educational experience would be found in
the foundational aspect. For the cosmopolitan vocation
espouses more than an exclusively disclosive notion of
truth. Its retrieval of the great constructions of the human
spirit is done from the basis of a developing foundational,
and so transformative, position on the integral dialectics
of the subject, community, and culture.

The general characteristics of my proposal are as
follows. One year of the curriculum here suggested is devoted to the exploration of the current situation in these
three dialectics; two years are devoted to a retrieval of how
we got to this point; and a final year focuses on the question of where we go from here. The first year centers on
awakening the question through the study and dialectical
appropriation of the thought forms of modernity and of
their reciprocal relationship with the organization of human affairs at the level of social values. The second and
third years would emphasize the study of cosmological and
anthropological thought forms in antiquity and in the development of the major civilizations of the world. The final year would focus on the critical mediation of cognitive
and existential praxis from the present into the future,
through the articulation and/or exercise of the scientific
and philosophic, literary and artistic, political and economic, religious and theological positions and orientations
that would evoke the world-cultural alternative to the longer
cycle of decline.

Under the semester system, the usual undergraduate curriculum totals something in the neighborhood of
128 hours. I suggest that sixty-four of these hours, or sixteen each year, be devoted to the core curriculum, with
support courses being added in accord with the needs of
individual students. Eight hours would be devoted each

semester to the core curriculum. In the first three years, six of these hours each semester would be concerned with the hermeneutic aspect of the program, and two with the foundational dimension. In the final year, all sixteen hours would be foundational in intent.

In the first year of the program, then, two six-hour hermeneutic courses — one each semester — would be taught by an interdisciplinary team of scholars whose expertise enables them to help students not only to study some of the representative primary sources of the modern period in science and philosophy, art and literature, economic and political theory, religion and theology, but also to exercise themselves critically in the intentionality that produced these sources and to grasp the objective correlatives of such intentionality at the level of the social order. These two hermeneutic courses would be divided as follows: in the first semester the course would be devoted to primary sources from the late medieval period (Machiavelli) through the first phase of the Enlightenment; in the second six-hour course, the same approach would cover the period from Kant's second *Critique* to the present. The two foundational courses during the first year — two hours each semester — would be devoted to a basic introduction to the self-appropriation of the modern scientific, scholarly, and modern-philosophic differentiations of consciousness.

The second and third years of the curriculum are concerned with the course of civilizational history that led humanity into the modern period. In their second year, students would be exercised in retrieving the various differentiations that resulted in what Jaspers and others regard as the axial period in the major civilizations of the world. Four traditions would be studied: the Chinese, the Indian, the Israelite, and the Hellenic. The emphasis would be placed on testing the hypothesis of independently originating axial breakthroughs from cosmological to some form and degree of anthropological and soteriological truth. Students would read in translation primary sources in these traditions, with the explicit intention of disengaging the differentiations among cosmological, anthropological, and soteriological mentalities.

The foundational aspect of the curriculum in the second year, and again in the third, would focus upon furthering students' self-appropriation of intentional consciousness, and upon introducing them to the self-appropriation of symbolic consciousness. An effort would be made to enable them to contrast and relate to one another their symbolic and theoretic procedures. Within the realm of theory, they would be called upon to contrast the modern praxis of scientific intelligence with which they became familiar in their first year with the classical ideals of science expressed in the works of Plato and Aristotle, whom they will study in the second year. Thus their appreciation will be heightened of the characteristic difference between modern and classical thought forms. An effort would be made, too, to enable the students to discover their own mythopoetic imaginations and to integrate this discovery with their ongoing appropriation of intelligence and rationality. Thus the notions of intellectual and psychic conversion become central to the foundational dimension of the second and third years.

The hermeneutic theme of the third year of the curriculum would be religion and culture. The axial religions would be studied in greater depth precisely as religions, and attention would be directed to the question of religious dialectic both within the religious traditions taken singly and among them. Presuming that most of the students would come from a Christian background, specific attention would be devoted to the intentionality behind and worlds opened in front of New Testament texts. The

relationship of religious to personal and cultural values
would be studied. The process of mediating the Christian
differentiation in contemporary terms would also be begun, and students would thus be invited to experience what
it is to do theology. The question, too, of the development
of religious doctrine in the various traditions would be studied, and an effort made to understand the respective manners in which the task of mediating religion and culture
eventually had to give rise, at least in some of these religions, to a technical theology distinct but not separate from
living religion. The continuing foundational aspect of the
third year would include an introduction to the self-appropriation of one's dialectical capacities and of one's religious orientations.

Finally, in the fourth year of the curriculum, emphasis shifts to the predominance of the foundational aspect.
The theme of the fourth year is the integration of theory
and praxis. The intention is, first, to arrive at an
understanding of the options regarding foundational issues that lie behind current methods being employed in
various fields; and second, to move to a resolution of these
dialectical conflicts by coming to one's own position on
foundational issues. The accent is on being able to give an
account of one's own foundational stance. The emphasis
shifts from an intellectual life *in oratione obliqua*, understanding and reporting on what others have said and done,
to an intellectual life *in oratione recta*, saying and doing
oneself, mediating the movement from the present into
the future.

Obviously, the entire thrust of the curriculum and
the intellectual and emotional demands it imposes make
it probable that only a small number of students might be
able to participate in it. Selecting these students will be
difficult. Moreover, because of the demands upon faculty
for individual contact with students, most of the faculty

engaged in such a program would have to be freed from other responsibilities. To adopt this kind of curriculum as an alternative option involves, then, at least a rearrangement of financial priorities, if not downright financial sacrifice, on the part of an academic institution. Let me conclude, then, with the persuasion that such sacrifices are called for on the part of educational institutions genuinely devoted to the continuing transformative influence of a humanistic and religious heritage. For the goal of this program is to arrive at the foundations of a new style of interdisciplinary collaboration in the understanding and making of humanity. The hope is that the students would graduate from the program with a commitment to precisely this kind of ongoing collaboration with one another and with their professors — a commitment, I might add, that is strong enough to enable them to endure the sacrifices that are entailed when one decides to commit one's life and one's intellectual and psychic energies to the reversal of the longer cycle of decline before it reaches the point of no return.

Notes

[1] Bernard Lonergan, *Method in Theology* (see above, chapter 1, note 1) 31-32.

[2] See Bernard Lonergan, *Insight* (see above, chapter 1, note 20) 207-18/232-44.

[3] Ibid. 236-38/261-63.

[4] Bernard Lonergan, 'The Absence of God in Modern Culture,' in *A Second Collection* (see above, chapter 5, note 3) 101-16.

[5] See Friedrich Heiler, 'The History of Religions as a Preparation for the Cooperation of Religions,' in *The History of Religions: Essays*

in Methodology, ed. Mircea Eliade and Joseph Kitagawa (Chicago: University of Chicago Press, 1959) 142-53.

[6] See John McMurtry, *The Structure of Marx's World-view* (see above, chapter 7, note 27) 177-87. 1993 note: On the changed situation vis-à-vis Marxism, see above, chapter 3, note 3.

[7] See Eric Voegelin, *The World of the Polis*, and *Plato and Aristotle* (see above, chapter 8, note 1).

[8] Lonergan, *Insight* 623-24/646-47.

[9] Ibid. 238-42/263-67.

[10] Ibid. 723-24/744-45.

[11] On the need for a religiously and theologically transformed cosmopolis, see ibid. 633/656.

[12] Lewis Mumford, *The Transformations of Man* (see above, chapter 1, note 6) 120-36.

[13] Lonergan, *Insight* 225-32/250-57.

[14] David Tracy, *The Analogical Imagination* (see above, chapter 7, note 14) 6-14.

[15] Lonergan, *Insight* 212/237-38.

[16] Ibid. 218/243.

[17] See Robert M. Doran, *Psychic Conversion and Theological Foundations* (see above, chapter 1, note 9).

[18] Lonergan, *Insight* 472-75/497-99.

[19] Ibid. 187-96/212-20.

[20] Ibid. 241/266.

21 Eric Voegelin, *Israel and Revelation* (see above, chapter 1, note 8) 56.

22 Karl Jaspers, *The Origin and Goal of History*, trans. Michael Bullock (New Haven: Yale University Press, 1967) 25-26.

23 See Bernard Lonergan, 'Dimensions of Meaning' (see above, chapter 9, note 9).

24 See Bernard Lonergan, *Verbum* (see above, chapter 5, note 51) 25-26.

25 Lonergan, *Insight* 226-32/251-57.

26 Doran, *Psychic Conversion and Theological Foundations* 94-95.

27 Lonergan, *Insight* 416-21/441-45.

28 Ibid. 230-32/255-57.

29 Ibid. 398-401/423-26.

30 Frederick Lawrence, '"The Modern Philosophic Differentiation of Consciousness" or What is the Enlightenment?,' in *Lonergan Workshop* 2, ed. Fred Lawrence (Chico, CA: Scholars Press, 1978) 238.

31 Frederick Lawrence, 'Political Theology and "The Longer Cycle of Decline" (see above, chapter 7, note 25) 238.

32 Ibid. 240. The Lonergan quotation is from 'The Role of a Catholic University in the Modern World,' in *Collection* (see above, chapter 9, note 9) 32.

33 Lawrence, 'Political Theology ...' 240.

34 Ibid. 242.

Part Three

———

Hermeneutics and Foundations

13 Self-knowledge and the Interpretation of Imaginal Expression

My intention in this paper is to indicate the relation of psychic conversion to the interpretation of imaginal expression.

By psychic conversion I mean gaining a capacity for internal communication in the third stage of meaning, through the attentive, intelligent, rational, and responsible negotiation of one's own spontaneous elemental symbolizing, as the latter occurs in such events as one's dreams. As a conversion, psychic conversion is a transformation of the repressive censorship vis-à-vis neural demands for psychic integration and conscious representation, into a constructive censorship in their regard.[1] As occurring in complementarity with religious, moral, and especially intellectual conversion, psychic conversion is a dimension of the foundational reality of a generalized empirical method that takes its stand on the self-appropriation of human interiority. In fact, if my previous arguments are correct,[2] psychic conversion brings to completion the quest for the heuristic structure of foundations that achieved its first decisive systematization in the eleventh chapter of Lonergan's *Insight*, where there is reached the explanatory position on human knowing with which one enters the third stage of meaning.

By imaginal expression I mean all linguistic discourse, whether oral or written, that unfolds on, and is meant to

be responded to on, the psychological and literary levels
of expression as contrasted with the scientific and philosophic levels. The notion of levels of expression is introduced in Lonergan's discussion of interpretation in *Insight*.[3]
There modes of expression are classified, not in terms of
language, style, or genre, but in terms of the sources of
meaning both in the speaker or writer and in the hearer or
reader. While scientific expression originates centrally in
the sources of explanatory understanding in a speaker or
writer and is meant to reproduce such cognitional sources
of meaning in a hearer or reader, and while philosophic
expression originates centrally in the critical reflection of
a speaker or writer and is meant to reproduce such critically reflective sources of meaning in a hearer or reader,
imaginal expression originates centrally simply in the experience of the speaker or writer or in an artistically ordered set of experiential elements, and is meant (1) to effect in the hearer or reader purely psychological conditioning at the experiential level of sensations, memories,
images, emotions, conations, associations, bodily movements, and spontaneous intersubjective responses, or (2)
to elicit a more or less comprehensive and determinately
ordered emotional response, or, finally, (3) to convey insight, stimulate reflection, or prompt evaluation, but in an
indirect or suggestive manner.

The category of imaginal expression, then, is open
enough to include several diverse literary genres. What
qualifies it as a distinct level of expression is that its intended response from hearer or reader consists in an ordering of psychic sensitivity and, in some cases, in the in-
sinuation of insights through this ordering, or in the calling forth of judgments either by the display of the field of
evidence in which the judgments could be verified, or by
the affective shaping or reinforcement of a moral or religious, or an amoral or antireligious, horizon. The elicited

responses would be ordered in some pattern of experience other than the intellectual: that is, in the dramatic, the practical, the aesthetic, the biological, the moral, or the religious pattern of experience. Emphasis is placed in such expression and intended response on that level of consciousness that we properly call the psyche, on the first level of awareness, on either the manipulation or the stimulation of that dimension of our intentionality whose criterion of authentic performance is attentiveness.

My paper, then, represents an attempt to advance the kind of interpretation theory that is already well underway in Lonergan's writings, and that in many ways, precisely because of the centrality of the notion of levels of expression, has advantages over the more prevalent hermeneutic theories employed in much contemporary philosophical and theological discussion. For this reason I hope that I may be excused for devoting the first two sections simply to an exposition of my interpretation of the relationship in Lonergan's thought between foundations and interpretation. I concentrate on this relationship for two reasons. First, I believe that it is here that Lonergan's contribution to contemporary hermeneutic theory becomes most apparent. Second, only within this framework can I speak of the significance of psychic conversion for interpretation, since psychic conversion is a dimension of foundational reality. The relation of psychic conversion to interpretation will be treated in the third section. I conclude the paper with a suggestion regarding the dialectical sublation of structuralist methodology into the interpretation of narrative that is made possible by Lonergan's understanding of foundations complemented by my notion of psychic conversion.

1   Foundations and Interpretation:
The Position of *Insight*

Since psychic conversion is a matter of foundational reality, we must begin our discussion with a study of the relations between the functional specialties of foundations and interpretation. What in general is the relationship between explanatory self-knowledge and interpretation? First, we shall explore these relations as they appear in *Insight*, before the notion of functional specialization became explicitly differentiated; then we will study the same relations as they appear in *Method in Theology*,[4] where the breakthrough has been achieved to the structure of theological operations and of the comprehensive reflection on the human condition that is grounded in theological foundations. Our specific concern in studying both of these works centers on the interpretation of what I have called imaginal expression.

1.1   Mystery and Myth

The functional equivalent in *Insight* of what was later to become the specialty 'foundations' lies in the three basic positions on knowing, the real, and objectivity that are exposed, respectively, in the eleventh, twelfth, and thirteenth chapters of this book.[5] The functional equivalent of the later specialty 'interpretation' is explained in the seventeenth chapter, 'Metaphysics as Dialectic.' What is the relationship offered there between the three basic positions and the method of interpretation?

The explicit problem of *Insight*'s seventeenth chapter is the interpretation and dialectical negotiation of philosophical texts. And from the beginning, the relationship that is affirmed between the foundational positions of cognitional analysis and the objectives of interpretation is quite direct. '[W]e propose to ask whether there exists a single base of operations from which any philosophy can be interpreted correctly, and we propose to show that our cognitional analysis provides such a base.'[6] But before addressing himself to the interpretation of philosophical texts, Lonergan offers, *from the same base*, a set of suggestions that are relevant to the concerns of this paper. He presents 'a genetic account of the radical meaning of mystery and myth, of their significance and function, of the grounds of their emergence, survival, and disappearance,'[7] and he treats the questions of whether mystery and myth are to be regarded as cognate to earlier stages of metaphysics in its latent and problematic phases, and whether they vanish as metaphysics becomes both explicit and critically grounded.

By 'mystery' Lonergan means 'symbolic expressions of positions,' and by 'myth,' 'symbolic expressions of counterpositions.'[8] By referring to positions and counterpositions, he is assuming that his cognitional-theoretic foundations are relevant to the interpretation and evaluation of prephilosophic levels of expression as well as to the philosophical level that is his central concern in this chapter. It is his notion of metaphysics that establishes the connection.

For Lonergan, explicit and adequate metaphysics consists in the intelligent grasp, reasonable affirmation, and responsible implementation of the integral heuristic structure of proportionate being. Thus metaphysics is, as it were, a detailed and open-ended corollary to *Insight*'s functional equivalent of the later specialty foundations — that is, to the explicit and adequate self-knowledge that is attained in the affirmation of the basic positions on knowing, the real, and objectivity. The implementation of this integral heuristic structure of proportionate being involves the philosopher in the reorientation of contemporary common sense and in the reorientation and integration of contemporary scientific knowledge, through advancing those assertions that are coherent with the basic positions on knowing, the real, and objectivity, and reversing those assertions that cannot be reconciled with these basic positions.

The affirmation of the basic positions that constitutes the functional equivalent in *Insight* of what later would become the specialty 'foundations' (1) depends on the prior development of science and the prior philosophical clarification of general issues that enabled Lonergan to devote the first ten chapters of *Insight* to 'a study of insight in mathematics, in classical and statistical science, in common sense and its fourfold bias, in the ambiguity of things and bodies, and in the reflective understanding that leads to judgment';[9] (2) issues in the distinctions between the activities of experiencing and imagining, understanding, and judging, and so in the distinctions not only between positions and counterpositions on the basis of an accurate and universally applicable criterion of reality and of real distinctness, but also between explanation and description on the basis of the rigorous detachment of the intellectual pattern of experience that makes of the knower 'an inconspicuous term in the real that is affirmed';[10] and (3) enables one to acknowledge the heuristic and progressive character of human intelligence, to distinguish between anticipations of insight and the actual achievement of insight, and between partial insight and mastery of a field or domain of human knowledge.

Now such a foundational base enables one not only to understand the general significance of the symbolic expressions that Lonergan calls mystery and myth, both in themselves and in the development of the human mind and of human language, but also to distinguish between the expression of positions in mystery and the expression of counterpositions in myth, and so to discredit the latter while still paying due allegiance to the former. For, when we speak of mystery and myth we are concerned with the intimation of unplumbed depths that accrues to our psychic feelings, emotions, and sentiments,[11] and with the linguistic expression of such an intimation; and this intimation corresponds on the psychic level to our intellectual and rational anticipation of being, through which, because of our unanswered questions, we know of an unknown. Our orientation by the notion of being, or the desire to know, is an orientation into a known unknown, and it calls for a corresponding orientation on the psychic level to participation in some cosmic meaningfulness. Moreover, just as being is differentiated into the variable spheres of what is already known and of what remains to be known and so is intended as to be known, so the psychic orientation is differentiated into the variable realms of 'the sphere of reality that is domesticated, familiar, common' and 'the sphere of the ulterior unknown, of the unexplored and strange, of the undefined surplus of significance and momentousness.'[12] It is in the latter sphere that we find the primary field of mystery and myth, where affect-laden images and names are employed to mediate the known unknown.

Now, while mythic consciousness thinks that its images and names so mediate the known unknown as to make it known, the attitude of mystery preserves the images and names rather as expressions of the cosmic orientation of a psychic level of subjective events linked to an unrestricted notion of being. Mythic consciousness, then, is 'an untutored desire to understand and formulate the nature of things,'[13] while mystery complements the unrestricted openness of our intelligence and reasonableness that is the concrete operator of our intellectual development with 'a corresponding operator that deeply and powerfully holds our sensitive integrations open to transforming change.'[14] Mystery survives the development of science and metaphysics, because 'even adequate self-knowledge and explicit metaphysics may contract but cannot eliminate a "known unknown," and ... they cannot issue into a control of human living without being transposed into dynamic images which make sensible to human sensitivity what intelligence reaches for or grasps.'[15] And so, while mythic consciousness is the lack of self-knowledge, and myth is the opposite of metaphysics, mystery is the necessary and permanent imaginal counterpart and complement of the unrestricted desire to know whose concrete unfolding in history is the source, among other things, of adequate and explicit self-knowledge and of a derivative adequate and explicit metaphysics.

The images that qualify as mystery or as myth, precisely as images, are operative on the first, experiential level of consciousness. They function 'within the psychic syndrome of associations, affects, exclamations, and articulated speech and actions.'[16] But as symbols and as signs, these images stand in correspondence with intellectual dynamism. As symbols, they are simply linked with the known unknown. As signs, they are linked with some interpretation that would understand the image.[17] Such interpretations, moreover, are manifold, for the question of the goal of human finality 'receives countless answers, pragmatic or conceptual, naturalistic, humanistic, or religious, enthusiastically positive or militantly negative.'[18] But correct interpretation of such symbolic utterances can now be based in the explicit and adequate self-knowledge that affirms the self as a unity of empirical, intelligent, and rational consciousness, and that recognizes the imaginal operator of psychic development as the sensitive correlative to an unrestricted intellectual intending of being. Such interpretation will not be a matter, then, of reconstructing in ourselves the experiences of others and of uncritically adding our own intellectual viewpoints which these others did not share. Rather, because one understands what a viewpoint is, how viewpoints develop, and what the dialectical laws are that govern their unfolding, one's interpretation of such utterances will be a matter of recovering the viewpoint of the past by approximating the insights, judgments, beliefs, and decisions that made the words and deeds, the feelings and sentiments, of another 'the activities of a more or less intelligent and reasonable being.'[19]

Cognitional analysis, then, is foundational for the interpretation of the imaginal deliverances both of mythic consciousness and of the openness of mystery to human intelligence's unrestricted objective. Such interpretation will be essentially dialectical, for the interpreter knows that the sensitive field of mystery and myth is the locus of the origin, the expression, and the application of intelligent and rational contents and directives; that the integrating activities of the intellectual and rational levels stand in a dialectical unity-in-tension with the integrated activities of the sensitive level; and that because the intellectual and rational activities are either the proper unfolding of the detached and disinterested desire to know or a distorted unfolding due to the interference of other desire, the sensitive activities themselves are involved either in the mysteries of the proper unfolding or in the myths into which these mysteries are distorted because of the aberrations of intellectual and rational performance.[20] The primary issues, then, in the interpretation of imaginal utterance have to do with the cognitional authenticity of the human spirit.

The interpretation of mystery and myth, finally, is not limited to the study of historically prescientific and prephilosophic utterance. The tense opposition of sensitive and intellectual operations is the source of a permanent challenge to the dominion of the detached and disinterested desire to know. The advance of science and philosophy may mean simply that later myths are now complemented and reinforced by corresponding philosophies and made historically effective 'through the discoveries of science and the inventions of technology.' Myth, then, is '*the permanent alternative to mystery.*'[21]

1.2   The Universal Viewpoint and the Interpretation of Imaginal Expression

Within the context of *Insight,* what is ultimately at stake in both imaginal expression and its interpretation is the question of truth: more precisely, the sensitive psychic complement of the intellectual and rational intending through which alone truth can be attained. Consequently, the foundational appropriation of one's intelligent and reasonable intending is a constituent feature of any methodically adequate interpretation that would formulate the viewpoint, the intentionality, that corresponds to and produces the content of the original imaginal expression. Nor is such a notion of interpretation to be classified among the various romantic notions of hermeneutics, according to which interpretation is a matter of repeating in experience and expression the inner experience of the original author. What is at stake here is something quite different: the articulation, through the medium of interiorly differentiated consciousness, of the *horizon* that comes to expression in the original text. One need not choose between an interpretation that articulates a 'world behind the text' (romantic hermeneutics) and one that articulates a world disclosed 'in front of the text.'[22] In understanding and articulating the horizon of the text, the interpreter captures the simultaneously world-constitutive and self-constitutive meaning of the original expression. A scientific interpretation of *imaginal* expression, then, would understand and formulate for a contemporary audience or readership at least the ordering of psychic sensitivity that was the response intended in the original expression, and, depending on the given instance, perhaps also the insights that were intended to be emergent from such an ordering, or the judgments for which such an ordering was to display the sensitive or imaginal field of evidence. The particular ordering of sensitivity intended, as well as the insights and judgments insinuated, are to introduce the reader or hearer into participation in the horizon of the original expression.

A hermeneutic theory that would account for and promote such interpretation must indicate a basis from which the interpreter can assign grounds for his or her interpretation that enable one to transcend the limitations and errors inherent in the biases of one's own common sense. Such a basis must be a heuristic device that accounts in principle for the development of *all* viewpoints and *all* intentionality. One needs to specify a technical instrument that puts one in possession of the constants of *all* subjectivity. These constants would be common to the recipients of the original expression and the recipients of the interpretation. They lie behind the genesis, the development, and the dialectical unfolding of all viewpoints. While they are always expressed in culturally, historically, and linguistically relative forms of expression, in themselves they transcend all relativity to particular audiences and readerships, since they are at the origin of all expression, and thus are universally human.

The discovery of these constants constitutes what Lonergan calls a universal viewpoint. 'By a universal viewpoint will be meant a potential totality of genetically and dialectically ordered viewpoints,'[23] 'a heuristic structure that contains virtually the various ranges of possible alternatives of interpretations.'[24] The concern of a universal viewpoint is with *acts* of meaning, the insights and judgments that are expressed or insinuated in texts, the intentionality that produced the original expression. One's familiarity with these acts is rooted in one's self-appropriation of one's own experience, understanding, and critical reflection.

> There are the external sources of historical interpretation, and in the main they consist in spatially ordered marks on paper or parchment, papyrus or stone. But there are also sources of interpretation immanent in the historiographer himself, in his ability to distinguish and recombine elements in his own experience, in his ability to work backwards from contemporary to earlier accumulations of insights in human development, in his ability to envisage the protean possibilities of the notion of being, the core of all meaning, which varies in content with the experience, the insights, the judgments, and the habitual orientation of each individual.[25]

The base or foundation of this ordered totality of viewpoints is self-knowledge: the positions on knowing, being, and objectivity. The viewpoints are ordered genetically, in that they are arranged as series of discoveries through which human subjectivity could advance to its present position. They are ordered dialectically, in that adequate self-knowledge enables one to compare and contrast the many formulations of discoveries on the basis of whether they are coherent or not with the basic positions. Because of such an ordered totality, one 'can reach a concrete presentation of any formulation of any discovery through the identification in personal experience of the elements that, as confused or as distinguished and related, as related under this or that orientation of polymorphic consciousness, could combine to make the position or counterposition humanly convincing.'[26]

The universal viewpoint differs radically from universal history and from Hegelian dialectic in that the totality, the ordering, and the ordered viewpoints are all *potential*. The totality is not a series of known contents but a heuristic structure whose contents are sequences of unknowns whose relations are only generically determinate. The genetic ordering heads toward sequences of discoveries, but of discoveries that could be and indeed were made in a variety of manners. The dialectical ordering heads toward the furthering of positions and the reversal of counterpositions, but the oppositions are by no means as clear-cut as the antitheses of the basic positions and counterpositions. What is ordered, finally, is the sequence of viewpoints, and this sequence is itself 'advancing from the generic to the specific, from the undifferentiated to the differentiated, from the awkward, the global, the spontaneous to the expert, the precise, the methodical.'[27]

The foundations, again, of a universal viewpoint lie in a fact: the universe of meanings consists in 'the full range of possible combinations (1) of experiences and lack of experience, (2) of insights and lack of insight, (3) of judgments and of failures to judge, and (4) of the various orientations of the polymorphic consciousness of man.'[28] Thus: 'in the measure that one grasps the structure of this protean notion of being, one possesses the base and ground from which one can proceed to the content and context of every meaning. In the measure that one explores human experience, human insights, human reflection, and human polymorphic consciousness, one becomes capable, when provided with the appropriate data, of approximating to the content and context of the meaning of any given expression.'[29]

Now the notion of a universal viewpoint combines with the notion of levels and sequences of expression to generate an upper blade of generalities or presuppositions for methodical and accurate interpretation of the expressions of another. That is to say, the interpreter must be familiar not only with the lower blade of techniques for dealing with the documents and monuments through which others have expressed their meanings, but also, and foundationally, with the manner in which meanings form a genetically and dialectically related sequence of unknowns, and with the manner in which expressions develop from the undifferentiated to the specialized.[30] The scientific interpretation that emerges from such familiarity is a matter of an adequate and accurate differentiation of the protean notion of being by a set of genetically and dialectically related determinations[31] of patterns of experience, accumulations of insights, and sets of meanings[32] — *and 'no more.'*[33]

The application to imaginal expression of the universal viewpoint and of the notion of sequences of modes of expression is complicated by the fact that such expression unfolds on, and is responded to on, the prescientific and prephilosophic psychological and literary levels of expression. The intended response may insinuate insights or display the field of evidence for judgments, but the level of consciousness from which the expression primarily emerges and on which it must be responded to is the experiential level. Moreover, if the interpretation is to be scientific, it must do more than convey a new set of images and associations from which its recipient can reach the insights and form the judgments through which the original expression can be interpreted. A scientific interpretation must itself formulate these insights and judgments, which themselves concern in the present instance an expression whose source of meaning is experiential and whose term of meaning is, perhaps, the psychological correlative of what could be or is meant to be affirmed or denied.

Despite this added difficulty, it seems that the various canons of a methodical interpretation offered by Lonergan still obtain. Thus, the interpretation must convey the psychic correlative of some differentiation of the protean notion of being. It must do so in an explanatory fashion, taking account of the genetic sequence of such differentiations, of the dialectic of positions and counterpositions, of the symbolic expressions that psychically correspond to such alternatives, of the possibility of the differentiation and specialization of modes of expression, and of the psychic or imaginal correlatives of such differentiation and specialization. Again, the interpretation will be at first hypothetical, but it will increase in probability or approximate certainty by coming into coherence with the universal viewpoint, with the genetic sequence of modes of expression, and with the possible gaps that might exist between meaning, on the one hand, and available resources of expression, on the other. Finally, the interpretation will be, not logical, but intelligent, and so it will take into account the nonsystematic component of fields of meaning, of expression in relation to meaning, of expression in relation to dynamic psychic constellations in the original author or speaker, and of documents in their origins, production, and survival.

1.3 Summary

Our exposition and interpretation of the theory of hermeneutics that appears in Lonergan's *Insight* has not covered all the details of the theory. Our intention has been to indicate the intimate connection that Lonergan posits there between the foundational positions on knowing, being, and objectivity, and the task and goal of interpretation. We have studied that relation in respect to Lonergan's genetic account of those imaginal expressions that qualify

for the titles of mystery and myth, and in respect to the
notion of a universal viewpoint as horizon for a scientific
interpretation. We have extended the import of Lonergan's
discussion of the universal viewpoint so that it includes
more explicitly an account of the horizon that *Insight*'s basic
positions would constitute for the interpretation precisely
of imaginal expression. Thus we may now move on to a
discussion of the relations that seem to obtain between
foundations and interpretation in *Method in Theology*, where
the notion of functional specialization has emerged with
differentiated clarity. Once again, we shall pay special heed
to this relation as it affects the interpretation of imaginal
expression.

2   Foundations and Interpretation: The Position of *Method in Theology*

The issue of the relationship between foundations and interpretation becomes more complex in *Method in Theology*. Four points seem to call for attention: the expansion
of the foundational position on the subject, the explicit
differentiation of functional specialties, the difference between the intellectual hermeneutics of the functional specialty 'interpretation' and the evaluative hermeneutics of
the functional specialty 'dialectic,' and the issue of the upper
blade of the universal viewpoint as this is transposed into
the context of *Method in Theology*.

2.1   The Expansion of the Foundational Position on the Subject

The central development in Lonergan's thought between
Insight and *Method in Theology* concerns the expansion of
foundations. The basic position on the subject includes
but now goes beyond the position on the knower. There is

affirmed a fourth level of consciousness, a level on which we apprehend potential values, evaluate, deliberate, discern, decide, and act. In *Insight*, this level was compacted into intelligent and reasonable consciousness; in *Method in Theology*, it is recognized as involving operations quite distinct from, and sublating, the operations of intelligent inquiry and reasonable reflection through which the real world is known. Fourth-level operations, moreover, constitute, not a notion of being, but a notion of value. Thus, as the position on being is a corollary of the position on knowing, so the position on value is a corollary of the position on deciding. And the basic position on objectivity is implicitly expanded so as to include an affirmation of the affective and existential dimensions of self-transcendence.[34]

The details of the expanded foundational position are familiar enough to those who have followed Lonergan's development to need no further elaboration here. It is sufficient to indicate that, while the self-affirmation of the knower is now equated with a philosophic conversion, foundations consist in the objectification not only of this conversion but also of moral and religious conversion. The suspicion already arises that, if previously cognitional analysis was posited as providing a base of operations from which both philosophical and imaginal texts could be interpreted, a further differentiation now appears in that base, a nuanced clarification that includes existential analysis, the objectification of the moral and religious self-transcendence of the interpreting subject.

2.2   The Explicit Differentiation of Functional Specialties

The suspicion is verified when one reflects on the implications of the fact that the expansion of the basic position on the subject is what made possible the breakthrough to the differentiation of functional specialties in the first place.

Correlative to the fourth level of intentional consciousness are the functional specialties of dialectic and foundations. Only these functional specialties make possible the
transition from the first phase of theology, which studies
the past, to the second phase, which directly addresses the
present and the future.[35] The link from the critical mediation of the past into the present to critical mediation in the
present and from the present into the future is intrinsically dependent upon exposure and resolution of the issues of cognitive and existential authenticity. These issues
arise as questions from the very performance of the tasks
of studying the past in interpretation and history; they are
explicitly confronted in dialectic, and they are resolved in
foundations. The expansion of the basic position on the
subject and the correlation of the cardinal functional specialties of dialectic and foundations with fourth-level objectives means that appealing to authenticity as the criterion of positions to be developed and of counterpositions
to be reversed involves more than the appropriation of one's
own intelligence and rationality. It entails also the appropriation of oneself as a moral and religious being. The adequate self-knowledge that can ground one's own philosophical and theological positions is a more complicated
achievement than it was in *Insight*. It involves the self-affirmation of the moral and religious, as well as of the intellectual, subject.

Foundations, moreover, specifies directly the grounding only of the last three functional specialties: doctrines
or positions, systematics, and communications. And even
with regard to these three sets of tasks, the objectification
of the three conversions and the consequent derivation of
general and special categories to be employed in the second phase of theology is only a partial foundation. Also
foundational is the work of the first four functional specialties: research, interpretation, history, and dialectic.

> We are seeking the foundations, not of the whole of theology, but of the last three specialties, doctrines, systematics, and communications. We are seeking not the whole foundation of these specialties — for they obviously will depend on research, interpretation, history, and dialectic — but just the added foundation needed to move from the indirect discourse that sets forth the convictions and opinions of others to the direct discourse that states what is so.[36]

This statement raises a host of problems. In *Insight*, Lonergan was seeking a 'single base of operations from which any philosophy can be *interpreted* correctly,'[37] and he specifies that the equivalent of foundations in *Insight* is directly foundational of the task of interpretation. In *Method in Theology*, on the other hand, the expanded set of foundational positions, which includes the positions of *Insight*, is explicitly affirmed as foundational, not of interpretation, but only of the second phase. Are we to infer that there has occurred a fundamental transposition of the issue of the relation between foundations and interpretation? Have we moved from a position according to which adequate self-knowledge is foundational of interpretation, to a position in which interpretation and adequate self-knowledge are co-foundational of one's own statement of truth? Or is the relationship between foundations and interpretation more complicated, and the transposition of the issue consequently less drastic?

A study of the relevant sections of *Method in Theology* would indicate that the latter alternative is the correct one. Not only are the categories derived in foundations employed in all eight functional specialties,[38] but also there

is explicitly affirmed an interdependence, first, of foundations and dialectic, and secondly of dialectic and interpretation. In fact, all eight functional specialties are involved
in at least an indirect interdependence.[39] Moreover, interpretation itself is said to be related to and dependent upon
the other seven functional specialties, including foundations.[40] What, then, is the relationship that emerges in the
chapter on interpretation between adequate self-knowledge
and the tasks of interpretation? And how does this relationship move into the issues of dialectic?

2.3   Intellectual Hermeneutics and Evaluative Hermeneutics

Interpretation, or intellectual hermeneutics, comprises
three tasks: understanding the text one is studying, judging the accuracy of one's understanding of the text, and
stating to one's contemporaries what one has judged to be
the correct understanding of the text. The texts with which
Lonergan is concerned in the chapter on interpretation in
Method in Theology are a matter, not of philosophical, but
of commonsense, expression.

> Horizons, values, interests, intellectual devel-
> opment, experience may differ. Expression may
> have intersubjective, artistic, symbolic compo-
> nents that appear strange. Then there arises the
> question, What is meant by the sentence, the
> paragraph, the chapter, the book? ... Such in
> general is the problem of interpretation.[41]

It is in regard to the first of the three tasks of interpretation, that of understanding the text, that there emerges a
discussion of the relation between self-knowledge and interpretation.

Lonergan's procedure here, as in *Insight*, prescinds from a discussion of lower-blade techniques — form criticism, redaction criticism, literary criticism, etc. — and moves rather to a discussion of the levels of conditions of possibility for accurate interpretation. That is, the steps that Lonergan unfolds as intrinsic to the understanding of texts involve a move from proximate to more remote conditions of possibility, until the final step, that of self-knowledge, is reached; and this final step is not strictly part of one's task or method as an interpreter, but is 'an event of a higher order, an event in [one's] own personal development.'[42] Each of the conditions of possibility of interpretation involves one in the self-correcting process of learning, but the final condition involves a familiarity that one gains, not in learning the method of interpretation, but in learning the art of living. The concern of interpretation is to understand 'what happened to be the objects, real or imaginary, intended by the author of the text.'[43] One's initial resources for fulfilling this task lie in one's knowledge of the language in which the text is written, and in the amplitude of one's own accumulated experience, understanding, and judgment. Even with these resources, one's assumptions regarding precisely what it is that the text intends may be mistaken. Then one must acknowledge that one's knowledge of the object is not sufficient for passing an accurate interpretation on to others; one must 'note one's every failure to understand clearly and exactly and ... sustain one's reading and rereading until one's inventiveness or good luck have eliminated one's failures in comprehension.'[44] But a third and more remote exegetical condition may also be required. One may have to appropriate the common sense of the people to whom the author belongs and whom the author is addressing in the text. One may have to extend one's self-correcting process of learning to the point of coming to understand 'the author himself, his nation, language, time, culture, way of life, and cast of mind.'[45] In order to understand the objects intended in the text, one may need more than one's own general and potential knowledge about these objects, and more than the rereading and inventiveness that clear up lesser problems of miscomprehension. To be an interpreter, one may have to be a scholar.

But the series of stages in the self-correcting process of learning involved in understanding the object intended in the text can move decisively beyond the developments intrinsic to the process of becoming an expert in exegetical methods. Even with a knowledge of the common sense of another people, even with the sustained rereading of the text, even with a knowledge of the language in which the text is written and the general and potential knowledge of the objects that necessarily is concomitant with the knowledge of the language, it may happen that one is still unable to understand the text. The self-correcting process of learning may have to be pushed to the limit of effecting a radical change in oneself before one is able to understand the objects intended in a text. One may have to come to a revolution in one's own outlook or viewpoint. 'The major texts, the classics, in religion, letters, philosophy, theology, not only are beyond the initial horizon of their interpreters but also may demand an intellectual, moral, religious conversion of the interpreter over and above the broadening of his horizon.'[46] And following upon such a conversion, one may have to rethink the entire issue from the basis of one's new and more profound viewpoint. One may be dealing with that kind of writing that 'is never fully understood. But those that are educated and educate themselves must always want to learn more from it.'[47] One may be dealing with a writing that grounds an entire tradition, that creates the very milieu in which it can be studied and understood, that actually produces in the interpreter the preunderstanding from which it can be correctly interpreted. Or one may be dealing with a writing that departs from an authentic tradition, that grounds a recasting of the intended objects in such a way that it adapts them to a biased set of assumptions and convictions grounded in a flight from conversion. One may be pushed to the limit of determining which is the case. But one can decide only if one has oneself faced the issue of intellectual, moral, and religious conversion and come to some conclusion for oneself on these foundational matters. One can decide only if the event of coming to understand oneself has occurred in one's personal development as a human subject.

At this point, then, we have moved away from the tasks of scholarly or intellectual interpretation to evaluative interpretation. We have moved from the functional specialty 'interpretation' to the functional specialty 'dialectic.' We have raised the very questions that are to be resolved in foundations. And it is clear how these questions impinge on interpretation. For without having faced these dialectical and foundational questions, we may not be in a position to achieve the very purpose of scholarly interpretation. We may simply not be able to understand the objects that are intended in the text that we are studying. And coming to the position of being able to understand these objects may no longer be a matter of one's development as a scholar, but of one's growth as a human being. We are now actually *encountering* the past, where encounter is a matter of 'meeting persons, appreciating the values they represent, criticizing their defects, and allowing one's living to be challenged at its very roots by their words and by their deeds.'[48] Scholarly interpretation of some texts demands that one have put one's self-understanding to the test, by admitting into one's treatment of the text this existential encounter with the text's horizon.

We can see, then, how the issues of foundations now affect the task of interpretation. These issues state the limit of the conditions of possibility of understanding a text, the limit of the self-correcting process of learning that may be required in order to understand, the limit of familiarity with intended objects that may be needed in order to understand the objects that in fact are intended in a given text.

2.4   The Existentially Transformed Universal Viewpoint

As we have seen, the relationships between foundations and interpretation are more complicated in *Method in Theology*, not only because of the explicit differentiation of the functional specialties, but also because of the greater complexity of the foundational issues themselves. In addition to the basic positions on the knower, on the real, and on objectivity, there are basic positions on the moral agent, on value, on affectivity, on the religious subject, on the divine, and on love. There is still affirmed, however, 'the notion of a potential universal viewpoint that moves over different levels and sequences of expression.'[49] In fact, the sequences of expression are more clearly differentiated than they were in *Insight*.[50] But the universal viewpoint is now reached 'by advocating a distinct functional specialty named dialectic.'[51] And in dialectic the issues are raised, not only of knowing, but also of choosing and of relating to the divine. The universal viewpoint thus becomes the upper blade, not only for a series of differentiations of the protean notion of being and of the imaginal counterparts of these differentiations, but also for a series of differentiations of the notion of value and of the imaginal counterparts of these differentiations. In fact, the base from which an accurate interpretation can be given consists now, not only of a cognitional theory that contains positions on the basic philosophic issues of knowing, reality, and objectivity, but also of a transcendental analysis of the notion of value, of human subjectivity's natural desire for the knowledge and love of God, and of the heuristic structure of the soteriological satisfaction of that natural desire.[52] But the function of the universal viewpoint remains basically the same, even if it is expressed in a more differentiated understanding of the relationship between the foundational issues and the tasks of interpretation.

3   **Psychic Conversion and Interpretation**

I have already stated that I regard psychic conversion as an aspect of foundational realty. If I am correct, then psychic self-appropriation is a constitutive feature of one's foundations. My task in the present section is to indicate, on the basis of the previous analysis of the relations of foundations and interpretation, the pertinence of psychic conversion for the interpretation of imaginal expression.

The clue that opened me upon the notion of psychic conversion lies in the expansion of the basic position on the subject that, as we have seen, represents the central development in Lonergan's thought between *Insight* and *Method in Theology*. The notion of value that is fourth-level consciousness is such that potential values are first apprehended in intentional feelings. And such feelings themselves are related intimately to symbols. 'A symbol is an image of a real or imaginary object that evokes a feeling or is evoked by a feeling.'[53] There are, then, imaginal counterparts, not only to the notion of being, as in *Insight*, but also, and most intimately, to the notion of value. In fact, it seems reasonable to argue that, if Lonergan is correct concerning the relationships between intentional feelings and values, on the one hand, and between these same feelings and symbols, on the other, then if one were to come to the point of genuine familiarity with the spontaneous elemental symbolizations of one's own psyche, one would also gain a familiarity with the affective responses through which one apprehends and initially moves toward the good. One would be discovering and appropriating the aesthetic and dramatic base of one's morals and of one's religion. One would be gaining explanatory understanding of one's own story, of the movement of one's own life precisely as that movement is experienced and symbolically reflected by the sensitively psychic level of one's consciousness. One would be in a position to appropriate both the first level of consciousness, the experiential level, and the fourth level as it sublates this experiential component and the two intellectual levels of consciousness into the affectively intentional response to the good. One would be significantly aided by such a change in oneself in the concrete self-appropriation of one's own being as an existential subject. One would be, perhaps, approximating the same explanatory understanding of the experiential and existential levels of one's consciousness as Lonergan enables of the intellectual and rational levels. One would perhaps even be bringing to completion the foundational quest that reached its decisive turning point, its genuine systematization, its first formative discovery, in the self-affirmation of the knower, but that has already been extended by Lonergan himself to an affirmation of higher levels of consciousness than those through which we know what is so. One would be providing oneself with a set of defensive circles to safeguard the authenticity of one's being as an intellectual, moral, and religious subject.[54]

The foundational role of psychic conversion for the task of interpretation appears most directly in the hermeneutic of imaginal expression. The self that one has come to know is a self that not only inquires and understands, reflects and judges, and so is a notion of being, but that also evaluates and deliberates, decides and acts, and so is a notion of value. By the very ontological constitution of such a self, there inevitably will be released imaginal counterparts of one's intentions of being and of value. Both intentions, then, are connected with the symbols that reveal the dramatic component, the story, of one's intentionality. To disengage that story intelligently, rationally, responsibly is to gain a greater depth of understanding of oneself as a cognitive intention of being and as an existential intention of value. Such disengagement is a decisive aid in answering the questions, What do I really want? What am I doing to achieve what I really want? Is what I want really worth while? Is what I am doing to achieve it in keeping with genuine self-esteem, or is it a promotion of my own advantage at the expense of others, or of the advantage of my group at the expense of other groups, or of shortsighted practicality at the expense of ultimate issues and long-term consequences? Am I an agent of the shorter or longer cycles of decline or of their reversal? Am I part of the problem or part of the solution?

The solution, of course, lies in self-transcendence, and psychic conversion is a conversion of the censorship that admits or refuses to admit those imaginal materials that are needed for insight, reflection, and decision — for intellectual, rational, and moral self-transcendence.[55] It is a conversion of the preconscious collaboration of imagination and intelligence through which the materials are presented out of which I can make a work of art out of my own life. It is the condition of the possibility of dramatic artistry in the third stage of meaning, that is, in that stage in which such artistry is strictly dependent upon self-appropriation.

Much work will have to be done to relate the notion of psychic conversion to the depth-psychological systems of Freud and Jung. That work will reveal the significance

and necessity of a correct position on self-transcendence
if one wants to understand the human psyche.[56] But my
task at present is not to construct this elaboration, but to
proceed to the question of the relation that obtains between psychic conversion as foundational and the interpretation of imaginal expression.

The relationship can be succinctly stated: come to
know as existential subject the contingent figures, the structure, the process, and the archetypal and anagogic spontaneity of your own psyche, and you will come into possession of an expanding base and an intelligible pattern
illuminating the imaginal counterparts of spiritual desire
that come to expression in those texts that originate from
and are meant to be responded to on the psychological
and literary levels of expression. That is: (1) appropriate
the relationships that obtain among the levels of consciousness[57] as Lonergan has delineated these levels; (2) discover
the relationship between the symbolizations of your own
psyche and the authentic or inauthentic orientation of your
intellectual, rational, and existential intentionality; (3) distinguish the modalities of these symbols and their respective meanings as either personal or archetypal or anagogic;
(4) and you will be able to understand imaginal expression as the psychic correlative of some differentiation of
the polymorphic intellectual and existential consciousness
of human subjectivity as this consciousness either remains
faithful to the exigences of intentionality or departs from
the desire to know and the desire for the genuine good.

If psychic conversion is as foundational as intellectual conversion, it will stand in the same relationship to
the task of interpretation as does the affirmation of the
positions on knowing, the real, and objectivity. Moreover,
I believe that psychic conversion will be the instrument
through which moral and religious conversion are able to
assume their own foundational stance alongside intellec-

tual conversion as the existential condition of the possibility of scientific interpretation. For it is through psychic conversion that one is enabled to appropriate the moral and religious dimensions of one's own consciousness. What one comes to through such an appropriation is not simply a further set of positions that can be set over against basic antitheses. Rather, one arrives at an explanatory unfolding of the story of one's own existence as a moral and religious agent. The story is uncovered in explanatory fashion because one has reached the standpoint from which one can, by insight, fix terms and relations by one another. The insight in question is an insight into the symbols that elementally and spontaneously proceed from one's own sensitive psyche. The insight grasps the relations that obtain, not only among the various dimensions of these symbols, but also between these symbols and the unfolding of one's intentionality as an intelligent and existential being-in-the-world. The insight is verified as one tries it out. And the verified insight enters the constitution of the habitual intellectual, moral, and religious orientations that one adopts as a subject. The orientations provide an expanding base for the interpretation of the imaginal expressions of others, because these others too are dynamic unities-in-tension of sensitive psychological consciousness and intentionality. Their elemental symbolizing, too, is the sensitive psychological counterpart and complement of the protean notions of being and value. One's universal viewpoint is enriched as one comes to know the relations that obtain between one's sensitive psychological symbolizations and one's intention of being and value. One is able to move more readily to that interpretation of imaginal expression that explains such expression as the psychological correlative of what could be, or is meant to be, not simply affirmed or denied, but also chosen or rejected. One understands symbolic language as complementary on the

psychic level to the differentiations of the notions of being
and value achieved by the subject of such language. Psychic
conversion thus enters into the dialectical base of
interpretation, and finds its most direct relevance to interpretation when one is treating texts that are already written in the symbolic mode, texts whose expression, then,
originates from and is intended to be responded to on the
prescientific levels of human expression.

4   **The Sublation of Structuralism into
      Interpretation**

I conclude with a few methodological suggestions regarding the dialectic of structuralism and hermeneutics and
with a tentative claim that psychic conversion may perhaps be relevant to the debate.

    'Structuralism,' it would seem, like 'existentialism,'
is a term that is used to refer to markedly different methodologies and ideologies. For Jean Piaget, structuralism is
a study of systems of transformations-under-laws, where
'the structure is preserved or enriched by the interplay of
its transformation laws, which never yield results external
to the system nor employ elements that are external to it.
In short, the notion of structure is comprised of three key
ideas: the idea of wholeness, the idea of transformation,
and the idea of self-regulation.'[58] Unless I am mistaken,
however, the structuralism of Piaget differs notably from
that of Claude Lévi-Strauss, for whom the systems in question result not at all from the terms within the system, but
solely from the differences among the terms, the differential elements; for whom, moreover, this system of differences exists only on an axis of simultaneities that is to be
sharply distinguished from an axis of successions or alter-
nations; and for whom, finally, the unconscious nature of
the systems, their existence and functioning on a

nonhistorical level of the mind, leads to the development
of an anti-humanistic and anti-hermeneutical philosophy
for which genetic growth is an arbitrary notion, culture is
reduced to nature, and 'the ultimate goal of the human
sciences [is] not to constitute but to dissolve man.'[59]
Piaget's notion of structure as it functions operatively in
his thought corresponds quite well, it seems, to that expressed by Lonergan when he speaks of human knowing
as a formally dynamic structure.[60] The principal difference between this notion and that of Lévi-Strauss seems
to be with respect to the relative priority of synchronic
and diachronic relations within the totality. The conflict of
Lévi-Straussian structuralism with hermeneutics seems to
be rooted in the priority assigned by the former to unconscious, automatically functioning, and codified relations
of simultaneity at the expense of genetically or dialectically unfolding relations that permit a semantic comprehension.

What perhaps has not been sufficiently acknowledged
by the hermeneutic protagonists in the debate, however, is
the relevance to semantic understanding of the notion of
structure itself as diachronic. It would seem, too, from my
admittedly limited reading of efforts at structural exegesis, that the functioning notion of structure that is frequently employed is not the generalized structuralism of
synchronicity that is featured, for example, in Lévi-Strauss's
The Savage Mind, but is, rather, germane to the notion of
a formally dynamic and diachronic structure that seems
to be the functioning notion in Piaget's *Structuralism*. Variations on the conflict appear when Lévi-Strauss indicates
that the differences between 'primitive' classifications and
modern science are a function, not of different stages of
mental development, but of different synchronic levels of
knowledge;[61] while those who hold the contrary view do
not dispense with structural relations among levels of con-

scious performance, but rather arrange the structure in a diachronic fashion that accounts for genuine development.[62] Lévi-Strauss's option is picked up and applauded by John Dominic Crossan, for whom what matters are 'certain witnesses for change without progress and for evolution without improvement,'[63] and for whom 'evolutionary *progress* is simply a piece of major Western arrogance.'[64] But it would seem that, if hermeneutics is to continue to dispute the claims that arise from Lévi-Straussian brands of structuralism — claims that are not simply exegetical and so relevant to lower-blade techniques, but meta-methodological and so affecting the upper blade of the universal viewpoint and of the levels and sequences of expression — hermeneutical understanding will have to incorporate into its procedures the explanatory perspective of formally dynamic and diachronic structures, and to point out to proponents of structuralism that it is in fact a diachronic notion of structure that they frequently are employing and should employ if they wish to correlate structure and meaning.

Among the imaginal expressions for whose interpretation psychic conversion may be foundational are narratives. Narratives have also been the focus of much structuralist exegesis. If I am correct in my claim regarding the foundational role of psychic conversion, one of the elements that it provides the interpreter is the possibility of an explanatory understanding of stories. But the base that is psychic conversion is itself an explanatory understanding of one's own story; and that understanding, as it emerges from the attentive, intelligent, reasonable, and responsible negotiation of one's own elemental symbolizing, is a matter of fixing in a diachronic manner the terms and relations of one's own spontaneous symbolic system, and the terms and relations that obtain between this system and one's intelligent, reasonable, and responsible intentionality. The symbolic system is structured; so is intentionality; and so, finally, is the interaction of symbolizing and intending. But the structuring in each case is diachronic. And the story that is told by the symbolic system is the story of one's own development or reversal, both of which are revealed precisely in the diachronic structuring of the relations that obtain among the terms of the system.

The question arises, then, whether the transposition of structuralism from the field of linguistics to that of human studies does not inevitably introduce into the very notion of structure a diachronic primacy that perhaps can be dispensed with in linguistics. Structuralism changes its own very structure when it becomes a methodological tool for the study of human relations. And surely, structuralism is changed with my proposal or tentative suggestion of a diachronic comprehension of narrative. But hermeneutics has been changed no less. The hermeneutics of narrative becomes, on the basis of psychic conversion, explanatory understanding of the diachronic structure of a story. It becomes a matter of fixing terms and relations by one another, on the basis of one's knowledge of the terms and diachronic relations that obtain in one's own story. The relations are those of emergence, of development, of conversion, of decline, of reversal, of breakdown. Perhaps through the complementary mediations of the self that are intentionality analysis and psychic self-appropriation, one comes into possession of the ground theme of every story. And perhaps what psychic conversion specifically provides the interpreter is foundational familiarity with that ground theme as it is expressed on the very imaginal level of consciousness from which the narratives one is studying have emerged.

It may be, then, that the hermeneutics of narrative is best understood as a diachronic structuralism. It is certainly true that in such an understanding our notions both

of hermeneutics and of structuralism would be changed.
But such change is precisely what happens in any dialectic
in which the tension of the opposites is not prematurely
displaced.

> A dialectic is a concrete unfolding of linked
> but opposed principles of change. Thus, there
> will be a dialectic, if (1) there is an aggregate of
> events of a determinate character, (2) the events
> may be traced to either or both of two prin-
> ciples, (3) the principles are opposed yet bound
> together, and (4) they are modified by the
> changes that successively result from them.[65]

Such a notion of dialectic seems to support my still quite
tentative suggestion that the hermeneutics of narrative
might itself be profitably understood in terms of a
diachronic application of transformed structuralist insights.

5   Conclusion

The intention and scope of this paper have been deliberately quite limited. All that I have attempted to do is to
indicate what I understand to be the relation between my
work on psychic conversion and Lonergan's positions in
Insight and *Method in Theology* on the relation of foundations to interpretation. I am quite confident that Lonergan's
hermeneutic theory is of crucial importance to contemporary debates in the fields of both literary criticism and
hermeneutics. Lonergan provides, I believe, access to a
quite unique reinstatement of the subject as center of the
interpretive process. I do not believe that his position is
subject to the critiques of Cartesian and Husserlian subjectivity that have influenced many of the most influential
literary and hermeneutical theories. And I do believe that

his understanding of the relation between foundations and interpretation can do much to resolve the present impasse that these disciplines seem to have reached.

Nonetheless, I do not intend this paper as an attempt to argue these beliefs. I have explicitly limited myself to indicating the complementary relation of psychic conversion to Lonergan's foundations, as these foundations impinge on the tasks of interpretation. Moreover, before Lonergan's position on hermeneutics can be fruitfully related to contemporary debates in literary criticism and interpretation theory, the relations between his notion of the dialectic of the subject which constitutes his explicit foundations and the dialectics of community and culture which relate these foundations to society will have to be articulated in a manner which shows the pertinence of these relations to theories of literary criticism and hermeneutics. The present paper indicates simply and exclusively the grounds from which I believe anyone convinced of the crucial importance of Lonergan's position on the subject would enter the present discussion in these fields. And no doubt before one would be able to make any impact on these fields, one would have had to demonstrate a grasp of the issues at stake in the current debates. These are all projects yet to be undertaken. But I hope the present paper contributes to the basic positions from which further dialogue and dialectic in these areas may proceed.

Notes

1 See Bernard Lonergan, *Insight* (see above, chapter 1, note 20) 190-203/214-27.

2 Robert M. Doran, *Psychic Conversion and Theological Foundations* (see above, chapter 1, note 9).

3 Lonergan, *Insight* 568-73/592-95.

4 Bernard Lonergan, *Method in Theology* (see above, chapter 1, note 1).

5 '[I]n any philosophy, it is possible to distinguish between its cognitional theory and, on the other hand, its pronouncements on metaphysical, ethical, and theological issues. Let us name the cognitional theory the basis, and the other pronouncements the expansion.

'... [T]he inevitable philosophic component immanent in the formulation of cognitional theory will be either a basic position or else a basic counterposition.

'It will be a basic position (1) if the real is the concrete universe of being and not a subdivision of the "already out there now"; (2) if the subject becomes known when it affirms itself intelligently and reasonably and so is not known yet in any prior "existential" state; and (3) if objectivity is conceived as a consequence of intelligent inquiry and critical reflection, and not as a property of vital anticipation, extroversion, and satisfaction.

'On the other hand, it will be a basic counterposition, if it contradicts one or more of the basic positions.' Lonergan, *Insight* 387-88/412-13.

6 Ibid. 530-31/554.

7 Ibid. 531/554.

8 Bernard Lonergan, '*Insight* Revisited,' in *A Second Collection* (see above, chapter 5, note 3) 275.

9 Lonergan, *Insight* 535/558.

10 Ibid. 539/562.

11 Ibid. 532/555.

12 Ibid. 532/556.

13 Ibid. 543/566.

14 Ibid. 546/570.

15 Ibid. 548/571.

16 Ibid. 533/557.

17 On image, symbol, and sign, see ibid. 533-34/557-58.

18 Ibid. 534/557-58.

19 Ibid. 541/564.

20 Ibid. 548/571-72.

21 Ibid. 548-49/572. Emphasis added.

22 This distinction appears frequently in David Tracy's discussions of interpretation. See, for example, *The Analogical Imagination* (see above, chapter 7, note 14) 120, and the texts referred to in the same book on 145, note 67.

23 Lonergan, *Insight* 564/587.

24 Ibid. 564/588.

25 Ibid. 565/588.

26 Ibid. 565/589.

27 Ibid. 566/589.

28 Ibid. 567/590.

29 Ibid.

30 Ibid. 578/600-601.

31 Ibid. 581/604.

32 Ibid. 585/608.

33 Ibid. 582/604. Emphasis added.

34 See Frederick Crowe, 'An Exploration of Lonergan's New Notion of Value,' *Science et Esprit* 29:2 (1977) 123-43; see also Robert M. Doran, 'Subject, Psyche, and Theology's Foundations' (see above, chapter 1, note 13).

35 On the two phases of theology, see Lonergan, *Method in Theology* 133, 140.

36 Ibid. 267.

37 Lonergan, *Insight* 530-31/554, emphasis added.

38 Lonergan, *Method in Theology* 292.

39 Ibid. 144.

40 Ibid. 153.

41 Ibid. 154.

42 Ibid. 170.

43 Ibid. 156.

44 Ibid. 159-60.

45 Ibid. 160.

46 Ibid. 161.

47 Ibid., quoting Friedrich Schlegel's description of the classic.

48 Ibid. 247.

49 Ibid. 288.

[50] See the section 'Stages of Meaning' in ibid. 85-89.

[51] Ibid. 153.

[52] 1993 note: It is important that I not be interpreted as claiming that the natural desire to see God or what in the next chapter will be called the notion of transcendent mystery is a fifth-level notion. My references to the 'fifth level of consciousness' in *Theology and the Dialectics of History* have been so interpreted by Michael Vertin, in his article 'Lonergan on Consciousness: Is There a Fifth Level?', *Method: Journal of Lonergan Studies* 12 (1994). I have never held that what in some writings I call a fifth level of consciousness is a *notion* in Lonergan's sense of that term. What I call the notion of transcendent mystery is identical with what in *De ente supernaturali* (Toronto: Regis College edition, 1971) Lonergan calls the obediential potency for the absolutely supernatural, or again with what Lonergan calls the natural desire to see God (*Collection*, chapter 5), or with what in *Method in Theology* he calls the transcendent exigence. It is identified in *Theology and the Dialectics of History* as 'an obediential potency for the self-communication of God in revelation and grace, for the self-communication that begins to fulfill the transcendent exigence that consciousness is.' It is true that, as Vertin notes, my references to the fifth level in *Theology and the Dialectics of History* are less clear than they are in the other writing that Vertin interprets (correctly) and criticizes, 'Consciousness and Grace' (*Method: Journal of Lonergan Studies* 11:2, 1993, 51-75), where the fifth level is clearly the inchoate *satisfaction* of that natural exigence, and so is grace. But *Theology and the Dialectics of History* itself speaks of the fifth level as a resting from the striving of intentional consciousness (31).

This note is not meant in any way to detract from the value of Vertin's article; he has made a serious contribution to clearing up a decisive issue. But he has not interpreted correctly my position in *Theology and the Dialectics of History*. What he has in fact called our attention to is the significance of the hermeneutical canon of residues (*Insight* 613-16). *Theology and the Dialectics of History* took ten years to write. In the course of that time my thought on this issue developed, but the articulation did not always keep pace. Earlier passages were not always rewritten, perhaps the shift in viewpoint was not clearly noticed, or if it was noticed, the earlier articulation was not adequately corrected. At no point, however, would I have answered 'Yes' to the question, Is what you are calling the fifth level of consciousness a notion in Lonergan's sense of that term? Perhaps I may offer the hermeneutic key that the passages that speak of a notion of transcendent mystery, as defined above, were written rather late in the process. May I point out as well that the lack of clarity that Vertin correctly finds in some of my expressions on this issue also affects the following statement of Lonergan himself: 'conversion ... is total surrender to the demands of the human spirit: be attentive, be intelligent, be reasonable, be responsible, be in love.' *Method in Theology* 268.

53 Ibid. 64.

54 On the notion of defensive circles, see Lonergan, *Insight* 118/141.

55 On the censorship, see ibid. 189-96/212-20. On the shorter and longer cycles of decline, ibid. 222-28/247-53. On the relation of the dialectic of community to the dialectic of the subject, ibid. 218/243.

56 For the pertinence of Paul Ricoeur's study of Freud to the project I envision, see Robert M. Doran, *Subject and Psyche* (see above, chapter 1, note 11) chapter 3. The basic dialectic with Jung will be over the issue of a distinction to be drawn among the orders of elemental symbols. I have found quite helpful Northrop Frye's discussion of archetypal and anagogic symbols. See his *Anatomy of Criticism: Four Essays* (Princeton: Princeton University Press) 95-128. For the rudiments of my psychological use of this distinction, see my paper 'Aesthetic Subjectivity and Generalized Empirical Method' (see above, chapter 1, note 27).

57 1993 note: An example of the lack of clarity that Vertin picked up on (see above, note 52) and that grounded his interpretation can be given here: the original version of this paper had 'the five levels of intentional consciousness.' There are four, not five, levels of *intentional* consciousness (see above, chapter 10).

58 Jean Piaget, *Structuralism* (New York: Basic Books, 1970) 5.

59 Claude Lévi-Strauss, *The Savage Mind* (Chicago: University of Chicago Press, 1973) 247.

60 Lonergan, 'Cognitional Structure,' in *Collection* (see above, chapter 9, note 9) 206.

61 Lévi-Strauss, *The Savage Mind* 15.

62 See Lonergan, *Method in Theology* 85-99.

63 John Dominic Crossan, *The Dark Interval: Towards a Theology of Story* (Niles, IL: Argus Communications, 1975) 27.

64 Ibid. 33.

65 Lonergan, *Insight* 217/242.

14 Psychic Conversion and Lonergan's Hermeneutics

1 Introduction

In an important section of his *Anatomy of Criticism*, Northrop Frye writes: '[T]here are two fundamental movements of narrative: a cyclical movement within the order of nature, and a dialectical movement from that order into the apocalyptic world above.' He notes that 'the movement to the demonic world below is very rare, because a constant rotation within the order of nature is demonic in itself.'[1]

Such an observation has a ground in the critic's own differentiation of desire, the desire that Frye maintains is the center of the order of words,[2] and, further, in the critic's sensitive appropriation of that differentiation.[3] What Frye expresses here is also the fundamental element in my critique of the Jungian hermeneutic of archetypal symbolism. For Jung does not distinguish the two narrative movements of which Frye speaks, but collapses the elementally meaningful symbols of the narrative of the individuating subject into a 'constant rotation within the order of nature.' Without descending to the demonic world below, Jung plays with the demonic in the world of the here and now. Constant rotation is symbolized for Jung in the mandala, the symbol of wholeness. Thus Erich Neumann, one of the most creative and original thinkers in the Jungian

school, writes, 'So long as man shall exist, perfection will
continue to appear as the circle, the sphere, and the round,
and the Personal Deity who is sufficient unto himself, and
the self who has gone beyond the opposites, will reappear
in the image of the round, the mandala.'[4] The mandala is
the self beyond the opposites, and that self is the image of
the primal deity sufficient unto itself. But the restriction
of the self to constant rotation in the order of nature is a
rejection of the apocalyptic movement to the world above,
a repudiation of the supernatural,[5] and, precisely as such,
a choice for the demonic. The identification of such a restricted self with the image of God is an apotheosis of the
self, not as the mystery of divinization by grace, but as the
myth that expresses acquiescence to the primordial temptation, 'You shall be as gods.'[6]

The position in Jung's work can be advanced, and
the counterposition reversed, by realizing that the conflict
of opposites must be differentiated into two distinct realizations of the single but complex notion of dialectic.[7] There
are various dialectics of contraries, among which is the
dialectic of consciousness and the unconscious. Jung remains one of the most astute guides to their negotiation.
But there is also the dialectic of contradictories between
good and evil. The entire series of dialectics of contraries
can reach with God's grace an ever precarious integrity
beyond that tendency of our sinful nature to disequilibrium[8] which theology calls concupiscence. But the dialectic of contradictories cannot be resolved by ambitioning
an integrity beyond its opposite poles. For here there is
'not a struggle between any opposites whatever but the
very precise opposition between authenticity and
unauthenticity.'[9] The ambition to resolve this dialectic
through an integration of good and evil is precisely what
constitutes the essence of the demonic. To choose constant rotation within the order of nature when invited to

acquiesce to the movement of grace represented in the anagogic symbolization of the movement to 'the apocalyptic world above' is, in Bernard Lonergan's terms, to refuse to surrender to the relentless transformation of 'the integrator' by 'the operator.'[10] In this case the operator is not only the natural desire for what cannot be achieved within the resources of nature, but also the supernatural gift of grace responding to nature's yearnings. And the refusal is no integration of good and evil; it is choice of constant rotation within a presently achieved flexible *circle* of ranges of schemes of recurrence, when the invitation to a supernaturally transformed finality is to transcend the circle to a new and higher integration effected by an 'otherworldly love.' Such a choice

> rests on man's proud content to be just a man, and its tragedy is that, on the present supposition of a supernatural solution, to be just a man is what man cannot be. If he would be truly a man, he would submit to the unrestricted desire and discover the problem of evil and affirm the existence of a solution and accept the solution that exists. But if he would be only a man, he has to be less. He has to forsake the openness of the pure desire; he has to take refuge in the counterpositions; he has to develop what counterphilosophies he can to save his dwindling humanism from further losses; and there will not be lacking men clear-sighted enough to grasp that the issue is between God and man, logical enough to grant that intelligence and reason are orientated towards God, ruthless enough to summon to their aid the dark forces of passion and of violence.[11]

This is not to negate, but to relativize, the mandala as symbol of the flexible circle of ranges of schemes of recurrence. The mandala is a legitimate elemental symbolization of a temporary integration of the various dialectics of contraries that consolidate human development. It becomes demonic when it is willed as constant rotation, and so when it becomes the symbol of a consolidated resistance against the transformative dynamism of 'the operator.' What is good is the process of ever higher organizations of the dialectics of contraries resultant from the fact that we are incarnate spirits. What is evil is the displacement of these dialectics in one direction or the other, the capitulation to the tendency of sinful nature to disequilibrium. And what is demonic is the choice of a constant rotation within that sinful nature, against the pressure of the heightened tension consequent upon the fact that the solution to the problem of evil is supernatural.

Now the foregoing comments began with an observation on the foundations of a particular judgment on imaginal expression made by one of the foremost literary critics of our time. They moved to a critique of the hermeneutics of imaginal expression offered by a particular school of depth psychology that lacks precisely those foundations. But the positive observation on Frye and the critique of Jung are both based in the work of Bernard Lonergan, and witness to my conviction that the significance of Lonergan's work for the hermeneutics of imaginal expression in general and literary criticism in particular is as great as is the importance of his work for understanding and developing philosophic positions and for understanding and reversing philosophic counterpositions. That the work of Lonergan can ground a critique and reorientation of depth psychology has been a constant theme in most of my work. The connection of the symbols studied by depth psychology with the literary universe mapped out by Frye would lead us to suspect that Lonergan's significance for a hermeneutic of all imaginal expression, including literary, is far-reaching and momentous.

I cannot develop here a full Lonergan-inspired hermeneutics of the symbolic. I will argue, though, that there are grounds in the principal elements of Lonergan's theory of interpretation for a hermeneutics of the imaginal that might enable someone someday to write the generalized poetics that has occupied hermeneutic thinkers at least from Dilthey to Ricoeur;[12] and that the notion of psychic conversion that I have tried to develop on the grounds of Lonergan's work might provide an important ingredient in the foundations of a Lonergan-inspired hermeneutics of imaginal expression. I will first review what I regard as the elements in Lonergan's notion of interpretation that I think would be the most important facets of his thought for the development of a generalized poetics. Second, I will show the connection of psychic conversion with these elements. Third, I will apply the position worked out in these two sections to several examples. This final section will suggest how a Lonergan-inspired poetics might reflect back on the Jungian hermeneutics of symbolic expression, to reorient its account of the sequences of imaginal expression in the direction of a hermeneutics of the symbolic expressions of the emergence of consciousness as transcendental notion of being, of the good, and of absolute mystery.[13] I had hoped to conclude with a further development that I will have to postpone due to the length of the paper. But I cannot resist at least mentioning it, especially since it has influenced my interpretation of the hermeneutic theory of *Insight*.

Lonergan first treats interpretation in a chapter devoted to metaphysics. The first sentence of this chapter begins with a statement of his intention to meet Hegel's challenge that philosophers 'not only ... account for their own views but also ... explain the existence of contrary convictions and opinions.'[14] And the last sentence of the chapter states that the challenge has been met in a way quite distinct from that of Hegel himself. I propose that we are to interpret Lonergan on the interpretation of differentiations of the notion of being and the interpretation of the symbolic expressions of these differentiations as offering the heuristic structure of a history of the *being* of meaning, a history that has to be contrasted not only with Hegel's dialectical necessitarianism, but also with Heidegger's poetic meditations on the destiny of Being mediated in the temporal appropriation of Being in the *Verstehen* of *Dasein*. This proposal is confirmed by the first two sections of *Method in Theology*'s chapter on communications, treating respectively 'Meaning and Ontology' and 'Common Meaning and Ontology.'[15]

2   **Lonergan's Hermeneutics and the Interpretation of Imaginal and Literary Expression**

The hermeneutics of *Insight* has a philosophic finality. It would show how 'the historical series of philosophies would be regarded as a sequence of contributions to a single but complex goal.'[16] That goal is the self-appropriation of the polymorphism of human consciousness. It is grounded in the self-affirmation of consciousness as empirical, intelligent, and rational notion of being. The implementation of the philosophical hermeneutics of *Insight* would yield a phenomenology of spirit, where spirit is notion of being. The phenomenology would represent philosophy's appropriation of its own genesis, an appropriation at once concrete, historical, dialectical, and as with Hegel's *Phenomenology*, partly foundational of further development *in oratione recta*. When integrated with the later sea change that became functional specialization, it would be differentiated into the essential elements of the first five functional specialties of a methodical philosophy.

The pertinence of the hermeneutics of *Insight*, however, extends beyond its explicit objective. Both the base and the objective of the hermeneutic theory lie in the appropriation of the *polymorphism* of human consciousness. Most directly for the concerns of *Insight*, of course, this polymorphism is the source of diverse and conflicting cognitional theories, so that there is possible a hermeneutic 'general theorem to the effect that any philosophy, whether actual or possible, will rest upon the dynamic structure of cognitional activity either as correctly conceived or as distorted by oversights and by mistaken orientations.'[17] But if we direct our self-appropriating attention to the polymorphism as such, in the light of the correct conception of the dynamic structure of cognitional activity, we will find a clue to the understanding and evaluation of extraphilosophic utterances and texts as well. In fact, if not in explicit intention, the hermeneutic theory of *Insight* is a development of a position on 'a single base' from which not only 'any philosophy' but any nonphilosophic text as well 'can be interpreted correctly.'[18]

That single base is human desire, the same desire that for Northrop Frye is the 'center of the order of words.' Its limits, Frye says, are 'not the real, but the conceivable, ...the world of fulfilled desire emancipated from all anxieties and frustrations.'[19] By differentiating within that polymorphic desire, first a notion of being, and then a notion of value, and by understanding both of these as manifestations of a 'natural desire to see God,' a transcendent exigence, Lonergan turns Frye's 'self-contained literary universe'[20] into an intentional structure, an order that is only provisionally centripetal. It is centripetal as a region of withdrawal, but the withdrawal is for the sake of a return to 'concrete living in its concrete potentialities.'[21] Art, including literary art, thus becomes, without the instrumentalization of didacticism, a 're-creation of the liberty of the subject, the recognition of the freedom of consciousness' beyond environmental or neurobiological determinisms.[22] It enables us to explore 'the full freedom of our ways of feeling and perceiving'[23] beyond all instrumentalizations of experience.

Potentially emergent from the implementation of the hermeneutic theory of *Insight*, then, is a phenomenology, a phenomenology not only of the explicit philosophic achievements and mistakes of humankind, but also of other constructions of the human spirit, including artistic and imaginal literary constructions. To emphasize the hermeneutics of *Insight* as a source for literary criticism is not to take an unnecessary detour around the path that would lead most directly to our objective. This is clear already from the fact that Lonergan begins his discussion of hermeneutics with 'a genetic account of the radical meaning of mystery and myth, of their significance and function, of the grounds of their emergence, survival, and disappearance.'[24] The path to our objective, I believe, will be smoothed by complementing Lonergan's hermeneutics in *Insight* not only with the further differentiations found in his later work, but also with the position on psychic conversion. But it is the hermeneutics precisely of *Insight* that provides the essential point of articulation of the position on psychic conversion with Lonergan's theory of interpretation, even if the essential advances of *Method in Theology* have to be included in any complete account.

What makes *Insight* a particularly apt vehicle for developing a hermeneutics of the imaginal and for articulating psychic conversion with Lonergan's position is the fact that there is explicit attention paid throughout *Insight*, and in particular in the treatment of interpretation, to the dialectical unity in tension of psyche and intentionality. The notion of being and the principle of correspondence between the operators of intellectual and psychic development constitute the major contributions of *Insight* to a hermeneutics of the imaginal. Moreover, as we will see, the dialectic within consciousness between the spirit and the sensitive psyche is the basic element in the explication of psychic conversion. For it is the *causa cognoscendi* of the more radical dialectic of consciousness and the unconscious. This dialectical unity in tension is, I think, more presupposed than explicitly adverted to throughout *Method in Theology*.

The basic notion in the hermeneutics of *Insight*, then, is the notion of being. When coupled with *Method's* notion of value, with the transcendent exigence, and with the soteriological differentiation of consciousness created by the divine response to that exigence of our nature, it grounds a semantics of desire and fulfillment that constitutes the upper blade of a generalized hermeneutics for reconstructing the constructions of the human spirit through which the world has been mediated and constituted by meaning. To this upper blade there can eventually be added, as I will argue in the next section, a psychic or imaginal complement, a semantics of transcendental imagination as sensorium of transcendence, that will greatly aid interpretation of literary texts. But the addition is possible in virtue of the principle of correspondence already explained by Lonergan. And this principle implies that the semantics of imagination would contribute as well to the interpretation even of philosophic texts. For it would enable the interpreter to understand and express what would be the sensitive appropriation on the part of the author being interpreted of what that author thought was intelligently grasped and reasonably affirmed in the positions or counterpositions of his or her philosophic expressions. That is to say, there is an archetypal, figurative, mythic resonance even to those expressions that have their source, not in the sensitive psyche, but 'in a reflectively tested intelligent ordering of experiential elements' or 'in the addition of acts of will, such as wishes and commands, to intellectual and rational knowledge,' and that are meant to be responded to 'on the three levels of experience, insight, and judgment, or ... not only on the three cognitional levels but also in the practical manner that includes an act of will.'[25] Hermeneutics is a theory of interpretation of both literary and post-literary ranges of expression, and a theory of both intellectual and evaluative or transformative interpretation of these texts. In all of these applications, its upper blade entails Lonergan's transcendental notions and the principle of correspondence between these notions and the sensitive psyche. Lonergan's 'single base of operations' remains the ultimate foundation, even with the complement of psychic conversion, for from this base is derived, by the principle of correspondence between sensitive desire and the notions of being, value, and transcendence, the criterion for distinguishing symbolic expressions of positions from symbolic expressions of counterpositions, and for locating with precision the relative placing of the levels and sequences of expression.

Thus imaginal expression is to be interpreted, in pure formulations,[26] as the sensitive appropriation of the particular differentiations of the higher notions attained and symbolized by the author whose text is being interpreted. Discourse that unfolds on, and that is meant to be responded to on, the psychological levels of expression as contrasted with scientific and philosophical levels, is, then, the expression of sensitivity's consolidation of and adaptation to the differentiations of the polymorphic set of transcendental notions that the consciousness of its author has reached. *Insight* grounds this affirmation in three steps.

First, it posits a principle of correspondence between the operator of intellectual development and a psychic operator. Second, it identifies the operator of intellectual development precisely as the notion of being. And third, it locates in the notion of being both the ground and the objective of scientific or methodical interpretation. Let us consider the third of these steps first, since in the last analysis it is the crucial factor.

The notion of being is the ground of scientific interpretation, in that the upper blade of appropriate hermeneutic performance has two components, both of which are based in the notion of being. The first component regards meaning, and it consists of 'the assertion that the protean notion of being is differentiated by a series of genetically and dialectically related unknowns'[27] that are to become known precisely through methodical interpretation. That is, first, the universe of meanings consists of

> the full range of possible combinations (1) of experiences and lack of experience (2) of insights and lack of insight (3) of judgments and of failures to judge, and (4) of the various orientations of the polymorphic consciousness of man.[28]

And, second,

> in the measure that one grasps the structure of this protean notion of being, one possesses the ground from which one can proceed to the content and context of every meaning. In the measure that one explores human experience, human insights, human reflections, and human polymorphic consciousness, one becomes capable, when provided with the appropriate data,

of approximating to the content and context
of the meaning of any given expression.[29]

The second component of the upper blade concerns expression itself, and it lies in 'the assertion that there is a
genetic process in which modes of expression move towards their specialization and differentiation on sharply
distinguishable levels.'[30] But the source of the notion of a
sequence of expressions on distinct levels is the notion of
being. That is to say, first, that there are different levels of
expression insofar as the expression has its source

> (1) simply in the experience of the speaker, as
> in an exclamation, or (2) in artistically ordered
> experiential elements, as in a song, or (3) in a
> reflectively tested intelligent ordering of expe-
> riential elements, as in a statement of fact, or
> (4) in the addition of acts of will, such as wishes
> and commands, to intellectual and rational
> knowledge.
>
> In turn, the hearer or reader may be in-
> tended to respond (1) simply on the experien-
> tial level in an intersubjective reproduction of
> the speaker's feelings, mood, sentiments, im-
> ages, associations, or (2) both on the level of
> experience and on the level of insight and con-
> sideration, or (3) on the three levels of experi-
> ence, insight, and judgment, or (4) not only on
> the three cognitional levels but also in the prac-
> tical manner that includes an act of will.[31]

Next,

> Besides levels of expression, there also are se-
> quences. Development in general is a process

from the undifferentiated to the differentiated, from the generic to the specific, from the global and awkward to the expert and precise. It would simplify enormously the task of the interpreter if, from the beginning of human speech and writing, there existed and were recognized the full range of specialized modes of expression. But the fact is that the specializations had to be invented, and the use of the inventions presupposes a corresponding development or education of prospective audiences or readers.[32]

The source of the invention of specialized modes of expression lies in the insights through which the notion of being is differentiated. And the same notion of being that grounds hermeneutic method is also its objective. That is, the canon of relevance for a methodical hermeneutics 'demands that the interpreter begin from the universal viewpoint *and* that his interpretation convey some differentiation of the protean notion of being.' And the canon of explanation demands that this differentiation 'be not descriptive but explanatory. It will aim at relating, not to us, but to one another, the contents and contexts of the totality of documents and interpretations.' An explanatory differentiation of the notion of being will thus account for 'the genetic sequence in which insights gradually are accumulated,' for 'the dialectical alternatives in which accumulated insights are formulated, with positions inviting further development and counterpositions shifting their ground to avoid the reversal they demand,' and for 'the possibility of the differentiation and specialization of modes of expression.'[33]

The notion of being that is the ground and objective of adequate interpretation is the authentic orientation of

human consciousness as the desire to know, as a concrete
and dynamic unity of empirical, intelligent, and rational
operations generating the true judgments in which the real
is known. It is thus the operator of intellectual development. And human consciousness is itself a unity in tension of the sensitive psyche with the intentionality of the
human spirit. It is the latter element, the spiritual, that
makes of human consciousness a notion of being, where
'being is (or is thought to be) whatever is (or is thought to
be) grasped intelligently and affirmed reasonably.'[34] But

> because the integrating activities of the intel-
> lectual level and the integrated activities of the
> sensitive level form a dialectical unity in ten-
> sion, it follows (1) that the intellectual activi-
> ties are either the proper unfolding of the de-
> tached and disinterested desire to know or else
> a distorted unfolding due to the interference
> of other desires, and (2) that the sensitive ac-
> tivities, from which intellectual contents emerge
> and in which they are represented, expressed,
> and applied, either are involved in the myster-
> ies of the proper unfolding or distort these
> mysteries into myths.[35]

The term 'mystery' means for Lonergan the symbolic expression of a position, and the term 'myth' the
symbolic expression of a counterposition.[36] The dialectical unity in tension of the psyche and the spirit thus exhibits 'a principle of correspondence between otherwise coincidental manifolds on each lower level and systematizing
forms on the next higher level.' Thus 'the principle of dynamic correspondence calls for a harmonious orientation
on the psychic level, and from the nature of the case such
an orientation would have to consist in some cosmic di-

mension, in some intimation of unplumbed depths that accrued to man's feelings, emotions, sentiments.'[37] Thus imaginal expressions, the elemental meanings found in the spontaneous symbolizing of the psychic operator, can and should be interpreted as symbolic of differentiations of the notion of being that is human consciousness. Moreover, such expressions consolidate these differentiations in the dialectical unity in tension of the subject; for

> as the cognitional and volitional appropriations of truth are solidary with each other, so also they condition and are conditioned by adaptations of human sensibility. Here the basic problem is to discover the dynamic images that both correspond to intellectual contents, orientations, and determinations, yet also possess in the sensitive field the power to issue forth not only into words but also into deeds ... [A]s intellectual development occurs through insights into sensible presentations and imaginative representations, so also the intelligent and reasonable control of human living can be effective only in the measure that it has at its disposal the symbols and signs by which it translates its directives to human sensibility.[38]

As with the interpretation of the philosophic meanings with which *Insight* is primarily concerned, then, so with the interpretation of elemental symbolic meanings, 'if [one's] understanding is correct, it will provide a differentiation of the protean notion of being, and it will provide no more.'[39] This interpretation will be expressed in 'pure formulations,' that is, in formulations that 'proceed from the immanent sources of meaning to determine differentiations of the protean notion of being.'[40] But it will be expressed as well in hypothetical expressions that transpose the pure formulation into the equivalent content that would proceed from the particular viewpoint behind the expression being interpreted. Knowledge of this particular viewpoint is a function of one's understanding of the levels and sequences of expression, and so of the differentiation of the notion of being which the author was capable of expressing. The hypothetical expression must approximate or coincide with the actual expression being interpreted, and if it does, it may be pronounced a probable or correct interpretation.

The materials are completely in place, I believe, in chapter 17 of *Insight* for a remarkably thorough and illuminating theory regarding the interpretation of elemental meanings. The principal elements in that theory would be, first, the position that interpretation in general is to determine differentiations of the notion of being, and second, the position that such differentiations would have psychic correlatives and correspondences in the realms dialectically differentiated by mystery and myth. These latter expressions would be understood as themselves symbolic precisely of the differentiation of the notion of being reached by the individual whose work is being interpreted. The history of elemental human symbolizing would be understood, on such an analysis, as the history of the sequences of expression of the dialectic of the psyche with the intentional consciousness that is a notion of being. This dialectic is the source of the understanding of symbolic expressions. These expressions are elementally meaningful dramatizations of the successive differentiations of the notion of being that constitute the history of human consciousness. The understanding of these expressions will be verbalized in pure formulations to the extent that it grasps these expressions precisely as symbolic of the differentiation of consciousness itself as a notion of being.

Such differentiation is, consequently, the ground of the meaning of symbolic expression. From the pure formulation the interpretation will proceed to the hypothetical formulation that would correspond to the original speaker's or writer's context. To the extent that the hypothetical expression truly matches the real expression, the interpretation may be judged to be true.

What *Method in Theology* would add to this analysis is the distinct relevance of the notion of value and of absolute transcendence for an understanding of the heuristic anticipation that authentic human consciousness is. The position suggested in the previous paragraph can be expanded in light of *Method in Theology*, then, by adding to the expression 'differentiations of the notion of being' the phrase 'or of the notion of value' and the phrase 'or of the transcendent exigence.' Thus, the upper blade of hermeneutic method becomes the assertion that the notions of being and of value, and the transcendent exigence of human consciousness, are differentiated by a series of genetically and dialectically related unknowns. Pure formulations will proceed to determine differentiations of the notion of being or of the notion of value or of the transcendent exigence. Hypothetical expressions will transpose the pure formulation into an equivalent content that will be appropriate to the original writer's viewpoint not only as regards being but also as regards value and as regards transcendent mystery. Correct understanding will provide a differentiation of the notion of being or of the notion of value or of the transcendent exigence, and nothing more. Within these notions 'the transition from one differentiation to another is the quite determinate and determinable process' not only of 'changing patterns of experience, accumulations of insights, and sets of judgments'[41] but also of decisions and of distinctly religious experience. The canon of relevance demands that the interpretation con-

vey some differentiation of either the notion of being or
the notion of value or the transcendent exigence, and the
canon of explanation that the differentiation be explanatory. The basic principle by means of which the
hermeneutic theory is applicable to elemental symbolic
meaning is the same dialectical unity in tension of the
psyche and the spirit that was the ground of extending to
the psyche the hermeneutic theory of *Insight*. For, as regards the notion of value, the apprehension of values occurs in feelings,[42] and these feelings are reciprocally related to symbols, in that a symbol is an image of a real or
imaginary object that evokes a feeling or is evoked by a
feeling.[43] And as regards the transcendent exigence and
its incremental satisfaction in religious experience, we know
already from *Insight* that there is a religiously transformed
universal viewpoint, in which

> the solution will be not only a renovation of
> will that matches intellectual detachment and
> aspiration, not only a new and higher collabo-
> ration of intellects through faith in God, but
> also a mystery that is at once symbol of the
> uncomprehended and sign of what is grasped
> and psychic force that sweeps living human
> bodies, linked in charity, to the joyful, coura-
> geous, wholehearted, yet intelligently controlled
> performance of the tasks set by a world order
> in which the problem of evil is not suppressed
> but transcended.[44]

The principal assertions of this section can be stated
succinctly as follows.

First, the position of chapter 17 of *Insight* on the
hermeneutic upper blade of the notion of being, when
combined with the principle of correspondence between

the operators of intellectual and psychic development, grounds a hermeneutics of the meanings carried in such embodiments as symbols and literary language.

Second, to this upper blade may be added *Method*'s differentiation of the notion of value and the articulation of the transcendent exigence whose fulfillment in religious love is made foundational in *Method in Theology*.

Third, the principle of correspondence remains in effect with these further differentiations, so that the meanings carried in these embodiments would be interpreted as expressing a sensitive appropriation of some differentiation of the notions of being, value, and transcendence reached by the one expressing himself or herself in these carriers of meaning.

3   Psychic Conversion and the Interpretation of Imaginal Expression

The position on the meaning of elemental symbolic expressions as imaginally correspondent to differentiations of consciousness as a notion of being, a notion of value, and a transcendent exigence has radical implications for the reorientation of depth psychology. A science of the psyche grounded in the science of intentional consciousness provided by Lonergan would regard the elemental meanings expressed in the spontaneous symbolic deliverances of the psyche in such events as dreams and other occurrences at the same level, as symbolic precisely of differentiations of consciousness as a notion of being, a notion of value, and a true exigence for unrestricted intelligibility, unconditioned truth, unqualified goodness. Because of the dialectical unity in tension of human consciousness as at once psychic and spiritual, the dream of a human being, especially if it is archetypal or anagogic, symbolizes oneself as a more or less differentiated and authentic notion of being, of value, of God. Interpreting the dream is understanding oneself precisely in the differentiations one has achieved of the notions of being, of value, and of God that one *is*. Such interpretation of oneself grounds one's interpretation of the elemental symbolic productions of others, past and present, as indications of a genetic and dialectical series of differentiations of these notions. A reoriented depth psychology thus becomes a dimension of the upper blade of a methodical hermeneutics.

Such a position on the genuine objective of depth psychology can be grounded rather conclusively, I believe, in what Lonergan has written about the psyche and its symbols. *Insight* grounds the position on the elemental symbol as a sensitive expression of consciousness as notion of being. This is precisely the significance of the section on mystery and myth in the chapter devoted to interpretation. *Method in Theology* unites symbols to the notion of value by the medium of the feelings in which values are apprehended and with which symbols stand in a relationship of reciprocal evocation. *Method in Theology* speaks in this context of the significance, from a basic point of view, of the existential approach to the interpretation of dreams.[45] Finally, as we just have seen, *Insight* highlights the symbolic dimensions of the transcendent exigence and its supernatural fulfillment, by speaking of the mystery that at once symbolizes the uncomprehended, signifies our limited grasp of it, and empowers the life of charity that would further the reign of God in this world.

What I now must do is relate psychic conversion to this position. Psychic conversion is a transformation of the subject, a particular dimension or set of events in the full conversion process. Its peculiar finality lies in consolidating the integral and basic dialectic of the subject toward which each of the other dimensions of conversion — religious, moral, intellectual — makes its proper contribution. The integrity of the dialectic of the subject is the goal of the entire and precarious process of conversion. For the tendency to distort the dialectic of the subject is what is meant by the theological category 'concupiscence,' and conversion is the change of direction effected by grace, a movement away from that distortion and towards an ever precarious integrity. Psychic conversion is a defensive circle, as it were, around the contributions of the other, more foundational, dimensions of conversion.

The first step in understanding psychic conversion, then, lies in understanding the dialectic of the subject. Dialectic, as I have argued elsewhere,[46] is a single but quite complex notion in Lonergan's work. The complexity of the notion has to be brought under some control, and I have tried to do this on the basis of the distinction between consciousness and knowledge. Thus, there is a duality both to knowledge and to consciousness. The duality of knowledge is broken through the self-affirmation of the knower that represents the first and foundational step, not in conversion but in self-appropriation, in the movement to the stage of meaning governed by interiorly differentiated consciousness. But the duality of consciousness is to be, not broken, but preserved and strengthened. The duality of consciousness is a dialectic of contraries, whereas the duality of knowledge grounds a series of dialectics of contradictories. Both instances of dialectic are discussed in Lonergan's work, though not in the terms of contraries and contradictories; and the distinction of consciousness and knowledge provides a thorough grounding of such a complex use of the single term 'dialectic.'

Dialectic, moreover, is a feature of the upper blade of the heuristic structure of human science. It 'stands to generalized method, as the differential equation to classical physics, or the operator equation to the more recent physics.'[47] It is 'applicable to *any* concrete unfolding of

linked but opposed principles that are modified cumulatively by the unfolding.'[48] The complexity of the notion
derives from the fact that the opposition to which dialectic
is applied can be one either of contrariety or of contradiction. When the opposition is one of contrariety, the linked
but opposed principles are to work harmoniously, in functional interdependence. When the principles are so operating, the dialectic is an integral dialectic of contraries.
But when one of these principles is dominant over the other,
the unfolding of the changes resultant from the principles
is a distorted dialectic of contraries. And 'the essential logic
of the distorted dialectic is a reversal. For dialectic rests
on the concrete unity of opposed principles, the dominance
of either principle results in a distortion, and the distortion
both weakens the dominance and strengthens the opposed
principle to restore an equilibrium.'[49]

When the opposition is one of contradiction, however, the linked but opposed principles cannot function
harmoniously with one another. Then there is 'not a
struggle between any opposites whatever but the very precise opposition between authenticity and unauthenticity.'[50]
Then the resolution of the conflict involves opting for one
alternative and rejecting the other. But the dialectic of
contradictories is related to the dialectic of contraries in
that authenticity is a function of opting for the integral
dialectic of contraries, and inauthenticity a function of
opting for or capitulating to the distortion of the dialectic
of contraries. The integral dialectic of contraries is the
objective of the process toward authenticity that is conversion.

In the dialectic of the subject, the radical contraries
are neural demands for psychic integration, which constitute 'the unconscious,' and the orientation of dramatically
patterned intentionality. This radical dialectic of the subject is the *causa essendi* of a derived dialectic that is prior

quoad nos and so the *causa cognoscendi* of the more radical dialectic. The derived dialectic is the dialectic within consciousness between the sensitive psyche and the spirit that constitutes the unity in tension of the subject of which we spoke in the previous section. The radical dialectic is the *causa essendi* also of a dialectic within the psyche itself, between the psyche's vertical finality to participation in the life of the spirit and the regressive tendency 'ever backwards' that figures so prominently in Freudian speculation. This regressive tendency is a function of the limitations imposed by the neural base and its particular schemes of recurrence. The dialectic of the psyche can be understood in the terms provided by Paul Ricoeur's masterful interpretation of Freud, where a Freudian archeology of the subject is joined with a teleology that Ricoeur derives from reflection on Hegel's *Phenomenology*. But, since the archeology affects the psyche, perhaps it would better be understood from an interpretation of some of the more positive tendencies in the psychology of Jung than through an appropriation of Hegel.[51]

Of the orientation of dramatically patterned intentionality that is one pole of the radical dialectic of the subject, Lonergan writes:

> [I]n so far as [the] thrust of the self regularly opts, not for the merely apparent good, but for the true good, the self thereby is achieving moral self-transcendence; he is existing authentically; he is constituting himself as an originating value, and he is bringing about terminal values, namely a good of order that is truly good and instances of the particular good that are truly good. On the other hand, in so far as one's decisions have their principal motives, not in the values at stake, but in a calculus of the

> pleasures and pains involved, one is failing in
> self-transcendence, in authentic human exist-
> ence, in the origination of value in oneself and
> in one's society.[52]

At its root this orientation 'consists in the transcendental
notions that both enable us and require us to advance in
understanding, to judge truthfully, to respond to values.'[53]
Moreover, 'this possibility and exigence become effective
only through development. One has to acquire the skills
and learning of a competent human being in some walk of
life. One has to grow in sensitivity and responsiveness to
values if one's humanity is to be authentic.'[54] And such
'development is not inevitable, and so results vary. There
are human failures. There are mediocrities. There are those
that keep developing and growing throughout a long lifetime, and their achievement varies with their initial background, with their opportunities, with their luck in avoiding pitfalls and setbacks, and with the pace of their advance.'[55] The 'direction of development' that is orientation undergoes a change for the better through conversion. Then 'one frees oneself from the unauthentic. One
grows in authenticity. Harmful, dangerous, misleading
satisfactions are dropped. Fears of discomfort, pain, pri-
vation have less power to deflect one from one's course.
Values are apprehended where before they were overlooked.
Scales of preference shift. Errors, rationalizations, ideologies fall and shatter to leave one open to things as they are
and to man as he should be.'[56]

The orientation of the dramatic subject[57] is, then, a
response to the dialectic of contradictories, to that dialectic that has to do not with any opposition whatever but
with the very precise opposition between authenticity and
inauthenticity. But precisely that orientation, that response,
is in dialectical tension with the unconscious, with neural

Theology and Culture 463

demands for psychic integration. And here the dialectic is in principle one not of contradictories but of contraries. Only inauthenticity transforms it into a dialectic of contradictories. The conscious and the nonconscious are to cooperate harmoniously in one's development, and they will do so in proportion to one's authenticity. They will do so, too, insofar as one correctly apprehends the starting point, the process, and the term of any stage of this development, and acts on this knowledge. This apprehension and consequent action constitute what Lonergan calls the law of genuineness.

> Every development involves a starting point in the subject as he is, a term in the subject as he is to be, and a process from the starting point to the term. However, inasmuch as a development is conscious, there is some apprehension of the starting point, the term, and the process. But such apprehensions may be correct or mistaken. If they are correct, the conscious and unconscious components of the development are operating from the same base along the same route to the same goal. If they are mistaken, the conscious and unconscious components, to a greater or less extent, are operating at cross-purposes. Such a conflict is inimical to the development, and so we have the conditional law of genuineness, namely, that if a development is conscious, then its success demands correct apprehensions of its starting point, its process, and its goal.[58]

This law is not only conditional, however, but also analogous. 'What it demands will be spontaneous in some cases and in others only obtained through more or less extensive self-scrutiny.'[59] The need for self-scrutiny is spoken of in *Insight* as dependent on the extent to which 'errors have become lodged in the habitual background whence spring our direct and reflective insights,' so that 'if we relied upon our virtual and implicit self-knowledge to provide us with concrete guidance through a conscious development, then the minimal series [of apprehensions that make a development conscious] so far from being probably correct would be certainly mistaken.'[60] But we may also speak, I think, of self-scrutiny as a requirement proportionate to the stage of meaning that one has reached. A subject intent on interiorly differentiated consciousness will be moved by this intention to the exploration of what a less differentiated subject would not be moved to investigate.

Psychic conversion serves to aid one in attaining a proper understanding of the starting point, the process, and the goal of any stage of one's development. It fulfills this function insofar as, by transforming the censorship over neural demands from exercising a repressive control to administering their entry into consciousness in a constructive fashion, it renders accessible to conscious negotiation the neural demand functions that, strictly speaking, constitute the unconscious. These demand functions are a coincidental manifold on the neural-physiological level, but they reach integration in conscious images and accompanying affects. Thus by interpreting these images and affects, one reaches an understanding of the nonconscious components of development. Images are the proximate materials for insight, and insight is a step along the way to the judgments through which the real is mediated by truth. Moreover, knowledge of fact is merely a base for the consequent judgments of value and the decisions through which one constitutes oneself and one's world as works of genuine or inauthentic dramatic art. The intention of artistry on the dramatic stage of life governs the entire process of achieving authenticity, and provides the most appropriate paradigm for praxis.

Among the images through which neural demand functions reach a higher integration are dreams. Dreams have been emphasized by the depth psychologists as a major source of data on the unconscious, and I support this emphasis. For in the dream, the censorship over neural materials exercised by the orientation of dramatically patterned intentionality is somewhat relaxed, so that the dream provides a closer and more trustworthy approximation to the materials one must understand and negotiate if one is to have a correct apprehension of the various stages of a development than do many other images more subject to biased manipulation and control. An inauthentic orientation of dramatically patterned intentionality will exercise what Lonergan calls a repressive censorship over the neural demands that would achieve conscious integration in images and concomitant affects. Thus it would institute a distortion in the dialectic of contraries between consciousness and the unconscious. But that distortion manifests itself in dreams, and the manifestation provides one with the images through whose interpretation one can move to a correction of the distortion. An authentic orientation would exercise a constructive censorship regarding the same demands, so that the images that are required for developing self-understanding and self-constitution are permitted to find their way into consciousness joined with their appropriate affective responses. Dreams will also display this integrity of the imaginal field in an authentic subject. Thus Jung can emphasize quite correctly that dreams are sometimes compensatory and sometimes complementary to the orientation of the conscious ego. They will be compensatory to the extent that the dialectic of the subject is distorted; the compensation is precisely for the sake of providing the materials through which an intelligent, rational, and responsible subject can take the steps to correct the distortion in the constitution of his or her being as a subject.[61] Dreams will be complementary to the extent that one is already on the path toward a relative integrity in the subjective dialectic. They will confirm the path one has taken, and consolidate one's orientation on that path. Furthermore, attentiveness to dreams through a respectful remembering, intelligent interpretation, and careful existential negotiation through intrasubjective dialogic communication establishes in the subject a habitual openness to the deliverances of the unconscious in other forms besides dreams, that is, in the very flow of waking sensitive consciousness itself. Such a habitual negotiation of the unconscious through the intermediary of the sensitive, imaginal, and affective flow of empirical consciousness is the state in which one abides insofar as one has undergone, and remains in, what I am calling psychic conversion.

Psychic conversion is a change of attitude on the part of the dramatically patterned orientation of consciousness with respect proximately to the sensitive psyche and remotely to the unconscious. This change is in effect a transformation of the censorship exercised by consciousness over neural demands, a transformation from a repressive to a constructive exercise of control over what will be allowed to come into consciousness in the first place. It establishes what Jung called 'the transcendent function,'[62] where the word 'transcendent' expresses, not what it means in Lonergan's term 'the transcendent exigence,' but the capacity of the ego to go beyond itself to the negotiation of the unconscious.

The dialectic of contradictories that affects proximately the orientation of conscious intentionality — the dialectic of authenticity and inauthenticity — will inevitably be resolved in a manner that makes of the dialectic of contraries between this same conscious orientation and the unconscious either an integral or a distorted dialectic. Psychic conversion is an extension of the full conversion process, which changes the direction of one's orientation, so that the repressive censorship becomes constructive. It thus helps to establish the habitual integrity of the dialectic of the subject.

The course of events issuing from an integral dialectic of the subject moves in a direction quite opposed to that resultant from a distorted dialectic. As the censorship becomes constructive, one's orientation becomes character, in Philip Rieff's sense of this term as the restrictive shaping of possibilities.[63] It becomes the responsible exercise of conscious finality. It becomes virtue. And the underlying neural manifold becomes a more pliable support and instrument of artistic world constitution and self-constitution. But to the extent that the censorship is repressive, there occurs a cumulative fragmentation of the neural manifold. This fragmentation is described quite exactly by Lonergan in his treatment of the censorship.[64] Demands for affects are unhinged from appropriate imaginal counterparts and joined to incongruous cognitive elements. Moreover, the orientation of the dramatic subject becomes fixed in a determinate but regressive direction. There needs to be opened a commerce between the conscious and the unconscious components of development, and for that to happen there is required a change in the very orientation of the subject. That change is what I have meant by psychic conversion, the transformation of the censorship exercised by one's dramatic orientation from a repressive to a constructive functioning in one's development.

The avenues to psychic conversion are many. While I continue to agree with the depth psychologists on the importance of dreams, I would add that in some respects, the path taken is less important than the transformation itself. All of these avenues complement one another, and none has exclusive prerogatives. What is essential is the transformation itself. My principal caution to those who would emphasize other avenues besides the dream is by way of a mild hermeneutic of suspicion. That is to say, Yes, there are other ways, but if one's dreams are presenting materials that one does not want to face, then to embark on these other ways to the neglect of the dream is to escape from the task at hand into an inauthentic aestheticism.

There is, however, a further advantage to the inclusion of dream interpretation among the resources on which one relies in moving toward a habitual abiding in the tension of the radical dialectic of the subject. This advantage is of particular importance in relating psychic conversion to the issues of hermeneutics. For dreams make available in a unique way one's own peculiar symbolic system, and, when they are archetypal or anagogic, they also enable one to experience the participation of one's own symbolic system in the mythic adventure through which humanity has participated in the drama of existence. The symbolic represents a particularly difficult field for hermeneutics, since in a sense it is furthest removed from the systematic-theological, the rigorously conceptual and intellectual. As we have seen, Lonergan has emphasized that the more systematic a work is, the less difficult is the task of interpretation, whereas the more a work moves in and is addressed to the sensitive and imaginal dimensions of the subject, the more difficult it is not only to interpret such a work but also to find an appropriate horizon of hermeneutic understanding valid for all such interpretation.

Paul Ricoeur has insisted that the interpretation of such works cannot radically proceed from, but rather must inform, self-knowledge. In this respect I have disagreed with him. As Lonergan holds that, if one truly understands what it is to understand, one possesses a fixed base and an invariant pattern opening upon all further developments of understanding, so I would hold that if one comes to know the imaginal structure and process of one's own psyche as higher integration of coincidental neural manifolds, one will come into possession of an expanding base and an intelligible pattern enabling one to understand symbolic expressions of human desire as these are found in other cultural and religious objectifications in the course of human history.[65] Ricoeur insists that we can understand human experience only by understanding human expressions. Obviously I do not deny that study of the symbolic and imaginal productions of the human spirit is a rich and essential dimension of self-understanding. But I reject the exclusivity of Ricoeur's approach. I believe that a reoriented depth psychology can enable us to understand human symbolic expressions through a more radical and concrete understanding of one's own experience, as this experience reaches an intrasubjective expression in the symbolic articulations of the psyche. These symbolic expressions are understood as reflective of the differentiation of consciousness as a notion of being, a notion of value, and a transcendent exigence. Just as the theological functional specialty 'foundations' is informed by one's interpretation of the past and one's appropriation of a historical interpretation, while on the other hand this interpretation and appropriation are themselves grounded in the foundational self one is, so one's understanding of one's own psyche is informed by one's interpretation of the symbolic expressions available from past history, while this interpretation is itself grounded in the self one is and knows oneself to be.

I have noted Lonergan's sympathy for the existential approach to the dream. The sympathy is grounded in his position on the relations of feelings, on the one hand, to values, and on the other hand, to symbols. Feelings are, as it were, the middle term that links elemental symbols to

the issues of existential orientation. As values are apprehended in feelings, so symbols are images that evoke feelings or are evoked by feelings. The elemental symbols that
are our dreams are thus intimately related to the question
of one's orientation as existential subject responsible for
the constitution of self and world in originating freedom.
Thus these symbols must be sublated to the level of originating freedom itself if they are to be negotiated properly.
They are not to be simply interpreted, much less wallowed
in at the sensitive level itself. The interpretation must be
correct, and here, as elsewhere, a correct interpretation is
possible. And the correct interpretation must be acted
upon, if the finality manifested in the very appearance of
the dream is to come to fruition. The acting in question
here is, first of all, the intrasubjective dialogic communication that can be established through such techniques as
Jung's 'active imagination,'[66] but it does not remain here.
From the outset it must be oriented to the free and responsible constitution of the self as originating value in
the community and in history.

  The grounds or foundations of the possibility of correct interpretation of a dream lie precisely in the same
universal viewpoint and position on levels and sequences
of expression that for Lonergan is the source of the possibility of a correct interpretation of texts. Conversely, the
application to elemental symbols of these elements of the
upper blade of hermeneutic method can result in a satisfactory theory of such symbols. That theory itself would
join the other elements of the heuristic procedures of a
methodical hermeneutics as an incremental addition to
the integral heuristic structure of proportionate being. The
'being' here is the being of meaning, meaning as being.

  While I am in complete agreement with Lonergan's
preference for the existential approach to the dream, since
this approach places the dream more explicitly in the con-

text of the notion of value than do either Freudian or Jungian hermeneutic systems, I would add that important ingredients of an as-yet-incomplete theory of dreams will be provided by both Freud and Jung. Ernest Becker has begun to work out an existential reinterpretation of Freud that I find most fruitful.[67] As for Jung, his essential and lasting contribution is the insistence on the transpersonal dimensions of some dream symbols, or on what he has called the archetypal. He has correctly criticized Freud for overlooking the significance of this dimension of the elementally symbolic. There are data of consciousness in the form of transpersonal dreams that cannot be accounted for in the terms provided by the Freudian theories of repression and the personal unconscious. Jung has recognized these data and tried to understand them. But, as I indicated at the beginning, his understanding tends to compact all transpersonal dream symbols under one category, the archetypal, whereas there are at least two distinct dimensions to the transpersonal symbolic realm. We can continue to speak with Jung of a basic duality of dream symbols, namely the personal and the transpersonal; but I would add to this position the thesis that we must subdivide the category of the transpersonal into the archetypal and the anagogic.

Archetypal symbols are taken from nature and imitate nature. Thus a maternal symbol in an archetypal dream represents not one's mother but the nourishing or, as the case may be, destructive character of the psyche itself. The symbol is 'chosen,' as it were, by reason of personal associations with one's own mother. But the associations have a transpersonal significance, and it is the latter that the dream embodies. Anagogic symbols are also taken from nature or, sometimes, from history, but, so far from imitating nature, they represent the supernatural — the involvement of the subject in the *mysterium iniquitatis*, on the one hand, and the redemptive mystery of God's grace, on the other hand. Thus they simultaneously symbolize and effect the transformation of the subject and the world under the power of the divinely originated solution to the mystery of evil.[68] They are experiences of grace. In this sense they are sacramental, giving the very transformation of energy become conscious in the psyche which they symbolize.

Psychic conversion is thus related to Lonergan's hermeneutics insofar as, by effecting the transformation of the censorship from a repressive to a constructive functioning in one's development, it provides access to the images which either express the differentiations of the notion of being, of the notion of value, and of the transcendent exigence achieved by the subject in question, or consolidate these differentiations in the sensitive appropriation of their truth, thereby increasing their probability of survival.

The principal points made in this section can be summarized under four headings. First, the position maintained in the previous section regarding the interpretation of elemental symbols grounds a reorientation of depth psychology, according to which the elemental meanings analyzed and interpreted by this science are understood as sensitive appropriations of differentiations of the notions of being, value, and transcendence.

Second, the self-knowledge or psychic self-appropriation that such a science renders possible enters into the upper blade of one's interpretation, history, and evaluation of the elemental meanings expressed by others, in that it provides one with a potential totality of genetically and dialectically related elemental embodiments of differentiations of consciousness.

Third, a reoriented depth psychology thus enters into the upper blade of a methodical and dialectical hermeneutics.

Fourth, psychic conversion, as the transformation of the censorship from a repressive to a constructive functioning, makes available important data for this understanding of oneself. By making possible an understanding of one's own elemental embodiments of differentiations of the notions of being, value, and transcendence, it provides a base and pattern from which one proceeds to understand other such expressions of the differentiation of consciousness as notion of being, notion of value, notion of absolute mystery. As informing foundational self-knowledge, it enters into the grounds of a methodical hermeneutics of the elemental meanings embodied or carried in such vehicles as symbols and literary language.

Perhaps further clarity can emerge from a contrast of this position with the Jungian hermeneutics of symbolic expressions.

4   Clarification by Contrast

In this final section, I will come full circle on my opening remarks by arguing that Lonergan's hermeneutic upper blade complemented by the depth psychology just sketched provides a more adequate foundation for the interpretation of elemental symbolic expression than is found in Jungian thought, and serves to reorient the Jungian hermeneutic by providing a criterion for distinguishing mystery from myth, symbolic expressions of positions from symbolic expressions of counterpositions. I will rely on Erich Neumann's book *The Origins and History of Consciousness*, since this book bears some affinities with my position on the interpretation of elemental symbols and is expressly concerned with a hermeneutic for understanding the development or sequences of imaginal expression. For Neumann, as for the position presented here, the history of the sequence of archetypal symbols is to be under-

stood as a series of symbolic expressions of the differentiation of consciousness.[69] A few comments must suffice to
show the enrichment and clarification that could be
brought to Neumann's work and to the Jungian psychology on which it relies, when one understands the consciousness whose differentiation is expressed in the elemental
meanings of symbolic expressions to be a notion of being,
a notion of value, a notion of God.

First, some terminological clarifications are in order. The title of the English translation of Neumann's book
is misleading. The original German title *Ursprungsgeschichte
des Bewusstseins* is better translated the *History of the Origins (or Arising) of Consciousness*. Moreover, the 'consciousness' whose arising and development is being studied is
the ego. The closest approximation in Lonergan to what
Jungians mean by the ego or by consciousness, I think, is
the orientation of dramatically patterned intentionality as
one understands oneself to be and has sensitively appropriated that understanding. That understanding may or
may not correspond to the self one is. Whether it does or
does not depends largely on whether conscious and unconscious, and intentional and psychic, components of
development are working in harmony with one another,
from the same base, along the same route, towards the
same objectives. Neurosis develops to the extent that these
components are in conflict with one another, and psycho-
sis when the ego's defenses against its intrasubjective antagonists collapse in some definitive fashion. Neumann's
study concentrates on the archetypal symbols that express
the arising and development of an ego increasingly capable
of orienting itself in life in harmony with the other
intrasubjective forces and relying on their resources and
able to tap into them. The ego is faced as well with the
danger of surrendering its potential of originating freedom,
with the possibilities of self-deception and illusion, and

with the perils of being overwhelmed by all that is 'other' within the very constitution of the subject. Thus the term 'consciousness' has for Neumann and for Jungians in general a more restricted meaning than it has for Lonergan.

Conversely, the term 'the unconscious' has a more inclusive meaning for Neumann and for Jungians than it has for Lonergan. It denotes not only the neural manifold, but also all of the psychic integrations of that manifold that have not been objectified or made part of the ego, and that influence one's orientations without one being reflectively cognizant of their effects.[70]

Again, the Jungian terms 'collective unconscious' and 'transpersonal elements of the psyche' correspond to what for Lonergan is the *sense* of the unknown, the cosmic dimension, the intimation of unplumbed depths that accrues to our feelings, emotions, and sentiments, and that expresses itself in the affect-laden images and names that are the primary field of mystery and myth.[71]

Thus Neumann's work can be understood, in Lonergan's terms, as a study of the affect-laden images that accompany, express, and indeed catalyze the transformation of the psychic dimensions of consciousness under the force of the development of particular orientations of the subject as originating freedom and of particular self-objectifications of dramatically patterned intentionality. My thesis is that Neumann's already extremely rich and suggestive account would only be strengthened by understanding consciousness far more broadly as transcendental notion or pure question heading for being, value, and transcendent mystery, and by understanding psychic development and elemental symbolic sequences of expression in accord with the principle of correspondence between the intentional and the psychic operators in that consciousness. On the basis of such an understanding of the psyche, Neumann, and Jungians in general, would be provided with a critically based criterion they now lack for differentiating in the realm of the symbolic between position and counterposition, mystery and myth.[72]

For Neumann as for Lonergan, there is a 'dialectic between consciousness and the unconscious' that, when it is transformed and liberated, gives birth to integrated human personality.[73] Nonetheless, the terminological clarifications that I just indicated are very important. Without them, the poles of the dialectic are not correctly apprehended. After the crucial and basic distinction of consciousness and knowledge, the most important step is the distinction of a dialectic of contraries from a dialectic of contradictories. Without such a distinction, one runs the risk of confusing two different kinds of opposites, those which can be and should be integrated with one another, and those which call for a choice of one pole of the dialectic and a rejection of the other. The confusion manifests itself in many Jungian treatments of the problem of good and evil. If good and evil are considered to be opposites in the same way as intentionality and the psyche, or consciousness and the unconscious, or the masculine and feminine components of the psyche itself, an attempt will be made to integrate good and evil, to achieve a position beyond these opposites in the same manner as one attempts to achieve a position beyond contraries. Such an attempt rests on a profoundly destructive and demonic illusion. Jung comes quite close to recognizing the distinction of the different kinds of opposites when he writes, '[I]nstinct is not in itself bad any more than spirit is good. Both can be both.'[74] But the position is not maintained consistently even in Jung's own writings, and some of his followers have abandoned this insight and attempted to achieve for themselves and to encourage in others an integration of good and evil analogous to the integration of consciousness and the unconscious that represents the genuine dialectic of the subject.

Next, what is symbolized by the archetypal or, better, transpersonal symbols that Jung has recovered for us is the emergence not so much of consciousness itself, since what Jung calls the collective unconscious is itself, at least to a large extent, already a conscious sense of the unknown invested with an intimation of unplumbed depths. It is rather the emergence of an integral dialectic in consciousness between that psychic *sense* of the unknown and the various higher differentiations of consciousness, under the orientation of dramatically patterned intentionality that constitutes what Jungians call the ego. This integral dialectic, in turn, is grounded in the more radical dialectic between the whole of consciousness, as both psyche and spirit, both sense of the unknown and question, on the one hand, and the genuinely unconscious neural manifold, on the other hand.

To this clarification there can be added the persuasion of Lonergan that the entire set of dialectically related events that constitute the human subject or self is to be understood on the grounds of the perspective afforded by understanding the possibilities of differentiating consciousness. Lonergan brings needed clarifications to the issue of precisely what the possibilities of the differentiation of consciousness are: possibilities of the emergence of consciousness as an unbiased and dialectically structured notion of being, notion of value, notion of transcendent mystery. The authentic emergence of the *ego* then would be understood to lie in the *self-affirmation* of the subject as precisely an unrestricted notion of being, the good, and world-transcendent mystery.

Finally, then, I would locate in the clarification of these possibilities the precise contribution that Lonergan can make to Jungian psychology. If Jung can show the way to a recovery of the primary field of mystery and myth, Lonergan can provide the criterion for distinguishing mystery from myth. In Lonergan's work there is a sharper, more precise, and more complete account than can be found elsewhere of the possibilities of various differentiations of consciousness, and so of the ultimate foundations from which the archetypal and transpersonal symbols of the psyche are to be understood and discriminated.

The directives, then, for a hermeneutic of symbolic expression are the following. First, work out with Lonergan's help an understanding of consciousness as a notion of being, a notion of value, and a notion of transcendent mystery. Second, add to that the principle that dictates a correspondence between the operators of development in intentional consciousness so understood and the operators of development on the psychic level of consciousness. And third, correlate the latter operators with the transpersonal symbols that Jungian psychology has recovered. Then you will have the grounds for understanding these symbols as not only expressing but also effecting precisely through these expressions the energic transformation of the sensitive dimensions of consciousness as the 'sensorium of transcendence' that 'makes sensible to human sensitivity what human intelligence reaches for or grasps.'[75]

One of the most important clarifications that such an approach brings to the Jungian understanding of transpersonal symbolism, and the only one that I can dwell on here, is the distinction between integrator and operator. Most of Neumann's work in *The Origins and History of Consciousness* is easily adjustable to the position on the psyche as the sensitive correlative to intentional orientations. But the distinction of integrator and operator would enable a reorientation at the precise point where it is needed. And it will do so without reversing any of the genuine positions afforded by the Jungian understanding of the psyche as the primary field of mystery and myth. Jung has made genuine and irreversible advances beyond the Freudian understanding of the psyche. In fact, the distinction of integrator and operator will be in the interest of the genuine Jungian concern, which is to study the transpersonal symbols that not only express but also catalyze the emergence of the individuated ego. But that ego will now be understood as a dramatically patterned orientation to self-transcendence toward what is, what is good, and what is the unsurpassable ground of all that is and of all that is good. Elemental symbolic meanings, then, will mean the differentiation of consciousness as such a set of transcendental notions, and will be understood as effecting the energic transformation of the sensitive component of consciousness in correspondence with the differentiation of the intelligent, rational, existential, and religious components. Such a distinction, too, coupled with the principle of correspondence between psychic operators and the operators of consciousness as notion of being, notion of value, notion of transcendent mystery, will give to Jungian psychology the solid criteria it now lacks for distinguishing between mystery and myth, between symbolic expressions of positions and symbolic expressions of counterpositions.

An examination of the starting point and the conclusion of Neumann's study will display the need it has for a distinction between integrator and operator. Neumann discovers eight stages in the *Ursprungsgeschichte* of the individuated ego. The first three represent stages in the cosmological myth. They are repeated in the ontogenetic development of the modern ego. The first of these stages, and the only one on which I will concentrate here, is that of 'the uroboros,' where 'the ego is contained in the unconscious,' and so where consciousness is completely undifferentiated from the unplumbed depths accruing to exclusively psychic consciousness. The appropriate symbolizations of the beginning are the symbolizations of the darkness that precedes the creation of light. In this darkness psyche and world are one. 'There is as yet no reflecting, self-conscious ego that could refer anything to itself, that is, reflect. Not only is the psyche open to the world, it is still identical with and undifferentiated from the world; it knows itself as world and in the world and experiences its own becoming as a world-becoming, its own images as the starry heavens, and its own contents as the world-creating gods.'[76]

The self-containment of the darkness that precedes the light is expressed especially and universally in symbols of the circle, the sphere, the round. Here there are as yet no before and after, no above and below, and in fact no differentiated opposites at all. 'Living the cycle of its own life, it is the circular snake, the primal dragon of the beginning that bites its own tail,' the self-begetting uroboros.[77] But, as we saw at the beginning of this paper, for Neumann and for Jungians in general, 'so long as man shall exist, perfection will continue to appear as the circle, the sphere, and the round; and the Primal Deity who is sufficient unto himself, and the self who has gone beyond the opposites, will reappear in the image of the round, the mandala.'[78] The symbolism includes preeminently the womb, 'the primordial symbol of the place of origin from whence we come,'[79] as well as 'anything deep — abyss, valley, ground, also the sea and the bottom of the sea, fountains, lakes, and pools, the earth, the underworld, the cave, the house, and the city ... anything big and embracing which contains, surrounds, enwraps, shelters, preserves, and nourishes anything small.'[80] The symbol perdures in images of restoration, where differentiated opposites achieve a new integration after their conflict has effected their seeming destruction.

Much of this analysis can be confirmed from the approach suggested here. Let us consider, for example, the descriptions of the New Jerusalem in both the Old and New Testaments. Even after the emergence not only of soteriological but also of at least incipient anthropological symbolizations originally in conflict with the cosmological constitutive meaning of preindividuated consciousness, they show the permanent significance of such symbols of the beginning, and the transformations they can undergo. A striking Old Testament instance occurs in Ezekiel 48.30-35, and thus in a writing that also manifests the emergence of individuated consciousness in Israelite religion (see Ezekiel 18.5-32). Cosmological symbolization is not replaced, only relativized, by the emergence of what, following Eric Voegelin, we can call anthropological symbolization.[81]

Many of the symbols expressive of the identity of self and world in the beginning are maternal.

> All the positive maternal traits are in evidence at this stage, when the ego is still embryonic and has no activity of its own. The uroboros of the maternal world is life and psyche in one; it gives nourishment and pleasure, protects and warms, comforts and forgives. It is the refuge for all suffering, the goal of all desire. For always this mother is she who fulfills, the bestower and helper. This living image of the Great and Good Mother has at all times of distress been the refuge of humanity and ever shall be; for the state of being contained in the whole, without responsibility or effort, with no doubts and no division of the world into two, is paradisal, and can never again be realized in its pristine happy-go-luckiness in adult life.

> The positive side of the Great Mother seems to be embodied in this stage of the

uroboros. Only at a very much higher level will
the 'good' Mother appear again. Then, when
she no longer has to do with an embryonic ego,
but with an adult personality matured by rich
experience of the world, she reveals herself
anew as Sophia, the 'gracious' Mother, or, pour-
ing forth her riches in the creative fullness of
true productivity, as the 'Mother of All Living.'[82]

There are also negative aspects to the force expressed
in this symbolism, however. For it is an image of the force
that counteracts what is specifically human, the orientation to the differentiation of consciousness. As such, it symbolizes not life but death.

The Great Mother takes the little child back
into herself, and always over uroboric incest
there stand the insignia of death, signifying final dissolution in union with the Mother. Cave,
earth, tomb, sarcophagus, and coffin are symbols of this ritual recombination, which begins
with burial in the posture of the embryo in the
barrows of the Stone Age and ends with the
cinerary urns of the moderns.[83]

The unknown character of the beginning symbolized by the uroboros is a source of the sense of mystery
that will ever remain a feature of human consciousness.
The autarchy of the uroboric stage becomes narcissistic
only when the stage persists beyond the time when ego
consciousness should begin to emerge in its own right.
Nor is a return to the symbolism of this stage to be viewed
as necessarily and exclusively regressive.

[T]he development of the ego, of consciousness, of personality, and, lastly, of individuality
itself is actually fostered by the autarchy whose
symbol is the uroboros. In many cases, therefore, the appearance of uroboric symbolism,
especially if its formative and stabilizing character is strongly marked as, for instance, in the
mandala, indicates that the ego is moving toward the self, rather than in the direction of
objective adaptation.[84]

In the symbols associated with the 'Great Round,'
then, we have a clear example of the manner in which one
and the same elemental expression can indicate positions
or counterpositions. On this Neumann is clear. But what
are his criteria for distinguishing mystery from myth? How
does a Jungian know when the uroboros is symbolic of
creativity and when it indicates regression and a death wish?
Criteria are provided by the distinction between integrator and operator. The distinction relativizes the primacy of
mandala symbolism, without discounting its importance
in the life of a mature adult. Symbols reminiscent of the
uroboric stage reflect and, in fact, catalyze integration. They
represent and, in a very definite sense are, the self as integrator. But in addition to the self as integrator there is the
self as operator, and 'the operator is relentless in transforming the integrator.' The mandala is 'the subject as he
is functioning more or less successfully in a flexible *circle*
of ranges of schemes of recurrence.' The operator is 'the
subject as a higher system on the move.'

The integrator resides in successive levels of
interrelated conjugate forms that are more familiar under the common name of acquired
habits. But habits are inertial. The whole ten-

dency of present perceptiveness, of present affectivity and aggressivity, of present ways of
understanding and judging, deliberating and
choosing, speaking and doing is for them to
remain as they are. Against this solid and salu-
tary conservatism, however, there operate the
same principles that gave rise to the acquired
habits and now persist in attempting to transform them. Unconsciously operative is the finality that consists in the upwardly but indeterminately directed dynamism of all proportionate being. Consciously operative is the detached and disinterested desire raising ever further questions. Among the topics for questioning are one's own unconscious initiatives, their
subsumption under the general order intelligence discovers in the universe of being, their
integration in the fabric of one's habitual living. So there emerges into consciousness a concrete apprehension of an obviously practicable
and proximate ideal self; but along with it there
also emerges the tension between limitation and
transcendence; and it is no vague tension between limitation in general and transcendence
in general, but an unwelcome invasion of consciousness by opposed apprehensions of oneself as one concretely is and as one concretely
is to be.[85]

The dialectic of limitation and transcendence is in
the pure case a dialectic of contraries representing a genetic relationship. But when the tension is displaced, the
opposed apprehensions of oneself can become contradictory, and the dialectic becomes one of contradictories. The
dynamics are expressed in the following account:

To fail in genuineness is not to escape but only to displace the tension between limitation and transcendence. Such a displacement is the root of the dialectical phenomena of scotosis in the individual, of the bias of common sense, of basic philosophical differences, and of their prolongation in natural and human science, in morals and religion, in educational theory and history.[86]

On the basis of the principle of correspondence, we may say that, if the mandala as integrator is not complemented by symbols of the self as operator, a displacement occurs in the direction of limitation. If symbols of the self as operator are not accompanied by symbols of present levels of integration, a displacement has occurred in the direction of transcendence. '[T]he perfection of the higher integration does not eliminate the integrated.'[87] Jungian psychology, with its emphasis on the symbols of the self as integrator, complements, but also needs to be complemented by, Lonergan's insistence on the relentless transformation of the integrator by the operator, where the principal operator in question is consciousness as an unrestricted notion of being, of the good, and of transcendent mystery.

I will conclude by risking interpretation of several examples of imaginal expression, so as to provide an illustration of what I am talking about. The first example is a very important dream of Jung's. The second interprets the symbolic significance of the Oedipus and Orestes cycles. The third example is the image of the Heavenly Jerusalem in the concluding chapters of the Book of Revelation. Jung's dream manifests a refusal of the relentless transformation of the integrator by the operator. The Oedipus and Orestes trilogies display the psychic tension caused by a world-

constitutive differentiation of the notion of being. In the
Oedipus story, we find the tragic failure of consciousness
to differentiate, and in the Orestes story we see the difficulties entailed in the differentiation, and witness the conditions of its success. And in the concluding images of the
Bible we see the transformation of the cosmological
mandala symbolism under the pressure of a soteriological
differentiation of consciousness.

The dream of Jung's that I will interpret here is an
invitation to Jung to transcend the mandala of present levels of integration under the force of consciousness as a
notion of transcendent mystery. In the dream Jung rejects
the invitation, and given the fact that the dream of refusal,
as he admits, prefigured his writing of his most problematic book, *Answer to Job*, the book most suggestive of the
integration of good and evil, the refusal of the operator is
linked with the failure to distinguish contradictories from
contraries, and so with the potential present in Jungian
psychology for promoting the attempt to integrate good
and evil in the same way as one would integrate the genuine dialectic of the subject.

The dream, as narrated by Jung in his autobiographical reflections, is quite complex. Before it manifests itself
as an invitation to submit to the transcendent exigence, it
displays a quite intimately related invitation to transcend
the lifelong problems that Jung had with his father, problems that, because his father was a clergyman, deeply influenced his relation to Christianity and to religious questions in general.

At the beginning of this extraordinarily significant
dream, Jung's father fetches from a shelf a heavy folio volume of the Bible bound in a fishskin, opens it to the Old
Testament and to the Pentateuch in particular, and begins
to deliver an extraordinarily profound interpretation of a
certain passage. '[H]is argument was so intelligent and so

learned that we in our stupidity could not follow it.'[88] The 'we' are Jung himself and two other psychiatrists. In the next scene, Jung and his father enter a house which Jung's father indicates is haunted, and where they could hear loud noises made by its preternatural inhabitants. Let me now quote the remainder of Jung's presentation of the dream.

> We then entered the house, and I saw that it had very thick walls. We climbed a narrow staircase to the second floor. There a strange sight presented itself: a large hall which was the exact replica of the *divan-i-kaas* (council hall) of Sultan Akbar at Fatehpur Sikri. It was a high, circular room with a gallery running along the wall, from which four bridges led to a basin-shaped center. The basin rested upon a huge column and formed the sultan's round seat. From this elevated place he spoke to his councilors and philosophers, who sat along the walls in the gallery. The whole was a gigantic mandala. It corresponded precisely to the real *divan-i-kaas*.
>
> In the dream I suddenly saw that from the center a steep flight of stairs ascended to a spot high up on the wall — which no longer corresponded to reality. At the top of the stair was a small door, and my father said, 'Now I will lead you into the highest presence.' Then he knelt down and touched his forehead to the floor. I imitated him, likewise kneeling, with great emotion. For some reason I could not bring my forehead quite down to the floor — there was perhaps a millimeter to spare. But at least I had made the gesture with him. Suddenly I knew — perhaps my father had told

me — that that upper door led to a solitary
chamber where lived Uriah, King David's general, whom David had shamefully betrayed for
the sake of his wife Bathsheba, by commanding his soldiers to abandon Uriah in the face of
the enemy.[89]

Jung indicates that the portion of the Bible which
his father was interpreting was probably Genesis. He interprets the fishskin on the Bible as symbolic of the muteness and unconsciousness of fishes. He admits that his father does not succeed in communicating, due partly to
the stupidity of himself and his companions, and partly to
their malice. Uriah, he says, is a guiltless victim, a prefiguration of Christ. And for Jung, the figure of Uriah meant
his own mission to speak publicly about 'the ambivalence
of the God-image in the Old Testament,' and prefigured
as well the loss of his own wife by death. 'These were the
things that awaited me, hidden in the unconscious. I had
to submit to this fate, and ought really to have touched my
forehead to the floor, so that my submission would be complete. But something prevented me from doing so entirely,
and kept me just a millimeter away.'[90] The result, prefigured by the dream, as Jung admits, was *Answer to Job*, the
one book Jung said he would not revise.

My own interpretation of the dream runs counter to
Jung's at several points. His father is trying to get something across to him and to his psychiatrist colleagues, something very important. 'It dealt with something extremely
important which fascinated him.'[91] But neither Jung nor
his psychiatrist friends can understand what his father is
trying to say. The fishskin around the Bible is a symbol not
of mute unconscious stupidity but of salvation. It is the
Ichthus. The passage his father is interpreting, if indeed it
was Genesis as Jung seems to think, is allusive to *God's*

'answer to Job,' 'Where were you when I laid the foundations of the earth?' (Job 38.4). The dream indeed prefigures *Answer to Job*, but Jung's father is trying to urge him *not* to go in the direction that would lead him to write that book. His father is communicating an urgent message to him and to psychiatry, to acknowledge the transcendent exigence and submit to it, to integrate it with their knowledge of the archetypal sense of the unknown which they have discovered. Jung and his friends cannot understand the message, but, as Jung himself says, their incomprehension is due not only to stupidity but also to their desire not to understand what was being said. His father tries again, by showing him the alternative, the haunted house, the occult realm where people try to achieve a position beyond all opposites, including the contradictories of good and evil, the realm of the demonic. This is the Great Round as something to be transcended, not abided in; it is the Self chosen by the ego as supreme principle, but understood by Jung's father as something to be transcended in adoration of the Highest Presence. Even the fact that the invitation occurs on the second floor of the house may be significant. The second floor may be the second level of consciousness, the level which an idealist does not transcend. At any rate, Jung will not submit to the invitation to transcend the Self, especially as the symbol of such transcendence is the mystery of innocent suffering represented in Uriah the Hittite. It is not impossible that Uriah figures in the dream not because Jung's wife was to be taken from him but because of certain facts regarding Jung's marital relations that have only recently become known.[92] Jung would not submit to the relentless transformation of the integrator, the perfect and gigantic mandala that becomes demonic when it is apotheosized, and the result is available in the religious position of Jung's alternative answer to Job, an answer in which the problem of coming to terms with evil is made radically, not the problem of human beings, but the problem of God. For Jung, we help God come to terms with God's own 'shadow problem' by integrating evil into the self beyond the opposites. This was Jung's choice, made in the face of and contrary to an eloquent invitation from his father to submit to the gift of redemption offered by the same Highest Presence who laid the foundations of the earth. The meaning of the dream is not archetypal but anagogic, not natural but supernatural, not simply psychological but religious. The dream indeed prefigures *Answer to Job*, but is an important and urgent message that Jung *not* write this book, but rethink his position. He refused, and the dream catalyzed that refusal, appropriated it at the sensitive level of Jung's consciousness. '[A] constant rotation within the order of nature is demonic in itself.'

My interpretation in no way denies the positive significance of mandala symbols as expressive and catalytic of integration. It simply adds to this emphasis the insistence on the relentless transformation of the psychic integrator by the psychic operator in correspondence with the operators of consciousness as a notion of being, a notion of value, a transcendent exigence. Nor is the enduring significance of the cosmological symbolism to which the mandala belongs to be denied. Such symbolism is to be integrated with the anthropological symbolism that emerges with the differentiation of intentional consciousness from the cosmological psyche. Such an integration constitutes a dialectic of culture analogous to the dialectics in the subject between intentionality and the psyche and between the whole of consciousness and the unconscious.

Next, some of the great Greek tragedies display in imaginal and narrative form the anthropological symbols that expressed the differentiation of the notion of being from psychic enclosure in the great maternal round, the differentiation that was occurring in the axial period of Greek civilization in which these tragedies were composed. The time was a period of the gestation of differentiated consciousness, and the dramas express in imaginal language the differentiation of the notion of being that was going forward. From the upper blade of the hermeneutical method that I am suggesting, the Oedipus story is, *pace* Freud, the dramatization of the awful precariousness of the emerging differentiation of the notion of being from the Great Round, and the Orestes cycle is the dramatization of its success, the breakthrough, the *miraculum Graecum.* The success requires not the elimination but the transformation of the psychic furies under the persuasion of the psyche, the mother, as wisdom, as Sophia, in the person of Athena. As wisdom, the psyche guarantees to these psychic realities a permanent place in the underground of the city built by the intelligence that was emerging in its own right. As long as the psychic powers are allowed their abode in the depths, they are the Eumenides, the favorable psychic forces that wish us well. These myths are elemental symbolic articulations of the emergence of a world-constitutive differentiation of the notion of being.

Different from these are the scriptural articulations of the differentiation of the transcendent exigence. In their most unrelieved aspect, these articulations take the form of apocalypse. But, as Frye indicates, there is a point beyond the apocalyptic, where 'the undisplaced apocalyptic world and the cyclical world of nature come into alignment.' This Frye calls 'the point of epiphany,' where heaven and earth achieve their connection. While Frye finds the most common settings of such symbols to be 'the mountaintop, the island, the tower, the lighthouse, and the ladder or staircase,'[93] I think we may include in a preeminent fashion the final vision of the Heavenly Jerusalem

in the Book of Revelation. For here the mandala symbolism of cosmological consciousness has undergone an
anagogic transformation, without losing any of its original
archetypal significance. The anagogically transformed cosmological mandala is the redemption of the self-enclosed
psyche. In contrast with the scene in Jung's dream, the
throne in the center of the mandala is now the seat of no
'lord of this world,' the seat not of the apotheosized self
but of the Lamb slain before the foundation of the world,
the innocent victim, the suffering servant who bore the sin
of many and whose bride is now the holy city, the integrity
of the anagogically transformed wholeness of redeemed
nature and history. The solution is 'a new level on which
human living develops and rejoices.' Its constituents are
'absolutely supernatural, because their sole ground and
measure is the divine nature itself. Then faith includes
objects beyond the natural reach of any finite understanding. Then hope is for a vision of God that exhausts the
unrestricted desire of intelligence. Then charity is the trans-
port, the ecstasy and unbounded intimacy that result from
the communication of the absolute love that is God himself and alone can respond to the vision of God.'[94]

> Then he showed me the river of the water of
> life, bright as crystal, flowing from the throne
> of God and of the Lamb through the middle of
> the street of the city; also, on either side of the
> river, the tree of life with its twelve kinds of
> fruit, yielding its fruit each month; and the
> leaves of the tree for the healing of the nations.
> There shall no more be anything accursed, but
> the throne of God and of the Lamb shall be in
> it, and his servants shall worship him; they shall
> see his face, and his name shall be on their fore-
> heads. And night shall be no more; they need

no light of lamp or sun for the Lord God will
be their light, and they shall reign for ever and
ever. (Revelation 22.1-5)

Notes

[1] Northrop Frye, *Anatomy of Criticism* (see above, chapter 13, note 56) 161-62.

[2] Ibid. 118.

[3] On the sensitive appropriation of truth, see Bernard Lonergan, *Insight* (see above, chapter 1, note 20) 561-62/584-85.

[4] Erich Neumann, *The Origins and History of Consciousness*, trans. R.F.C. Hull (Princeton: Princeton University Press, 1971) 11. On symbols as carriers of elemental meaning, see Bernard Lonergan, *Method in Theology* (see above, chapter 1, note 1) 67. On the important category of elemental meaning, Lonergan writes: 'In the potential act [of meaning] meaning is elemental. There has not yet been reached the distinction between meaning and meant. Such is the meaning of the smile that acts simply as an intersubjective determinant, the meaning of the work of art prior to its interpretation by a critic, the meaning of the symbol performing its office of internal communication without help from the therapist. Again, acts of sensing and of understanding of themselves have only potential meaning. As Aristotle put it, the sensible in act and the sense in act are one and the same. Thus sounding and hearing are an identity: without ears there can be longitudinal waves in the atmosphere but there cannot be sound. Similarly, data are potentially intelligible, but their intelligibility in act coincides with an intelligence in act.' Ibid. 74. See also ibid. 62-63, 66-67. The meanings with which we are concerned in this paper are embodied in more than one carrier of meaning. They are linguistic, for we are concerned with literary criticism and the interpretation of texts. But they are also artistic and/or symbolic. On carriers of meaning, ibid. 57-73.

[5] I will show this below in an interpretation of a dream of Jung's, an interpretation that differs from Jung's own.

[6] On mystery and myth, see Lonergan, *Insight* 531-49/554-72.

[7] On the differentiation of dialectic, see my paper 'Duality and Dialectic' (above, chapter 4) and chapter 3 of *Theology and the Dialectics of History* (see above, chapter 1, note 3). It is in 'Duality and Dialectic' that I first identified Lonergan's notion of dialectic as a single but complex notion.

[8] See Bernard Lonergan, 'Finality, Love, Marriage,' in *Collection* (see above, chapter 9, note 9) 17-52, at 51.

[9] Lonergan, *Method in Theology* III.

[10] Lonergan, *Insight* 476/501.

[11] Ibid. 729/750.

[12] See Wilhelm Dilthey, 'The Imagination of the Poet: Elements for a Poetics,' in Dilthey, *Selected Works*, vol. 5, *Poetry and Experience*, ed. Rudolf A. Makkreel and Frithjof Rodi (Princeton: Princeton University Press, 1985) 29-173; Paul Ricoeur, *Freud and Philosophy* (see above, chapter 5, note 16).

[13] 1993 note: See above, chapter 13, note 52, on my meaning of 'notion of transcendent (or absolute) mystery.'

[14] Lonergan, *Insight* 530/553.

[15] 1993 note: This position on an ontology of meaning in chapter 17 of *Insight* is offered in chapter 19 of *Theology and the Dialectics of History*. That chapter is based on a paper written for the 1987 Lonergan Workshop at Boston College.

[16] Lonergan, *Insight* 389/414.

[17] Ibid. 530/553.

[18] Ibid. 530/554.

[19] Frye, *Anatomy of Criticism* 119.

[20] Ibid. 118.

21 This point is made in chapter 9 of Bernard Lonergan, *Topics in Education* (see above, chapter 2, note 15).

22 Ibid. 232.

23 Ibid.

24 Lonergan, *Insight* 531/554.

25 Ibid. 569/592. Thus Frye can go so far as to wonder, at the end of *Anatomy of Criticism*, whether it is not the case that 'the verbal structures of psychology, anthropology, theology, history, law, and everything else built out of words have been informed or constructed by the same kind of myths and metaphors that we find, in their original hypothetical form, in literature.' Frye, *Anatomy of Criticism* 352.

26 Pure formulations 'proceed from the immanent sources of meaning to determine differentiations of the protean notion of being. Such differentiations may be either the contents of single judgments or the contexts constituted by more or less coherent aggregates of judgments. In either case they are pure formulations if they proceed from an interpreter that grasps the universal viewpoint and if they are addressed to an audience that similarly grasps the universal viewpoint.' Lonergan, *Insight* 580/602.

27 Ibid. 578/600.

28 Ibid. 567/590.

29 Ibid.

30 Ibid. 578/601.

31 Ibid. 569/592.

32 Ibid. 571-72/594.

33 Ibid. 586-87/609-10. Emphasis added.

34 Ibid. 567/590.

35 Ibid. 548/571.

[36] Bernard Lonergan, '*Insight* Revisited' (see above, chapter 9, note 35) 275.

[37] Ibid. 532/555.

[38] Ibid., pp. 561-62/585. Nor is such a position vitiated by the fact that the symbolic meanings that would be interpreted as elemental expressions of differentiations of the notion of being are themselves not explanatory meanings. For there is possible 'an explanatory interpretation of a nonexplanatory meaning.' That is, 'The original writer's meaning may have its source in insights into things as related to him, and in all probability he will have neither a clear notion of what is meant by insight nor any distinct advertence to the occurrence of his insights. Still, *ex hypothesi*, he had the insights and they provided a source of his meaning; moreover, the insights he had were or were not different from the insights of other earlier, contemporary, and later writers; and if they were different, then they stood in some genetic and dialectical relations with those other sets. Now it is through these genetic and dialectical relations that interpretation is explanatory. It is through these genetic and dialectical relations that explanatory interpretation conceives, defines, reaches the insights of a given writer. Accordingly, it in no way involves the imputation of explanatory knowledge to a mind that possessed only descriptive knowledge. It is concerned to reach, as exactly as possible, the descriptive knowledge of the writers P, Q, R, ..., and it attempts to do so, not by offering an unverifiable inventory of the insights enjoyed respectively by P, Q, R, ..., but by establishing the verifiable differences between P, Q, R, ... Because it approaches terms through differences, because the differences can be explained genetically and dialectically, the interpretation of nonexplanatory meaning is itself explanatory.' Ibid. 587-88/610.

[39] Ibid. 582/604.

[40] Ibid. 580/602.

[41] Ibid. 585/608.

[42] Lonergan, *Method in Theology* 37.

[43] Ibid. 64.

[44] Lonergan, *Insight* 723-24/744-45.

45 'Most significant from a basic viewpoint, there is the existential approach that thinks of the dream, not as the twilight of life, but as its dawn, the beginning of the transition from impersonal existence to presence in the world, to constitution of one's self in one's world.' Lonergan, *Method in Theology* 69.

46 Robert M. Doran, 'Duality and Dialectic' (above, chapter 4) and chapter 3 of *Theology and the Dialectics of History*.

47 Lonergan, *Insight* 244/268.

48 Ibid. 244/269. Emphasis added.

49 Ibid. 233/258.

50 Lonergan, *Method in Theology* 111.

51 Paul Ricoeur, *Freud and Philosophy*. See Lonergan, *Method in Theology* 67-68, for the suggestion of the complementarity of Freud and Jung, and Robert M. Doran, *Subject and Psyche* (see above, chapter 1, note 11) chapter 3, for a study of Ricoeur's interpretation of Freud that concludes with the suggestion that a better teleological partner to Freud's archeology would be found in Jung's analytical psychology.

52 Lonergan, *Method in Theology* 50.

53 Ibid. 51.

54 Ibid.

55 Ibid. 51-52.

56 Ibid. 52.

57 On the priority of the dramatic pattern of experience, see Robert M. Doran, 'Dramatic Artistry in the Third Stage of Meaning' (see above, chapter 1, note 28).

58 Lonergan, *Insight* 475-76/500.

59 Ibid. 476/501.

60 Ibid. 476/500-501.

61 Again, 'the essential logic of the distorted dialectic is a reversal. For dialectic rests on the concrete unity of opposed principles; the
dominance of either principle results in a distortion, and the distortion
both weakens the dominance and strengthens the opposed principle to
restore an equilibrium.' Ibid. 233/258.

62 C.G. Jung, 'The Transcendent Function' (see above, chapter
5, note 8).

63 See Ernest Becker, *The Denial of Death* (see above, chapter 2,
note 10) 266.

64 Lonergan, *Insight* 191-96/214-20.

65 See Doran, *Subject and Psyche*, chapter 3. See also Doran,
'Paul Ricoeur: Toward the Restoration of Meaning,' chapter 1 in *Intentionality and Psyche* (see above, chapter 1, note 2).

66 On active imagination, see C.G. Jung, *Mysterium Coniunctionis*,
trans. R.F.C. Hull, vol. 14 in The Collected Works of C.G. Jung, Bollingen
Series XX (Princeton: Princeton University Press, 1970) 494-96. See
Jung's appropriate caution, p. 496: 'As a rule there is a marked tendency
simply to enjoy this interior entertainment and to leave it at that. Then,
of course, there is no real progress but only endless variations on the
same theme, which is not the point of the exercise at all.' That the dream
is symbolically related, not only to the notion of value, but also to the
notion of being is exemplified in the dream narrated by the chemist
Friedrich August Kekulé, in which there was provided the image he
needed for his insight into the structure of the benzene ring. The desire
to know 'can invade the very fabric of [our] dreams.' Lonergan, *Insight*
4/28. I am unable to locate the reference to Kekulé. As I recall, when he
reported his findings to his colleagues, he advised them to pay attention
to their dreams. That the dream sometimes bears a direct relation also
to the transcendent exigence, and is anagogic in meaning, will be shown
below when I interpret a dream of Jung's.

67 Ernest Becker, *The Denial of Death*.

68 To these must be added dreams that are not symbolic at all,
that is, such events as prescient and synchronistic dreams relating quite

directly and, as it were, literally, to events and persons in history or in the life of the individual. That such dreams occur is undeniable. How they are to be explained constitutes a major scientific problem to which, as far as I know, no adequate solution has been provided. Jung's theory of synchronicity, approved by the physicist Wolfgang Pauli, at least recognizes the fact of such events. But a truly explanatory account of such data, an account that probably will have to draw at once on physics, psychology, and philosophical theology, has yet to be presented.

[69] Neumann's work interested Lonergan. I know of Lonergan's interest from conversations with him in the winter of 1973-1974 at Regis College. Indications of his interest can be found in the references to this book that appear in *A Third Collection* (see above, chapter 2, note 9). See the index, 'Neumann, Erich.'

[70] 'The twilight of what is conscious but not objectified seems to be the meaning of what some psychiatrists call the unconscious.' Lonergan, *Method in Theology* 34, note 5.

[71] Lonergan, *Insight* 531-49/554-72.

[72] I must emphasize the notable correspondence of objectives in the positions of Lonergan and Neumann. Both are aware of the post-Enlightenment neglect of the primary field of mystery and myth, and of the consequent danger of the perversion and derailment of sensitivity due to the hybris of the ego or originating freedom. A major contribution of Jungian psychology to the implementation of Lonergan's program lies in its contribution to the overcoming of the modern neglect of the field of mystery.

[73] Neumann, *The Origins and History of Consciousness* xxiv.

[74] C.G. Jung, 'On the Nature of the Psyche' (see above, chapter 5, note 20) 206.

[75] Lonergan, *Insight* 548/571.

[76] Neumann, *The Origins and History of Consciousness* 6.

[77] Ibid.

[78] Ibid. 11.

[79] Ibid. 14.

[80] Ibid.

[81] Eric Voegelin, *Israel and Revelation* (see above, chapter 1, note 8) 56.

[82] Neumann, *The Origins and History of Consciousness* 15.

[83] Ibid. 17.

[84] Ibid. 34-35.

[85] Lonergan, *Insight* 476-77/500-502.

[86] Ibid. 478/503.

[87] Ibid. 475/499.

[88] C.G. Jung, *Memories, Dreams, Reflections* (see above, chapter 1, note 24) 218.

[89] Ibid. 218-19.

[90] Ibid. 219-20.

[91] Ibid. 218.

[92] See Vincent Brome, *Jung: Man and Myth* (New York: Antheneum, 1978).

[93] Frye, *Anatomy of Criticism* 203.

[94] Lonergan, *Insight* 724-26/745-47.

Part Four

Toward a Systematic Theology

In this paper I will present in summary fashion some insights reached along the way toward writing the first installment on a systematic theology.[1] I began with the assumptions, first, that, if a theology mediates between a cultural matrix and the significance and role of a religion within that matrix,[2] then the first task in constructing a contemporary systematic theology would involve working out basic terms and relations for understanding the cultural matrix being addressed; and second, that these terms and relations would be found by reflecting on Bernard Lonergan's understanding of the structure of society, especially in the seventh chapter of *Insight*.

The first assumption was significantly expanded, however, as the work proceeded, and the expansion was largely due to following through on the second assumption. For what Lonergan offers is not simply guidance for the sizing up of a given situation. His reflections on society and its immanent dialectic of community contain a key to the heuristic anticipation of an understanding of the intelligible core of historical process itself. After several years of work, I have come to see that the principal general categories of a systematic theology can be derived from reflecting on Lonergan's contributions to an understanding of history. The significance of this insight for the construction of a systematic theology lies in the fact that

Christian doctrines can thus be understood in the context of a general-categorial understanding of history. Systematic theology becomes throughout a theological theory of history, as the realities named by the special categories are mediated with the realities articulated in the general categories of a theory of history.[3] Systematics thus becomes praxis, in that it articulates the meaning constitutive of Christian fellowship, witness, and service as the latter exercise a catalytic agency in evoking an alternative situation more closely approximating the reign of God in this world.

My first assumption, then, while broadened far beyond its original scope and range, retains an element of truth. The understanding of theology as mediating between a cultural matrix and the significance and role of a religion within that matrix does imply that the theologian addresses one situation only to evoke another one. A mediating theology has not only a disclosive but also a transformative function with respect to its situation. In the perspective provided by Lonergan's understanding of the entire theological enterprise as constituted by eight distinct but related functional specialties, where the first four specialties mediate in indirect discourse from the past into the present, and the second four in direct discourse from the present into the future, the burden of the transformative function falls upon the second phase. What remains true from my first assumption is that a theologian working in the second phase — in foundations, doctrines, systematics, and communications — has to understand, and articulate his or her understanding of, the situation which is being addressed and of the alternative situation which one would evoke. But the widening of the scope and range of this assumption involved for me the grasp of what I would call the heuristic structure of *any* situation, the a priori element involved in the theological understanding of history itself. I will attempt to set forth here the basic elements of this understanding.

1   The Analogy of Dialectic

The principal categories that I would offer to express an understanding of the structure of history are *the analogy of dialectic* and *the integral scale of values*. These will become the principal general categories of a systematic theology that would understand the meaning of Christian doctrines in the light of an understanding of history. The realities named in the principal Christian doctrines — in David Tracy's summation 'God, Christ, grace; creation-redemption-eschatology; church-world; nature-grace, grace-sin; revelation; faith, hope, love; word-sacrament; cross-resurrection-incarnation'[4] — are to be understood in this systematic theology within the overall context of the dialectics of the subject, culture, and community, as these dialectical processes are related to one another by the structure of the scale of values.

The dialectic of the subject and the dialectic of community are discussed by Lonergan in the chapters on common sense in *Insight*.[5] The dialectic of culture is my own contribution. The scale of values is set forth by Lonergan in *Method in Theology*,[6] and my own efforts have been to understand three of the levels of value — social, cultural, personal — as constituted, respectively, by the three dialectics of community, culture, and the subject, and to specify the relations which prevail among the various levels of value both from below and from above. What would these relations be in a line of pure progress in history? How does the breakdown of these relations enable us to achieve some understanding of the dynamics of decline? These are questions to which I would suggest a response. The category of the analogy of dialectic expresses my understanding of the dialectics of the subject, culture, and community. And I try to relate these to one another by specifying their respective functions within the integral scale of values.

Each of the three dialectics is internally constituted as 'a concrete unfolding of linked but opposed principles of change.'[7] The principles constitutive of the dialectic of the subject are neural demands for psychic integration and conscious representation, on the one hand, and the censorship over these demands exercised by dramatically patterned intelligence and imagination, on the other hand.[8] The principles constitutive of the dialectic of community are spontaneous intersubjectivity and the practical intelligence that institutes the technological, economic, and political structures of society.[9] The principles constitutive of the dialectic of culture are cosmological and anthropological constitutive meaning, which are two diverse but interrelated sets of insights regarding the direction that can be found or missed in the movement of life.[10] The dialectics are analogous, first, in that each is an embodiment of the creative tension of limitation and transcendence constituting an unfolding of linked but opposed principles of change;[11] second, in that each is a dialectic of contraries, not of contradictories; and third, in that in each case the integrity of the dialectic is a function of a third principle of higher synthesis beyond the principles internally constitutive of the respective dialectic.

A dialectic of contraries, as opposed to a dialectic of contradictories, is a particular realization of the single but complex notion of dialectic in which the constitutive principles are to work harmoniously in the unfolding of the changes that emerge from their interaction. The processes of individual, social, and cultural change proceed along a line of pure progress to the extent that they are marked by the integral unfolding of the changes emergent from both of the constitutive principles of the relevant dialectic.[12] A dialectic of contraries is a matter, not of either/or, but of both/and: both neural demand functions and the constructive censorship; both spontaneous intersubjectivity and practical common sense; both cosmological and anthropological meaning and truth. The dialectics of the subject, community, and culture are integral dialectics to the extent that the processes of change that they constitute are a function of the harmonious interaction of both of the opposed principles of change internally constitutive of the dialectic. Each dialectic becomes distorted when the changes are a function of the dominance of one principle over the other, that is to say, when the dialectic of contraries is treated as if it were a dialectic of contradictories — either neural demands or the (now repressive) censorship, either spontaneous intersubjectivity or practical (and now exclusively instrumentalized) intelligence, either cosmological or anthropological (become mechanomorphic) constitutive meaning. In a distorted dialectic, each internally constitutive principle is displaced from its normative function in the concrete unfolding of linked but opposed principles, and the displacements affect the entire process of change emergent in the skewed dialectic.

A dialectic of contradictories does function, however, with respect to a third principle of higher synthesis responsible for the integrity of the respective dialectics. The integral dialectic of neural demand functions and the censorship is a function of the charity that Lonergan calls universal willingness.[13] The integral dialectic of spontaneous intersubjectivity and practical common sense is a function of genuine cultural values. And genuine cultural values, themselves constituted by the integration of cosmological and anthropological meaning and truth, are a function of a soteriological differentiation of consciousness. A dialectic of contradictories operates with respect to these principles of higher synthesis: either universal willingness or some blend of the biases; either authentic or inauthentic culture; either soteriological meaning and truth or bondage to a one-sided vision of reality that either overly immanentizes the ultimate measure of integrity (the cosmological horizon) or renders this measure so inaccessible to the questing mind and heart (the anthropological horizon) that it is eventually rejected altogether (the death of God and the end of history proclaimed by some contemporary post-structuralists).

2   The Dialectic of Community

'Society' is a generic term embracing five elements: technological institutions, the economic system, the political order, primordial intersubjectivity, and culture. Culture has two dimensions: the everyday level of meanings and values informing a given way of life, and the reflexive or superstructural level of scientific, philosophic, scholarly, and theological objectifications.

I said above that there is a dialectic of community internally constituted by the linked but opposed principles of spontaneous intersubjectivity and practical intelligence. Spontaneous intersubjectivity is one of the five elements constitutive of a society. Practical intelligence is the source of three of the other elements: technology, the economic system, and the political order. The dialectic of community is the concrete unfolding of the changes that result from the tension of spontaneous intersubjectivity with the dimensions of society emergent from commonsense practicality. The integrity of the dialectic, and so of the society that it informs 'rests on the concrete unity of opposed principles; the dominance of either principle results in a distortion, and the distortion both weakens the dominance and strengthens the opposed principle to restore an equilibrium.'[14]

The integrity or distortion of the dialectic of community is a function, proximately, of the everyday level of culture, and remotely of the reflexive scientific, scholarly, philosophical, and theological dimension of culture. '[I]f men are to meet the challenge set by major decline and its longer cycle, it will be through their culture that they do so.'[15] Spontaneous intersubjectivity, technology, economic relations, politics, and the everyday level of culture constitute the infrastructure of a society; the reflexive level constitutes a society's superstructure. Culture, in both its everyday infrastructural and its reflexive superstructural dimensions, is the condition of the possibility of the integrity of the dialectic of spontaneous intersubjectivity and the technological-economic-political structures created by practical intelligence for the sake of social order.

In *Insight* Lonergan speaks of a dimension of consciousness that he calls cosmopolis, which informs an intellectual collaboration that assumes responsibility for the integrity of the dialectic of community by attending to the cultural values operative at both the infrastructural and superstructural levels of culture. The integrity of the dialectic of community is a function of neither of the principles internally constitutive of the dialectic, but of culture. Culture is to see to the harmonious cooperation, the creative tension, of intersubjectivity and practicality, through which the community becomes, if you want, a work of art. Authentic cultural values constitute a higher synthesis of the internally constitutive poles of the dialectic of community, a synthesis upon which the integrity of the dialectic depends. Conversely, the breakdown of the dialectic is due to a culture that either has been 'forced into an ivory tower of ineffectualness by the social surd' or has 'capitulate[d] to its absurdity' by becoming practical.[16] Cosmopolis assumes the responsibility of preventing either of these defaults of transpractical intelligence in the constitution of the meanings and values informing a given way of life.

The analysis to this point is transcendental. It is grounded in the concrete unity-in-tension that is human consciousness itself, the unity-in-duality of sensitive spontaneity and ordering intelligence.[17] Any situation is constituted in part by a particular condition, more or less integral or distorted, of the dialectic of community. But a theology that would mediate between a cultural matrix and the significance and role of Christian faith within that matrix must specify more concretely the factors that constitute the particular dialectic that the theology would address. I understand the significant dialectic of community today to be global. Almost every regional cultural matrix today must be understood in terms of planetary structural realities at the levels of technology, economics, and politics. These realities have been created in large part by the exploits of competing and escalating imperialistic systems. I use the term 'imperialism' in accord with a modification of Joseph Schumpeter's definition: 'the objectless disposition on the part of a state to unlimited forcible expansion.'[18] The modification is to the effect that such a disposition can constitute either a state or an economic macrosystem controlling even states. At its base imperialism is constituted by a neglect of the limitation poles in the three dialectics of community, culture, and the subject: a neglect of spontaneous intersubjectivity, of cosmological constitutive meaning, and of aesthetic participation in the movement of life. The distortions of imperialistic praxis represent a skewing of the threefold dialectic in the direction of transcendence: of practical intelligence become exclusively instrumental reason, of anthropological meaning become mechanomorphic nihilism, of censorship become repressive of the major portion of the materials through which persons can make a work of art out of their lives. And in each case the distortion weakens the dominant principle and calls forth the reversal of the derailed dialectic by evoking the contribution of the neglected element. But the suppressed element, when awakened, can be just as tyrannical as was its suppressor. From the suppressed intersubjectivity, there can result mob violence; from neglected cosmological meaning, a demonic entrapment on the great mandala that would measure on purely intracosmic standards whatever human integrity it still acknowledges; from the repressed psyche, a psychotic breakdown.

The task is one of reversing the distortion of the dialectic of community due to the ascendancy of the practical intelligence that institutes technological, economic, and political structures, over the contrary but essential exigences of intersubjective spontaneity; this task is in part the responsibility of the cosmopolitan intellectual collaboration that, by assuming responsibility for the integrity of culture, is, in Hannah Arendt's words, to 'develop a new guarantee which can be found only in a new political principle, a new law on earth, whose validity this time must comprehend the whole of humanity while its power must remain strictly limited, rooted in and controlled by newly defined territorial entities.'[19] The combined facts, that, first, technological institutions, an economic system, and a political order are constitutive elements of society, and second, that these realities are to be understood ultimately in global terms, lead to the conclusion that the dialectic of community is today a global tension. Because culture is the condition of the possibility of the integrity of the dialectic of community, cosmopolitan intellectual collaboration is confronted with a demand for the generation of world-cultural values capable of synthesizing the internally constitutive poles of a global dialectic of community.[20]

The perversions of the dialectic of community constituted by the objectless disposition to forcible expansion that is imperialism are rooted in the aberration of intelligence that Critical Theory calls the exclusive instrumentalization of reason, and Lonergan the general bias of common sense. Practicality or instrumental intelligence in origi-

nating and developing capital and technology, the economy
and the state, can be properly subordinate to the constitution of the human world as a work of art only by being
brought into and maintained in a state of taut balance or
poised equilibrium with spontaneous intersubjectivity. And
this is possible only by the subjection to the higher,
noninstrumentalized specialization of intelligence that constitutes and indeed generates authentic cultural values. For
this it needs to be invested with the detachment that is
required to honor long-range, ultimate, and theoretical
questions. The dramatic artistry of subjects in community
requires that detachment if it is to preserve intact the delicate and nuanced unfolding of the dialectic of intersubjectivity and practicality in the constitution of the social order. The function of culture is to render intellectual comprehension of, and existential engagement in, social reality critical, dialectical, and normative: critical, because any
social situation is a compound of the intelligible and the
unintelligible, the good and the evil, and one must able to
judge the difference; dialectical, because our intellectual
and existential participation in society must advance the
intelligible and good dimensions of the situation and reverse the unintelligible and evil dimensions (the dialectic
of contradictories), and because the intelligible and good
are a function of the integral dialectic of intersubjectivity
and practicality (a dialectic of contraries) and the unintelligible and evil are a function of the distortion of this dialectic; normative, in that neither of the principles internally constitutive of the dialectic is the immanent form of
the intelligibility and goodness of the situation. That intelligibility and goodness must be rooted in the higher synthesis of cultural meanings and values embracing both poles
of the dialectic in a concrete unity-in-tension.

　　　One of the major principles of the transcendental
analysis of historical process — a principle that will be-

come clearer when we discuss the scale of values — is that only cultural values commensurate with the proportions of the social dialectic can assure the integrity of the dialectic itself. This means that if the social dialectic itself is of global proportions, the culture that would sustain it in its integrity must be in some sense a world culture. The integral dialectic of community today calls for schemes of recurrence in the social infrastructure that are both global and alternative to the schemes that emerge from the competing and escalating imperialisms. These alternative schemes depend upon a set of cultural values that are both different from those informing the imperialistic systems and capable of uniting in crosscultural community and collaboration the members of the various regionally circumscribed cultural traditions of humankind. Cosmopolis today must see to the generation of those cultural values, at both levels of culture. The possibility and necessity of the vast interdisciplinary effort required to meet this task constitute the intellectual context of a contemporary Christian systematic theology. Such a theology must be part of that wider interdisciplinary collaboration, employing categories used in other fields as well, but also providing its own special categories. I propose the general systematic rubric of the analogy of dialectic, as a framework in which theology can assume these responsibilities.

3   The Integral Scale of Values

The position just stated regarding the relation between the dialectic of community at the level of the social order and the need for cultural values commensurate with the demands of the common good implies a particular stance on the scale of values in general which we must articulate before moving on to other instances of dialectic. The pertinence of the dialectics of culture and the subject for an understanding of history will emerge in the course of our discussion of the integral scale of values and especially of the relations among the various levels of the scale.

Lonergan presents the following account of the scale of values:

> [W]e may distinguish vital, social, cultural, personal, and religious values in an ascending order. Vital values, such as health and strength, grace and vigor, normally are preferred to avoiding the work, privations, pains involved in acquiring, maintaining, restoring them. Social values, such as the good of order which conditions the vital values of the whole community, have to be preferred to the vital values of individual members of the community. Cultural values do not exist without the underpinning of vital and social values, but nonetheless they rank higher. Not on bread alone doth man live. Over and above mere living and operating, men have to find a meaning and value in their living and operating. It is the function of culture to discover, express, validate, criticize, correct, develop, improve such meaning and value. Personal value is the person in his self-transcendence, as loving and being loved, as originator of values in himself and in his milieu, as an inspiration and invitation to others to do likewise. Religious values, finally, are at the heart of the meaning and value of man's living and man's world.[21]

I would offer the following understanding of the scale of values.

First, technology, economic relations, and the legal and political stratum of society, in dialectical relation with intersubjective spontaneity, with the dialectic constituted as a function of the everyday level of culture, compose the *infrastructure* of a healthy society.

Second, the *superstructure* of such a society lies in the reflexive, objectifying dimension of culture.

Third, the infrastructure is thus constituted by the vital, social, and everyday cultural levels of value, and the superstructure by reflexively articulated cultural values.

Fourth, beyond these levels of value constitutive of the infrastructure and superstructure of society lie the levels of personal and religious value.

Fifth, the relations among the levels of value may be understood in part as follows: the higher levels condition the schemes of recurrence of the more basic levels, while problems in the effective recurrence of the more basic levels offer an occasion for, and establish the proportions to be met by, the questions that prompt the needed developments at the higher levels. Thus religious values condition the possibility of personal integrity. Personal integrity conditions the possibility of genuine cultural values. At the reflexive level of culture such integrity would inform the cosmopolitan intellectual collaboration of which we spoke above, one function of which is to keep alive in the infrastructure a concern for the integrity of cultural values. Cultural integrity conditions the possibility of a just social order, where justice is a function of the integral dialectic of community. And a just social order conditions the possibility of the equitable distribution of vital goods in such a way as to assure liberation not only from hunger and misery but also from servitude and personal degradation, from hopelessness and meaninglessness. Conversely, problems in the effective recurrence of vital goods for the whole community can be met only by a reversal of distortions in the dialectic of community at the level of social values. A new dynamic equilibrium between intersubjective interaction and technological, economic, and political changes demands a transformation at the everyday level of culture. The latter transformation frequently calls for and depends upon reflexive scholarly and theoretical developments at the superstructural level of culture. And new cultural values at both levels call for changes at the level of personal integrity. The latter, finally, depends for its sustenance and consistency on the religious development of the person.

There are, then, two basic and mutual sets of relations among the levels of value: a movement from above downwards determines the integral functioning of the scale; a movement from below upwards demands the creativity that will result in new developments, further differentiations, at the higher levels.

Sixth, the integrity of the superstructure thus conditions that of the infrastructure.

Seventh, the breakdown of infrastructural integrity consequently calls for developments at the superstructural level of culture.

And eighth, the personal integrity of the individual and the authenticity of his or her religious life, while they lie beyond both infrastructure and superstructure, are essential to the integral unfolding of historical process.

A society, then, is composed of an infrastructure and a superstructure. But the condition of any given society depends on what in fact constitutes these two dimensions of that society. The society is healthy to the extent that its infrastructure is constituted by the dialectical tension of intersubjective interaction with the technological, economic, and political institutions emergent from practical intelligence. The cultural values operative at the everyday level determine the integrity of this basic social dialectic.[22] But the breakdown of everyday cultural values can at times be reversed only by prolonged and difficult collaborative scholarly and theoretical labor at the superstructural level, labor that aims at either the restoration of cultural values that have been eclipsed, or, as in periods of epochal change such as our own, the generation of a new and more inclusive set of cultural values. The cultural values in general of a healthy society are constituted by the operative assumptions consequent upon the pursuit of the beautiful in story and song, ritual and dance, art and literature; the pursuit of the intelligible in science, scholarship, and common sense; the pursuit of the true in philosophy and theology; and the pursuit of the good in all questions regarding the normative relations among the elements constitutive of the human world. The values constituting cultural integrity are the transcendental values of the beautiful, the intelligible, the true, and the good. The operative assumptions that they engender to govern a particular way of life would permit the subordination of practicality in the origination and development of capital and technology, the economy and the state, to the construction of the human world, of human relations, and of human subjects as works of art; they would see that practicality is maintained in a taut balance with the exigences of intersubjective communication and interaction, and so would guard against the exclusive instrumentalization of intelligence and reason responsible for the current distortions of the dialectic of community.

Personal and religious values are to be understood in relation to the values internally constitutive of the social infrastructure and the cultural superstructure. While they lie beyond these, they are not for that reason to be regarded as constituting a realm of privacy irrelevant to cultural and social process. While the values that constitute cultural integrity condition the possibility of an integral dialectic of community at the level of social values, these cultural values in turn can be promoted only by persons of moral and intellectual integrity. And the person as a self-transcendent originator of values in self and world does not exist, is in fact an impossibility, without the gift of God's grace. Higher levels of value thus condition the possibility of the recurrent realization of more basic levels: no personal integrity without divine grace, no genuine cultural values without personal integrity, no good social order without cultural integrity, and no vital values for the whole community without a good social order. The movement from above downwards among the levels of value is thus the movement of conditioning. The movement from below, on the other hand, is in part one of differentiation and creativity. Problems in the effective realization of more basic levels are solved by new developments at higher levels, developments which must be commensurate with the problems they are meant to solve. Thus a breakdown of the schemes of recurrence supplying vital values to the whole community calls for a higher integration of the dialectic of community, whether through new technological developments, new economic relations, new forms of political organization, through the adaptation of the sensitive spontaneity of intersubjective groups, or through some combination of these various elements of the dialectic. The conversion of the dialectic of community from distortion to integrity calls for either the restoration of cultural values that have suffered eclipse or the differentiation of new, more inclusive, and more refined cultural values. Cultural values are authentic to the extent that they meet the proportions of the problems generated by the distorted dialectic of community. Whether eclipsed cultural values are to be restored or, as in periods of axial cultural changes, new cultural values are to be generated, a conversion of persons to a new level of integrity in their constitution of the world, of human relations, and of themselves as works of dramatic art is required. And because the sustained integrity of self-transcendent persons is impossible without the gift of the divinely originated solution to the problem of evil, the whole process is in effect a supplication for an ever more refined and purified relationship with God.

What is required of the relations among technology, the economy, and politics if these practical arrangements, while a product of instrumentalized intelligence, are to be a function of the integral praxis that would constitute the human world as a work of art, and so if they would emerge in creative tension with the intersubjective base of community? The primary requirement is that legal and political institutions be an element not of the superstructure but of the infrastructure of society. Genuine cultural values keep the political in its place in the infrastructure, where it is to mediate between culture in its everyday dimension and the economic and technological institutions of a society, with a view to placing and maintaining these in dialectical relation with intersubjective interaction. Thus, while the mediation from the superstructural to the infrastructural level of culture is one function of cosmopolis, the mediation from the infrastructural level of culture to the economy, to capital formation, and to the intersubjective community is the responsibility of the authentic political specialization of common sense.

On the other hand, when the integral scale of values is neglected, as in the societies spawned by the competing and escalating imperialisms, legal and political institutions slip out of the infrastructure and constitute the lowest level of a mendacious superstructural edifice erected for the sake of preserving a distorted dialectic between practicality and the intersubjective community. Law and politics then become a function of economic relations rather than the guarantee of the dialectic between these relations and intersubjective groups. Slipping out of the infrastructure, they become a mendacious but quite public determinant of the meanings and values informing the way of life of

segments of the community. They usurp the prerogatives
of culture. Genuine culture retreats into the margins of
society. The effective culture is merely the creation and
instrument of distorted practicality. When the political
specialization, defaulting on its legitimate and necessary
infrastructural function, invades the domain of culture,
genuine culture surrenders its function of autonomously
determining the meanings and values that, through political integrity, would otherwise inform the economy and the
institutions of technology as dialectical counterparts of
intersubjective interaction. As culture retreats, morality and
religion follow suit, and become merely private concerns.
The entire structure of the scale of values is upset by the
derailment of the political: a derailment that is rooted in
the loss of the tension of practicality and intersubjectivity
which it is the responsibility of culture to inform and of
politics to implement and maintain.[23] The authentic political specialization of common sense is to meet the recurrent problem of effective agreement through rational
persuasion guided by genuine cultural values. But under
the dominance of the distortions generated by bias it becomes in a recurrent fashion the inauthentic instrument
of the process that produces the social surd. The subordination of the genuine function of politics to the distorted
dialectic of community can be prevented only by an everyday culture that has not become instrumentally practical.

   I follow Lonergan in maintaining that an authentic
everyday culture depends on the development of a dimension of consciousness that recognizes and implements the
immanent norms of intelligence and indeed of the entire
scale of values. This cosmopolitan mentality operative at
the superstructural level is to generate and support, first, a
culture in which '[d]elight and suffering, laughter and tears,
joy and sorrow, aspiration and frustration, achievement and

failure, wit and humor, stand not within practicality but above it;'[24] second, a philosophy that appropriates a normative order of inquiry; and third, a human science that is not only empirical but also critical, dialectical, and normative, because grounded in that philosophic appropriation.

Culture, philosophy, and human science, then, are reflexes of a distorted infrastructure only when they have surrendered to the exclusive instrumentalization of intelligence and reason responsible for the distortion. The genuine relation of superstructure and infrastructure is quite the reverse of that which Marx discovered in capitalism and which, ironically, his followers promoted in state socialism. Theology is to evoke a superstructure that, through the philosophy, the human science, and the culture it sponsors, would have a profound impact on the everyday cultural, the political, the economic, and the technological dimensions of the infrastructure.

4   The Dialectic of the Subject

The cultural superstructure can influence the social infrastructure and direct it toward integrity only if it takes its stand on the immanent duality of consciousness that gives rise in the first place to the dialectic of community. At the level of the dialectic of community, this duality manifests itself in the tension of spontaneous intersubjectivity and practical intelligence. But its more radical manifestation is to be found in a dialectic constitutive of the subjects composing a society. The integrity of the dialectic of the subject at the level of personal value is the condition of the possibility of the cultural values that would guarantee an integral dialectic of community at the level of social values.

The dialectic of the dramatic and existential subject is a tension between neural demand functions and that preconscious collaboration of imagination and intelligence that Freud called the censorship and that Lonergan helps us understand within a more inclusive horizon than that available to Freud. The dialectic of the subject constitutes a second instance of the analogy of dialectic.

The integral dialectic of the subject is a condition of the possibility of the cosmopolitan collaboration that assumes the integrity of culture as its responsibility; for it is the immanent intelligibility of personal value as the ground of cultural values. The dialectic of the subject figures in the scale of values in such a way that, while personal integrity grounds the authentic function of culture in a movement from above downwards *among the levels of value,* distortions in the realm of personal value are statistically almost inevitable if personal development is solely a matter of a movement from below upwards *in human consciousness*; and these distortions are to be understood precisely in terms of a breakdown of the integral dialectic of the subject, due to some blend of the several biases that distort the concrete unfolding of the linked but opposed principles of neural demand functions and the censorship. A higher integration in the subject that functions from above downwards in human consciousness is required if persons of integrity are to be available to promote the cultural values that can sustain the integral dialectic of community in the social order. That higher integration is effected by the gift of charity, as the latter imparts an antecedent and in the limit universal willingness. This willingness constitutes the immanent intelligibility of religious values.

The dialectic of subjective development functions within the dialectic of community. The dialectic of community sets the conditions that stimulate our vital spontaneities and mold the orientation of our intelligence as the latter negotiates, with the help of imagination, the spontaneities stimulated by the social situation. These spontaneities, as neural demand functions, constitute one pole of the dialectic of the subject. The other pole consists of the dramatic intelligence in collaboration with imagination that, as censor, negotiates the neural demands. A creative tension of neural demands and the censorship analogous to that which we have already seen between intersubjective spontaneity and practical intelligence is required for the integrity of the dialectic of the subject. The dialectic is distorted in the direction of limitation when neural demands overwhelm intelligent, reasonable, and responsible powers of negotiation; it is distorted in the direction of transcendence when these powers of negotiation become repressive of the very factors they are meant to attend to. In either case a reversal of the distortion is invited through an appeal to the claims of the neglected factor.

The ground of our capacity to shape the elements stimulated by the dialectic of community into a work of dramatic art, through the constructive rather than repressive functioning of the censorship, lies in the sensitive psyche's relative aesthetic liberation from both neural process from below and instrumentalization from above. Then intelligence can artistically subordinate neural process to psychic determinations. The censorship is the collaboration of the psyche, through imagination, with intelligence in the effecting of this subordination. It is constructive if oriented to insight and responsible decision, and repressive if directed against these. In my own interpretation of this matter, the orientation of the censorship against insight can be rooted in either of its constitutive elements: in intelligence itself, as in general bias, or in the psychic component, as in the other forms of bias, each of which impairs the psyche's aesthetic liberation from the neural undertow and so its ability to collaborate with intelligence in admitting images into consciousness for insight. As we move from individual through group to dramatic bias, the problem becomes progressively more a problem of psychic development; dramatic bias is the least available to conscious control and free self-correction.

Just as the integrity of the dialectic of community is grounded, not in either of its internally constitutive principles taken singly, but in the higher synthesis provided by authentic cultural values, so the dialectic of the subject is grounded, not in neural demands nor in the censorship, but in the higher synthesis of an antecedent universal willingness that must be offered and accepted as a gift, as grace, as a feature of personal development not achievable on the basis of one's own immanent resources. If the movement from below in conscious development is not met by a movement from above, development will almost inevitably fall victim to some blend of the biases. The movement from above is the gift, the grace, of an antecedent and in the limit universal willingness, of the detachment of divinely bestowed charity. Without this grace, a functioning relation of conditioning from above downwards among the levels of value is impossible; for the highest level of value would lie in the personal, and bias would prevent an integral development precisely at that level. Personal integrity is not self-grounding. Only a living relationship of partnership and love with the absolute limit of the process of going beyond renders possible sustained development. That relationship is the communication of a willingness that conforms, not to inadequately developed human intelligence, but to God's understanding of the world order which God has chosen and created and which God sustains in being through the whole course of its emergent process.[25]

5   The Dialectic of Culture

Cultural values mediate between personal values and social values. If the latter two levels of value are constituted by an integral dialectic of limitation and transcendence, we may suspect that the same is true of authentic cultural values. But our discussion of the issue of cultural values and of a dialectic of culture is more convincing if it proceeds not from some a priori base of transcendental analysis, however valid, but from a concrete consideration of the crisis of cultural values in a situation where the dialectic of community is globally distorted by the competing and escalating agents of imperialistic ambition. Our attention can shift at this point, then, to the relations that obtain *from below upwards* among the levels of value. The social-infrastructural dialectic of community today is a matter of global proportions, due to the socioeconomic relations and political realities that constitute a globally interdependent commonwealth. These relations and realities demand the generation of cultural values that are more complex in structure and inclusive of more historically transmitted materials than would be the cultural values that might function as ordering factors for less extensive and more regionally circumscribed technoeconomic and political relationships. The meanings and values, the culture, adequate to the proportions of a globally interdependent technological, economic, and political order in dialectical relationship with what is now a crosscultural inter-subjectivity, are at best emergent in our situation. Theology today is to mediate what Christians believe as true and value as good, not so much with a relatively stable set of cultural meanings and values as with an emergent and potentially more differentiated set adequate to a global social order. For a systematic theology to mediate Christian faith with the contemporary cultural matrix is for it to participate in the emergence of a new matrix informed by cultural values suited to the proportions of the global social relations that they are to order. The transformation of culture on a global scale is the condition of the possibility of a humane infrastructural order for a global society.

The needed transformation of culture will emerge in part from the retrieval, crosscultural communication, philosophic reference-specification, and dialogically achieved integration of our presently available, historically transmitted knowledge of, and attitudes toward the world, God, ourselves, and the sense of our lives. Following Eric Voegelin, I find these presently available patterns of cultural meaning and value to be threefold: cosmological, anthropological, and soteriological symbolizations of the primordial experience of participation in a movement with a direction that can either be found or missed. I propose that cosmological and anthropological constitutive meaning constitute a dialectic of culture whose integrity is grounded in neither of its internally constitutive poles, but in the soteriological differentiation of consciousness that theology is to mediate with cosmological and anthropological insight and truth in such a way as to promote an integral dialectic of culture.

Like the dialectics of the subject and of community, then, the dialectic of culture is a dialectic of contraries. Both poles are to be affirmed, each in its appropriate relation to the other. The dialectic of culture is another instance of the tension of limitation and transcendence, with the cosmological pole a limiting factor and the anthropological the promoter of transcendence. The integrity of culture is a function of the concrete unfolding of cosmological and anthropological insight and truth; the inauthenticity of culture is a function of the breakdown of this integral unfolding due to the displacement of the tension toward one or other pole.

Cosmological symbolizations of the experience of life as a movement with a direction that can be found or missed find the paradigm of order in the cosmic rhythms. This order is analogously realized in the society, and social order determines individual rectitude. Cosmological insight thus moves from the cosmos, through the society, to the individual. As such it is more compact than anthropological insight, where the measure of integrity is recognized as world-transcendent and as providing the standard first for the individual, whose ordered attunement to the world-transcendent measure is itself the measure of the integrity of the society. Anthropological insight moves from God through the individual to the society. The dialectic of culture, like every dialectic of contraries, is a concrete unfolding of these linked but opposed principles of change.

These two ways of experiencing and understanding the participatory engagement of consciousness in the movement of life are characterized by quite contrasting experiences of time. Cosmological constitutive meaning has its roots in the affective, biologically based sympathy of the organism with the rhythms and processes of nonhuman nature. Anthropological truth is, on the contrary, constitutive of history as the product of human insight, reflection, and decision. A first approximation to the relation between them would contrast cyclical and linear time; but in fact, cosmological time is not precisely cyclical nor is anthropological time linear. The issue is one of schemes of recurrence with greater or lesser probabilities of emergence and survival due to the relative constitutive contribution of insight, reason, and decision. Cosmological consciousness, alone, binds human schemes of recurrence too stringently to those that inform cosmic process, while anthropological consciousness, alone, is insensitive to its biologically based, rhythmic participation in nonhuman nature, and given the necessary technical skills will promote a relatively post-historic mode of existence in contrast with the relatively prehistoric existence of the cosmological societies. The distortions of the dialectic would thus take the form either of anthropological consciousness losing affective sympathy with nature as it constitutes history, or of

cosmological consciousness succumbing massively to a
fatalism that it supposes is inscribed in cosmic rhythms. A
contemporary soteriology must display the deliverance effected by the divinely originated solution to the mystery of
evil, not so much from cosmological existence as from
mechanomorphic perversions of anthropological truth. The
integral dialectic of cosmological and anthropological truth
under the higher synthesis of the soteriological differentiation would provide an ecumenically available set of
meanings and values to inform the social infrastructure of
a global communitarian alternative to the imperialistic distortions of the dialectic of community. Because such a set
of cultural meanings and values is not yet an established
feature of life, theology's mediation of the soteriological
vector with the contemporary situation will itself contribute to the crosscultural generation of the cultural values of
a world-cultural humanity. In mediating faith and culture,
theology will be constituting the very meanings and values
of a new cultural order.

6   Conclusion

My hope is to construct or at least anticipate a systematic
theology that would understand Christian and theological
doctrines in the light of an understanding of historical process. Such a systematics would have as its central general
categories those that I have expressed in this paper.

It remains to be stated how such a systematics would
be not only academic and praxis-oriented, but also
ecclesial.[26] The academic and praxis-oriented characteristics have been developed at some length in this paper. I
will conclude with some comments about the ecclesial
context of this systematic theology, hoping thereby to illu-
minate the realm of religious values, whose integral functioning is the condition of the possibility of the integrity of
the entire scale of values.

From the discussion of cultural values, it is clear that the systematic theology that I have in mind would evoke remotely a transecclesial world-cultural communitarian alternative to the totalitarian potentials of the competing and escalating imperialistic systems. But it would evoke proximately the church as a catalytic agent of this alternative. The most satisfactory model of the church within this perspective is that of the community of the suffering servant of God. Theology is both an intellectual ministry to that community and a component of that community's ministry in the world. Thus not only must theology as an intellectual enterprise satisfy criteria of rigorous method, so that systematic theology is genuinely systematic and not a matter of 'rough coherence,' and not only must theology as historically situated receive its agenda from the exigences of its contemporary situation; it also must as ecclesial be radically pastoral, prophetic, and kerygmatic, evoking the church as a community of witness, fellowship, and service with a disclosive and transformative role to play in the contemporary historical situation. As such, it must be carried on within a horizon of Christian self-understanding that is articulately objectified in categories that are at once continuous with the tradition and pertinent to the ever new demands of the prevailing situation. These categories must articulate the constitutive intelligibility of the praxis of the reign of God that itself constitutes ecclesial ministry. That praxis, a matter of 'doing as Jesus did,' lies in a participation not only in Jesus' ministerial proclamation and enactment of the kingdom, but also in the paschal self-offering through which the alternative situation announced and evoked in Jesus' proclamation and praxis became embodied, however precariously, in a real historical community. As the principal catalytic agency of Jesus himself lay in his redemptive suffering, so the principal catalytic agency of the community called and empowered to do as Jesus did will lie in its participation in the law of Jesus' cross. The constitutive intelligibility of the community of disciples, that through which alone the church can be truly an incarnational sacrament of Jesus to the world and an eschatological sacrament of the world itself, lies in this innermost elemental feature of the divinely originated response to the human problem of evil.

The inner form of the catalytic agency of suffering servanthood lies in fidelity to the integral scale of values through which the distorted dialectics of the subject, culture, and community are transformed into the concrete unfolding of linked but opposed principles of change that constitutes as integral dialectic.[27] The categories of suffering servanthood name the religious values that condition the possibility of the personal integrity that in turn can promote the cultural values needed to inform a global dialectic of community capable of assuring the equitable distribution of vital goods to the one family of humanity under God in history.

Notes

[1]   Robert M. Doran, *Theology and the Dialectics of History* (Toronto: University of Toronto Press, 1990).

[2]   Bernard Lonergan, *Method in Theology* (see above, chapter 1, note 1) xi.

[3]   On general and special categories, see ibid. 281-93.

[4]   David Tracy, *The Analogical Imagination* (see above, chapter 7, note 14) 373. Lonergan offers an interrelation, grounded in method, of five sets of the special categories in *Method in Theology* 290-91.

[5]   Bernard Lonergan, *Insight* (see above, chapter 1, note 20) 187-206/210-31, 211-18/237-44.

6 Lonergan, *Method in Theology* 31-32.

7 Lonergan, *Insight* 217/242.

8 Lonergan, *Insight* 189-91/212-14. On the ultimate primacy of the dramatic pattern of experience, see my paper 'Dramatic Artistry in the Third Stage of Meaning' (see above, chapter 1, note 28).

9 Lonergan, *Insight* 211-18/237-44.

10 On cosmologial and anthropological constitutive meaning, see Eric Voegelin, *Israel and Revelation* (see above, chapter 1, note 8) 56. On the experience of life as a movement with a direction to be found or missed, see Voegelin, 'The Gospel and Culture' (see above, chapter 8, note 46).

11 Lonergan, *Insight* 472-79/504.

12 '[D]ialectic is a pure form with general implications; it is applicable to any concrete unfolding of linked but opposed principles that are modified cumulatively by the unfolding; it can envisage at once the conscious and the nonconscious either in a single subject or in an aggregate and succession of subjects; it is adjustable to any course of events, from an ideal line of pure progress resulting from the harmonious working of the opposed principles, to any degree of conflict, aberration, breakdown, and disintegration.' Lonergan, *Insight*, 244/268-69.

13 Lonergan, *Insight* 624/646-47. Some Jungians do not differentiate contraries from contradictories. The ego and the unconscious are contraries to be synthesized in a higher unity; good and evil are contradictories, the only resolution of which is a choice of one or the other. See Robert M. Doran 'Jungian Psychology and Christian Spirituality' (see above, chapter 1, note 33).

14 Lonergan, *Insight* 233/258.

15 Ibid. 236/261.

16 Ibid. 237/262. On cosmopolis, 238-42/263-67.

17 Cosmopolis 'stands on a basic analysis of the compound-intension that is man.' Ibid. 241. On the transcendental grounding of the

dialectics of contraries in the unity-in-duality of consciousness, see chapter 3 of *Theology and the Dialectics of History*.

18 Joseph Schumpeter, *Imperialism/Social Classes* (see above, chapter 11, note 20) 6.

19 Hannah Arendt, *The Origins of Totalitarianism* (see above, chapter 7, note 2) ix.

20 On world-cultural humanity, see Lewis Mumford, *The Transformations of Man* (see above, chapter 1, note 6) 137-68.

21 Lonergan, *Method in Theology* 31-32.

22 Note that the basic social dialectic is between practicality and intersubjectivity, not (as Marxists maintain) within practicality (the dialectic of forces and relations of production). For an approximation to our position, see Jürgen Habermas, 'Labor and Interaction: Remarks on Hegel's Jena *Philosophy of Mind*,' in Habermas, *Theory and Practice*, trans. John Viertel (Boston: Beacon Press, 1973) 142-69.

23 My analysis differs from the Marxist position on at least four counts: first, the more dominant role assigned to the dialectical functioning of intersubjective spontaneity in the infrastructure; second, the consequent subordination of practicality to the dramatic constitution of the world as a work of art; third, the recognition of cultural integrity's responsibility for the infrastructural dialectic; and fourth, the inclusion of the legal and political in the infrastructure of society.

24 Lonergan, *Insight* 236/261.

25 1993 note: In my first attempt to transpose systematic categories from a scholastic metaphysical context into the context demanded by interiorly and religiously differentiated consciousness, I have found it necessary to make a further distinction here. Aquinas distinguished the habit of charity, here identified with what Lonergan calls universal willingness, from sanctifying grace. The former is an operative habit rooted in a potency, the will, while the latter is an entitative habit rooted in the essence of the soul. This distinction is carried over by Lonergan in *De ente supernaturali* and in *De Deo trino*, but is not maintained when he speaks in *Method in Theology* of a dynamic state of being in love without conditions or qualifications or restrictions or reservations, and

identifies this dynamic state, not with the habit of charity but with sanctifying grace. See *Method in Theology* 289. What I am here calling 'a living relationship of partnership and love with the absolute limit of the process of going beyond' is initiated by that absolute limit, by God, in the communication of God's own life to us. That created communication of divine life is what a theoretical or metaphysical theology called sanctifying grace, and I suggest that its counterpart in intentional and religious consciousness is not the dynamic state of being in love — that is the operative habit of charity, universal willingness — but a resting in God's love for us. See Robert M. Doran, 'Consciousness and Grace' (see above, chapter 13, note 52).

26 1993 note: Obviously, my debate here is with David Tracy's understanding of systematic theology. I have refrained from including in this volume a complete chapter on Tracy that initially was to be part of the work ('Theology as Public Discourse: A Critique of David Tracy's Agenda for Theology'), because my profound personal and professional respect for Tracy prevents me from attempting a public debate before I have had the opportunity to discuss these matters with him in a more dialogical fashion. If the comments here suggestive of Tracy's proposals are not based on an adequate interpretation of his work, then I ask that they be taken only in their positive intention as programmatic suggestions for a systematics that I would want to attempt on my own, and not as a criticism of another's proposals on the same matter.

27 For a more extensive elaboration of this theme, see Robert M. Doran, 'Suffering Servanthood and the Scale of Values' (above, chapter 7). 1993 note: I have argued extensively in *Theology and the Dialectics of History* that the relationships that I posit among the levels of value support the liberation theology doctrines of a preferential option for the poor and of their hermeneutically privileged position in the interpretation both of the tradition and of the situation. More recent reflections on my experience of pastoral ministry among people with AIDS have led me to see that the servanthood of the church's ministers is secondary. The primary carriers of the grace of being suffering servants of God in the Deutero-Isaian sense are the poor themselves. Whatever share the rest of us have in that grace is due to them and to their invitation to us to participate in their lives.

DATE DUE

			Printed in USA

HIGHSMITH #45230